Maranatha!

**A Study of
Unfulfilled
Prophecy**

Maranatha!

**A Study of
Unfulfilled
Prophecy**

Harry Bultema

Foreword by
Daniel C. Bultema

KREGEL PUBLICATIONS
Grand Rapids, Michigan 49501

Translated from the Dutch by Cornelius Lambregtse.

Library of Congress Cataloging-in-Publication Data

Bultema, Harry.
  Maranatha! A Study of Unfulfilled Prophecy.

  Bibliography: p.
  Includes index.
  1. Bible—Prophecies.   2. Second Advent.
3. Eschatology.   I. Title.
BS647.B7913   1985   236   85-24027
ISBN 0-8254-2263-9

Printed in the United States of America

CONTENTS

6 / Contents

ACKNOWLEDGMENTS

With a deep sense of gratitude, I humbly acknowledge the faithful efforts of Mr. Cornelius Lambregtse in translating this book from Dutch into English. A special note of thanks is extended to Timothy F. Conklin, Executive Director of Grace Publications, Inc., and Dale DeWitt, Professor of Theology at Grace Bible College, who confirm the value of *Maranatha!* as an important contribution to one's understanding of the development of twentieth-century American theology. I am deeply indebted for their encouragement and expert editorial work on the manuscript. Special thanks also to my dear wife for her patience and support during my own work in bringing *Maranatha!* back into print.

My deep appreciation goes to my brother, John Bultema, to other members of the Bultema family, and to many relatives and friends for their valued help and encouragement.

My heartfelt thanks is given to Robert L. Kregel, Harold J. Kregel and Paul W. Bennehoff of Kregel Publications for their expert advice and wonderful cooperation in getting this English edition published.

(See also the Foreword)   DANIEL C. BULTEMA

FOREWORD TO THE ENGLISH EDITION

One of the precious truths in the special revelation given to the Apostle Paul is the blessed hope of Christ's coming to catch away members of the body of Christ, both those who have died and those in Christ who are living (1 Thess. 4:13-17; Titus 2:13).

The truth of the coming of Christ burned in my father's heart. He yearned for others to be moved to an expectation of the blessed hope of Christ's-any-moment return. He expressed this so appropriately in the Preface to the first edition of *Maranatha!*, "We have no more ardent desire than that many a child of God in these dark days (which according to prophecy will become even darker) may be led to a prayerful examination of the prophetic Scriptures, and above all to a sober and ardent expectation of the blessed return of the Lord. If it (this book) were to have these fruits, how great our joy and gratitude would be. May the Lord grant this."

If these words were appropriate over one-half century ago, they are even more pertinent today, when we too . . . "look for the Savior, the Lord Jesus Christ, who shall change our vile body, that it may be fashioned like unto His glorious body, according to the working, whereby He is able to subdue all things unto Himself" (Philippians 3:21).

Maranatha! was first published in Dutch in 1917. My father, of Dutch heritage, pastored many of his kinsmen—Dutch immigrants who settled in the Midwest. God graciously used the initial printing of *Maranatha!* to lead many people into the precious truth concerning the imminent coming of Christ.

Perhaps someone will ask, "What has led to the translation and publication of this book in English?" One reason relates to the many other writings of my father. *Maranatha!* was his first major written work. In those days, there seemed to be a special excitement and the spirit of expectancy of the Lord's return. The first edition was so blessed of the Lord that a second printing was published a few months later. His *Commentary on the Book of Daniel* soon followed. Then he produced his *Commentary on Revelation* followed by *Typology of Scripture* and Commentaries on *Zechariah* and *Isaiah,* all published in Dutch.

Later other books and pamphlets were published in English. God's stamp of approval and blessing attended each one. His practical *Commentary on Isaiah* was translated from Dutch into English and published in 1981. This 640-page volume is even now a tool in God's hands to stir hearts concerning prophetic truth.

The Spirit of God has graciously blessed my father's prolific pen, and we therefore sense the urging of the Lord to publish *Maranatha!* in English.

This book caused no small stir when it was first published. It led my father out of the Christian Reformed Church, which he highly esteemed. Upon reflection, he later wrote, in 1921, "I loved the Christian Reformed Church with all that was in me, and I labored night and day for her welfare and now I am an outcast. If I had only been uncertain in my mind about the two avenged points, namely; that Christ was the King of Israel and Head of the Church; and that Israel and the Church were not identical, then I could easily have retracted for the sake of peace and for the sake of the brethren. As it was, however, I was not in doubt about them. I had weighed and re-weighed, tested and tried them under the searchlights of God's Word, and to retract them as falsehoods would have been the most grievous sin on my part."

My father continued to have a host of friends in the denomination, and many were led to love premillennial truth through his persuasive preaching and teaching.

"He, being dead, yet speaketh" through this English edition. My prayer echoes my father's " . . . that many a child of God may be led . . . to a sober and ardent expectation of our Lord's return."

"Looking for that Blessed Hope, and the glorious appearing of the great God and our Savior, Jesus Christ" (Titus 2:13).

Autumn, 1985   Daniel C. Bultema

PREFACE TO THE
SECOND DUTCH EDITION

It is with a deep sense of gratitude to God that we are writing a brief preface to the second edition of this book on unfulfilled prophecy. Our boldest expectations have been far surpassed in every respect. The book is eagerly bought, read, and discussed. This must partly be explained, of course, by the energetic effort of the publisher, and partly by favorable reviews, which we gratefully acknowledge. But it also proves that our people hunger for the truths that relate to the blessed return of the Lord. This gladdens us greatly, for we are convinced that in these days of apostasy and worldliness, the only thing that can keep us as a Church and as individuals safe from the massive turning away from God is the ardent expectation of the returning Christ.

Those who say, "My Lord tarries in coming," are the unfaithful slaves who, according to the presentation of the Savior, reveal a twofold characteristic: 1) they begin by beating their fellow slaves out of the house and 2) they invite the drunkards in and get drunk with them. Those slaves, on the other hand, who expect Him, have their loins girded and their candles burning. "Anyone who has this hope in Him," says the Apostle of love, "purifies himself, as He is pure."

This edition might be called an expanded one. In essential points, however, no changes have been made. Only here and there we eliminated or changed a complete sentence, in response to kind advice, to which we always respond with an attentive ear and a grateful heart. "He giveth power to the faint; and to them that have no might he increaseth strength. Even the youths shall faint and be weary, and the young men shall utterly fall: But they that wait upon the Lord shall renew their strength" (Isa. 40:29-31).

May this be the rich experience of the soul of each and all of God's children!

Muskegon, Michigan, July, 1917   HARRY BULTEMA

PREFACE TO THE
FIRST DUTCH EDITION

It is not wholly without diffidence that we offer the following pages, dealing with still-unfulfilled prophecy, to our fellow Christians. This will be no surprise to anyone who is acquainted with the true situation.

In the first place, the subjects discussed here belong to the most difficult in this area of theology, fraught with many pitfalls, so that it is well-nigh impossible to get through this task unscathed.

Second, in regard to the last things there is generally great ignorance. This is not an accusation, but a statement of undeniable fact. Notwithstanding all the instruction in the doctrine of salvation, it seems that in our circles no progress is being made with regard to these truths, for not only the membership but also many preachers will on occasion gladly admit that they "know nothing of these things." In many instances their faces reveal some regret when admitting this, which betrays that they would like it otherwise, but they themselves don't know how. Yet ignorance is less of a problem than prejudice. Ignorance may result in misunderstanding and confusion, but it is willing to be instructed. Prejudice is not only shortsighted, but also refuses to see what lies beyond its own field of vision. Prejudiced people refuse to learn because they are narrow-minded, one-sided, and partial. Now it may be said that Reformed people have a broad view. But it cannot be denied, alas, that with regard to the last things they are often not only ignorant, but in many cases also lamentably restricted.

Taking these things into consideration, as well as the fact that the writer cannot boast of experience, erudition, titles, or fame, it must be clear to everyone that we send this book into the world with much reservation.

On the other hand, we have a great deal of liberty in offering these pages to our people. For the basic thought of this expository labor—*the literal fulfillment of prophecy*—obtains in our turbulent times its most outstanding justification. We see before our eyes that all nations have become angry; that there is distress of the nations with perplexity, when the sea and the waves are roaring (Rev. 11:18; Luke 21:25-26). The great apostasy, which has been foretold to come at the end of this dispensation, has, according to the opinion of some students of prophecy, commenced. The fig tree, Israel, begins to bud again as a sign that summer is nigh at hand (Luke 21:29-30).

Moreover, our dark and terror-filled times are at the travail of a new dispensation. They constitute the dark that precedes the rising of the Sun of Righteousness. They are heralds of Shiloh, whom the nations will obey. For that reason they make the believers in Scripture optimistic in the true sense of the word. According to the admonition of our Savior, the believers must lift up their heads when these things *begin* to come to pass, because their redemption is drawing nigh.

The author believes that these things *have begun* to take place, and therefore he lifts up his head courageously, joyfully, and longingly, knowing that the redemption is nigh. It is in this confidence, that the day of Christ is close at hand, that he has written this book. He considers it a privilege and a duty to express this openly and emphatically. Without wanting to sound a false alarm, he wishes, by this study, to guide his fellow believers also to the glad expectation of the coming of the Lord, who is coming soon, even though He might tarry another century.

The subjects treated do not in every respect form a complete unit. A systematic treatment of unfulfilled prophecy is simply not possible. Nevertheless, I have attempted to do so as far as possible, so that the chapters are not totally disconnected. Our main purpose has been, however, to highlight the expository aspects of these subjects, for we consider it irresponsible to speak or write about religious subjects without letting the Word of the Lord speak most of all.

Those who do not adhere to this view of prophecy will naturally find much that is not to their liking. This by no means implies that the opinion expressed herein goes contrary to the meaning of the Spirit. A study such as this cannot, of necessity, be to everyone's liking. Some will feel that too much, others that too little, is given. Some people will disagree with one statement, others with something else. Maybe one will shrug his shoulders in doubt about a certain point, while someone else may be moved to incredulous laughter. And since the book goes contrary to predominant views, the possibility exists that someone may throw it away as a heretical, if not contemptible, work. For more than one traditional notion is mercilessly discarded, and this may easily evoke anger.

So many questions present themselves in connection with the return of the Lord that the attacking of a cherished idea is unavoidable. This will evoke opposition. Honor from men is sweet to the flesh, so we should no more expect it than despise it; one can hardly consider such things a calamity, however, if he wishes to be a follower of Him who never accepted honor from men, but considered everything an abomination before God that was in high esteem with men.

In general, the tone of this study is by no means hesitant. There is a reason for that. I should be guilty of gross hypocrisy, if I were to write in a tone of uncertainty; for that would be similar to guessing on the part of the wise Master, when, on the basis of prayerful study and research of God's Word, there is a conviction in the heart that is as solid as a rock. Regarding the *manner* and *place,* the *context* and the *circumstances,* however, we do not dare to speak with a similar certainty. Further careful examination of Scripture may furnish much more light, although these matters cannot be considered of the greatest importance. We notice that man usually speaks most on the things on which Scripture speaks least. By nature we hate Scripture, and it is only due to the work of God in us that fills us with reverence for it.

Concerning the sources of my convictions, the following must be understood. Regardless of how much we owe to certain persons and sources (see the historical outline), there is nevertheless not a single book(let) on the Millennium or any chiliastic person or system that moved us to this study. It is only by the Word of the Lord that we were led to these comforting truths. This Word has also been our main source, with the exception of the historical outline. To avoid the appearance of erudition we have not mentioned all the scriptural references, nor added a bibliography.* It was also the Word of

*These have been added for this English edition by the publishers.

the Lord that convinced us unquestionably of the truth of the reign of Christ, as well as of the courage of conviction that otherwise would be lacking to promote this truth publicly. And although several friends and colleagues urged me to write on these things, it was mainly the light of the Word that led me. Likewise the Word alone, as the sword of the Spirit, can be the weapon against the opponents of the doctrine of the reign of Christ. All else will avail little. No pious deliberations, nor the phantoms and shadows of the past, though ever so venerable in themselves, will avail anything against the light of the future as it is reflected by the prophetic Word. We wish to stand or fall with this Word.

We hope that our readers will not be like the people of Sychar before they had heard Christ, nor like the Hebrews, but like the Bereans who examined, in the light of the Word, whether these things were so. We do not wish to see any authority being attached to what we have to say except as it has been garnered from the infallible Word of God. The thoughts of men are less than vanity itself, whereas no tittle or iota of God's Word will fall to the ground, no matter how despised. "All flesh is as grass, and all the glory of man as the flower of grass. The grass withereth, and the flower thereof fadeth away: But the Word of the Lord endureth forever." And so let also our work perish if it be not according to His Word!

It will be evident to the reader that no foolish attempts have been made to figure out the time of the return of the Lord. All such predictions are dishonoring to God and have done much harm to the study of prophecy. One will therefore find no prophecy from us, but simple reflections on the unfulfilled predictions of the Lord. Nor will one find a false alarmism that speculates on the fear or mere reflection of human curiosity. We have no more ardent desire than that in these dark days, which, according to prophecy will become even darker, many a child of God may be led to a prayerful examination of the prophetic Scriptures, to a careful consideration of the signs of the times, and above all to a sober and ardent expectation of the blessed return of the Lord. If it were to have these blessed fruits, how great our joy and gratitude would be! May the Lord grant this!

Muskegon, Michigan, April, 1917   HARRY BULTEMA

Part I
Prophecy

Chapter 1

A CONSIDERATION OF PROPHECY AND ITS EXEGESIS

Prophecy is a special form of God's revelation to His people. It is divine truth that reveals the future to us. Soothsaying, which is found among all nations, shows that man has a deep-seated need for knowledge regarding the future. The Lord Himself has put this need in man, and He has provided for this need by revealing in His Word the main events of the future.

Scripture contains more prophecy than many believers think. During the emergence of modernism and higher criticism, the statement was constantly made that Scripture contained very few prophecies. And since many orthodox people accepted and repeated this, believers are more influenced by it than they realize. The Church as a whole does not take prophecy very seriously, even though it shines as a light in this dark world. In a certain respect, all of Scripture is prophetic. But in the sense we mean it here—and if we include the prophetic psalms and parables, the promises, types, and the many predictions in the historical books—prophecy occupies almost half of the whole body of revelation.

Only part of this prophetic Scripture has been fulfilled. At the first coming of Christ, a minor portion of the Old Testament predictions were completely fulfilled. More were fulfilled in the destruction of Jerusalem, the dispersion of the Jews, and the decline of the heathen kingdoms.

When we subtract the fulfilled prophecies from the sum total of prophecy, we come to the surprising discovery that hardly half of the prophetic word has been completely fulfilled. This means that about a fourth of the entire Scripture may be called unfulfilled prophecy. The very first prophecy of salvation, the mother promise, has not been completely fulfilled (Rom.

16:20; Rev. 20:10). The second prophecy concerning the nations of Shem, Ham, and Japheth has not been wholly fulfilled, but is still being carried out daily before our eyes. The third prophecy we find in the promise given to Abraham, Isaac, and Jacob, and this too, as we later hope to show, has by no means been wholly fulfilled. The fourth prophecy we find in Genesis 49, where we read that the dying patriarch blessed his sons. But a statement such as we find in verse 10, that the nations will be obedient to Shiloh, is still awaiting a grand future.

In order to know the prophetic part of Holy Scripture, we must first know the entire Scripture. We need the Bible in its entirety, as well as in its parts. This part, too, God has given for the benefit of His people. The Holy Spirit did no superfluous work when thousands of years ago He revealed the prophecies that are still unfulfilled. The theory that the intent of prophecy will be understood only at its fulfillment is contrary to both Scripture and experience. "For whatsoever things were written aforetime were written for our learning, that we through patience and comfort of the Scriptures might have hope" (Rom. 15:4). "All scripture is given by inspiration of God, and is profitable for doctrine, for reproof, for correction, for instruction in righteousness" (2 Tim. 3:16). The Lord rebuked the disciples on the way to Emmaus because they were slow of heart to believe all that the prophets had spoken. The Savior considers the failure to understand prophetic Scripture a result of ignorance. As for experience, unfulfilled prophecy has, under the old dispensation, made many a Jew wise unto salvation. Even the scribes in Jesus' day knew many things from unfulfilled predictions. And in the new dispensation, countless Godfearing people have been comforted by the Lord's future promises. We need only think of the still-unfulfilled promise of Christ's coming again.

Many Scripture passages command us to study prophecy (Matthew 16:3; Mark 13:23, 28, 33; Daniel 9:2-3, 20-27; 2 Peter 1:19; Revelation 1:3, and others). God looks with pleasure on all who tremble before His Word and conduct themselves according to it. And it is His will that we search His entire Word. The Hebrews are just as strongly reproved for being satisfied with the rudiments of God's Word as the Bereans are praised for diligently examining the Word. If people evaluate their own word highly, would the Lord not do so with regard to His infallible Word?

Since the Lord anticipated that His people would greatly disregard His prophetic Word in the ages to come, He has given special promises to spur them on to such study. In Daniel 12:10 we are told that wise people will understand prophecy; and in verse 4 the promise is given that, as a result of examining prophecy, knowledge will be increased. The prophetic Book of Revelation has a special promise at both the beginning and the end for those who attentively read, hear, and obey.

Many believers neglect the study of the prophetic Word. Arguments against the study of prophecy are valid when directed toward its misuse, but not with regard to the study itself. What would we think of a soldier who only wanted to watch, and not do battle or reconnoiter the enemy? Nevertheless, that is the situation in the Reformed Churches in the Netherlands, America, and South Africa.

One objection is that prophecy is dark, or obscure. This complaint is contrary to the Word of the Lord, which tells us that it is a light shining in a dark place. Every believer who prayerfully and continually examines prophecy will agree with this statement. Anyone who complains about the darkness of prophecy, be he a professor or day laborer, indicates that he has not allowed the light of prophecy to illuminate his mind and heart as he should. The opening of God's words gives light and understanding, but only to the simple, not to those who think they already know it or who claim that it cannot be known. In His light we see the light. Other people allow themselves to be confused by the greatly divergent explanations of prophecy. Perplexed by the quantity and variations of prophecy, they see nothing but a maze, and conclude that the best course is to avoid advancing too far into it. This suggests a great weakness of character or spiritual weakness, or perhaps both.

In Israel, whoever refused to listen to the prophets had to be killed. Why? Because the prophet brought a message from God. Whoever rejected a prophet rejected God Himself. But what must we say then of those who refuse to listen to the voice of prophecy? Do the Scriptures of prophecy have no message?

Or dare we confidently declare that their message is too obscure to pay attention to? If the trumpet of prophecy indeed gave such an uncertain sound, who would then prepare himself for battle? According to such a view, the prophets are barbarians, for Paul says that when someone speaks to me and I do not understand him, then he is a barbarian to me (1 Cor. 14:11). Paul tells such people to keep silent (v. 28).

It seems to us, however, that the number of those in the believing church who sense that the general attitude to prophecy on the part of believers is not right, is great indeed. The vague explanations of prophecy do not satisfy them. They seem too unreal to them. They instinctively feel that by and large the very natural and human element of prophecy has not been taken into account, that the prophets themselves have never even thought of the things that many exegetes put into their mouths.

THE MISUSE OF PROPHECY

While the disregard of prophecy is harmful, misinterpreting it is even worse. We wish to call attention to some of the main misuses of prophecy. When I speak of the term "misuse," I do not wish to be malicious. It is my firm conviction, based on the Scripture passages in the Old and New Covenants, that we are dealing with misunderstandings. These misconceptions must be corrected before we can study prophecy effectively.

Christ's Humiliation Rather Than His Exaltation

We mention as a misuse the teaching that the core of prophecy is in the humiliation of Christ. Actually, the core of prophecy is in the exaltation of Christ. Certainly the prophets also spoke of Christ's suffering (Luke 24:26; Acts 3:18; 1 Peter 1:11). The prophets presupposed both crib and cross, and usually cast their eyes on the King of Glory. Even in the main portions dealing with the humiliation of the Messiah, such as Psalm 22, Isaiah 53, and Zechariah 9 and 11, they speak in passing, as it were, of His humiliation, but more directly of His exaltation. They never deal at length with His humiliation, but they do speak in long passages of His exaltation.

This was, of course, not because of any shortsightedness on

the part of the prophets. They could have dealt with the Messiah in His humiliation just as extensively as they did with the Messiah of Glory. For it was the Spirit of the Lord that urged them on and qualified them.

So we are far from dealing with anything accidental. Here we find divine wisdom. The secret of any true world view is to look at the end. That is where not only Asaph and Habakkuk but also all the patriarchs, psalmists, and prophets obtained their peace of mind. "Let every thing that hath breath praise the Lord"—that is the principle and basic thought of all of them. It will take place fully when every knee bows to Christ and every tongue confesses to the glory of the Father that He is the Lord.

At the end of the road one sees the justification and reconciliation of the passion; the end proves the value of the beginning. At the end, God's counsel will be completely fulfilled. The actual comfort of the prophetic Scriptures emerges only when one learns to look at their great conclusion. Believers become followers when the Apostle considers that the sufferings of this present time are not worthy to be compared with the glory that shall be revealed. Even more, they become followers of the Christ who, for the joy that was set before Him, endured the cross and despised the shame.

Thus, the prophets did not dwell on the cross, instead they looked at the development of the great world drama. They did not see the goal of Christ's coming in His priestly work (which was also important), but in His kingly work. Christ came down into the manger to get to the cross, and up to the cross to get to the throne. Hence this King of Glory does not exclude the cross, but includes it. Christ comes back as the crucified One. The crowned Christ is the crucified Christ. We must always place His cross in the middle, but we must consider His crown as the end goal of His mediatorial work. Then the preaching will not be merely soteriological and concern itself with the salvation of the individual, but cosmological, so that the world-encompassing nature of Christ's work comes clearly into view.

It will be argued that Paul in 1 Corinthians 2:2 said that he determined not to know anything save Jesus Christ and Him crucified. According to some, Paul meant to say that he always wanted to speak of the cross or the crucifixion as an act. But the

Apostle said nothing of the kind. He wanted to know nothing save Jesus Christ, not as a famous rabbi or world sage as some Corinthians might have liked, but in the continuous meaning of a crucified One. He used the participle, which points to the eternal value of the cross. Even though he preached the glorified Christ, he presented Him in the form of a crucified Christ.

Christ's death, and the ransom obtained by it, is the main point of the gospel and will remain so forever. The death of the Lord is the awe-inspiring means to a glorious goal. The cross is not a goal but a means. The prophets usually looked past the means to the glorious end goal of all things.

The Church as Center of Prophecy

Another misuse, and a no less serious one, consists in the desire to see the church everywhere in prophecy. This is all the more regrettable since this has been a common misunderstanding for many years. It must appear presumptuous to contest it. We are fully convinced, however, that if anyone wants to find mention of the Church in prophecy, he can find nothing at all, for the simple reason that the prophets knew nothing of the Church of Christ.

As Scripture teaches us plainly, this was a secret; it was a mystery to them. Indeed, it was the mystery that throughout the preceding ages was hidden from all saints and prophets. Scripture tells us this repeatedly and emphatically (Acts 10:34; Rom. 16:25-26; Eph. 3:5-6; Col. 1:26-27; 1 Tim. 3:16). Later we will return to this important principle in the study of prophecy for it concerns not only the exegete of prophecy, but also our concept of the Church and, as a result, our total calling in life and the practice of godliness.

However, anyone who is of the opinion that the Church as the body of Christ must be found everywhere, and who approaches prophecy with this thought in mind to explain it, will be guilty of the strangest absurdities and falsifications of Scripture. The six heavy volumes by Vitringa and the four unwieldy tomes by Hellenbroek on Isaiah serve as proof that learned and Godfearing men who proceed from this faulty premise cannot avoid all manner of contradiction with themselves.

In this misuse, divergent concepts, such as Jacob, Zion, Judah, Israel, Ephraim, are all applied to the Church, but only when reference is made to the future glory. Glorious indeed will be the state of the Church, or the Church State, in the future. But when judgments are announced upon the same persons, these judgments are applied to the Jews. At one moment the Church is the worm Jacob, and at the next, a Kingdom that will rule over all, and of which the kings of the earth will be the nursing fathers and the queens the nursing mothers.

In the prophets we must not look for the Church, but for Israel and its promised glory. We may apply all these truths to the Church as well, but application is something quite different from explanation. Of the Church it can be said, "All things are yours," hence also the Old Testament prophets. The Church shares in the complete Christ and also in all the promises, which in Him are yea and amen. No matter how much we wish to apply to the Church, we must never make the mistake of explaining prophecy in terms of the Church. For if we do, the word of prophecy will afford no light, but instead we shall shed much darkness.

Spiritualizing Bible Truths

Again, closely related with the preceding misuse, we mention the method of spiritualizing in the exegesis of prophecy. It is hard to say in what this method consists, for its most outstanding feature is the lack of a method and a clearly defined principle. Its advocates have never given a formal definition or set of rules. David N. Lord in his *Laws of Figurative Language* says of it, "It is an unscientific and crude invention without any ground to justify the setting aside of clear and unambiguous language." Indeed, F. Bettex correctly calls exegetical spiritualizing "one of the craftiest inventions of the liar from the beginning." The famous Jew, Adolph Saphir, says with sadness, "It is from the arsenal of the orthodox that the armor has been taken to attack the fundamental truths of the gospel." Dr. A. B. Simpson calls it, "The greatest heresy of the present day."

With this method of exegesis the most ridiculous things have been derived from Scripture, or rather, put into it. It has for centuries filled people with an aversion to prophecy. The cause of this method lies in the error, which, although it wished to be biblical, seized this means to evade the force of the words. Origen, the leading heretic among the Church Fathers, is generally considered the father of spiritualistic exegesis. With him it was a trick to eliminate the Millennium from the doctrine of faith, and to justify the salvation of all men and devils.

The great Church Father, Augustine, also committed the same error. In his famous work, *De Civitate Dei,* he uses this method with relation to the Church, and with this he became the father not only to Rome's concept of the Church but also of several other heresies. Rome can appeal to him for the doctrine of purgatory, the teaching that the believers cannot have assurance of faith, the teaching of the necessity of persecuting heretics, and other falsehoods.

It is to be regretted that in the exegesis of prophecy, scholars did not proceed from permanent, simple, and natural rules, and that they did not attach sharp and definitive meanings to frequently recurring concepts such as Jacob, Judah, Jerusalem, Zion, Ephraim, and Canaan. In all other branches of science this would most certainly have been done.

It was correctly assumed that prophecy must be taken in a deeply spiritual sense, but a spiritual explanation is quite different from a spiritualized one. The Rationalistic writers also applied this method of exegesis to the New Testament, in particular to Christ's teachings, and thus they arrived finally at the symbolic exegesis of David Strauss. The men of higher criticism apply it to the historical books, while they in turn explain the prophets from an exclusively historical-grammatical approach.

Just as much as it cannot be denied, even so is it to be regretted that the Reformed writers of today have not altogether abandoned this method of Scriptural exegesis. We only need look at eschatology as it is practiced by our leaders Kuyper and Bavinck; also Sikkel, *Holy Scripture and Its Exegesis;* Dr. J. Woltjer, *The Word: Origin and Explanation;* Dr. F. W. Grosheide, *New Testament Exegesis;* Dr. G. Warfield, *The Apocalypse and the Millennium;* the Rev. H. Hoekstra, *Chiliasm.* With this method anything can be taught or can be argued away. Zeegers, in his *Logica,* gives a striking example of this manner of exegesis, which we freely pass on here.

Three sons, when opening and reading their father's will, came across these words, "I order and command my sons that during the first three years after my death they shall never wear a golden button on their robe." This was followed by a lengthy penal provision. The oldest of the three sons, however, was skilled in languages and criticism. Confidently he claimed that the word *button* mentioned by the testament must not be taken literally but figuratively. *Button,* he said, is *knoop* in Dutch, *Knopf* in German, *knapp* in Swedish, *knap* in Danish, *chaep* in Anglo-Saxon, *knob* in English, and is related to the following Dutch words, *knobbe, knubbe, knoest, knap, heuvel,* and the Icelandic *gnipa,* to stick out, to be elevated, and so it can, in relation to one's back, have no other meaning than hump, hunch. The youngest brother, however, could not agree with this learned explanation, since the adjective *golden* before button could not very well refer to a fleshy protuberance on the back. But his learned brother argued that this was no problem at all, since *golden* in this context had to be taken in an allegorical, mythological sense. To this the youngest replied that their father could not have wished for punishment of a hunchback, to which the oldest brother sharply and sarcastically answered that anyone of that opinion was not qualified to take part in an explanation.

This method of biblical interpretation often renders its adherents satisfied with their own insights, for almost without exception the spiritualizers look down with great contempt on those who adhere to the words as they appear. Spiritualizing seems so genuinely spiritual, whereas the simple and obvious explanation seems so earthly and carnal. But we must never forget that the cross of Christ has the appearance of evil.

The results of this method of spiritualizing are disastrous. Israel remains throughout all ages the warning example. Israel spiritualized and blurred the suffering of Christ and all that pertains to it, just as we often do with regard to the future glory of Christ and everything connected with it. Israel had learned and believing leaders. There was not a hair on their heads that doubted the inspiration of Scripture. They knew which was the greatest commandment. They knew where the Messiah was to be born. They generally taught the people from Scripture in such a manner that the Savior could say, "Do as they teach you." They manifested great zeal in the preservation and defense of the Scriptures. And still this nation and these scribes did not recognize their Messiah in the suffering Mediator. On the contrary, *on the basis of their Scriptures,* they put Him to death. They believed the Scriptures of truth and yet not all the truth of the Scriptures.

Israel's guilt is great, for she murdered her sovereign King. The old prophets, as we have already seen, spoke relatively little about the first coming, and much about the Messiah of Glory in His second coming. The ratio is about 350 times concerning the second coming to 10 concerning the first coming. We have much more light and far more means for understanding this point than Israel did.

Today Satan uses this method more than ever before, and he thereby evaporates all truths that stand in his way. He has nothing against the Bible, providing you do not understand and explain it in its natural and reasonable meaning. And the same holds true for the sects and theological currents that follow in his steps.

The Swedenborgians use this method with the deepest conviction. Without any trouble they reason away the return of Christ.

The Freemasons have blurred the Bible as a symbol. In one of their writings they literally say, "The Bible must not be understood literally but according to its meaning." Without any difficulty they, too, reason away the future work of Christ and dissolve everything into the victory of glorious principles, a happy time of brotherhood and enlightenment.

The modern Reformed Jew simply does with Isaiah 53 what many do with Isaiah 54, namely, spiritualize it; he sees in it his suffering nation.

Christian Scientists and the Theosophists, too, have no objections to the Bible whatsoever, provided you understand it in a figurative or, more correctly, symbolical sense. In short, it can be said of modernism in all its branches that it has no ill will against the Bible, if only you will take it in a metaphorical sense, i.e., if you are willing to falsify it.

This method of spiritualization runs counter to verbal inspiration, to the law of language, and the law of reason.

1. *A poetic or spiritualistic interpretation of Scripture is in conflict with a sound view of inspiration.*

Scripture itself emphasizes that it is verbally inspired. Moses appeals repeatedly to God's authority, in Leviticus forty-four times and in Numbers eighty-seven times. The same is said of David (2 Sam. 23:2; 1 Kings 8:15). Solomon, too, says the same (1 Kings 8:56). In the prophets we find again and again the same statement (Isa. 1:2; Jer. 1:4; Ezek. 1:3). If God is speaking of earthly glory for Jerusalem, must we then make it into spiritual glory for the Church? Gabriel wants Daniel to understand his *words*. Do not the words contain the intent and meaning of the Spirit? As a rule, Israel understood it this way; that is the reason why the letters and dots were carefully counted when preserving Holy Scripture. In Jeremiah's day, the leaders of Israel were degenerate, yet they adhered to the literal meaning of what the prophet Micah had spoken (Jer. 26:11; cf. Mic. 3:12). The man of God of Bethel and Daniel also took it in the same way (1 Kings 13:9-10; Dan. 9). Understand the words. This rule is demanded by verbal inspiration. This truth is totally ignored by the spiritualization method.

2. *Such interpretation clashes with the laws of language.*

Prophetic language contains divine laws that may not be disregarded. Language is the carrier of thoughts. It expresses ideas and does not hide them. Professor Louis Berkhof in his *Hermeneutics* says on page 193:

> Moreover, we must not be misled by thinking that the language of the prophets was wholly symbolic and that among themselves they adhered to a kind of composite of symbolical thought-forms in which they constantly poured their preaching. Some were of the opinion that this was actually the case and judged that no justice was done to the prophets if their words were taken in their ordinary meaning.

God is not a man that He should lie, and therefore He means exactly what He says, nothing more and nothing less. As the true God, He gave every word its own meaning. Will He not remain true to Himself and demand that the interpreters give each word its actual meaning? He does not hide His thoughts, but reveals them in His words. In them He speaks to the little children, and He speaks perfectly.

The Holy Spirit has an excellent knowledge of language; indeed, in the final analysis He is the only One with a perfect knowledge of language. Can it be imagined that this Person with an infallible knowledge of language would mean things differently than the way He speaks them? Asking this question is answering it already in the negative. We can safely say that the spiritualizers misjudge both the language and the object of revelation.

3. *This manner of interpreting prophecy must be discarded as being in conflict with the law of thought.*

It is in the highest degree inconsistent and unreasonable. At present we need not say much about this. DaCosta and others have often remarked that when the majority of exegetes come across the curses and judgments upon the Jews, they resort to the term Israel, as it always appears in the Old Testament. But when, a few verses further on, mention is made of blessings, then the Jews suddenly become the Church. This conflicts with the reasonable and hermeneutical rule that in the same context the terms must be taken in the same sense, without adding or deleting anything. Everyone must agree that this would be dishonest and unreasonable.

We find the same type of presentation with regard to the first coming of Christ and His second coming. With regard to His first coming, all emphasis is put on the literal fulfillment, and correctly so, for everything is literally fulfilled to the smallest details. But when the same exegetes come to Christ's return, His future reign, and all the mediatorial work He will then do, they let everything evaporate into a mist. The later Jews spoke of two Messiahs, Messiah-ben-Joseph was the suffering Messiah and Messiah-ben-David the reigning Messiah. The exegetes, it is true, do not have two Messiahs, but they do have something that is hardly any better, namely, a twofold rule of exegesis with regard to the Messianic prophecy, a literal and a figurative interpretation. Is it not high time that we begin explaining matters in connection with Christ's second coming in the light of the literally fulfilled prophecy of His first coming?

We see the same thing in connection with the past and the future of the Jews. With respect to past judgments and dispersion of the Jews, everything is explained, with a measure of satisfaction, quite literally. And no wonder, for Scripture has been literally fulfilled in the dispersion of the Jews. The curse and dispersion are taken literally, but the gathering and blessings are spiritualized into the conversion of the heathen, the extension of the Church, or something similar.

We could go on pointing out numerous absurdities. For example, some exegetes apply Zechariah 14:20-21 to the New Testament Church, and hence completely spiritualize it. But why then is the ass in Zechariah 9:9 not seen as a spiritual ass, and the thirty pieces of silver in 11:12 likewise? And why not also the wounds in the hands (13:6), or the shepherd (13:7)? The dispersion of the Jews mentioned in the first chapters is literal. These interpreters are agreed on that. But when in chapter 12 the restoration of the Jews is emphatically foretold, this is taken in a different sense. That Christ's feet will stand on the Mount of Olives at His second coming must of course be explained as referring to His ascension, or something entirely different. No one has the right to explain the fulfilled things literally while explaining the unfulfilled things any way but likewise literally.

Chapter 2

RULES FOR EXPLAINING PROPHECY

The manner in which we explain prophecy governs our expectation of the future. Therefore it is important to point out some rules for explaining prophecy.

Prophecy must be taken and explained literally. This requires further explanation. "Literal interpretation" does not satisfy completely, as it makes us think of a senseless and unspiritual explanation totally devoid of the spirit of differentiation. The exegesis of prophecy should always be deeply spiritual, without spiritualizing. By a literal explanation, we mean that the words of prophecy should be explained in a simple, natural, unrestrained manner, and that we must not depart from the literal meaning except when forced to. Ever since the teaching of the German theologian, Johann Albrecht Bengel, the term *realistic* explanation has been used, but this expression does not satisfy either. We should much prefer the term *natural* explanation, but the reader might think of it as naturalistic, unspiritual, or even carnal. Nor does *organic* explanation express fully what we mean. So we must be satisfied with the term *literal*. In any case, this is the most common name in our country.

The literal explanation takes into account that Old Covenant prophecies often are unaware of place and time, and that they frequently see the great facts of salvation projected on one large mirror. On their grand canvasses they often paint within the same frame the first and second coming of Christ, the outpouring of the Holy Spirit, and the destruction of Jerusalem.

This view by no means denies that a rich treasury of poetry, imagery, types, and symbols is to be found in prophecy. In all of Scripture, and specifically in the prophets, we find much poetic expression. This use of poetry by the prophets may be ascribed to various possible causes. Their language was poorer than ours, their imagination richer. They lived closer to nature and particularly closer to God, so that their normal expression of reality seems poetic to us.

The use of literal interpretation does not imply that all prophecy must be taken with *inflexible* literalism. A literal or realistic explanation does no violence to the rules of good style. Throughout life we have countless expressions that cannot be taken literally. We say, for instance, the spirit *escaped* from the body. In a strictly literal sense the spirit did not flee from the body. We also say, the sun comes up, the evening descends, the night spreads its veil, the church bells call us to the house of God, the wear and tear of time, and so on. These are all expressions that cannot be taken in a strictly literal sense. A sound, literal explanation will never overlook this figurative style of writing.

We read, for example, in Daniel 2:37-38 that God had given the beasts of the field and the fowls of the heaven into the hand of Nebuchadnezzar. If we were to take this literally, we would end up with the greatest absurdity. Must we therefore apply the spiritualizing method and say that "the beasts" means evil men, and "the birds" dirty men? This would be equally absurd. We have here, quite simply, a poetic expression. We read in the same chapter, "Thou art this head of gold." This cannot be meant literally, of course. The resurrection of dry bones (Ezek. 37:1-10), too, cannot be explained literally. But, when the meaning of this image is given, it must be explained in terms of Israel's restoration, not in terms of regeneration, the call of the heathen, the flourishing of the Church, or anything of that kind.

Genesis 9:26-27 contains Noah's prophecy to his sons. Bible students are agreed that this prophecy is literally fulfilled in the history of the nations. But are we now living in the tents of Shem? Thus the way some want to spiritualize Revelation 20 is just as ridiculous, since the chain with which Satan was bound could not possibly be a literal chain. Christ's instruction, "Buy a sword," can hardly have been meant literally. At the Lord's

Supper, He said, "This is my body," which cannot be taken literally. He also said, I am the Bread, I am the Way, I am the Door, I am the Vine, and so on. It must be obvious that the chain with which Satan is bound is pure imagery.

Patrick Fairbairn in his book on prophecy constantly attacks a literal exegesis. In order to illustrate what he considers the absurdity of this method, he explains the first promise concerning Christ made to Eve as referring to the enmity between man and snakes. He then uses this interpretation as a proof against literal exegesis. And yet, we ask, has not this prophecy been fulfilled? Has there not been throughout the ages bitter enmity between Satan and Christ, and between the children of darkness and those of light? Is it not dishonest to oppose the natural explanation of Scripture in this way? Bible students believe that throughout Scripture the serpent is a type of Satan, and the seed of the woman is a reference to Christ and His people.

Proof for the legitimacy of a literal explanation of Scripture is abundant. God has used human language to reveal His message. When someone says to me, "I shall bring my son back," I do not take it to mean something different, but I take it literally. Why should we not do the same with regard to Holy Scripture? Professor Louis Berkhof says in his *Sacred Hermeneutics,* "Unless the opposite is quite obvious, we must proceed from the premise that we must take the words of prophecy in their common meaning." If we take the words of prophecy differently than in their ordinary meaning, prophecy is no longer revelation, but becomes a concealment of thoughts. Whoever had the liveliest fantasy would be the best exegete. Prophecy would not be light, but rather darkness.

Moreover, verbal inspiration requires a literal explanation. This rule is so obvious that it should not need to be emphasized.

FULFILLED PROPHECY

All prophecy which has been fulfilled has been fulfilled literally. We conclude from this that prophecy which has not yet been fulfilled will in the future also be fulfilled literally.

According to the men of higher criticism, the Scripture contains a long list of unfulfilled prophecies (see for example Prof. Abraham Kuenen, *Prophets and Prophecy in Israel;* cf. also Prof. Arthur Pierson, *A Study on the Writings of Israel's Prophets*). If God's predictions in the past had been proven false, then God's people would have reason to fear that much of the promised salvation would not be forthcoming.

Professor Pierson refers to the cities of the Philistines. He is of the opinion that the prophets unanimously announced the destruction of these cities, and that this prophecy has not been fulfilled, since Gaza still exists and Ashkelon was a prominent city at the time of the crusades. But he himself admits that only a few traces are left of the old glory of the five Philistine cities and that they shared in the lot that befell all of Palestine.

Ezekiel predicted the total destruction of Tyre. Newton, Keith, Urquhart, and Fairbairn have unanimously shown in their books on prophecy that this prediction has been literally fulfilled. The Lord has literally made of this proud trade city a bare rock, a place where they "spread their nets in the midst of the sea."

Jeremiah's prophecy regarding Damascus supposedly has remained unfulfilled (Jer. 49:23-27). For this city is still standing and flourishing to the present day and is, according to Pierson, the seat of the Turkish pasha, with a population of over 150,000. Because of a lack of information, we cannot point to a literal fulfillment here. We know that Syria, of which Damascus was the capital, had been occupied by Nebuchadnezzar during his campaign to the west and after the conquest of Egypt at Carchemish. There are several other possibilities: a) This prophecy is not speaking of a complete and eternal destruction of the city, b) Damascus may be representative of all of Syria, as is frequently the case in Scripture. Capitals are usually the heart of the nation, but the city itself may not suffer the misery of total destruction, c) It may have been destroyed but soon afterwards rebuilt, d) We may have here, as some think, a later supplement of Amos 1:4-14, in which case we find the fulfillment in 2 Kings 16, e) The prophecy is not particular but general, and so the final fulfillment may lie in the future. This explanation seems most probable to us. Whatever the case, no one has the right to claim that this prophecy is not and will not be fulfilled.

Pierson also refers to Moab and Ammon. According to several prophets, the two would lose their nationality and Israel would witness their enemies' downfall. It is nevertheless certain, says Pierson, that Moabites and Ammonites were still in a flourishing condition well into the seventh century A.D. But do we not see that it has been literally fulfilled since that time? The nation of the Jews will, according to the prophets, never pass away, and this miracle nation has already witnessed the "rise, glory, and destruction" of many nations and states. In his list of unfulfilled prophecies, Pierson also points to Edom, Egypt, Ethiopia, and Babylon. According to other writers, all the predictions in regard to these cities and nations have been literally fulfilled. Professor Kuenen is forced to admit, in view of the irrefutable facts, that all these prophecies "in some respects can nevertheless not be considered as totally unfulfilled."

When we speak of already fulfilled prophecies, we speak of literally fulfilled prophecies. Let us further look into this important fact. In Holy Scripture we find six kinds of fulfilled prophecy.

1. Prophecies regarding the heathen nations.
2. Prophecies regarding the Jews.
3. Prophecies regarding the first coming of Christ.
4. Prophecies regarding Christ Himself.
5. Prophecies found in the historical books.
6. Prophetic references to times.

1. *Prophecies regarding the heathen nations.*

With respect to this, it is sufficient to refer the reader to the above mentioned authors, and besides these to Isaac DaCosta, *Israel and the Nations;* F. Bettex, *The Bible the Word of God;* D. Nelson, *Unbelief the Greatest Malady of Our Times;* and Dr. Arthur Pierson, *Many Infallible Proofs.*

2. *Prophecies regarding the Jews.*

We shall not elaborate on this here, since later we must deal more specifically with Israel. Now we refer only to Leviticus 26. It speaks of blessings if Israel would be obedient, and miseries if she would be disobedient. History has taught that Israel was disobedient. And what do we see presently? We see that all those threats have been literally fulfilled.

There would be famine in Israel (Lev. 26:26). This has been literally fulfilled (see Lam. 2:12; 2 Kings 25:3; Ezek. 4:16; 5:12).

Israel would eat the flesh of her children (Lev. 26:29). It was literally fulfilled at the destruction of Samaria (see 2 Kings 6:28ff), at the first destruction of Jerusalem (Lam. 2), and at the second destruction of Jerusalem.

Israel's land and cities would be destroyed (Lev. 26:30-32), and thus it happened.

Israel would be scattered among the nations. Everyone knows how literally this has been fulfilled.

Israel would always be persecuted (vv. 33, 36). It has been literally fulfilled in her woeful history of blood and tears.

The land would lie desolate for a long time (vv. 33, 36). This has been literally fulfilled; from A.D. 70 it lay desolate until our very own day.

Israel would not be utterly destroyed (vv. 39, 44). It has been literally fulfilled. The crusaders, the popes, the inquisitors, and the kings of the earth together have not been able to destroy this people. The burning bush cannot be consumed.

All of these prophecies have been literally fulfilled. But what happens when the reader comes to verses 40-46, which speak of Israel's conversion and restoration? In at least as clear terminology as in the preceding verses, they speak of her downfall and misery. Some interpreters throw all sound rules of language and logic to the wind and "spiritualize" these verses. The same is true with Deuteronomy 28, 29, and 30, with Hosea 3, and with Luke 1:3-33. A text is cut in halves; one half is interpreted literally and the other spiritually. The Mormons do the same with numerous passages of Scripture. Oh that the day might come when people would treat the prophecies consistently!

3. *Prophecies concerning the first coming of Christ.*
These have been realized. All of these, without any exception, have been literally fulfilled, as is evident from the parallels.

Prophecy	Fulfillment

He would be born from the seed of the woman

Genesis 3:15 "... her seed; it shall bruise thy head." | Galatians 4:4 "... made of a woman."

He would be from the seed of Abraham

Genesis 22:18 "And in thy seed shall all the nations of the earth be blessed." | Matthew 1:1 "... Jesus Christ, the son of David, the son of Abraham."

Christ out of the tribe of Judah

Genesis 49:8 "Judah, thou art he..." | Hebrews 7:14 "For it is evident that our Lord sprang out of Judah."

Christ out of the seed of David

Jeremiah 23:5 "I will raise unto David a righteous Branch." | 2 Timothy 2:8 "Remember that Jesus Christ of the seed of David was raised from the dead."

Christ out of a virgin

Isaiah 7:14 "Behold, a virgin shall conceive..." | Luke 1:27 "...and the virgin's name was Mary."

Christ would be the Son of God

Isaiah 9:6 "Unto us a son is given." | Luke 1:35 "Therefore also that holy thing which shall be born of thee shall be called the Son of God."

The scepter would not have departed from Judah

Genesis 49:10 "The scepter shall not depart from Judah . . . until Shiloh come." | Matthew 2:1 "Now when Jesus was born in Bethlehem of Judea...in the days of Herod the king...."

He would be born in Bethlehem

Micah 5:2 "But thou, Bethlehem..." | Matt. 2:6 "And thou Bethlehem ..."

He would be called Immanuel

Isaiah 7:14 "...and shall call his name Immanuel." | Matthew 1:23 "...and they shall call his name Emmanuel."

His entrance into Jerusalem

Zechariah 9:9 "Rejoice greatly, O daughter of Zion; shout, O daughter of Jerusalem: behold, thy King cometh unto thee: he is just, and having salvation; lowly, and riding upon an ass, and upon a colt the foal of an ass." | Matthew 21:5 "Behold thy king cometh unto thee, meek, and sitting upon an ass, and a colt the foal of an ass."

His entrance into the temple

Malachi 3:1 "...shall suddenly come to his temple..." | Matthew 21:12 "And Jesus went into the temple of God..."

Prophecy	Fulfillment
His zeal for the house of God	
Psalm 69:9 "For the zeal of thine house hath eaten me up..."	John 2:17 "The zeal of thine house hath eaten me up."

And thus we could go on to show that without exception all of the approximately sixty or seventy fulfilled prophecies have been fulfilled literally. An excellent booklet on this subject is that of P. A. Sparenburg, *Prophecies Concerning the Messiah and Their Fulfillment.* From our earliest youth it has been hammered into us as children that what the prophets predicted of the Messiah has been literally fulfilled in Jesus Christ, the Savior. As believers in the Bible, we boast of this literal fulfillment of prophecy concerning the first coming of the Lord.

4. *Prophecies regarding Christ Himself.*

The predictions of Christ which have been fulfilled have been fulfilled literally.

Christ predicted that He would be betrayed (John 6:70; 13:21). He foretold His suffering and death (Matt. 16:21; 17:22; 20:18; Mark 8:31-33; 9:31-32; 10:32-34, 45; Luke 9:22; 18:33; 24:7; John 10:18; 15:13). He predicted His resurrection (see also Matt. 17:23; 20:19; 26:32; John 2:19-22).

Prophecy	Fulfillment
Called out of Egypt	
Hosea 11:1 "...and called my son out of Egypt."	Matthew 2:15 "Out of Egypt have I called my son."
His forerunner	
Isaiah 40:3 "The voice of him that crieth in the wilderness..."	Matthew 3:3 "The voice of one crying in the wilderness..."
Full of the Holy Spirit	
Isaiah 11:2 "And the spirit of the Lord shall rest upon him..."	Luke 4:1 "And Jesus being full of the Holy Ghost..."
A prophet like unto Moses	
Deuteronomy 18:15-18 "The Lord thy God will raise up unto thee a Prophet...like unto me..."	John 1:45 "We have found him, of whom Moses in the law...did write ..."
A priest after the order of Melchizedek	
Psalm 110:4 "Thou art a priest for ever after the order of Melchizedek."	Hebrews 5:6 "Thou art a priest for ever after the order of Melchisedek."

Prophecy	Fulfillment

A mediator of the New Covenant

Malachi 3:1 "Behold, I will send my messenger...of the covenant..."	Hebrews 12:24 "And to Jesus the mediator of the new covenant..."

He would perform miracles

Isaiah 35:5-6 "Then the eyes of the blind shall be opened, and the ears of the deaf shall be unstopped."	Matthew 11:5 "The blind receive their sight...and the deaf hear..."

The state of His humiliation from the manger to the cross

Isaiah 53:3-5 "He is despised and rejected of men...but he was wounded for our transgressions..."	Philippians 2:7 "But made himself of no reputation, and took upon him the form of a servant..."

Christ foretold His ascension to heaven (Luke 22:69; John 6:62; 7:33; 8:21; 14:28; 16:5; 20:17), and His coming again (Matt. 16:27; 24:30; 25:31; 26:64; Mark 8:38; 13:26; 14:62; Luke 21:27; John 14:3).

He predicted the outpouring of the Holy Spirit (John 14:26; 15:26; 16:7). He anticipated His glorification (Matt. 16:28; 17:1; Mark 9:1-2). He predicted the destruction of Jerusalem, giving many details. Without knowing about this prediction Josephus wrote of the literal fulfillment. (See also Dr. William Patton, *The Judgment of Jerusalem*, and the Rev. J. Kok, *The Coming of the Son of Man*).

Regardless of the imagery, we must come to the conclusion that the great Prophet Himself made predictions that have so far been literally fulfilled. This fact should be sufficient to prove that the remaining prophecies will be fulfilled in God's time. When interpreting prophecy we must stay as close to the simple meaning of the words as possible. Richard Hooker, sixteenth century theologian, once said, "When interpreting Holy Scripture I adopt as an infallible rule that when the literal meaning is reasonable and acceptable, the explanation that is farthest removed from the literal is usually the worst."

5. Prophecies found in the historical books.

The prophecies in the historical books have been literally fulfilled. For the sake of brevity we limit ourselves to the books of Kings.

Prophecy	Fulfillment
1 Kings 1:30 "Even as I sware unto thee by the Lord God of Israel, saying, Assuredly Solomon thy son shall sit upon my throne in my stead; even so will I certainly do this day.	1 Kings 1:48 "Blessed be the Lord God of Israel, which hath given one to sit on my throne this day, mine eyes even seeing it."
2 Kings 1:52 "But if wickedness shall be found in him [Adonijah], he shall die."	1 Kings 2:25 "Benaiah...fell upon him that he died."
1 Samuel 2:31 "Behold, the days come, that I will cut off thine [Eli's] arm, and the arm of thy father's house, that there shall not be an old man in thine house."	1 Kings 2:27 "So Solomon thrust out Abiathar from being priest unto the Lord; that he might fulfill the word of the Lord, which he spake concerning the house of Eli in Shiloh."
1 Kings 2:33 "Their blood shall therefore return upon the head of Joab, and upon the head of his seed for ever" (cf. 2 Sam. 3:39).	1 Kings 2:34 "So Benaiah...fell upon him, and slew him."
1 Kings 2:37 "For it shall be, that on the day thou goest out, and passest over the brook Kidron, thou shalt know for certain that thou shalt surely die."	1 Kings 2:46 "Benaiah...went out, and fell upon him, that he died."
1 Kings 3:12 "...neither after thee [Solomon] shall any arise like unto thee."	1 Kings 5:12 "And the Lord gave Solomon wisdom, as he promised him" (cf. 1 Kings 10:23).
1 Kings 5:5 "Thy son, whom I will set upon thy throne in thy room, he shall build an house unto my name" (cf. 2 Sam. 12ff.).	1 Kings 6:14 "So Solomon built the house, and finished it" (cf. 1 Kings 8: 19-20, 24-26).
1 Kings 9:7 "Then will I cut off Israel out of the land which I have given them; and this house, which I have hallowed for my name, will I cast out of my sight; and Israel shall be a proverb and a byword among all people" (cf. Deut. 29:24ff.).	2 Kings 25:9, 11 "And he [Nebuchadnezzar] burnt the house of the Lord... the remnant of the multitude, did Nebuzaradan the captain of the guard carry away" (cf. the entire history of the Jews).
1 Kings 11:11-12 "I will surely rend the kingdom from thee, and will give it to thy servant. Notwithstanding in thy days I will not do it for David thy father's sake: but I will rend it out of the hand of thy son."	1 Kings 12:16, 19-20 "What portion have we in David? Neither have we inheritance in the son of Jesse. So Israel rebelled against the house of David unto this day...and made him [Jeroboam] king over all Israel."

Prophecy	Fulfillment
1 Kings 13:2 "O altar, altar, thus saith the Lord; Behold, a child shall be born unto the house of David, Josiah by name; and upon thee shall he offer the priests of the high places that burn incense upon thee, and men's bones shall be burnt upon thee."	2 Kings 23:15-20 Look up this section, read it, and gratefully admire it. About three hundred forty-five years after the prophecy, all was literally fulfilled. This gripping history puts to shame all those who claim that prophecy does not deal with particular, and is even less fulfilled in details. For more prophecies that also give exact names, dates, and places, the reader is referred to Isaiah 23:15ff.; 44:28; 45:1; Jeremiah 25:11ff.; Daniel 9:24ff.
1 Kings 13:22 "Thy [the man of God at Bethel] carcase shall not come unto the sepulchre of thy fathers."	1 Kings 13:24 "A lion met him by the way, and slew him" (cf. v. 26).
1 Kings 14:5 "For it shall be, when she cometh in, that she shall feign herself to be another woman."	1 Kings 14:6 "And it was so,...why feignest thou thyself to be another?"
1 Kings 14:13 "For he only of Jeroboam shall come to the grave, because in him there is found some good thing toward the Lord."	1 Kings 14:18 "And they buried him."
1 Kings 11:36 "And unto his son will I give one tribe, that David my servant may have a light alway before me in Jerusalem."	1 Kings 15:4 "Nevertheless for David's sake did the Lord his God give him a lamp in Jerusalem, to set up his son after him, and to establish Jerusalem."
1 Kings 14:10 "Therefore, behold, I will bring evil upon the house of Jeroboam, and will cut off from Jeroboam him that pisseth against the wall, and him that is shut up and left in Israel, and will take away the remnant of the house of Jeroboam, as a man taketh away dung, till it be all gone."	1 Kings 15:29 "And it came to pass, when he reigned, that he smote all the house of Jeroboam; he left not to Jeroboam any that breathed, until he had destroyed him, according unto the saying of the Lord, which he spake by his servant Ahijah the Shilonite."
1 Kings 16:3 "Behold, I will take away the posterity of Baasha, and the posterity of his house; and will make thy house like the house of Jeroboam the son of Nebat."	1 Kings 16:12 "Thus did Zimri destroy all the house of Baasha, according to the word of the Lord, which he spake against Baasha by Jehu the prophet."

Prophecy	**Fulfillment**
Joshua 6:26 "And Joshua adjured them at that time, saying, Cursed be the man before the Lord, that riseth and buildeth this city Jericho: he shall lay the foundation thereof in his firstborn, and in his youngest son shall he set up the gates of it."	1 Kings 16:34 "In his days did Hiel the Bethelite build Jericho: he laid the foundation thereof in Abiram his firstborn, and set up the gates thereof in his youngest son Segub, according to the word of the Lord, which he spake by Joshua the son of Nun."
1 Kings 17:1 "And Elijah...said unto Ahab, As the Lord God of Israel liveth, before whom I stand, there shall not be dew nor rain these years, but according to my word."	1 Kings 17:7 "Because there had been no rain in the land."
1 Kings 17:14 "For thus saith the Lord God of Israel, The barrel of meal shall not waste, neither shall the cruse of oil fail, until the day that the Lord sendeth rain upon the earth."	1 Kings 17:16 "And the barrel of meal wasted not, neither did the cruse of oil fail, according to the word of the Lord, which he spake by Elijah."
1 Kings 18:1 "I will send rain upon the earth."	1 Kings 18:45 "And there was a great rain."
1 Kings 20:13-14 "And behold, there came a prophet unto Ahab king of Israel, saying, Thus saith the Lord, Hast thou seen all this great multitude? Behold, I will deliver it into thine hand this day; and thou shalt know that I am the Lord. And Ahab said, By whom? And he said, Thus saith the Lord, Even by the young men of the princes of the provinces."	1 Kings 20:19-20 "So these young men of the princes of the provinces came out of the city...And they slew every one his man: and the Syrians fled."
1 Kings 20:28 "And there came a man of God, and spake unto the king of Israel, and said...therefore will I deliver all this great multitude into thine hand, and ye shall know that I am the Lord."	1 Kings 20:29 "And the children of Israel slew of the Syrians an hundred thousand footmen in one day."
1 Kings 20:36a "Then said he unto him, Because thou hast not obeyed the voice of the Lord, behold, as soon as thou art departed from me, a lion shall slay thee."	1 Kings 20:36b "And as soon as he was departed from him, a lion found him, and slew him."

Prophecy	**Fulfillment**
1 Kings 20:42 "And said he unto him, Thus saith the Lord, Because thou hast let go out of thy hand a man whom I appointed to utter destruction, therefore thy life shall go for his life, and thy people for his people."	1 Kings 22:29-39
1 Kings 21:19 "Thus saith the Lord, in the place where dogs licked the blood of Naboth shall dogs lick thy blood, even thine."	1 Kings 22:38 "And the dogs licked up his blood...according unto the word of the Lord which he spake."
1 Kings 21:21 "Behold, I will bring evil upon thee, and will take away thy posterity, and will cut off from Ahab him that pisseth against the wall, and him that is shut up and left in Israel."	2 Kings 9:24-37
1 Kings 21:29 "Because he humbleth himself before me, I will not bring the evil in his days: but in his son's days will I bring the evil upon his house."	2 Kings 9:24-37
1 Kings 22:28 "And Micaiah said, If thou return at all in peace, the Lord hath not spoken by me."	1 Kings 22:37 "So the king died" (cf. v. 34).
2 Kings 1:4 and 6b "Now therefore thus saith the Lord, Thou shalt not come down from that bed on which thou art gone up, but shalt surely die."	2 Kings 1:17 "So he died according to the word of the Lord which Elijah had spoken."
2 Kings 2:10 "If thou see me when I am taken from thee, it shall be so unto thee" [namely, two parts of his spirit].	2 Kings 2:12-15 "And Elisha saw it ...The spirit of Elijah doth rest on Elisha."
2 Kings 3:17 "For thus saith the Lord, Ye shall not see wind, neither shall ye see rain; yet that valley shall be filled with water, that ye may drink, both ye, and your cattle, and your beasts."	2 Kings 3:20 "And it came to pass in the morning, when the meat offering was offered, that, behold, there came water by the way of Edom, and the country was filled with water."
2 Kings 3:18 "He will deliver the Moabites also into your hand."	2 Kings 3:24 "And smote the Moabites."
2 Kings 4:16 "And he said, About this season, according to the time of life, thou shalt embrace a son."	2 Kings 4:17 "And the woman conceived, and bare a son at that season that Elisha had said unto her, according to the time of life."

Prophecy	**Fulfillment**
2 Kings 4:43 "For thus saith the Lord, They shall eat, and shall leave thereof."	2 Kings 4:44 "And they did eat, and left thereof, according to the word of the Lord."
2 Kings 5:10 "Go and wash in Jordan seven times, and thy flesh shall come again to thee, and thou shalt be clean."	2 Kings 5:14 "And he was clean."
2 Kings 5:27 "The leprosy therefore of Naaman shall cleave unto thee."	2 Kings 5:27 "And he went out from his presence a leper as white as snow."
Leviticus 26:29 "And ye shall eat the flesh of your sons."	2 Kings 6:29 "So we boiled my son, and did eat him."
2 Kings 7:1 "Then Elisha said, Hear ye the word of the Lord; Thus saith the Lord, To morrow about this time shall a measure of fine flour be sold for a shekel, and two measures of barley for a shekel, in the gate of Samaria."	2 Kings 7:18 "And it came to pass as the man of God had spoken to the king, saying, Two measures of barley for a shekel, and a measure of fine flour for a shekel, shall be to morrow about this time in the gate of Samaria."
2 Kings 7:2 "And he said, Behold, thou shalt see it with thine eyes, but shalt not eat thereof."	2 Kings 7:20 "And so it fell out unto him: for the people trod upon him in the gate, and he died."
2 Kings 8:10 "The Lord hath shewed me that he [Benhadad] shall surely die."	2 Kings 8:15 "He died."
2 Kings 8:13 "The Lord hath shewed me that thou shalt be king over Syria."	2 Kings 8:15 "And Hazael reigned in his stead."
2 Kings 8:12 "Why weepeth my lord? And he answered, Because I know the evil that thou wilt do unto the children of Israel: their strong holds wilt thou set on fire, and their young men wilt thou slay with the sword, and wilt dash their children, and rip up their women with child." (See 1 Kings 21:21, 23.)	2 Kings 10:32; 12:17; 13:3, 7; Amos 1: 3-4. 2 Kings 6:19, 24-37; 10:1-11.
2 Kings 10:30 "And the Lord said unto Jehu, Because thou hast done well in executing that which is right in mine eyes, and hast done unto the house of Ahab according to all that was in mine heart, thy children of the fourth generation shall sit on the throne of Israel."	2 Kings 15:12 "This was the word of Lord which he spake unto Jehu, saying, Thy sons shall sit on the throne of Israel unto the fourth generation. And so it came to pass."

Prophecy	Fulfillment
2 Kings 13:19 "Whereas now thou shalt smite Syria but thrice."	2 Kings 13:25 "Three times did Joash beat him [Benhadad]."
2 Kings 14:25a "He restored the coast of Israel from the entering of Hamath unto the sea of the plain, according to the word of the Lord God of Israel."	2 Kings 14:25b "Which he spake by the hand of his servant Jonah...the prophet."
2 Kings 19:7 "Behold, I will send a blast upon him, and he shall hear a rumour, and shall return to his own land; and I will cause him to fall by the sword in his own land."	2 Kings 19:35-37.
2 Kings 20:9 "This sign shalt thou have of the Lord...shall the shadow ...go back ten degrees?	2 Kings 20:11 "And he brought the shadow ten degrees backward."
2 Kings 20:17-18 "Behold, the days come, that all that is in thine house, and that which thy fathers have laid up in store unto this day, shall be carried into Babylon: nothing shall be left, saith the Lord. And of thy sons that shall issue from thee, which thou shalt beget, shall they take away; and they shall be eunuchs in the palace of the king of Babylon."	2 Kings 24:12; 2 Chronicles 33:11; Daniel 1:3.
2 Kings 21:12 "Therefore thus saith the Lord God of Israel, Behold, I am bringing such evil upon Jerusalem and Judah."	2 Kings 25.
2 Kings 22:20 "Behold therefore, I will gather thee unto thy fathers, and thou shalt be gathered into thy grave in peace; and thine eyes shall not see all the evil which I will bring upon this place."	2 Kings 23:29 "And he [Pharaoh-necho] slew him [Josiah]."

These are examples of the literal fulfillment of only two historical books. We find the same phenomena in the other parts of Holy Writ. The Lord emphasizes that His Word was fulfilled exactly as He had announced. We can praise Him for His faithfulness, truth, and omniscience. Believers who nebulize His Word change the prophetic light to darkness. But His infallible Word will continue to shine in a dark place until the Morning Star Arises.

6. *Prophetic references to times.*

Prophetic periods which have been fulfilled, have been fulfilled literally. Many people do not realize that Scripture contains many prophetical time references. In connection with the millennial kingdom of peace, we are dealing with a most important matter, and so we are listing most of the time references that are found in Scripture.

Prophecy	**Fulfillment**

Adam

Genesis 2:17 "In the day that thou eatest thereof thou shalt surely die."	Genesis 3:7-9 depicts the fulfillment, implying their sense of shame, their knowledge of good and evil, and their fleeing from God. For is it not the wicked who flee when no man pursueth? From that day onward, death became part of life.

Noah

Genesis 6:3 "Yet his days shall be an hundred and twenty years."	Genesis 7:11. From the exacted lineation of time, it is clear that this prophecy was literally fulfilled.

The flood

Genesis 7:4 "For yet seven days, and I will cause it to rain upon the earth."	Genesis 7:10 "And it came to pass after seven days, that the waters of the flood were upon the earth."

Duration of the flood

Genesis 7:4 "I will cause it to rain upon the earth forty days and forty nights.	Genesis 7:12 "And the rain was upon the earth forty days and forty nights."

In Egypt

Genesis 15:13 "They shall afflict them four hundred years."	Acts 7:6 "...four hundred years." (Here, however, we are dealing with two different chronologies. The other is listed below.) Exodus 12:41 "And it came to pass at the end of the four hundred and thirty years, even the selfsame day it came to pass, that all the hosts of the Lord went out of the land of Egypt." In Galatians 3:17 Paul adopts this figure. This shows that this number is figured from the time that Abraham first moved into Egypt, not from the time that Jacob moved there. See also

Prophecy	Fulfillment
	Exodus 12:16ff. From Jacob's moving into Egypt to the exodus covers a span of no more than 215 years. The figure four hundred does not include the past years of Abraham's oppression.

The butler and the baker

Genesis 40:13 "Yet within three days shall Pharaoh lift up thine head."	Genesis 40:20 "And it came to pass the third day...that ...he lifted up the head of the chief butler."
Concerning the baker: Genesis 40:19 "Yet within three days shall Pharaoh ...hang thee on a tree."	Genesis 40:22 "But he hanged the chief baker: as Joseph had interpreted to them."

The seven years of abundance and famine

Genesis 41:29 "Behold, there come seven years of great plenty throughout all the land of Egypt."	Genesis 41:53 "And the seven years of plenteousness...were ended."
Genesis 41:30 "And there shall arise after them seven years of famine."	Genesis 41:54 "And the seven years of dearth began to come, according as Joseph had said."

The plague of hail

Exodus 9:18 "Behold, tomorrow about this time I will cause it to rain a very grievous hail."	Exodus 9:22-28.

Forty years in the desert

Numbers 14:34 "Ye...shall...bear your iniquities, even forty years."	Hebrews 3:17 "But with whom was he grieved forty years? was it not with them that had sinned, whose carcases fell in the wilderness?"

Seven days around Jericho

Joshua 6:4-5 "And the seventh day ye shall compass the city seven times... and the wall of the city shall fall down flat."	Joshua 6:15-16 "Only on that day they compassed the city seven times. And it came to pass at the seventh time...Joshua said unto the people, Shout; for the Lord hath given you the city."

Saul

1 Samuel 28:19 "Tomorrow shalt thou and thy sons be with me."	1 Samuel 29.

Prophecy	Fulfillment

Elijah

1 Kings 17:1 "There shall not be dew nor rain these years, but according to my word."	James 5:17 "And it rained not on the earth by the space of three years and six months."

Ahab

1 Kings 20:22 "At the return of the year the king of Syria will come up against thee."	1 Kings 20:26 "And it came to pass at the return of the year, that Benhadad numbered the Syrians, and went up ...to fight against Israel."

The famine in Samaria

2 Kings 7:1 "Tomorrow about this time shall a measure of fine flour be sold for a shekel."	2 Kings 7:18 "And it came to pass as the man of God had spoken to the king, saying, Two measures of barley for a shekel, and a measure of fine flour for a shekel, shall be tomorrow about this time in the gate of Samaria."

The Shunammite woman

2 Kings 8:1 "A famine...shall also come upon the land seven years."	2 Kings 8:2 "...seven years."

Ephraim

Isaiah 7:8 "And within threescore and five years shall Ephraim be broken, that it be not a people."	2 Kings 17:23. The fulfillment of this prophecy does not refer to the carrying into exile under Shalmaneser but under Esarhaddon, when the last remnant of Ephraim was carried away. Then this figure finds indeed literal fulfillment, for Ahaz ruled after this prophecy for another fourteen years. Hezekiah ruled after this prophecy for twenty-nine years. And the exile took place in the twenty-third year of Manasseh. This makes exactly sixty-five years.

Tyre

Isaiah 23:17. Tyre shall be forgotten for seventy years.	According to most commentators this refers to the domination of the first world power, namely, the Babylonians, as prophesied (see 2 Kings 25:27 and Jeremiah 25:11-12).

Hezekiah

Isaiah 38:5 "I will add unto thy days fifteen years."	2 Kings 20:7 "And he recovered."

Prophecy	Fulfillment

Exile

Jeremiah 29:10 "For thus saith the Lord, That after seventy years be accomplished at Babylon I will visit you, and perform my good word toward you, in causing you to return to this place."

Daniel 9:2 "In the first year of his reign, I Daniel understood by books the number of the years, whereof the word of the Lord came to Jeremiah the prophet, that he would accomplish seventy years in the desolations of Jerusalem."

Hananiah

Jeremiah 28:16 "This year thou shalt die."

Jeremiah 28:17 "So Hananiah the prophet died the same year."

Egypt's dispersion

Ezekiel 29:13 "At the end of forty years will I gather the Egyptians from the people whither they were scattered."

Here the correct references are lacking so that we cannot indicate the exact fulfillment. We know, however, that all the heathen nations around Israel, like Israel herself, were in bondage to Babylon for seventy years. Ezekiel prophesied during the time of the exile, so that, when he made this prophecy, about thirty years of it had passed (see Jeremiah 25:11-12 and Isaiah 23:17).

Nebuchadnezzar

Daniel 4:25 "And seven times shall pass over thee, till thou know that the most High ruleth in the kingdom of men, and giveth it to whomsoever he will."

Daniel 4:34 "And at the end of the days, I Nebuchadnezzar lifted up mine eyes unto heaven, and mine understanding returned unto me, and I blessed the most High, and I praised and honored him that liveth for ever, whose dominion is an everlasting dominion, and his kingdom is from generation to generation."

The chronological prophecy of Daniel 9:24-27 consists of three parts. The fulfillment of the first seven weeks is recorded in the books of Ezra and Nehemiah. The sixty-two weeks are literally fulfilled in the first coming of Christ. The last week, mentioned in verse 27, lies still in the future and will also be literally fulfilled. Since this prophecy has such far-reaching implications, we shall deal with it more specifically later on.

Thus far we have covered virtually all the Old Testament prophecies regarding future times that have already found their fulfillment. We can ignore Jonah 3:4, since this is obviously a conditional prophecy. The people repented and so the prophecy was withdrawn.

Hosea 6:2 is probably a mere saying or proverb, as are Job 5:19; Proverbs 6:16; 30:15, 18; and Amos 1:3. Such connections of two chronological numbers express the certainty and regularity of an act. Jesus also said to the Pharisees, "Behold, I cast out devils, and I do cures today and tomorrow, and the third day I shall be perfected." If we, with many exegetes, applied Hosea 6:2 to the resurrection of Christ, then we have again a time reference that has been literally fulfilled.

TIMES AND NUMBERS

When we turn to the New Testament, we find that all prophecies regarding certain times that have been fulfilled have been literally fulfilled. This includes the prophecy in Revelation 2:10 where it is foretold that the church at Smyrna will have a persecution of ten days. In A.D. 168 it experienced a persecution of ten days.

The fact that prophecies have been fulfilled is of the utmost importance for our total view of Scripture, and most of all for our expectation of the future. From it we can derive an argument against the widely accepted year/day theory of the Adventists and many Bible commentators. This theory claims that especially during the times of the prophets a day stands for a year. The scanty grounds on which this theory rests are Numbers 14:34 and Ezekiel 4:6. Even though excellent men like Augustine, Ambrose, Bengel, and others advocate this theory, the grounds are nevertheless much too weak, for what the Lord emphatically declares to be an exception, they make into a rule. All the calculations regarding the second coming of the Lord have resulted from this fatal theory. Finally, we see that of the roughly thirty-five chronological prophecies about thirty have been literally fulfilled. The main thing in Scripture is not the *time* but the *fact* of events.

And finally, with these facts before us, it will not do to evaporate the times that have not yet been fulfilled into a state of fog by means of the spiritualization theory. When, for instance, the Lord in Revelation 20 says *a thousand years* three times, and *the thousand years* three times, He means exactly what He says.

Intimately connected with the prophetic *chronology* are the prophetic *numbers*. What has been said of the times holds true also for the numbers. They must be explained literally and not symbolically. Scripture does not contain many numbers, yet there are some definite numbers (see Dan. 7:24; 8:14; 9:24-27; 12:11-12; Rev. 11:2-3; 12:6, 14; 13:5, 18). Note that they appear in the two most prophetic books of the Bible. It has been argued that these numbers must be explained symbolically. They are found in the most symbolical books, so the argument goes, and hence they must be explained symbolically. But the Lord wills that they be examined and explained (Dan. 9:2; 12:4, 10; Rev. 13:18).

Numbers are simpler than is usually thought. When we compare them with each other, we soon discover that all of them are based on one number, namely, the number seven. They are parts or multiples of the basic figure seven, which, with the number twelve, play the greatest role in Holy Scripture. We find "time and times and the dividing of time" (Dan. 7:25); "time, and times, and half a time" (Rev. 12:14); "time, times, and an half" (Dan. 12:7); "forty and two months" (Rev. 11:2; 13:5); "one week" (Dan. 9:27); "a thousand two hundred and threescore days" (Rev. 11:3; 12:6). One need not be a skilled mathematician to see immediately that we are dealing here with half of the figure seven. They are half of the unfulfilled week of Daniel, with which we must deal later.

We quote here a statement by E. Geurs, "Once again, we say simply that the most literal explanation, when it is not at variance either with the Bible itself or with sound logic, is at the same time the safest." That was the view of the early Church until Origen, who with his spiritualization partly destroyed the Eastern Churches.

LITERAL EXPLANATION

The literal explanation of prophecy rests mainly on literal inspiration. The following principles and rules result from this principle.

1. *No prophecy of Scripture should be interpreted humanly.*

The apostle Peter writes to the believers in 2 Peter 1:19 that they do well to take heed to the word of prophecy. With this, he gives the apostolic admonition that they must love it, and be guided by it, as it is a light that shines in a dark place.

But he hastens to add that if the prophetic word is to be a light to them, they must first have an indispensable knowledge concerning this word. First you must know this, he says, that no prophecy of the Scriptures is of any private interpretation (2 Peter 1:20). What he means by this is that prophecy may not be interpreted by the understanding and opinion of man, but only by the understanding and intent of the Spirit. He who gave it by inspiration is the One who must interpret it. This Word of God contains deep things, and He is the only One who searches the deep things of God. Man can no more produce an interpretation in accord with the meaning and intent of the Holy Spirit than make a true confession on the basis of flesh and blood. It is this important rule that usually is neglected by sects and heresies. They put their own meaning into the Word of prophecy. Only when we possess the anointing of the Holy Spirit, let it penetrate our lives, and apply it prayerfully to the interpretation of prophecy, shall we not err with regard to the Word. On the contrary, only then can we walk in the brightest light until the bright Morning Star arises. Only when we interpret through the Holy Spirit will the literal explanation be truly a spiritual interpretation.

In addition, Scripture must be compared with Scripture. Many have an aversion to doing this, for it requires hard study. Heretics often string a number of texts of the same sound together, with the intent of deceiving unsuspecting souls.

Scripture is one organic whole, with one Author and one main goal. For that reason we violate it, if we separate various texts or isolate certain truths out of their context. We must always compare various texts with like meaning and that should be in their context. In this way we honor the great Author of the words and surrender our own ideas to Him. He wants to bind our thoughts to the Word.

2. *We may not add to or subtract from prophecy.*

As was the case with the preceding rule, this holds true for the entire Scripture, but it is nowhere more violated than in the realm of prophecy. Anticipating this, Scripture, on its very last page, warns solemnly against this evil. That this warning was necessary has been proved in the history of the Church. The last prophetic book, as well as the whole body of prophecy, has often been avoided. Some Church Fathers, as well as Luther, had a certain aversion to the Book of Revelation because it so clearly teaches the doctrine of a millennium.

The Church of Rome has for ages committed the sin of adding to and subtracting from the Scriptures. For centuries she has considered herself the fulfillment of all prophecy, with the exception of the coming again of the Lord to judge the quick and the dead. By her traditions and many false doctrines, she has added to the word of prophecy.

The churches of the Reformation are by no means without guilt in this regard. They frequently committed the sin—not in theory, but in practice—of taking away from the words of prophecy. In their view and exegesis of prophecy, as well as in their concept of the Church, they have, alas, continued in the footsteps of Rome. We may not reproach the Reformers with this, for they had more than their hands full with combating Rome, the world powers, and the Anabaptists. In the area of theology they restored to us the authority of Scripture, justification by faith, and in part, at least, a pure government of the Church. But we must reproach the Reformation writers with having taken away from prophecy by their disuse and misuse of it.

If the Protestant churches in their confessions, standard theological works, and preaching had done justice to the entire body of prophecy, we today would not have so many sects that have made prophecy a hobbyhorse on which they run blindly.

3. *Israel is the heart of Old Testament prophecy.*

To Israel and by Israel the prophecies were pronounced over the nations. But of Israel itself, the coming Messiah is the heart. Thus we may call the Messiah the heart of prophecy. Everything revolves around the seed of the woman, the seed of Abraham, the seed of David, and the seed of the virgin. And in the New Testament the coming again of the Lord is the hope of the Church.

4. *Israel retains its own identity as a peculiar people from the beginning to the end of prophecy.*

Israel is a special people of God. This is made abundantly clear in Scripture (Gen. 15:1-15; 1 Chron. 17; Isa. 66:22; Jer. 31:3, 35-36; 33:22-26; Acts 10:45; Eph. 3:5-6; Col. 1:26-27; 1 Tim. 3:16).

Does not the ages-old history of this nation prove this clearly? It has never wanted or been able to unite itself with other nations, even though it was dispersed among all the nations. In every country Jewish people seem to retain a distinctive identity. Hence this nation, through its origin as well as its continued existence, is the abiding marvel of Jehovah. The Lord, however, never performs a miracle without a purpose. He has a reason for preserving Israel.

We shall also consider the remnant, which plays such an important part in the prophecy of the Old Covenant. No matter how hard Israel will be struck and afflicted by the judgments of God on account of its sins, it will never be totally exterminated. The remnant will be saved, as almost all the prophets tell us. Early in the Bible typical reference is made to this fact (Lev. 2:3, 10; 6:16; 1 Kings 18:19). Isaiah often spoke about it (1:9; 11:1, 11; 16:14), as did Jeremiah (23:3), Ezekiel (9:8; 11:13-25), Micah (2:12, 4:7; 5:7; 7:18), and Zephaniah (3:12-13, 18-19).

The underlying basis of the remnant is the idea of election; it presupposes sin and misery, and contains the prophecy of Israel's indestructibility and future restoration.

5. *According to the apostle Peter, the times of the restitution of all things is the subject of all the prophets* (Acts 3:21).

These times are not eternity; and far less this present dispensation in which all things are still devastated by sin. The expression refers to the same thing as the regeneration of which Christ speaks in Matthew 19:28, when the apostles will sit upon twelve thrones judging the twelve tribes of Israel. The expression, "the dispensation of the fulness of times," refers to the same circumstance, when all things will be gathered together under the one head, Christ (Eph. 1:10). The same is referred to again as "the kingdom of peace" of which all the prophets spoke. The current opinion of many people is that this present dispensation will last for a little longer or shorter time, but that on a certain future day, eternity will commence. This idea is absolutely unbiblical. There are numerous prophetic expressions in the New Testament that can refer neither to this dispensation nor to eternity. That this is always overlooked is partly due to ignorance about the last things and prejudice which blinds men's eyes.

We have never read a commentary or book on the prophets that dared deny that the prophets are speaking about a kingdom of peace. Everyone agrees that the prophecies are full of it. All writers, from the most radical critics to the staunchest orthodox thinker, and those in between who play the role of mediators, fully agree on this fact. Besides, one would be deliberately blind to deny this. But in the interpretation of these matters their ways separate widely. Those of a Reformed background usually ignore them or diffuse them into eternity as Abraham Kuyper did. Or, with J. H. Bavinck, they relegate them to the realm of poetic imagery. Or they interpret them by saying that these matters refer to the glorious state of the Church in the end time. The view of the latter we would rather call a false chiliasm.

Following the lead of Abraham Kuenen, the unbelieving critics usually ascribe these things to the enthusiasm of the prophets. According to Ernst Wilhelm Hengstenberg, the prophets were seers who depicted to Israel a glorious kingdom of peace in order to comfort the people. Riehm, in his *Messianic Predictions,* attacked this view with one of his own which implied that the prophets in most cases were mistaken. Some exegetes apply all these matters to the return from exile, and, in that connection, with the heyday under the Maccabees.

All these explanations fail to do justice to the prophets. When they predict Israel's conversion and glory as a nation, with Canaan as an eternal possession and the Messiah in their midst—as in Isaiah 2; 11; 40—66; Jeremiah 23; 30—33; Ezekiel 30—40, and so on—then all these things are still awaiting their complete fulfillment at the coming of the Lord. Numerous places in the Old Testament point to the future restoration of the Jews, which, according to Paul, will be like a resurrection from the dead for the entire world. By far, most of these scriptural references appear in connection with the coming of the Messiah for the judgment of the nations and the institution of the kingdom of peace. To refer these things frequently to the kingdom of peace causes difficulties. We are nevertheless convinced that only with this approach is justice done to the intent of the prophets; and only thereby is nothing taken away or added to the word of prophecy. The fact must not be overlooked that when interpreting the prophets, the Holy Spirit usually gives sufficient indications in cases where they must *not* be interpreted literally.

6. *When the Lord Himself gives an explanation of some vision, we must unconditionally adhere to it and consider this as the only correct one.*

This simple rule is often flagrantly violated.

This kind of explanation often appears in Holy Scripture. Dreams are always interpreted and some parables are explained. In all these cases, men usually adhere simply to this divine explanation. When in Revelation 1:20 the Lord says, "The seven stars are the angels of the seven churches; and the seven candlesticks which thou sawest are the seven churches," no one usually thinks of another interpretation. Nor does anyone look for another explanation when it is said in Revelation 19:8, "The fine linen is the righteousness of saints." Or again in verse 10, "The testimony of Jesus is the spirit of prophecy."

With regard to the exclusively prophetic sections, however, the simple indications given by the Holy Spirit Himself are frequently disregarded. In Revelation 11:4 we read, "These are the two olive trees, and the two candlesticks standing before the God of the earth." This text cannot be comprehended in a strictly literal sense, but that does by no means give us the right to spiritualize it. From a comparison of this statement with Zechariah 4, we can deduce that the Holy Spirit indicates that just as Joshua and Zerubbabel labored for the first restoration of Israel, so at its final restoration two men of God will be active in Jerusalem.

In Revelation 11:8 the great city is further defined as the city "where also our Lord was crucified." The Church Fathers were of the opinion that this referred only to Jerusalem. But in later ages it was thought that it referred to Rome, Paris, or what have you. In Revelation 12:9 the great red dragon is further delineated as "that old serpent," as "the Devil, and Satan," and as the one who "deceiveth the whole world." Yet some exegetes, notwithstanding this explicit explanation, are still thinking of the pope, the Antichrist, or the Roman Empire.

When it says in Revelation 17:9, "The seven heads are seven mountains," this is usually accepted as a literal statement. The same holds true for what immediately follows, "And there are seven kings," and the statement in verse 12, "The ten horns... are ten kings." And again the declaration of the Lamb in verse 14 is accepted with appreciation, "He is Lord of lords, and King of kings." In verse 15 no other interpretation of "the waters" is demanded than the one given there. In verse 18 the woman is said to be "that great city, which reigneth over the kings of the earth," and this is usually accepted as it stands.

But it must amaze us that the God-given explanation in Revelation 20:5 is silently ignored as though it were not given at all. In unmistakably clear terms it is stated as a specific explanation of the vision, "This is the first resurrection," yet this is usually brushed aside. Under no circumstances can it be said that this brief explanation is too obscure or that it prompts us to come to absurd conclusions. We recall in this connection a statement by the learned Dean Woodhouse, "When an interpretation is expressly given in a vision, that interpretation must be used as the key to the mystery, in preference to all interpretation suggested by the imagination of man."

We are of the opinion that the above-mentioned principles and rules are reasonable and scriptural, and hence we intend to abide by them in the subsequent pages of this book. Those who consider these rules fair will readily agree with the conclusions to which we come.

Chapter 3

THE SIGNS OF THE TIMES

Scripture teaches us that paying heed to the signs of the times is the duty of every believer. Christ called not only the Pharisees hypocrites because they did not discern the signs of the times, but also the multitudes for not discerning "this time" (Matt. 16:1-4; Luke 12:54-59). Not paying heed to the signs of the times is a greater sin than is commonly thought. It manifests a denial of His divine predictions, of His hand in history, and of His calling. Israel did not know its time, and therefore was not prepared for its time of visitation. Our struggle must be in accord with our times. This was understood by the men of Issachar, who were praised for their understanding of the times.

Sinful man wants to live his own life and shape his own future. His ways are always different from the Lord's ways. Israel's learned men craved spectacular signs from heaven, but they refused to see the actual signs. Before Jesus came, the signs were numerous, as they are today. Prophecies had been and were being fulfilled before their very eyes. The forerunner of the Messiah had come, but they called him a devil. Christ Himself performed many miracles, but they ascribed them to the powers of darkness. They did not see at all that the Kingdom of God had come to them in the person of the Messiah Himself. It was inexcusable on the part of the scribes not to see all of this.

The situation today is similar to what it was then. Many Christians are blind with regard to the signs of the time. The signs, drawn by the finger of the Almighty to warn and comfort us, tell us that the Lord is coming and that soon our warfare is ended. Isaac DaCosta made a distinction between the spirit of the time and the course of the times. The former is from the devil, the latter from God. We must diametrically oppose the former, and with the latter we must agree. But we must study and examine both in the searchlight of the prophetic word. Then they will loose us from the earth, for they cry out continually that this sinful world will soon crumble to dust when Christ will appear in brilliance out of Zion to cleanse and renew all things. This awe-inspiring event will dispose us to soberness and watchfulness. Whoever is fully aware of this can no longer love the present world.

Generally speaking, the signs of the times can be divided into positive and negative signs.

POSITIVE SIGNS

1. *A missionary zeal exists today such as has not been seen since the days of the Apostles.*

We may say that the Lord is blessing this effort. Everywhere He has given open doors, ready acceptance, and a rich harvest of blessings (see Matt. 24:14).

2. *Prophecy is studied more than ever before.*

In almost all countries the Lord has raised up godly and capable men who have searched the prophetic Scriptures and thereby unearthed treasures the Church had hardly discovered. And the multitude is still growing that looks forward eagerly to the coming of the Lord to take up His Church, to bind Satan, to restore Israel, and to set the groaning creation free. We recognize with gladness the fulfillment of the prophecy that toward the end time many will search the prophetic word, and the godly will understand it (Dan. 12:4, 10).

3. *Another joyful phenomenon is that true Christians will feel spiritually one in Christ more than ever before.*

The loveless exclusivism of former ages has almost disappeared. Calvinists and Lutherans during the time of the Reformation were filled with an almost devilish hatred toward one another. We say "filled" advisedly, for children were from their earliest youth in catechism classes filled with malice toward the other group. Just as much as we despise all compromise with the world, we rejoice in and welcome closer relations between true believers in Christ. In these closer relationships we see a glimmering of the joyful day when all Jesus' sheep will be one flock under one Shepherd.

4. *Today prophecy is manifestly being fulfilled.*

The fig tree (Israel) is beginning to bud (Luke 21:29-30). All the nations have become angry (Rev. 11:18). The horseman on the red horse has clearly gone out to remove peace from the earth (Rev. 6:4). And from day to day it is becoming more evident that the black horse of scarcity and famine has already gone out (vv. 5-6). Numerous antichrists tell us that it is the last hour (1 John 2:18). Other prophecies in these turbulent days have already been partially or totally fulfilled. We must remember, however, that we can never say as though with a stopwatch in our hand, "It is such and such a time on the prophetic clock."

5. *Signs among the Jews have appeared.*

This old nation is still beloved for the sake of the fathers. In spite of its woeful history, it is still, until this day, indeed especially in our day, the living proof of the veracity of Holy Scripture. Israel is a mass of fulfilled and unfulfilled prophecy. Many things the newspapers tell us about the Jews confirm the Scriptures. Zionism especially is a sign of far-reaching implications. For a study of Zionism seen in its prophetic significance we refer the reader to several small booklets on this subject by A. C. Gaebelein.

6. *In the entire civilized world there is a general impression that we have approached the end of the ages.*

With the worldlings, this manifests itself in a vague premonition, an undefined fear of things that will befall the world. But with the people of the Lord, the conviction becomes more general that Christ will soon come from the heavens. Everywhere we hear the midnight call, "Behold, the Bridegroom cometh; go ye out to meet him."

Socialism constantly makes mention of Christ's return. The victory of the red flag will be the coming of Christ and will bring the promised kingdom of peace. Mrs. Mary Baker Eddy identified the triumph of Christian Science with the coming of the Lord. The Order of the Star of the East, founded in 1911, has as Article I in its Declaration of Principles, "We believe that soon a great Teacher will appear in the world, and we wish to live in such a way that we may be worthy of Him when He comes." This Gentile order—which already has its adherents by the thousands in India, England, and America—is an invention of the prince of darkness to substitute the expectation of a great Intelligence for the blessed hope of the coming of the Lord. Christ is not returning to instruct the world as a teacher, but to judge it in righteousness as King.

The person in whom all these foolish people put their trust is no one else but the man of sin. In the light of the prophetic Word, we may readily call their special expectation of the godly a favorable sign of the times.

NEGATIVE SIGNS

All the signs of the times which are viewed as divine indications of the blessed return of the Lord must, without exception, be considered favorable, or positive. They emphatically tell us that this dark dispensation will soon be past and that the King of Peace is coming to establish a fullness of peace until the moon no longer exists.

We can speak of unfavorable or negative signs if we take them simply as phenomena of the day and not as the particular woes that precede the birth of a new world. (See Matthew 24:8.) The word "sorrows" refers to the travail of a woman giving birth. (Also see Romans 8:20-22.)

Scripture concerns itself with religion and moral life. Scripture also, though in passing, calls our attention to signs in other areas. We mention a few here.

1. *Intellectual signs of the times.*
Toward the endtime, knowledge will be increased (Dan. 12:4). The mockers of the last days, of whom Peter makes mention, will be scientific people. They speak of the constancy and unchangeableness of the laws of nature, as the modernists and evolutionists have done for the past half-century. They know of the patriarchs and they know of the future coming of the Lord. They know of the Flood and that the earth was changed by the Flood, but they don't believe there will be a future perishing of the world. They attempt to mock this fact away. And this weapon of mockery points us to a false science. Jude in his epistle points to an ungodly humanism that separates itself from God-fearing people, that seems to deny the existence of matter.

2. *The social sign of the times.*

Scripture references such as James 5:1-8, Revelation 6:5-6, and others point in this direction. The order presented here (war, famine) agrees with the order Christ indicates in Matthew 24, Mark 13, and Luke 21.

Christ also refers to social evils when He speaks of the days of Lot (Luke 17:28-30). Some people take this as a reference to homosexuality (see Genesis 19). This sin is representative of a reprobate mind (Rom. 1:28), as it is frequently found among old and new heathenism. The sin of Sodom is described in Ezekiel 16:49, where Ezekiel mentions the real cause—pride. The people wished to be their own lords and masters. All the other sins, such as *fullness of bread,* resulted from this one.

Sodom followed the centuries-old course of prosperity, luxury, wantonness, worldly-mindedness, and sensuality. And as usual, wantonness led to a *quiet complacency,* a false peace. The Sodomites were, moreover, avaricious. In all their luxury they neglected to remember those in misery. This resulted in God's judgment of the reprobate mind, to be followed shortly by a complete extermination. The people were too evil to live in this world.

With the expression "eating and drinking," the Savior obviously is thinking of their wantonness, with "buying and selling" of their avarice and greed, and with "planting and building" of their false security. They did all these things as if they were to go on forever, and as if the Lord in His anger was not ready to pluck up what He had planted and to break down what He had built.

Christ's reference to Noah's contemporaries indicates that the worldly situation regarding marital life will not be favorable at the end of this dispensation. From Genesis we know that many marriages had been contracted between a person who loved God and one who did not. The expression "sons of God" in Genesis 6:2 refers to the believing Sethites, rather than to angels, as some believe. God's people no longer wanted to be a separated poeple, or to keep themselves free from the pollution of the world. They turned away from the line of grace to move on in the line of the Canaanite development of sin. Marital life became more and more frivolous; they "took them wives of all which they chose." Their mingling with the children of the world tells us that they no longer sought the Lord. Indeed it tells us that they hardly used their minds. Moved by their passions and disregarding all limits of morality, they heedlessly plunged into marriage. In these unholy and ill-advised marriages, the Lord found the cause of the moral corruption that cried to heaven, which could only be washed away by the waters of the Flood. Carnal desires and the operation of the Holy Spirit are diametrically opposed to each other. When the salt had lost its savor and the people had degraded themselves to a tool of their lusts, the Spirit of God departed. The Lord no longer restrained this degenerated society, but allowed it to run blindly on toward its destruction.

Another hint at marital life in the last days is found in 1 Timothy 4:3. It speaks of people who will forbid marriage. Here we are not to think of imperial prohibition, but of general aversion to marriage. People prohibit what they do not like, what they want to do away with. Our forebears usually thought this was a reference to the Roman church, but these words do not wholly apply to her. For Rome, by making marriage a sacrament, has overestimated this institution rather than underestimated it. She forbids marriage only to her priests and nuns. Hence she is not motivated by a hatred of this divine institution, and that is what Scripture means by these words. We are reminded by this statement of the Apostle Paul of the hatred against marriage and the family as it is found in socialism, anarchism, spiritism, and other anti-christian movements.

Thus we see that at the end of time, the foundations of society and the family will be destroyed by sin.

3. *The political sign or the movements among the nations.*

From many statements in the prophets it is to be concluded that there will be a resurgent nationalism. The expression, *all the trees,* in Luke 21:29 undoubtedly refers to all the nations, just as the fig tree refers to the people of Israel. According to prophecy, the interests of the emerging nations will clash with each other. Scripture constantly speaks of the raging of the nations shortly before the return of the Lord (see, among other references, Isa. 17:12; Joel 3:9-10; Matt. 24:6-8; Luke 21:25-26; Rev. 9:14-21; 16:12-16).

Revelation 11:18 is an especially striking reference. It speaks of things that take place under the sounding of the seventh trumpet, and that is the trumpet of the consummation of things. All the nations are presented there as being angry. They burn with hatred against Christ and consequently also against each other, for in Christ is unity. He is the cement of the universe. All things exist through Him. But opposite this anger of the nations is, in striking contrast, the anger of the righteous Judge. The same verse also sharply contrasts the reward of the faithful and the reward of those who have corrupted the earth as God's creation.

People expect life to get better. But with Scripture in hand (especially such pronouncements as we find in Rev. 6:1-4, 11:18, and 16:12-15), we would not dare to claim that present miseries will speed away before the Lord returns. Already the deeply imbedded hatred and the complete blinding of the nations point out that we must not participate in the light-hearted cry of the false prophets of "peace, peace," and no danger. We must not look forward on this dark earth, but upward to the Word of the Savior, for there everything is light.

4. *Demoniacal signs, or the raging of the father of lies.*

Man in his course of sin began with the slogan that he wanted to be like God. Meanwhile, throughout the ages, he has walked in the steps of the devil. And throughout all the ages, the serpent and his seed continue their battle without any let-up against Christ and His seed. Just as Satan manifested his hellish activity in an accelerated measure at the first coming of Christ, so, according to prophecy, he will also do at His second coming. He will manifest great wrath, knowing that he has but a short time (Rev. 12:12). He will deceive the nations (Rev. 16:12-15) and cause them to clash with each other. Armageddon is his work. With "the energy of lies" he will work in the children of disobedience who have not loved the truth (2 Thess. 2:10). He will cause many foolish apostate people to pay heed to seducing spirits and doctrines of devils and to query the dead (2 Tim. 4:1-2).

This reminds us of the fifteen million spiritists in this country alone. Scripture-believing men, such as Haldeman, Gaebelein, Mauro, Mackenzie, Pollock, and Pink, all of whom have made an intensive study of spiritism, are unanimous in their judgment that it is not the spirits of deceased people who perform miracles, but the demons themselves. According to Scripture, consulting the dead is the work of the devil (see Lev. 19:31; 20:6, 27; Deut. 18:10-12; 32:17; Ps. 106:37; Isa. 8:19-20; 44:25; 47:9-13; Jer. 14:13-16).

5. *Religious signs or phenomena in the religious-moral realm.*
As already indicated, Scripture calls our attention particularly to these phenomena. Scripture does not hold out a glorious state of the Church, as so many theologians have dreamed about, but teaches a great apostasy. That will be the sign of the times par excellence. The Holy Spirit thought it necessary to emphasize this repeatedly. In an exceptional example, Paul in 1 Timothy 4:1 says that the Holy Spirit clearly foretells this apostasy. The Holy Spirit is the great Teacher of the Church, who makes known the things of the future, and is totally honest. Unlike the false prophets, He not only predicts the pleasant things, but also the unpleasant. He wishes to prevent a false peace of mind. For that reason He shows us the abysses of evil, so that we may not crash into them.

That which people want least, they hardly comprehend. We need think only of the disciples to whom the cross remained almost totally hidden, because they did not want it. The knowledge of the great apostasy from God and His Word is necessary for the Church. She can gain nothing and lose everything by disregarding this divine truth. She ought to know the nature of this dispensation, so she can be on her guard against apostasy and seduction.

If the churches of the Reformation had clearly understood this truth and had constantly been on their guard against apostasy, they would not have started dreaming of a glorious church-state on earth during this dispensation. Evidence that the Holy Spirit has revealed this truth is found in some fifty New Testament texts that refer to it directly or indirectly. The main text regarding this neglected truth is 2 Thessalonians 2:3, where the Apostle Paul says that the day of Christ does not come except a falling away come first. In the original Greek, he uses a definite article whereby he indicates that this apostasy (the word he uses) is well known to his readers. With this text should be compared, especially in the contexts where they appear, the following references: Matt. 24—25· Luke 18:8; 22:34-36; Rom. 11:22; Dan. 8:23; 12:10; 1 Thess. 5:1-6; 2 Thess. 2; 1 Tim. 4:1-7; 2 Tim. 3:1-5, 12; 4:1-3; James 5:1-8; 2 Peter 3:3-4; Jude 18-23; Rev. 3:14-22; 17—18. Whoever wishes to take the trouble to check these references will find that a general apostasy is clearly predicted, and that the evening hour of grace will be very dark indeed and will be almost like unto the dawning of the day of judgment.

Let us now go deeper into the nature and extent of this apostasy. When we speak of apostasy here, we do not mean the apostasy that has been known throughout the ages. Since mankind fell away from God, he has been sinking further and further. All those who do not seek their salvation in Christ as the Ark of Salvation will eventually sink away together with the apostate world.

We are referring here to the apostasy that will take place in Christendom itself. Such an apostasy is possible. Salt does not soon become tasteless, but it can lose its savor.

There is no falling away of those who are in Christ, and so the Church, seen as the body of Christ, can be fully assured that the gates of hell will not prevail against it. But just as assuredly as the Church as the body of Christ can never fall away, or decay, or even fall just once, a historical church as an institution can indeed fall away from grace. The history of the church sounds here a note of alarm. Whole groups of churches have indeed apostasized. Where are the prosperous churches of the first centuries in Asia Minor? Where those of Palestine? Of Egypt? Of Abyssinia? Except for a few, they have become apostate and God has wiped them away in order to let heathen and Turks flourish in their stead. Also in this connection it can be said, "Behold the . . . severity of God: on them which fell."

Hence the poison of forsaking God has always been active in the Church of God, but in the latter days we shall find an aggravation of it, both in depth and width. That will be the great falling away expressly predicted by the Holy Spirit, an apostasy that finds no equal in history. The seer on Patmos was given a vision of the apostate Church of the last days, and when he saw her, he marveled with a great marvel. In Revelation 18:7 this Church is depicted in a few powerful strokes. "She saith in her heart, I sit a queen, and am no widow, and shall see no sorrow." These words clearly bespeak her lazy security, her terrible pride, her lamentable frivolity, her spiritual blindness, and her cunning seductiveness. She is the antipode of the wife of the Lamb.

The one great sin of this apostate church is that she has not "held the Head" (Col. 2:19). While reaching out for the glory of this present world, she bade farewell to Christ. We see the same thing happening today in many apostate church denominations. Walking with God, which is the one thing needful for both the Church and for the individual believer, has been exchanged for traffic with the world.

Is the predicted apostasy already here, or is it still part of unfulfilled prophecy and therefore in the future? In answering this question we need to proceed carefully and refrain from false alarmism.

Some people believe that the predicted apostasy no longer lies in the future but has already commenced. The apostasy will not be completed until it has produced the man of sin. This tyrant will complete the apostasy, for he will not only be the child but at the same time the head of this apostasy. The apostasy is not an event of a day or a year, but rather a longlasting process. For salt does not suddenly turn from being fresh to being tasteless.

Although we attach great value to the opinion of learned and God-fearing men, we must nevertheless remember that men can err, even the most learned and most pious men. Even an entire generation can be grossly mistaken. Shortly before the year A.D. 1000, people were sure that the day of the Lord would dawn very soon. Many sold their houses and goods, and anticipated the imagined end. The year 1000 arrived, but not the day of wrath.

The situation becomes entirely different when the phenomena around us agree with what the prophetic Word says concerning the apostasy. We believe that this fact can hardly be denied.

A. In this connection we are thinking first of *higher criticism.* Some have applied science and erudition to rob the Word of the Lord of its power. Although they could not rob this Word of its eternal power, they succeeded in divorcing great masses of people from the discipline of the Word. These demolishers of the Bible have been the means by which thousands of young students have abandoned their faith in the Bible and the God of their fathers. They are mainly responsible for the spiritual misery of our age. They in particular are to blame that heresy has become the rule in our days and sound doctrine the exception. And this criticism is quite general. It has its proponents at nearly every institute of higher learning. Especially is the Netherlands a frontrunner in this God-dishonoring activity, and thereby has acquired a sad infamy on account of such men as Kuenen, Scholten, Pierson, Valeton, Eerdmans, etc.

Meanwhile, no one had better entertain the optimistic idea that these dark clouds will soon pass. It is to be feared that higher criticism will continue to batter against the rock of the Word. No matter how thoroughly this criticism is refuted, and no matter how much the excavations in the Near East contradict the vaunted results of higher criticism, these present-day scribes proceed with their destructive work, leaving many victims in their wake. We see schools that until recently remained faithful to "the faith which was once delivered unto the saints" abandon this in order to "give heed to seducing spirits."

B. The present-day concept of God is diluted. When the Word of God is ignored, it must follow that sound doctrine is disappearing. One idea which the world has of God is that of the *common fatherhood of God.* God is not a Sovereign, not a Judge, but the Father of all alike. This view is lauded as the product of increased insight. Its adherents teach the following:

1) There is *no Trinity.* When Jesus addressed God as Father, it is said He did not mean a part of the Godhead. Hence Unitarianism.

2) *God's honor* is not man's highest goal, *but man's happiness.* For does not a father have as his highest goal the happiness of his children? Hence Humanism.

3) We are not *adopted* as children by God, but we are all *born* as His children. Hence there is no necessity of a rebirth.

4) God does not punish people. He only chastens them unto correction. Which father does not seek the correction and improvement of his misbehaving children? Hence there is no lake burning with fire and brimstone.

5) Christ's death was only the death of a martyr, not a *substitutionary* death, for the Father was not angry and so did not need to be reconciled.

6) We should not speak of *grace,* for that does not agree with the concept *Father.* Neither should we use the words *Lord* and *Kingdom,* for they must be understood euphemistically. We must really pray, may the house of the Father come!

7) All men are brothers. Hence there is no separation or a communion of the saints.

A brief word of criticism is in order here. God is called Father in a fourfold way—in a general sense as the Creator of all mankind, as the Father of Israel, of the Son, and of the believers. The adherents of this doctrine believe that all people are God's children. But John 1:12 clearly teaches that only those who accept Christ as the One sent by the Father are the children of God. These present-day scribes are like the Jews who rejected Christ and yet boasted, "We have one Father—God." But what does Jesus say to them? "If God were your Father, you would love Me....you are of your father the devil, and you will do the lusts of your father" (see John 8:41-44). May all who name the name of Christ maintain that whosoever does not have the Son does not have the Father either. Only he or she who truly believes in Christ and loves Him from the heart can cast himself or herself at His Fatherly heart, saying, "Abba, Father!" On the other hand, whoever does not love Christ as the crucified Savior is anathema.

C. Ecclesiastical and religious life is in a sad condition. Many theological schools have professors who daily do what the infamous mocker, Voltaire, did as an exception more than a century ago. Some who do go to church are given stones instead of bread to eat. Thousands become the victims of the most soul-corrupting heresies. In every realm of life we see brazen opposition to the holy ordinances of God. Heathendom makes bigger gains in so-called Christian countries than Christianity in heathen countries.

Even in these distressful days, our children are as unconcerned as the contemporaries of Noah and Lot. Some people think of little more than games and sports and dancing and drinking. The black pictures Paul paints in 1 Timothy 4:1-3 and 2 Timothy 3:1-5; 4:3-4 are applicable to many church members. We see a general falling away from the only true foundation.

A humanistic optimism points to an irreligious state of the human heart. But this reality need not fill the believer with fear. They may conclude that the Lord remains faithful to His Word and carries out His counsel in all things. These signs are the darkness that precedes the dawn of redemption and the rising of the Sun of Righteousness. They are heralds of the Prince of Peace whom the nations will obey.

No salvation can dawn for this poor world as long as the Christ tarries, sin begets sin, Satan goes about to deceive the whole world, and Israel still wanders about on the face of the earth. The Deliverer will come out of Zion and turn away the wickedness from Jacob, and for the world this will be a resurrection from the dead. For that reason we sing along with the beloved poet:

> Earth, your salvation comes at last
> When all of Jacob's woes are past!

Before we look at this salvation, however, we first must speak of the results of the great apostasy, or the man of sin.

Chapter 4

THE ANTICHRIST

We have seen that before the Christ returns, the great apostasy must come. We wish to remind ourselves once again that this does not refer to a schism in the Church or to wickedness in the world, but to a general apostasy. It refers to baptized Christendom. That which bears the glorious name of church will depart from the living God. She who should be the immaculate bride of Christ, becomes a fallen woman who commits whoredom with the kings of the earth. She becomes a mother of the abominations of the earth. Modernism and rationalism in whatever form have not come as an enemy from the outside into the Church, but have been brought forth by the Church herself. And it is from this apostasy that the Antichrist will proceed. The apostasy itself is not the Antichrist, but he will be the fruit of the apostasy.

In theology the doctrine of the Antichrist occupies an important place today. Dr. Preuss, in his book on the Antichrist, gives two reasons for this: the rediscovery of the middle-east and a romantic tendency in our day. It seems to us better reasons could be advanced. Our entire present time is characterized by the sign of the last things. The newly revived interest in the prophetic Word simply had to be occupied with the mysterious personality of the man of sin. Added to this fact that the many anti-christian movements of our day increasingly draw the attention of our theologians. Finally this war [World War I] has already had its influence on everything. More and more the question is being asked whether possibly a super Napoleon will arise out of the confusion of the nations, who will prove to be the man of sin.

The doctrine of the Antichrist has never been totally ignored by the Church. Nor was this ever possible, for the Scripture mentions him repeatedly.

The *name* Antichrist is found only in the epistles of John. It is remarkable that John speaks of him as of a well-known entity among the Christians of his day (1 John 2:18-22; 4:3; 2 John 7).

The Apostle Paul mentions the Antichrist only once, but then quite extensively.

> Let no man deceive you by any means: for that day shall not come, except there come a falling away first, and that man of sin be revealed, the son of perdition; who opposeth and exalteth himself above all that is called God, or that is worshipped; so that he as God sitteth in the temple of God, shewing himself that he is God. Remember ye not, that, when I was yet with you, I told you these things? And now ye know what withholdeth that he might be revealed in his time. For the mystery of iniquity doth already work: only he who now letteth will let, until he be taken out of the way. And then shall that Wicked be revealed, whom the Lord shall consume with the spirit of his mouth, and shall destroy with the brightness of his coming: Even him, whose coming is after the working of Satan with all power and signs and lying wonders, and with all deceivableness of unrighteousness in them that perish; because they received not the love of the truth, that they might be saved (2 Thess. 2:3-10).

In chapter 13 of the Revelation of John, we find an even more extensive description of this abominable monster. The New Testament has depicted this sinister figure in great detail. What is predicted in the New Testament is by no means unknown in the Old.

In our opinion, however, there is no ground for the view of some who find the Antichrist in almost all of the books of the Old Testament; rather find there only nebulous references. Just as the teaching concerning Satan is not yet found clearly in the Old Testament, similarly there is an absence of the teaching concerning the Antichrist. God, knowing the weakness and ignorance of His people, did not want to terrify them with the anti-messiah, but wanted rather to gladden them with the true Messiah. Suppose that both the devil and the Antichrist had been fully depicted in the Old Testament, would not the Jews have easily succumbed to the sin of the heathen Persians and come to believe in two gods, a good one and an evil one? Therefore we must not look for a clear portrait of this lawless one in the Scriptures of the Old Testament. What is mentioned repeatedly is a formidable enemy of God and His people (Deut. 32:42; Ps. 8:2; 10:1-11; 18:14; 43; 52:1-5; 53; 55; 74; 140; Isa. 11:4; 14:4-17; 17:1; 30:31-33; 54:16; Jer. 23:19; 30:8, 23-24; Ezek. 23:1-8; Dan. 8:8, 23; 9:26-27; 11:21, 36; Nah. 1:11-14; Hab. 3:13; Zech. 11:17).

It is not justified, however, to apply all such references to the Antichrist. In some cases we are dealing with personal enemies, in others with the Evil One himself, while finally Daniel 11:36 and Zechariah 11:17 undoubtedly refer to the Antichrist.

It is apparently the will of God that His people will see, in every formidable manifestation of wrath against the seed of the woman, a prophecy of the day in which evil will fully manifest itself against the Messiah.

Thus such wicked persons as Cain, Nimrod, Pharaoh, Amalek, Midian, Goliath, Saul, Sennacherib, Rabshakeh, Nebuchadnezzar, Antiochus Epiphanes, Nero, and others were forerunners of the final great enemy, just as the holy men of God were types of the coming Redeemer. Already many prophecies of Scripture have been fulfilled, while others will obtain their ultimate fulfillment at the second coming of the Lord.

The most remarkable reference to the Antichrist is 2 Thessalonians 2. The following conclusions can be drawn from it:

1. *The Antichrist proceeds from the great apostasy.*

2. *The Antichrist comes immediately before the return of the Lord.*

The alarming confusion over the exegesis of 2 Thessalonians 2 and its greatly diverging explanations have resulted mainly from disregard of this truth: If we identify the coming of Christ, of which the context makes mention, with the destruction of Jerusalem, we will get a wrong view of the Antichrist. Then Nero or another Roman emperor becomes the man of sin, as though a heathen were able to deny both the Father and the Son of whom he never even heard. This fact also tells us that the pope cannot be the Antichrist.

3. *The Antichrist will then be revealed.*

This presupposes that he already existed before that. John could correctly say that he already was present in his day. Indeed, that there were many antichrists. We must make a clear distinction between the Antichrist of the last days and the spirit of the Antichrist, the antichristian element which has throughout all ages been operative even in the Church. We must also clearly distinguish the actual Antichrist from the pseudo-Christian and the types of the Antichrist, who John calls the antichrists. Thus we can say that the pope and many heretics, such as Arius, Pelagius, Joseph Smith, Charles T. Russell, Mary Baker Eddy, and others, are antichrists, but by the same token not any one of them, or even all together, are the true man of sin.

4. *The Antichrist is a person.*

He is not a system or order of persons, as is evident from the names given to him, as well as from the careful descriptions given by Daniel, Paul, and John. To apply these to a system leads to absurdities. Those who are of the opinion that the papal see is the Antichrist belong to a diminishing minority.

5. *The Antichrist is dreadfully haughty.*

He opposes God and exalts himself above all that is called God, or that is worshiped. Daniel speaks in the same terms about him; he calls him a king who does what he pleases. Scripture depicts the Antichrist as someone who wishes to do his own will. All self-willed religion is in essence antichristian, for what else does the devil do but follow his own will in everything?

6. *The Antichrist seats himself in the temple of God as a god.*

What is meant by the *temple of God?* This expression can mean three things: *a*) the believer (1 Cor. 6:19); *b*) the Church of Christ as the dwelling place of the Holy Spirit (1 Cor. 3:16-17); and *c*) usually the Jewish temple in Jerusalem (Dan. 9:27; Matt. 24:15; Mark 13:14; Luke 21:20). Since *a* and *b* are not possible here, we have no choice but to think of the temple the Jews will rebuild in Jerusalem. According to many, the

Antichrist will be a Jew, as the Jews and many Church Fathers have always thought. On the basis of Deuteronomy 33:22, Genesis 49:17, and Jeremiah 8:16, it has often been thought that the Antichrist would come forth out of the tribe of Dan. The remarkable omission of this tribe in the enumeration of the tribes of Israel in Revelation 7 has strengthened this view.

The Jews will return in unyielding unbelief and in their blindness rebuild the temple (see Isa. 66:1-6; Dan. 8:11; 9:27); in that rebuilt temple he will seat himself. Our marginal commentators and many exegetes simply ridicule this idea. But it must be remembered that most of the Church Fathers understood it this way. Even Origen and Jerome, who were strong opponents of the doctrine of a millennium, advance this exegesis of Daniel 8:9, Matthew 24:22, and 2 Thessalonians 2. Commenting on Daniel 8, Jerome says, "Most of us hold that this refers to the Antichrist, and say that everything that was foreshadowed by Antiochus will be actually fulfilled by the Antichrist." And Origen, who made his fruitless zeal to spiritualize everything into a system by which he could cast what he did not like to the winds, maintained the doctrine of a personal Antichrist and applied 2 Thessalonians 2:4 to his future activity in Jerusalem. On the viewpoint of the Church Fathers regarding these matters in general, see Geurs, *Israel and Her Future Restoration;* Seiss, *The Signs of the Times;* Cumming, *The Millennium;* Duffield, *The Prophecies;* Haldeman, *History of Premillennialism;* Silver, *The Second Coming in History and Scriptures;* Maitland, *The Apostolic School of Prophetic Interpretation.* We can hardly recommend these enough to anyone interested in prophecy, especially the first and last titles mentioned here.

7. *The Antichrist represents himself as God and demands worship from everyone.*

He will not begin, but rather end his career in this manner. His deification will be the end result of an ages-long process. We are not referring here to the long degenerative process of sin, but to the process of his personality. He does not appear as an atheist in the common sense of the word. We do not find him to be totally without religion, but rather to be the representative of false and self-willed religion. He does not deny the

Father and the Son because he does not believe that they exist, but because he does not *want* them to exist and because he himself wants to be both. He will honor the god Mauzzim [Heb. *elóah mâ uzzîm.*] (Dan. 11:38-39). This god represents the powers of nature, or, as others prefer, the spiritual powers in the air, the demonical powers. History teaches us that whoever elevates and glorifies matter perishes in it.

Dr. Abraham Kuyper thinks that Daniel is referring to the god of war. Pure naturalism usually leads to the subnatural, the demonic. The Antichrist's naturalism leads him in opposition to the Prince of princes (Dan. 8:25). He then will deny the Father and the Son (1 John 2:22). This denial develops into blasphemy (Rev. 13:6). He will be full of names of blasphemy (Rev. 17:3). Thus he will exalt himself above every god (Dan. 11:36). And the highest (or lowest) rung in this ladder will be that he presents himself as God, and then logically demands that the whole world worship him. From Revelation 13 it is clear that he will succeed in this.

The whole world will be amazed at him when it sees his great and marvelous power. It will admire him as the Unconquerable One. "Who is like unto the beast? Who is able to make war with him?" they initially cry out in amazement. And then, when they see that he has power over the military world, the world market, and the world of religion, they will begin to worship him. Seeing his marvelous signs and wonders, the apostates will apparently labor under the illusion that they are actually worshiping a divine being.

If we wonder in amazement how the Antichrist can go that far, Revelation 13 affords the answer. In this chapter we come across the word *give* six times. He does by no means have the power in himself to extract the worship of the world, but Scripture emphatically points out that this power is *given* him. It is given by the Lord for a righteous judgment upon the world that rejected Him. God will do two things at that time. First, He allows Satan to give his power, his throne, and his great authority unto the beast. Second, God sends into the hearts of the apostates a power of apostasy, literally, an energy of the lie, so that they will believe the lie. Christ did not want to accept the kingdoms of the world and their glory from the hand of the devil, but the Antichrist will have no objection whatsoever to doing so.

8. *Thus we see that the Antichrist comes at the initiative of Satan.*

He comes according to the will of Satan and with Satan's power and energy. Some exegetes take this expression to mean a generating act of the devil. In this regard, too, he would be a true anti-Christ. This would mean that just as Christ was conceived by the overshadowing of the Holy Spirit, the Antichrist would be conceived by Satan. Thus he would not be the incarnated devil himself, as still others understand it, but an offspring of the devil. This may be alluded to in the expression, *son of perdition.*

When one considers the embodied spiritual "appearances" of spiritism, the idea of Antichrist's generation by Satan is no longer improbable. We quote the Rev. S. J. Du Toit, who is of this opinion, from page 88 of his excellent booklet on *Unfulfilled Prophecies:*

> Now observe the phenomenon, which is nowhere else found in Scripture, that Satan is allowed to appropriate a bodily form which was often allowed to angels—something which he forever seems to covet greatly; he strives with Michael for the body of Moses, and the demons even pray to be allowed to enter into the swine (Luke 8:32). And must we not consider the many cases of demon-possession and of casting out of demons as so many aborted attempts to appropriate a bodily form over against the incarnated Word? Will not this fervent wish be granted him one day, whereby then the highest manifestation of Satan's power (*energeia*) will be revealed? Does not spiritism, in which already millions believe, move in this direction by breaking down the natural walls of separation and furthering an unlawful traffic between man and deceiving spirits?

Whatever the case, one thing is certain, that the Antichrist will be fully a demonic personality such as the world has never seen before. And just as his personality is unequalled anywhere, so will be his *influence.* He will literally control everything on this earth with his power of hell. He will cause the earth to tremble and the kingdoms to shake (Isa. 14:6). He will see that the laws and the times will be given into his hand (Dan. 7:25). He will, in an astonishing way, despoil everything (Dan. 11:36). To him will be given power over all kindreds and tongues and nations (Rev. 13). The ten kings will give their power and strength to him (Rev. 17:13). Hence he will be a world ruler such as has never before ruled on the earth. He will also far surpass all arch-tyrants because he will be able to support his power and influence by the most spectacular signs and wonders (2 Thess. 2:9; Rev. 13:13, 15). All the non-elect will worship him. Only the small number whose names are written in the Lamb's Book of Life will refrain from this abomination (Rev. 13:8). These faithful ones will therefore be killed (Rev. 13:15).

9. *The Antichrist will be restrained.*

Something will restrain the Antichrist, so that he will not appear too soon, but at his own time. The mystery of lawlessness was already in operation in Paul's days, so that the man of sin would have been revealed at that time if there had not been this restrainer. The question is now, what does Paul mean when he speaks of a restraining power? Who restrains the man of sin?

Answering this question poses great difficulties. In the first place there are two linguistic difficulties, for (1) he presents this power as being impersonal and as a masculine power; (2) the A.V. translators, in order to make 2 Thessalonians 2:7 a logically complete sentence, have inserted several words. The question is, however, whether these additions are correct and whether they correctly reflect the thought of the Apostle. Another difficulty is that we are dealing here with a sole reference. Nowhere else in Scripture do we read concerning this restraining power by which the Antichrist cannot be revealed. Possibly the greatest difficulty is that the Apostle assumes acquaintance with these things on the part of his readers, so he doesn't deem it necessary to name this power. It is not on account of cowardice or politics, as many think, that the Apostle refrains from mentioning the name of the restrainer, but because of sufficient knowledge. "And now ye know what withholdeth [him]," he writes.

Therefore it need not surprise us that the ideas vary greatly concerning this person, or of this *something,* that withholds. Until today the explanation of this text is still freighted with the idea given by our learned predecessor Hugo Grotius. He was of the opinion that Emperor Caligula was the Antichrist, since he demanded to be worshiped, and that his statue be placed in the temple at Jerusalem. The governor Vitellius [in the sources, the governor who actually was sent to carry out this policy is Petronius, the successor of Vitellius—Ed.], however, was kindly disposed toward the Jews, so he strenuously opposed the plans of the emperor. Therefore it is said that he was the restrainer. There is hardly a Roman emperor who has not been given the honor of being the restrainer.

Many Church Fathers thought that it referred to the Roman state, with its stern order of justice. Today many expositors are still of the same opinion. They who think that this epistle was written in the second century are usually thinking of some famous bishop.

Those who believe that every nation has its own angel usually think of a patron angel. Von Hoffmann, the famous expositor of the Erlangen school, thought of the archangel Michael.

Still others think it refers to the Counsel of God, which will disseminate the message of the Gospel over the earth, and that this is what withholds the man of sin from revealing himself. Those who identified the great apostasy with the French Revolution, and Napoleon I or III with the Antichrist, are thinking of the German Empire.

Today, those who do not believe in a verbal inspiration or the prophetic character of Scripture explain these words by Paul in a symbolic sense. Even Joseph Parker, who in England and America is renowned as being definitely orthodox, sees the text this way. See his commentary on this chapter of 2 Thessalonians.

Many think of Paul himself, or of all the apostolic preachers combined. Calvin, too, thinks it refers to the preaching of the gospel.

Chrysostom explains it as being the continuation of the special gifts of the Holy Spirit. He immediately adds, however, in that case the Antichrist must have already come, since the special gifts of the Spirit had long since ceased in the Church.

Premillennialists usually think of the Church itself, which will be removed by the rapture, or of the Holy Spirit, or of both at the same time, since the Holy Spirit indwells the Church.

Then there are those who think it refers to the principle of authority that is operative in the government, or to the sense of justice in man, or to the hold that truth has on the consciences of men.

Mrs. George C. Needham, in her thorough book on the Antichrist, argues that we must think of nothing or no one else but Satan.

From this brief summary of the widely divergent explanations, to which many more could be added, it is evident that the question of who the withholder is cannot be answered with complete certainty. This is one of the texts the Lord in His wisdom has left undetermined. We may not insist on one particular opinion to the exclusion of all others.

We prefer to think of the Holy Spirit as the Person who restrains or withholds, and of His general operation in the nations and the world in general, and in the Church in particular, as that *something* that restrains the Antichrist. For it is this Person in the divine economy of the work of the holy Trinity who is the author of common grace, which acts as a restraint in the whole world so that it does not run too fast towards its final judgment. Why was the first world ready for judgment? Was it not because the Holy Spirit chose to strive with the world? Why then cannot this be the case now also? If the Lord would not take away His Spirit from the world and thereby at the same time deprive it from common grace, then the entire world would not blindly follow after and worship the man of sin.

The question is often asked in connection with the rapture of the Church, "Why does the Holy Spirit tarry?" Our answer to this question is, "When the Lord catches up His Church out of the world to meet Him in the air, He will retrieve His Spirit." Only then can judgment come. We offer this idea to the reader, not as though it were the only true one, but as a viewpoint that agrees with the course of development of the first world, and also because it does not violate the context and the words themselves.

10. *The fall of the Antichrist.*

"Whom the Lord shall consume with the spirit of his mouth, and shall destroy with the brightness of his coming." He will be broken to pieces without hands (Dan. 2:34; 8:25). Human power cannot do away with him. Only Christ can do this, and He will crush him at His return. Without any judicial process, he will be sent to the lake of fire burning with brimstone (Rev. 17 and 19).

It is necessary to make a distinction between the Antichrist and the false prophet. The Antichrist is always depicted as a king who tries to imitate the royal supremacy of Christ. At the same time he will be the last head and representative of the Roman world power. But the Antichrist also wants to imitate the prophetic work and the marvelous gifts of the Spirit. For this he uses the false prophet as his helper, of which Revelation 13:11-18; 16:13; 19:20; and 20:10 tell us. This personage is the religious extension of the political Antichrist, and like the latter, he is a child of hell. He is in full agreement with the Antichrist and is his faithful and able servant.

No less than eight times we read in Revelation 13:11-18 that he makes certain things come to pass. In particular he is the performer of anti-christian signs and wonders. He even knows how to give life to the image of the beast, so that it can speak and bring down the multitudes to their knees in adoration before him. Apparently he will be even more deceitful than the actual Antichrist, for he has two horns like a lamb (Rev. 13:11). Horns are symbols of power, but here we see no crude royal horns, but horns of a lamb. Hence he will apply his power in a kind and sweet manner. He is a *beast* but in his cunning deceits he acts *like a lamb,* just as the mild and meek Savior. When asking of what his twofold power consists, we prefer to think of the power of science and religion. Being like the Antichrist in origin and nature, he shares with him the same fate. At the appearance of the glorified Christ, he is cast into the lake of fire and brimstone, and is soon followed by his consorts, the devil, death, and hades (Rev. 20:10, 14).

The Conqueror of these satanic personalities will now demand all our attention.

CHAPTER 5

THE LORD'S RETURN

When we speak of the return of the Lord, we are referring to the glorious truth that our Savior, who presently sits at the right hand of the Father and has a name above every name, will one day return bodily, visibly, audibly, and with great power to this earth. Other than the divinity and satisfaction of Christ, there is no truth the devil hates as much as this one. For many ages he succeeded in obscuring it. What has he not caused people to substitute for the return of the Lord! Judgments, such as earthquakes, wars, hunger, and pestilence; the outpouring of the Holy Spirit; the fall and destruction of Jerusalem; the establishment of the papal see, and the glorious Church State; the manifestation of Christ in man; the death of the believers; the victorious advance of the gospel; the separating and elevating power of the gospel; Socialism, Mormonism, Christian Science, Jewish Reform; and Christian civilization —all these things have at times been identified with the second coming of Christ.

Many times throughout the ages a time has been indicated as the year in which the Lord would return. It seems that mankind refuses to learn from history. Even in our day, outstanding men such as the astronomer, Dr. Totten of Yale, and Baxter and Dimbley of England, have proven themselves to be false prophets. According to the recently deceased arch-heretic Russell, [The reference is to Charles Taze Russell, founder of the Jehovah's Witnesses—Ed.] in 1914 all that existed would be turned upside down by the coming of the Lord. In that year the great world conflagration occurred, [World War I—Ed.] and now many of his blind followers are of the opinion that his prophecy materialized anyway.

THE TRUTH OF CHRIST'S RETURN

Meanwhile all these excesses have cast great doubt on this truth itself, so that many well-meaning Christians have branded the ardent expectation of the Lord's return as fanaticism or one-sidedness. The frequent misuse made of this truth through the cunning methods of the devil has possibly been one of the causes why today very little is preached or written in Reformed circles on the return of Christ. While the world has gone up in flames, we in the Netherlands and America are still too much engaged in "the doctrine of baptisms" and are seemingly not interested in progressing toward the return of the Lord. This truth is humiliating to the proud heart of man and manifestly does not fit with the ambitions of many. Whoever secretly loves the world more than Christ dares not look into the flaming eyes of the Judge.

It is to be feared that many people instinctively sense that waiting for Christ is a waiting for their own death and damnation. Still, with gratitude to God, it must be acknowledged that a change for the better is noticeable in this respect. To mention just one instance, more sermons are preached on the last book of the Bible than ever before. Nevertheless, it remains doubtful whether sufficient attention is paid to future things, especially the coming of Christ.

No truth appears so frequently in the New Testament as the return of Christ. According to the findings of Bickersteth, Birks, and Bonar in England, and of Brookes in America, Christ's return is mentioned more than three hundred times in the New Testament. If we add to this all those references that assume it, then it appears about once in every fifteen verses of the New Testament. When we receive a letter in which a dear friend repeatedly mentions one particular thing, we conclude that this special thing is considered of great importance by the writer. When someone in everyday life speaks often and much about one and the same matter, albeit in different words, we conclude that he considers the matter very important.

When Scripture speaks more often about the coming again of Christ than about any other doctrine, must we not conclude that the Lord considers this truth of the greatest importance? If that is the case, must we not do the same? We make bold to say that no one preaches the entire Word who does not unfold the return of the Lord in all its salvific significance. All of theology must degenerate if it does not pay attention to this teaching. Without this truth the holy temple of theology lacks its windows and its pinnacle. In the Old Testament there is hardly a Messianic prophecy that does not point via Golgotha to the blessed coming of the Lord. Hence it must be stated that whoever is silent on these things is guilty of tampering with the Word of the Lord (Deut. 4:2; 12:32; Rev. 22:19). Whoever omits the highest stage of Christ's glory must of necessity omit much more.

Such a person cannot unfold the events that are connected with the return of the Lord. Moreover, the Lord has emphatically commanded us not to keep silent on these things. The Greek word that most of the time is translated preaching [Gr. *Kerygma*] basically means, *announcing that the King is coming*. To preach that the Kingdom is coming presupposes the announcement that the King is coming. The three main points of Paul's preaching, and that of all the apostles were, Christ *for* us, *in* us, and *coming to us*.

The preaching of the return of the Lord will, by its very nature, be a preaching of Christ. Here more than in the case of any other truth, the unity and beautiful harmony of the one great work of the Lord for sinners can be pointed out. Here it can be shown that Christ entered the manger in order to go to the cross, and went on from the cross in order to ascend His throne. The cross, or better still, the slain Lamb, will be the focal point forever of the exalted Christ and the climax of the work of salvation. Everything will redound to the glory of a triune God.

The preaching of the Lord's return recommends itself specifically to the human conscience. It teaches man the total bankruptcy of all of world history outside of God. It knocks the worldly-wise from the pedestal of their philosophic pride and confronts them, together with all "the fat ones" of the earth, with the righteous Judge. This preaching tells the wanton man of today that his accumulated treasures will soon be cast to the moles and bats, and that the gold and silver that has not been transformed into good works will not follow him into eternity but will be a testimony against him. It tells the frivolous one, woe unto you who are now laughing, for you will howl and weep on account of the miseries that will befall you. It makes clear that the world is but a transition phase to a new heaven and a new earth, in which righteousness will dwell. To the mourning, it says that soon all tears will be wiped away and the suffering of this present time is not worthy to be compared with the glory that shall be revealed in us. It cries out to everyone that the time is short and therefore extremely serious. Finally, it satisfies the thinking mind, because it shows that with the return of the Lord the purpose of all things will be reached.

It is necessary that the Lord return. His cry on the cross may not be understood in the sense that He had already accomplished all of His mediatorial work. If He were not to return, He would not be the perfect Savior, and His first coming would lose all its significance. Prophecy, too, would lose its value and the entire Bible would be untrustworthy.

Christ still has much to do in the future. This Redeemer will not rest until He has accomplished all. He must raise the dead, gather, glorify, and reward His people, judge the nations, bind Satan, restore Israel, and renew creation. He must actually rule over the entire universe in order to bring to naught all power, rule, and authority, and to put all His enemies under His feet (1 Cor. 15:24-28).

As we see it, there is still another reason why we should greatly desire the return of Christ. We know that because of our unrighteousness He has been burdened with the shame of the cross. Now His shame has indeed been taken away from Him since He has been clothed with glory, indeed He has obtained a place at the right hand of God, but the glory surrounding Him is to this very day not seen by the world. What is taking place is that by means of preaching His glorification in heaven is brought to the knowledge of men, but almost all refuse to give credence. The number of those who believe without seeing is very small indeed; faith is truly not the possession of all. And thus on earth shame still rests on Christ. When the world saw Him for the last time, He hung as a dead man on the tree of shame and curse; is it not necessary then that the world, too, will behold Him in His heavenly glory so that it will cease mocking Him? There is no doubt about it. He must be glorified at the place where He was humiliated; where His cross once stood His throne must also be seen. Should we not long, then, for the day when the shame which our sins loaded down on Him will be taken away from Him? (Van Andel).

Christ's return is not only necessary for the sake of the Church, Israel, the nations, the Antichrist, Satan, and the entire creation, but also and not least of all, for His own sake. We must never lose sight of the fact that He has not climbed to the highest stage of His glory. Therefore He has not yet received all of the reward of His Father. Whoever loves Him must already, for that reason alone, ardently look forward to His return, for does not love always seek the good of the object?

THE PURPOSE OF CHRIST'S RETURN

What is the purpose of Christ's return?

The object of the Lord's return is always presented as *the judgment of the living and the dead.* This is not totally correct, however. Scripture clearly teaches us that the immediate purpose of His return is the complete deliverance of His people. The ultimate purpose cannot be but that of His first coming, which He expressed thus: "Father, I have glorified thee in the earth. Let everything that hath breath praise the Lord!" This was the keynote in all the utterances of the patriarchs, psalmists, and prophets. This ultimate goal Christ, as the great Representative of the Father, will bring about. Then every knee will bow unto Him and every tongue will confess that He is the Lord to the *glorification of the Father.*

In order to realize this immediate and main goal, Christ must first remove all that opposes Him and His people and judge the world in righteousness. Hence the judgment is not the *goal* but the awe-inspiring *means* He applies to quench the rebellion in creation in order to give the Father all the honor of His handiwork. To uphold the honor of God in every sphere of life is a saying that is often heard in orthodox circles, and it is correctly held before believers as a high calling, but in this dispensation it will always be to the Church more an object of hope than a glorious reality. The Church must indeed hope for it more fervently than for anything else, for it is not the Church but the Christ who is the perfect upholder of the honor of God in every realm of life. Let the Church ask first what the will of God is, for this is the only guideline of faith and life. Then it will never fall into the error of Rome which, "to the honor of God," led the sheep of Jesus to the slaughter.

THE RESULTS OF CHRIST'S RETURN

The *results* of the return of the Lord will be many and glorious. We shall mention only the results for the Church, for

Israel, for the world as an antichristian power, for the world as the object of God's love, and for the devil.

1. *The Church.*

By the grace of God, the Church is now already so rich that it has everything (1 Cor. 3:22; 2 Peter 1:3), that it can do everything (1 John 2:20). Nevertheless, believers are not fully redeemed even at their death, for the full redemption does not come until the redemption of their bodies, the gathering of all believers around the Christ at the highest stage of His glory, and the glorification of the entire creation. We may not detract anything from the salvation believers already have in Christ, but neither may we detract anything from the future salvation. Some elevate the present redemption at the expense of the future, but we may never forget that Scripture speaks far more often about the coming redemption than of the present one. It says that when men's hearts will fail for fear, and for looking after those things which are coming on the earth and the powers of heaven that will be shaken, then believers must lift up their heads, *for their redemption draws nigh.* The same statement appears in Ephesians 1:7 with regard to the present redemption by His blood. *Here* it speaks of a redemption brought about by a ransom, and there by His power.

The Apostle Paul does not want us to underestimate the present redemption, but neither does he want us to overestimate it, as he calls it the *firstfruits of the Spirit.* According to him, believers groan with the groanings of longing to be totally delivered from death. He is thinking here of the resurrection of the bodies of the believers. At that blessed resurrection our adoption as children will be completed, as then our bodies will be openly displayed as sharing in the redemption of the soul (Rom. 8:23).

To the extent that Christ's return draws closer, the redemption of the believers draws closer (Rom. 13:10). Christ not only delivers from sin, but also from this present evil world (Gal. 1:4), from the power of darkness (Col. 1:13-14), from all unrighteousness (Titus 2:14), from the wrath to come (1 Thess. 1:10), even if that means passing through the fire of judgment (1 Cor. 3:15). The *purchased possession* in Ephesians refers to the future. Believers are sealed unto the day of redemption, unto the day of Christ's return (Eph. 4:30). They are not appointed to wrath, but *to obtain* salvation (1 Thess. 5:9). According to Peter, salvation is prepared, ready to be revealed in the last time, at the Lord's return (1 Peter 1:5). For that reason the believers must hope to the end for the grace that is to be brought unto them at the revelation of Jesus Christ (v. 13). Christ is coming again unto the salvation of His own (Heb. 9:28).

That is the message throughout Scripture. The same idea is expressed in the often-used images of *sealing, firstfruits,* and *earnest* (Rom. 8:23; 2 Cor. 1:22; 5:5; Eph. 4:30). We are constantly reminded that believers have only a first installment of the full salvation and must wait for their full redemption. In the return of the Lord there is still new grace and mercy for the believers (Mal. 3:17; 1 Peter 1:13; 2 Tim. 1:18; Jude 21).

All the texts that present Christ or salvation as an object of hope point indirectly to the blessed return of the Lord. Scripture depicts even sanctification as obtaining its full effect and completion in the day of Christ, and not on the day of death, as is usually believed. At the death of the believers, only one half of our sanctification is completed, namely, the dying unto sin. But sanctification consists of two parts; it is also a complete dedication of the entire man to a triune God. And that cannot take place at death, since the body is still resting in the grave. Scripture frequently presents the glorification on the day of Christ as the completion of our sanctification (Phil. 1:6; 1 Thess. 5:23). The concepts of *redemption* and *salvation* in the New Testament have an eschatological inference.

In view of these Scriptural representations, many meditations and pious poems are one-sided. We quote one of them as an example, italicizing certain expressions:

> *Nothing,* sinner, great or small, need be added, Jesus died
> And thereby He has supplied *all* you need, He paid it *all.*
> When He hung there on the tree, He accomplished *everything;*
> Therefore death has lost its sting, you are saved and you are free.
> All is finished by God's grace, Jesus paid the price for you;
> *There is nothing more to do,* but for aye to sing Him praise.

In order to emphasize the all-sufficiency of the one perfect sacrifice by Christ, and to discourage all self-righteous attempts to earn salvation, a poem like this may have it merits, and hence some usefulness. Nevertheless, such sentiments, no matter how well intended and how true in themselves, will seldom obtain their intent, because they isolate the great and all-encompassing satisfaction by Christ as it is, completely separated from future redemption. This kind of writing can even be harmful to the life of hope, for the impression is given that there is nothing more to be done for our redemption, and also that there is nothing left to hope, to expect, or to long for. *"There is nothing more to do"*—if that is true, then we might as well shut our eyes to all the salvation of the future. Scripture nowhere speaks in this manner. It nowhere makes this kind of separation between His satisfaction and His future work. Even the three epistles that emphasize His sacrifice most strongly nowhere represent Christ's satisfaction in this manner.

We wish to be understood correctly. Our objection is by no means that too much emphasis is placed on the aspect of satisfaction. The opposite is rather true, not enough emphasis, because it is being isolated. A truth taken out of its context is at best a half-truth.

2. Israel.

Later we hope to return to the Church as well as to Israel, so that at the present we need not go into this matter in detail. Often the question is raised whether Christ will return after the conversion of the Jews or whether Israel will be converted after the Lord's return. Isaiah 59:20 and Romans 11:26 teach that Israel as a nation will be converted by the coming of the Lord. Zechariah 12:10-14, and many other texts, teach us the same.

We must visualize these matters as follows. First there will be a national revival in Israel, as well as in all the nations. We are told this three times in the parable of the budding fig tree. Because of Christ's curse it is withered for the entire duration of this dispensation. Shortly before the Lord's return the same tree will begin to bud again, as a sign that summer is at hand and the day of the Lord is approaching.

As a result of revived nationalism, Israel will partly return to the land of the fathers, not in a converted but in an unconverted state (Jer. 3:14; Ezek. 38:7-12; Zech. 12:1-8).

Then the first oppression by Gog and Magog will cast Israel into the great tribulation. According to Zechariah 12:2-3 and

Ezekiel 38 and 39, the great prosperity, power, and renown which Israel has obtained will arouse the envy of the nations and cause the ancient hostility of antisemitism to burst out as never before. Immense armies under the command of Russia[1] and instigated by the Antichrist will flood the Holy land (Isa. 25—26; 34:1-8; 59:17-19; Dan. 9:26-27; Joel 3:1-15; Zeph. 3:1-8; Zech. 12—14).

Next, when Israel's calamity has reached its zenith in the great tribulation, the Christ will appear and the Jewish people will see Him whom they have pierced (Zech. 12:10). Then they will cry out, "Blessed is he that cometh in the name of the Lord" (Matt. 23:39). Christ will descend on the Mount of Olives (Zech. 14:4), and a great earthquake will drastically change the appearance of the entire land. This earthquake partially solves the question of how Israel, which will be a great nation in the Millennium, can live in little Palestine.

The mourning of Israel for having rejected its Messiah will be great (Zech. 12:10-14; cf. Isa. 53). The fountain opened for the house of David will, however, wash away all its guilt. Israel will be converted in one day (Zech. 3:9) and sanctified (Zech. 14:20-21). Israel's calamity will have ended forever.

3. *The world as an Antichristian power.*

The world in this sense lies in wickedness (1 John 5:19), and its ruler and god is the devil (John 14:30; 16:11; 2 Cor. 4:4). It does not know the Father, the Christ, and the Holy Spirit, nor the believers (John 14:17; 17:25; 1 John 3:1). The world is the seed of the serpent, who always hates the believers and wars against them (John 15:18-19; 17:14). Therefore all who are friends of the world are enemies of God (James 4:4; 1 John 2:15-17; 5:4).

To expect optimistically that the world eventually will improve as civilization increases is unbiblical. Nothing on earth can make *this* world better. It simply is not God's intent to make it better, but to judge it in righteousness. Yet there are

---

[1]Today the general consensus is that Gog and Magog refer to northern nations, specifically Russia. Many feel that the basic word *rosh* ("chief") in Ezekiel 38:3 indicates this country by name. According to them the cities Meshech and Tubal are to be identified with the two important Russian cities of Moscow and Tobolsk. See the Scofield Bible at this point.

always many people who name the Name of Christ who are of the opinion that missions will one day convert the world. After centuries of missions and preaching, a dark night still covers the nations of the world. Not until Christ comes again will darkness flee and the morning of the new creation begin to dawn. When Christ returns, He will not meet a converted world, as postmillennialism dreams of, but a world that has reached the zenith of evil. It is the lostness of the present world that necessitates the return of Christ. To teach that the world is getting better or being converted is indirectly to deny that Christ is coming, for He will not come until the harvest of sin is ripe and the measure of sin is full.

Scripture teaches emphatically that the nations labor unto the very fire of judgment (Hab. 2:13) and that the apostate composition of things is kept in store as a treasure, reserved unto fire against the day of judgment (2 Peter 3:7). The burning of heaven and earth, however, will apparently not take place until after the Millennium, and then after the second rebellion of the nations when the devil has been released for a brief time (see Rev. 20:11; 21:1). But the world will already initially be purged by the judgment on the nations, the removal of the Antichrist and his helper, and the binding of Satan, as well as by the great signs and wonders that accompany the Lord's coming.

What is extensively described in Scripture is not the burning of the world *after*, but the judgment of the nations *before*, the kingdom of peace. A very extensive description of it can be found in the largest section of the Revelation of John, chapters 6—19. Failing to make a distinction between these two things has been the cause of much misunderstanding. Many people in our circles [Dutch Reformed—Ed.] think that the Lord can suddenly come one day to burn everything. We ought to know that the judgment begins with the judgment of the nations. This is not an act of one day, but will take some time, and in a sense the entire "day of Christ." In other words, during the entire kingdom of peace. Yet it is clear that the battle of Armageddon will take place immediately after the return of Christ. This battle of our great God, in which all the kings of the earth will be involved, will be fought in Palestine. From Revelation 16:12-18 the following facts can be concluded:

A) The nations are animated by the devil, the Antichrist, and the false prophet. This they do by means of the three unclean spirits like frogs.

B) The kings of the east are involved as well. There is no basis for the idea that this refers to the returning of Israel. Not only the kings of the east, but the entire world power, receives from God's hand its righteous retribution.

C) The time of this battle is the coming of the Lord. This is sufficiently evident from the parenthetic sentence of verse 15, "Behold, I come as a thief. Blessed is he that watcheth, and keepeth his garments, lest he walk naked, and they see his shame." This takes place under the sixth vial, which is the vial of the end, while the seventh, which immediately follows the sixth, is the vial in which everything is completed.

D) The location will be on the mountain of Megiddo, at the foot of which lies the great plain of Jezreel (Judg. 5:19, 2 Chron. 35:22). There Josiah, the God-fearing king of Judah, fell in battle. He was an outstanding theocratic king, but he fell before the heathen power of Egypt. And the theocratic king *par excellence* will crush all the nations. Without the shedding of blood there is no pardon. Without shedding of blood there is no retribution, either.

E) Immediately after the slaughter of the nations (see Isa. 63), judgments will be unleashed that usher in the end of the present world. An earthquake will erupt such as has never been seen before. It will not be merely local, but will cover the entire world. Because of its far-reaching effects, this earthquake has been the subject of several prophecies (cf. Isa. 2:19, 21; Hag. 2:6-7).

In Daniel we find the same description. The image Nebuchadnezzar saw in a dream represents the entire ungodly world power during the time of the heathen. The stone that fell on it and ground it to dust points toward Christ's coming in judgment. (On this judgment of the nations, see Isa. 66:15; Dan. 7:13; Matt. 13:40-41; Rev. 14:18-19; 19:19.) Few similies are used more often than that of *harvesting*. The harvest of the earth will become ripe, and the Lord as the great Husbandman will come to harvest and to purge His threshing floor.

4. *The world as the object of God's love.*

Death and Destruction cannot be the last word for God's creation. Has He not in Christ reconciled the world unto Himself? (See 2 Cor. 5:19.) Christ is not called in vain the Light, the Life, and the Savior of the world (John 1:6-9; 4:42; 14:6). Indeed, His plan to preserve it cannot fail (John 12:47). At His return He will reconcile unto God all things in heaven and on earth (Col. 1:20), and gather all things under one Head. Christ is the Firstborn among all creatures and the true Heir of all things. The kingdoms of this world or, better, the royal reign of the world becomes His (Rev. 11:15). He will reign until He has put all His enemies under His feet (1 Cor. 15:25).

All these glorious statements, which may not be reduced whatsoever, will then be fulfilled. The times of the heathen will come to an end, and the course of Israel's history will be continued. Only then will be fulfilled the oft-repeated promise that in Abraham all the nations will be blessed fully and far above expectation. Christ will truly and actually prove to be the King of Israel.

We make much of the fact that Christ was crucified under Pilate, and rightly so, but has he not also, as worldly judge, placed this statement above His cross, *This is Jesus the Nazarene, the King of the Jews*? Pilate, as the instrument of God, afforded here a true prophecy. The rulers of Israel hated the superscription in this form, but changeable and timid Pilate said, "What I have written I have written." Christ will ascend the throne as the King of the Jews, proving to the world that the object of God's good pleasure receives life from the dead. The Apostle Paul declares this emphatically in Romans 11:15.

5. *The devil.*

In a certain sense all the kingdoms of the world have been given to the devil. He deceives the entire world. The heathen serve him. He possesses great cunning, violent power, and wrath. With God's permission, he is able to perform signs and miracles and is even able to control the elements of nature. He is the most fearsome creature in all of creation. Scripture gives us the impression that he is a servant of God's justice unto the righteous judgment of God-forsaking mankind. Christ's return will bring deliverance from this cruel oppressor, who has so often vexed the souls of God's children. At the first resurrection, Satan will be deprived of his first prey. He will have the power of death, that is to say, the rulership over death. At the judgment of the nations, he will lose another part of his hold. When the Antichrist and the false prophet are cast down, Satan's most faithful helpers will be taken away from him. This strong one will be deprived of all his vessels by the stronger One.

Revelation 20:2-3 describes Satan's defeat: "And he laid hold on the dragon, that old serpent, which is the Devil, and Satan, and bound him a thousand years, and cast him into the bottomless pit, and shut him up, and set a seal upon him, that he should deceive the nations no more, till the thousand years should be fulfilled: and after that he must be loosed a little season" (cf. also Isa. 27:1; Rom. 16:20). With the devil gone, the greatest offense is banished from creation and the mother promise is fulfilled. Only then can we speak of a Kingdom of peace.

Hereafter we shall say more about the precious fruits of the Lord's return, but the little we have said thus far is already sufficient to express with the Rev. H. Pierson the ardent desire:

Come, O Lord Jesus! Why tarriest Thou any longer?
From one hour to the next it becomes more oppressive for Thy Church.
The oil is burning away and the lamps are going out;
Ah, how Thou testeth the love of Thy Bride!

The waiting is painful and the endless longing
Has already affected her eyelids with slumber.
The night weighs heavily, still she keeps hearing
Thy voice in her dreams and her members are languid.

Come, O Lord Jesus! Why tarriest Thou any longer?
Why tarriest Thou any longer?
From one hour to the next it becomes more oppressive for Thy Church.
More and more oppressive!

Part II
The First Resurrection

Chapter 6

THE FIRST RESURRECTION

It is a painful thing to a Christian when he must take a position contrary to that adhered to by his brethren. Indeed, it is so painful that many, for the sake of convenience, desist from doing so. But truth insists that we love it above everything else, even above peace. It is this love of the truth that compels us to take up the battle against the generally accepted teaching that there will be one common resurrection. We do not wish to combat the doctrine of a resurrection, for that is one of the most comforting truths of our eschatological hope, but the doctrine of a *simultaneous* resurrection of both believers and unbelievers. We also wish to show that a twofold resurrection —distinct not only in origin, nature, and purpose, but also in time—is definitely based on the Scriptures.

Holy Scripture is the source of knowledge for our examination. With regard to the doctrine concerning the last things, as well as to the entire body of the doctrine of truth, there has been far too much reasoning without an exegetical basis. For centuries exegesis has far too often been considered as an aid to the system of faith. This approach has done inestimable damage to the development of truth. Not only during the Middle Ages but also long after the Reformation the question was far more often asked what Plato, Aristotle, Augustine, and Jerome said than what the Scriptures say. And, alas, the tendency to view the once accepted ideas as irrefutable truth, without serious examination of the Scriptures, still continues. The only correct method in the development of truth is exegesis, not the traditional, and far less the philosophical-reflective type, but *biblical exegesis*. In our examination we wish to follow this method. Even then may our effort perish if it be not according to God's Word!

In this chapter we wish to make a few preparatory remarks.

1. *A first resurrection is possible.*

To God it is no greater miracle than one general or simultaneous resurrection. Hence the miraculous element need not intimidate anyone, for it is a wonder done by God's almighty hand. It is also possible from the point of view of those who are resurrected. If only one kind of person were lying in the graves, it would make no sense to speak of a twofold resurrection. Since, however, there are regenerated and unregenerated people resting in their graves, it makes sense to speak of a twofold resurrection.

2. *It is altogether reasonable.*

Not a single logical objection can be raised against a separate resurrection exclusive of believers. There is no inherent contradiction in this idea. There is no consciousness or feeling in man, at least not in unregenerated man, that opposes it. It is not contradictory to any sound concept. At best it can go contrary to a world of prejudice.

3. *It is not a futile error.*

Suppose that we were dealing here with a heresy, then it still would not be a fundamental, and hence futile error. For at this point we are *not* forced to abandon one single truth. It is not an assault on the Holy One Himself, nor does it deny anything of the holiness of His Word. If it did, we would reject it as heresy.

4. *Many saints have already been resurrected.*

This fact forces us to drop the idea of a general resurrection. Matthew 27:52-53 tells us that a partial resurrection has already taken place, "And the graves were opened; and many bodies of the saints which slept arose, and came out of the graves after his resurrection, and went into the holy city, and appeared unto many." We are told that they were saints and *many* of them arose by the power of Christ's death.

That these resurrected saints would once more have died is highly unlikely.

A) The word which is translated *appeared* points to immortal brightness and glory. It is the word that is used for Christ and the future glorification of believers. Most expositors believe with Calvin that they were resurrected with glorified bodies. Recently Dr. H. H. Kuyper also stated this in *The Herald.*

B) This would be at variance with the obvious purpose of this resurrection, which was to show the fruit of Christ's resurrection. It would have caused doubt if these saints would soon thereafter have died again. Nor does it seem possible that the Lord Jesus would have laid these believers once more in the grave, when they had been in the company of the glorified Christ.

C) In Psalm 68:18 and Ephesians 4:8 the word *captivity* must be translated as *captives,* and that most likely they are the believers who had been captives of death and the grave. This view is taken by various Church Fathers, Luther, Calovius, Alford, Owen, Nast, Olshausen, and many others. The saints would have to ascend into heaven sooner or later, and there would be no more suitable occasion than at the ascension of Christ Himself. Finally, Christ is bodily not alone in heaven.

5. *It is wholly in line with Reformed thought.*

Do we not teach, as Reformed people, that election governs all of man's life and that it has eternal effects? Whatever the redeemed and their glory will be one day is exclusively the result of God's election. Here we are dealing with election applied to the resurrection of the believers. Just as in the word *ekklesia,* the called-out assembly, the preposition *ek* points to the fact that the Church is the fruit of God's election. So the same preposition *ek,* which is often used in connection with the resurrection of believers, points out that this resurrection is a fruit of the election of grace. That is why it is often called elective resurrection. A pure development of the doctrine of resurrection will benefit the "heart of the Church." And, inversely, a deep respect for God's election will lead us all the more easily to a twofold resurrection.

This writer can personally testify that during this study the glorious truth of election has become increasingly precious to him. And is it not significant that American Methodists have attacked premillennialism on the grounds that it is Calvinistic in regard to election? The Methodist author George W. Wilson expresses it thus, and he italicizes his words, "Every prominent premillennarian on the globe is a pronounced Calvinist on election." This reproach is high praise indeed!

6. *Most theologians writing on these matters agree in principle that there is a non-simultaneous resurrection.*

From the many examples available, we select only three. On Revelation 20:5, Abraham Kuyper says, "Hence the presentation is that the resurrection of the dead takes place at two moments; (1) the resurrection of the sealed ones among the dead; (2) that of the rest of the dead." But he adds, "Both take place without any difference in time." The astute Maccovius, after having discussed the great difference between the resurrection of the righteous and the unrighteous, says, "There will be a resurrection of all, not at the same moment, however, but consecutively. The Holy Spirit teaches this in 1 Corinthians 15:23." He, too, adds, however, that all this takes place at the same time.

Dr. J. H. Bavinck, as always very cautious, states it thus, "From this [namely the great difference between the resurrection of the believers and that of the unbelievers] it does *not yet follow with certainty* that both resurrections differ also in time, that the resurrection of the righteous differ also in time, that the resurrection of the righteous precedes that of the unrighteous with a shorter or longer time" (*Magnalia Dei*, p. 640). The words we italicized are significant. This learned man apparently admits that there may also be a difference in time.

7. *A non-simultaneous resurrection, albeit with a firm basis, is highly probable.*

This seems likely when we consider the separated character of the people of the Lord. This people shall dwell alone, as Baalam, by the prodding of the Holy Spirit, had to prophecy of Israel. It can hardly be assumed that this holy and separated people, who in no respect may be conformed to the world, at such a significant occasion as the resurrection will be found in the company of the doomed dead.

The Holy Scriptures teach us that God wants to keep the dissimilar and incongruous separated. We may not separate what God has united, but neither may we unite what He has separated. Why was it not allowed in Israel to hitch an ox together with an ass before the plow? Was this in itself such a calamity? Why was an Israelite not allowed to sow a field with a mixture of two different kinds of seed? Is that not, according to agriculturalists, good for the soil? Why was a Jew not allowed to wear two kinds of material in one piece of clothing? Would this impair one's health in any way? The answer to all these questions is simply that God does not want the unification of the dissimilar. He made everything according to its kind. In the nature of the different kinds of things He created, He placed boundaries which His creatures may not remove. Since in the work of re-creation He drew such deep demarcation lines of contrast between believers and unbelievers, is it imaginable that on Christ's return His people will be found in association with the wicked?

A non-simultaneous resurrection is probable because that of the believers differs from that of the unbelievers in cause, nature, and purpose.

Finally, a non-simultaneous resurrection is acceptable when we realize that the day of Christ is not a day in the narrower sense of the word, but a separate dispensation. Many make the mistake of interpreting the days of creation as long periods of time, even though it is evident that these were ordinary sundays. On the other hand, the day of the Lord is taken as an ordinary day of twenty-four hours, although it is equally evident that it is a whole dispensation.

Let it surprise no one that we call the day of the Lord a dispensation, for Scripture itself calls it that. It also calls this entire present dispensation of nearly two thousand years a day (Rom. 13:11; 1 Cor. 4:3-5; 2 Cor. 6:2; John 16:23, 26). John even calls the entire time between Christ's first and second coming a *last hour.* (On this, see also Bavinck, *Dogmatics,* IV, pp. 769ff.) With this in mind, it can readily be accepted that in the "last day" the Lord resurrects His people, together with the wicked. In that "day," all will arise from the grave, the godly in the morning and the godless in the evening.

Thus we have seen that the doctrine of the first resurrection, a resurrection of the believers exclusive of the wicked, must be considered possible and reasonable. In any case, we cannot speak of a general resurrection. Since this doctrine, being in line with Reformed thought, is in principle accepted by many theologians, we can speak of it as highly probable.

Before advancing the certain proofs for a twofold resurrection, we first wish to consider in the next chapter the objections.

Chapter 7

OBJECTIONS TO THE FIRST RESURRECTION

Objections are being raised to this doctrine of the first resurrection, and it would be unfair if we were not willing to listen to them. We will present the main and constantly recurring objections, and answer them briefly. The strongest one we keep for the last.

1. *"Our Reformed predecessors knew nothing about it."*
After some reflection it must be admitted that this says little or nothing. For, in the first place, these pious and wise predecessors had no monopoly on all wisdom. They were not the only diggers for and keepers of the treasures and truth of Holy Scripture. To them and their labors can be applied Article 7 of our Belgic Confession, of which the second part says:

> Neither may we consider any writings of men, however holy these may have been, of equal value with those divine Scriptures, nor ought we to consider custom, or the great multitude, or antiquity, or succession of times and persons, or councils, decrees or statutes, as of equal value with the truth of God, since the truth is above all; for all men are of themselves liars, and more vain than vanity itself: Therefore we reject with all our hearts whatsoever does not agree with the infallible rule, which the apostles have taught us, saying, "Prove the spirits, whether they are of God".

Second, this argument says nothing, since these fathers all but avoided the entire doctrine of the last things. They have not developed this body of belief, nor could they, since their concept of the Church was deficient. Matters would be entirely different if they had applied their powers to serious examination of Holy Scripture, and had laid down their obtained results in a Confession. In that case, this argument would still not be conclusive, but it would certainly be significant. However, this is not the case. Just about the same thing can be said of the Belgic Confession as was said of the fathers. During recent years more and more voices are raised about the inadequacy of our Confession, especially with regard to the last things.

Here we must add, however, that going back from the fathers to the grandfathers, the latter most certainly knew and accepted a first resurrection. The entire Church until the time of Constantine the Great was committed to this doctrine. Dr. Bavinck even mentions some fourteen Reformed fathers who were proponents of this viewpoint, so it will not do to say that the fathers knew or wanted nothing of it.

2. *"It is* Jewish."

If this argument were not heard or written down so often, we would not mention it here, for it really deserves no refutation. This argument always derives its strength from the evil passion of antisemitism. Most certainly it is Jewish. Abraham understood it, for the New Testament testifies that he believed that God was able to raise Isaac from the dead. Joseph adhered to it, otherwise why should he have commanded that his bones be carried to Canaan? Obviously Job found comfort in it, David sang of it, Isaiah shouted with joy about it, and the martyrs of the Old Covenant allowed themselves to be tortured, courageously refusing the proffered deliverance, "that they might obtain a better resurrection." It is found in Second Ezra and in the Testaments of the Twelve Patriarchs. At the time of Christ, the Jews generally believed in the resurrection of the righteous, separated from that of the unrighteous and kept separate by the reign of the Messiah. All the Jewish expositors have taught this.

If the doctrine of the first resurrection was generally known by the Jews in Jesus' day, this sheds light on the question of why this doctrine is not more clearly described in the New Testament. It is presupposed, rather than emphatically taught. This is a further strong confirmation of the doctrine. For if the Jews had harbored it as a false concept, we would have had a refutation of this error from Christ and His apostles, who always testified to the truth and against the lie and error. But we find such refutation nowhere. As we shall soon see, they did just the opposite.

3. *"Only one text supports this doctrine, and that is obscure, from which we can deduce nothing."*

This objection reasons the same as the preceeding one; it is repeated time and time again, without any proof. The conclusion in this statement rests on two untruths, and is therefore itself untrue. This one text refers, of course, to Revelation 20:5. This reference is the clearest of them all, but to call it the only one is untrue.

We must admit that not many texts in Scripture specifically refer to the first resurrection. And that is in keeping with the nature of Scripture, as it does not speak often of the resurrection. As is the case with most doctrines, this truth is assumed in numerous texts. All the references to and assumptions of the Lord's return (there are over three hundred) presuppose the separate resurrection of believers. The first task Christ will do at His coming will be to change the living believers and to resurrect the deceased ones. Since Scripture does not mention the resurrection often, let no one expect much scriptural proof for a twofold resurrection. It is remarkable, however, that all the references which speak of the resurrection, with the exception of about fifty, speak exclusively of the resurrection of the believers. That is so remarkable that Bernhard Weiss, R. Schmidt, and other theologians, denied that Scripture also taught the resurrection of the wicked.

But judgment presupposes the resurrection of unbelievers, which Scripture teaches emphatically (Dan. 12:2, John 5:28, Acts 24:15). This does not alter the fact that the resurrection of the believers stands in the foreground (Job 19:25-27; Ps. 73:23-26; Isa. 26:19-20; Ezek. 37; Hos. 6:2; 13:14; Matt. 22:32; Mark 9:10; 12:25; Luke 14:14; 20:34-36; John 6:39-41; Acts 4:2; Rom. 8:11, 23; 1 Cor. 6:14; 15:1-58; 2 Cor. 4:14; Phil. 3:11, 20; 1 Thess. 4:16; Heb. 11:35; Rev. 20:5).

If both believers and unbelievers were to rise together, the blessed resurrection would not be placed in the foreground. In that case the resurrection would not have been specialized, but would have been predicted in more general terms. No one text specifically speaks of the dead as one mass. In the two instances in the New Testament where they are mentioned together, the believers are mentioned first (John 5:28-29; Acts 24:15).

If Revelation 20:5 were indeed the only reference to the first resurrection, could anything be proven from that fact? It is often claimed by those who cannot escape from the weight of this text that it speaks of two actual resurrections, separated by a period of a thousand years. They say that this is an obscure reference, and no doctrine can be built on it. We are convinced that this opinion is incorrect in three respects.

A) We are *not* dealing with an obscure text here. The strong opponents themselves see immediately that it speaks of a two-fold resurrection. One can hardly call a text obscure when both friend and foe can tell you, "It says so."

Moreover the Holy Spirit Himself in Revelation 20:1-5 gives a brief, literal, and infallible explanation of this vision. Since the Holy Spirit, by way of clarification, emphatically states, "This is the resurrection, the first," we have no reason to complain about obscurity. This reference may be obscure to a prejudiced mind that decides to reject a first resurrection. We must not approach the Word of God with our presuppositions, expecting to conform it to our opinions. The "mind of the flesh" refuses to submit to the Word of God. And the greater such a mind is, the slower its subjection will be in most cases. Even a born-again mind will by no means always and unconditionally subject itself. We do not like to see the house of cards of our own cherished opinions knocked down. The Word demands, however, that we bring all thoughts and imaginations of the heart into its captivity. There is nothing that prevents us from comprehending the thoughts of God, to such an extent, other than the carnal thoughts of pious men. Therefore we would do well to approach Revelation 20:5 as if nothing had ever been said about it, or as a child who reads it for the first time. Then this text will be clear, and not subject to a twofold explanation.

B) The above-mentioned opinion is wrong because it suggests that the doctrine of the first resurrection appears only in Revelation 20:5. For proof of the opposite, see above and below.

C) Those who insist that we may not base a doctrine on a single Scripture text are wrong. If a certain text is obscure in everyone's opinion, then the Church will be wise not to build a doctrine on it. However, the Early Church, according to Henry

Alford and others, ascribed to this text a literal and natural meaning. They explained it simply as referring to a first resurrection. Even a single statement such as this should be highly esteemed if we are to take the verbal inspiration of Holy Scripture seriously. For there is nothing superfluous in Scripture. The whole and each of the parts, albeit not in like measure, are necessary for the people of the Lord. If it was proven that here a first resurrection is taught, then this reference alone would be sufficient for the Church to teach a two-fold resurrection. Therefore we consider all this talk that nothing can be concluded from one text as rationalistic arguments that truly do not evidence great reverence for the Word of the Lord.

It is very strange that, in regard to other single scriptural statements, there is not this kind of fear to conclude something from them and indeed to base fundamental doctrines on them. Just consider how many clear texts there are to prove the eternal generation of the Son, the outgoing of the Holy Spirit, the Counsel of Peace, the doctrine of the covenant of works, original sin, man's total powerlessness, and infant baptism. In not one of these cases a variety of texts are demanded, which can be consumed as readily as a sliced loaf of bread. Nor is this imperative.

Contrary to many sects, Christian tradition teaches that it is not imperative that a doctrine must be spelled out explicitly in the Bible. Truths that can be deduced matter of factly or by logical deduction are equally valid and binding. We need only to read what Dr. Heppe in his excellent thesis on the scriptural basis for the witness of the Holy Spirit says:

> A specific statement to prove that the general witness of the Spirit is immediately beyond all doubt to the believer cannot be found in Scripture. This must be frankly admitted from the onset. We need not fear that by admitting this we weaken our position. The Reformed position attaches relatively little value to whether a particular doctrine is mentioned in specific words in Scripture or not. Take any doctrine, and the big question is never whether some particular text but whether a basis for it can be found in the Word of God.

It seems strange that with regard to the doctrine of the last things, different demands are made. Why not argue here also on the basis of the nature of the matter itself, as is done for instance with regard to election, to Christ's resurrection from the midst of the dead, to the mystical union, to the total separation of unbelievers, to Christ's return with all His saints and to the judging of the saints, and so on.

And finally, that the Lord demands that we unconditionally believe Him even when He speaks only one word, is sufficiently evident from the history of salvation. How many indications did Israel of old receive regarding the Messiah? Looking back, and seen in the light of fulfillment, they may be clear to us, but to Israel they were general promises. Israel had to rely for many ages on two or three such promises with regard to the ardently longed-for future deliverance. We must not forget that the Word of God is weightier than man's word. Let no one take it lightly; we must never lose sight of the fact that God does not consider His people to whom He gives His revelation as fools but as wise people. And is not one word to the wise sufficient?

Thus we have seen that there are sufficient reasons to reject all arguing about *only one* and *an obscure* reference. This is only an excuse to escape the force of Revelation 20:5.

4. *"Scripture emphatically teaches a general and simultaneous resurrection."*

We have known the arguments for a general resurrection from our earliest youth. Only the Lord knows how much struggle and vexation of soul it costs to discard such deep-rooted opinions. But God's truth must be more precious to the believer than all human traditions, indeed more precious than this temporal life itself.

Scripture emphatically teaches a general resurrection, this objection argues, with reference to the following three texts: Daniel 12:2, John 5:28-29, and Acts 24:15. We wish to consider these texts briefly and consecutively.

Daniel 12:2 reads, "And many of them that sleep in the dust of the earth shall awake, some to everlasting life, and some to shame and everlasting contempt." It is not necessary to conclude a simultaneous fulfillment from a simultaneous prediction. This would fly in the face of the entire body of unfulfilled prophecy. The prophet is not pointing to the *time* of the resurrection but to the *fact* of such. He gives a clear hint concerning a non-simultaneous resurrection. This interpretation is more evident in the translations of such learned men as Tregelles, Bush, Whiting, and Seiss, which goes as follows: "And many of them, who are sleeping in the dust of the earth, will awake, these (many who awake) unto eternal life, and those (the rest of the sleeping ones who will awake to another time) unto shame and everlasting contempt."

The rabbis usually also thought of a non-simultaneous resurrection. The majority of expositors do the same. Those unwilling to do so have, as a rule, the same view as Van der Palm, who expresses his opinion thus:

> That this text is not referring to the actual resurrection of the dead may become clear also from the word *many;* but the disguised expression is derived from it to point out the undying fame of those who had been slain for this glorious cause and the indelible shame of those who had betrayed it.

In this manner this learned man attempts to get out of this dilemma.

John 5:28-29 says, "Marvel not at this: for the hour is coming, in the which all that are in the graves shall hear his voice, and shall come forth; they that have done good, unto the resurrection of life; and they that have done evil, unto the resurrection of damnation." This text is thought to teach a general resurrection. The word *hour,* it is claimed, clearly points to a simultaneous resurrection from the grave. Indeed, if anywhere, this text *seems* to contradict the teaching of a non-simultaneous resurrection. And yet we hope to make clear to the reader that this "indeed" only *seems* so.

The best exegete of a scriptural text is the context in which it appears. Let us look at verse 25 of the same chapter. There Christ says, "The hour is coming, and *now is.*" That hour has lasted more than nineteen hundred years, and encompasses this entire present dispensation. So with what justification can it be said that this is not the case with the word *hour* in verse 28? It is a rule in exegesis that a word usually has only one specific meaning in the same context. "When a word in the same context appears more than once, we must, as a rule, always ascribe the same meaning to it" (Louis Berkhof, *Hermeneutics,* p.98).

Furthermore we must keep in mind that John usually indicates this entire dispensation with the word "hour." Remember his fatherly admonition, "Little children, it is the last hour."

Finally, we are dealing here with prophecy. And in prophecy, time indications are never of predominant importance. The prophets, for instance, frequently mention things in one breath which later prove to be separated from each other by centuries (cf. for instance, Isa. 61:2 with Luke 4:21). It was not Christ's intent to pinpoint the time of the resurrection. Since the prophets in the Old Testament often makes no separation between His first and second coming, then it should not surprise us that we find no fixation of time for the resurrection.

Acts 24:15 reads, "And have hope toward God, which they themselves also allow, that there shall be a resurrection of the dead, both of the just and unjust."

What we said above also applies to this text. The simultaneous mention of the two-fold resurrection does not mean that the two will take place at the same moment. It was not the intent of the Apostle to point out the time. We must furthermore keep in mind that he is addressing Gentiles, who know nothing of the Messianic salvation. For that reason he speaks of two resurrections in general. For if there were only one general resurrection, there would be no reason whatsoever for the Apostle to say emphatically, "both of the just and unjust." In that case it would be sufficient to mention it with one word only. Then a differentiation in groups of people would not be necessary.

It must not escape our attention that here again the resurrection of the believers is mentioned first. This is the case, as we have seen, in all three texts which mention the two kinds of people in connection with the resurrection. Is this not of great significance, especially when we compare 1 Corinthians 15:23, 1 Thessalonians 4:17, and Revelation 20:5?

Finally, the context is again significant. Paul is speaking of Israel's hope in the resurrection. It is important to know what expectation the Jews had in this regard. It has been shown particularly by Bertholdt in his *Christologia Iudaeorum* that the Jews expected a first resurrection. Later exegetes of the New Testament tell us the same. According to L. W. Munhall, orthodox Jews in Palestine have a tradition that the first resurrection will take place in the Valley of Jehoshaphat, so they prefer to be buried there in order to share in the first resurrection.

Thus we have seen that these texts are not proofs of a simultaneous resurrection. Neither may they be used, when considered by themselves, to teach a first resurrection. When we consider them without prejudice in the light of Revelation 20:5 and other scriptural references, they point to two non-simultaneous resurrections, rather than to one general resurrection.

Chapter 8

OLD TESTAMENT PROOFTEXTS FOR THE FIRST RESURRECTION

We will now present positive scriptural proof for a first resurrection. We shall briefly discuss the most important Scripture texts that deal with it. By beginning in the Old Testament and continuing on until Revelation 20, we can observe the progressive development of a doctrine.

Isaiah 24:22

"And they shall be gathered together, as prisoners are gathered in the pit, and shall be shut up in the prison, and after many days shall they be visited."

For the sake of clarification we offer the reader the following suggestions and ask him or her to compare this text with Revelation 20.

1. We are dealing here with the day of judgment. To make sure of this, we must carefully consider the preceding and following context, which points to the time of the resurrection.

2. Who are they that will be gathered together and shut up in a pit? Isaiah 24:21 gives the answer. "The host of the high ones that are on high, and the kings of the earth." Some expositors think that the stars are meant by "host of the high ones on high." Most commentators, however, think the devil and the spiritual wickedness in the air are meant. The kings of the earth (cf. Rev. 16:12-16) are always, but especially toward the end, most closely associated with the deceiver of the whole world (Dan. 8:20-22; Ps. 2; Rev. 19:21). The devil with his hosts in the air has deceived the nations. But he will be banished from these high places, and with his deceived hosts on high and on earth he will be shut up in the bottomless pit (Rev. 20:3). Then he can no longer deceive the nations.

3. Satan and his hosts will remain in the bottomless pit for a long time. During this period, there will be peace on earth (Isa. 24:23 and Rev. 20:4), and the Lord with His people will reign over the earth. Hence His people have already arisen, while the wicked are still resting in the abyss. "After many days (literally, after a multitude of days) they shall be visited" (Isa. 24:22), i.e., punished. The devil and the wicked do not receive their full punishment until the end of the millennial kingdom of peace. At the beginning Satan is cast into the bottomless pit (Rev. 20:3), and at the end into *the lake of fire and brimstone.*

This text assumes a first resurrection and discusses a second. The text, taken in its context, presents the most beautiful harmony with Revelation 20.

Isaiah 26:14

"They are dead, they shall not live; they are deceased, they shall not rise." Here again we touch only on a few points.

1. This text does not say, though some think it does, that there will not be a resurrection of the wicked. Isaiah teaches this clearly enough (see also Dan. 12:2, John 5:29, Acts 24:15). Isaiah means that the wicked will not rise with the God-fearing, and will not reign with them in the kingdom of peace.

2. We have here a song which the redeemed people of the Lord sing about their former oppressors. For them, death has been swallowed up in victory (Isa. 25:8); throughout the whole earth the rebuke of His people has been removed and their tears have been wiped away from their eyes. Then they are no longer cross-bearers, but crown-bearers with Christ, for He has returned (Isa. 25:9) and destroyed the face of the covering cast over all people and the veil that is spread over all nations (Isa. 25:7). The first resurrection has taken place. The people mentioned in the song are not resurrected yet; they are still lying dead in their graves. Nor will they arise until the end of the kingdom of peace. They are the wicked; but "blessed and holy is he that hath part in the *first* resurrection" (Rev. 20:6).

These wicked dead will not reign again on earth as before. They remain in their graves until the hour of their judgment has struck (Rev. 20:10-15).

Isaiah 26:19

We shall use the translation of Van der Palm because it best verbalizes the meaning. Here we have the chorus, the final song, that is being sung by the redeemed:

> Now, now your dead live again,
> Now their corpses arise;
> They awaken with a shout
> Who dwelt in the dust!
> Your dew is as the dew
> That descends upon the herbs,
> And for the second time the earth
> Brings forth those who already had died!

1. The emphasis is first of all on *thy dead men.* These are the believers who die in Jesus. "Blessed are the dead who die in the Lord." Nothing can separate them from the love of God, not even death, for the mystical union is inseparable. These dead do not belong to death, but to the Lord, both in life and in death. It is an entirely different matter with the unbelieving dead. They do indeed belong to death in all of the fearful sense of the word. As servants of God's severe justice, Satan and death have received a certain right to claim them.

These dead of the Lord will have a glorious resurrection in contrast to the wicked, of whom it is said already in Isaiah 26:14 that they will not rise again. The Lord's dead will awaken with a shout of joy. We need not wonder at this when we remind ourselves that Paul already shouted victoriously at the prospect of the blessed resurrection.

"Your dew is as the dew that descends upon the herbs." The metaphor of water always spoke to Israel, but even more, that of the dew. During certain seasons, no rain fell and everything would have burned if a copious and refreshing dew had not stretched out its veil over the earth. What the dew did in the realm of nature, the Holy Spirit does in the realm of grace. Here He is compared to the dew, elsewhere to the wind, fire, and oil. Softly, but irresistibly, He descends upon the dry field of the dead, causing it to awaken to life and to blossom. This will also become manifest in the day of resurrection. Then He will make this immense cemetery of the world into a garden of delight for believers. When the Lord sent forth His Spirit, His people were created. He renews the face of the earth, when the wicked will be removed.

2. "And for the second time the earth brings forth those who already had died." These words refer to another than the blessed resurrection; they refer to the second resurrection. The first part of Isaiah 26:19 emphasizes that the dead are the property of the Lord. Here, as in verse 14, the emphasis is on the state of death and punishment. The dead are presented here as something that is most horrible. They are cast away as dead carrion. The earth vomits them up. They arise unto contempt, unto judgment, of which verse 20 speaks, as well as the first verses of chapter 27.

That we are dealing here with the resurrection of the wicked is evident from the words and their construction. The word used for these dead is *rephaim;* it really means *giants* and should be thus translated in Deuteronomy 3:11-12; 2 Samuel 5:18, 22; 21:16, 18; 23:13. But it also appears in the sense of phantoms in the realm of the dead (Job 26:5; Prov. 9:18; 21:6) which must be pictured as being without flesh and blood, but not wholly without the power of life. With a few exceptions, the word is used to refer to the wicked dead.

Nor is the word which is translated *cast out* one that we would expect in connection with the blessed resurrection of the believers. It has to do with the scornful casting away of the dead body or of a miscarried fetus. The text does not say that they will live or arise, but it depicts the earth as casting them up and throwing them away. They are not even worthy of a place in creation and therefore the earth casts them out as a worthless mass. Nothing valuable in God's creation ever gets lost. All the images Scripture uses point toward the fact that the wicked will blow away like chaff before the wind; they will be done away with like scum of the earth, burned like stubble, and cast out like carrion. Chaff, scum, stubble, and carrion have no worth. That which is cast away does not *stand.* Scripture usually depicts the righteous as *standing* before the Son of Man in judgment (Ps. 1:5; Dan. 12:13; Luke 21:36) with confidence (1 John 2:28; 4:17; James 2:13).

The wicked, on the other hand, are *cast away,* are cast down before His feet and beaten to death. They will not stand before the face of the Lord, but will be cast out into the outer darkness. The idea of resurrection in connection with the wicked is hardly ever encountered in God's Word. For the people of God the resurrection is a standing up in the full sense of the word, but for the wicked it is essentially a deep fall, a total rejection, a sinking away under the wrath of the Almighty.

Of course, we must not expect a clear indication of the long passage of time between the two resurrections in a prophecy of this nature. All expositors agree, however, that they see some kind of reference to time in the last clause of Isaiah 26:19. The marginal notes here state, "*After* thou hast felled the giants down to the ground." The conjunction *waw* often means afterward, for the second time (see Judg. 2:19).

Isaiah 27:12

"And it shall come to pass in that day, that the Lord shall beat off from the channel of the river unto the stream of Egypt, and ye shall be gathered one by one, O ye children of Israel."

Here again we consider the clearer translation of Van der Palm and quote it as follows:

> The day is dawning
> In which Jehovah will gather in the fruit,
> From the inundated banks of the River Euphrates,
> To the brook of Egypt:
> Then all of you will be garnered, one by one,
> Ye children of Israel.

Isaiah 27 is considered one of the most difficult chapters of Isaiah. Much is clarified, however, when we realize that here a song is sung on Israel's future re-acceptance, which, according to the Apostle Paul, will be a resurrection from among the dead of the entire world.

Beginning with verse 7, a few unexpressed objections are answered. In contrast to the glory celebrated in song, the first objection is that God has often beaten His people severely. The answer to this is that the Lord never struck His people as hard as did their enemies.

A second objection is that God had such a struggle with His people that he cast them into exile. This is refuted by saying that all this was done with measure and had as its object their purification from idolatry and idol-service.

A third argument points out that Jerusalem, the city of God, had been cast out and forsaken as a desert. Can this be reconciled with the great love of God of which the song speaks afterward? This is refuted by a twofold answer: a) Israel was a dry piece of wood, ready for the fire, a nation without understanding which had forfeited all grace. b) But Israel's cause is not hopeless. A happy day of deliverance will yet dawn for Israel (Isa. 27:12). Verse 13 describes the gathering of the living exiles, while verse 12 denotes the gathering of the deceased. Verse 13 uses the metaphor of a general who calls his soldiers together by sounding the trumpet (cf. Isa. 18:3; Matt. 24:31; 1 Cor. 15:52; 1 Thess. 4:16). Here we are not in agreement with the State Translation (Dutch Authorized Version) which takes this as referring to Cyrus and to the trumpet of the gospel. We believe this refers to the day of Israel's re-acceptance and restoration.

But first, before the gathering in of the living, the dead will be resurrected and gathered together, as Paul teaches in 1 Thessalonians 4:17. The original idiom shows that this does not mean that the dead will be gathered up one by one, but that all of them together, without exception, will be garnered as one precious fruit. The emphasis is not on separate persons but on the totality of elect and deceased Israel, as is most clearly evident from the exact mention of the place. This text speaks exclusively of God's people. Delitzsch, Nägelbach, and others see this text as referring to the first and separate resurrection.

Isaiah 66:24

From this text (as well as from Job 19:25-26; Hos. 6:2; Zech. 14:5), especially when considered in the light of clearer texts, many indications of a separate resurrection can be deduced. But we prefer to stay with only the clearer texts.

Ezekiel 37:1-14

We need not print this extensive section. It is that of the wellknown vision of the quickening of the dry bones. We make the following observations.

1. This section does not deal with the spiritual quickening of a sinner. Nor are we to think of the merely civil and social restoration from the first exile, because the people are converted, united, happy, and ruled by the Messiah. And we are not to think of the so-called general resurrection of the dead. The prophet sees only a great number of skeletons, translated

here as dead men. That word is not the word generally used for the dead. Finally, the context forbids taking it in this sense.

2. It is evident from the explanation that the Lord Himself gives of this vision, that it is an indication of the return and conversion of the Jews. This resurrection of the Jews from the graves of the nations is, according to Scripture, a metaphor and at the same time an important aspect of the first resurrection. When the Deliverer comes out of Zion, He will turn away the wickedness from Jacob, and the believers will arise from their graves.

3. Israel must have been acquainted with the metaphor used here, otherwise the vision would have missed its purpose. Those learned men who have studied this point say that Israel was aware of a first resurrection, but hardly knew anything of a general and simultaneous resurrection, of a resurrection of the wicked. This will explain why the prophets, apostles, and Christ spoke almost exclusively of the resurrection of the righteous. They taught the raising of the unbelievers (Acts 24:14-15; 26:7-8), but not as taking place with the believers.

Daniel 12:2

We have already discussed this verse, and for that reason we can now deal with it briefly. Earlier it was shown that these words do not serve as proof for a general resurrection. On the contrary, we shall briefly show that they point to a separate resurrection.

The many and widely divergent explanations can be reduced to three kinds. a) Daniel 12:2 refers to the restoration of Israel with the metaphor of a resurrection, as in similar instances in Isaiah 24—27; Ezekiel 37, and so on. b) Most commentators explain this text in terms of a mixed resurrection. They usually treat it as Barnes does, who says, "The natural and obvious meaning of the word *many* is this, that a great multitude of people will arise, but not all. That is the way we would take the word when used of other matters." Yet this expositor quite unscrupulously changes the meaning of the word *many* to *all.* This is how prejudice acts and how Scripture is violated as a result of bias. *Many* might mean *all,* but certainly *many of* cannot. No matter how we twist and turn this expression around, *many* clearly excludes a general resurrection. c) Today there are many (and this time "many" does not mean all!) who think the verse is speaking of a heterogeneous resurrection. To use this seems the correct view. In support of this view we point out the following:

1. The *min partitivus* (Heb. grammar) suggests the idea that a separation will take place. We know that at His coming the Lord will separate the goats from the sheep.

2. The demonstrative pronoun, as it appears here, has a distributive meaning. Hence it is to be translated *these* (who are well known) and *those* (who are totally different, or whose turn comes later).

3. The metaphor of sleep for the concept of death is used only when speaking of deceased saints. Here the wicked are not called *sleepers,* but only *those* (over there).

4. If it is argued that these different kinds are nevertheless mentioned in one breath, then we point out that Daniel does this quite frequently. In Daniel 9:26 Jerusalem's destruction and the cutting off of the Messiah are mentioned in one breath, although a period of forty years separated these events. In Daniel 11:2 Xerxes and Alexander are placed beside each other, although 120 years separated these kings. Isaiah mentions in one sentence the acceptable year of the Lord and the day of vengeance (Isa. 61:2; see also Isa. 7:9; Joel 2:29-31; Mal. 4:1-2 and all Messianic prophecies).

Daniel 12:13

"But go thou [Daniel] thy way till the end be: for thou shalt rest, and stand in thy lot at the end of the days." These words speak of the resurrection as is clear from the context. Here the emphasis is on the unique and comforting nature of the resurrection from the grave rather than on its non-simultaneousness.

1. Daniel, the greatly beloved man, who had been sick on account of the horrible things that would befall his people, is comforted here with his separate and blessed resurrection. If there were only one resurrection of both the evil and the good, it would be odd that the believers' attention is pointed to, and they are comforted with, their resurrection. Why then is that one powerful act of resurrection pointed out, and not the blessedness in general? All this becomes clear to us when we

realize that the first resurrection includes our reigning with Christ, whereas the other dead remain in their graves.

2. What does the expression *stand in thy lot* mean? The word *lot* is a reference to the casting of lots in Israel, whereby everyone could receive his own inheritance. What the meaning is here is not clear, and opinions vary greatly. Some think that it speaks of the first resurrection mentioned in Matthew 27:52-53. This idea is possible, but it cannot be proved. Also, the expression *end of the days* does not favor it. Others think it has reference to the Messianic Kingdom, the Millennium, as for instance Heinrich Gesenius; he refers in this connection to Revelation 20:6. Many think it refers to the reward of grace. Just as Paul speaks of that good thing he had committed to Him against that day, meaning the reward of grace, it is assumed that here mention is made of Daniel's own lot. The context favors this explanation, particularly in verses 2 and 3. The reward of grace supplies comfort and encouragement.

It seems to us that this refers to the first resurrection, together with the reward of grace, for these two concepts are closely connected in Scripture. The reward of grace is given when the Lord comes and immediately after the blessed resurrection. Just as the tribes of Israel received their portion of Canaan from the hand of the Lord, so, in that day, everyone will receive his reward according to his works. Because of this reward of grace, the first resurrection is the blessed one, and blessed and holy are those who share in it.

Chapter 9

NEW TESTAMENT PROOFTEXTS FOR THE FIRST RESURRECTION

Luke 14:14

"And thou shalt be blessed; for they cannot recompense thee: for thou shalt be recompensed at the resurrection of the just."

1. The stipulation "of the just" would be completely superfluous if Christ was thinking of a so-called general resurrection. For was there any compulsion for Him to mention the just only? In a perfectly natural way He speaks of the resurrection of the just.

2. The Jews took this in no other sense than that of a separate resurrection, for according to Bertholdt, Olshausen, Meyer, Van Koetsveld, Van Oosterzee, Munhall, and others, they distinguished between two separate resurrections. If they had been in error regarding this matter, Christ would not have supported them. Is it imaginable that the faithful Witness, the mouth of Truth, would have supported them in any error?

3. One of the Pharisees sitting at meat with Jesus, upon hearing Him make that statement, enthusiastically cried out, "Blessed is he that shall eat bread in the kingdom of God!" (John 14:15). This shows that the scribe was thinking of a separate resurrection of the people of the Lord.

4. Although not conclusive, it is significant that eminent, impartial expositors explain the statement in this vein. We mention here Gill, Dodridge, Van Oosterzee, Olshausen, Alford, Meyer, Lange, Moses Stuart, Ryle, and the rationalistic commentators.

Luke 20:35

"But they which shall be accounted worthy to obtain that world, and the resurrection from the dead, neither marry, nor are given in marriage."

Jesus made this statement in answer to the presentation by the Sadducees of the levirate marriage. They wished to corner Jesus and their opponents, for the latter taught that man arose as a sensual person and would continue to produce children in the next world. But Christ showed them that they erred because they did not know the Scriptures nor distinguish the dispensations, for in the next world there is neither marriage nor giving in marriage.

1. We are not dealing here with the resurrection *of* the dead, but the resurrection *from among* the dead. Ignoring a distinction between the two causes us to lose sight of a non-simultaneous resurrection. If that distinction had not been completely lost sight of, but had always been honestly admitted as is usually done in connection with Christ's resurrection, its opponents would have been forced to accept a first resurrection. When the little word *ek* is used in connection with the dead, it always means, as Van Andel usually translates it, *from among the dead.* Does this not clearly imply that not all will arise?

When this preposition is used in connection with Christ's resurrection, the translation is "from (among) the dead." Why is this not done also when the preposition is used with the resurrection of Christ's people?

Professor Ten Hoor makes the following remarks on the expression "*from* the dead."

> We are not dealing here with a resurrection *of the dead,* nor merely *from death,* but *from the dead,* from the midst of the dead, from the world of the dead, from the state of the dead. Hence it says that, of all the dead, Christ only arose, while at that moment all other dead remained in the state of death. By His resurrection Christ departed not only from the circles of the physically dead, but also from the circles of mortal mankind which lies under the judgment of death. By His resurrection He attains such a height that He is elevated above the realm of death. Hence by His resurrection He is higher than those whose souls are in heaven but whose bodies are still in the realm of the dead.

The professor sees this all clearly and sharply, but when the same expression is used, not once, but many times, for the resurrection of believers, then it holds no less true for them. And if it holds true for them, it proves a first resurrection.

2. The expression, "they which shall be accounted worthy," is remarkable. It evokes the question of whether there are people who will not be accounted worthy to obtain this special resurrection. Indeed, we must go a step further and say that this idea *must* be concluded from it. Imagine that we explained this clause in terms of a general resurrection. What meaning would we then give to this expression? Is the resurrection as such not an unavoidable matter? Can it seriously be said of the resurrection that one must be deemed worthy of it? Is it not equally required for all the children of men, and equally unavoidable? If we insist on a general resurrection, then it is impossible to retain this expression, for it is absurd to say of something that is unavoidable that one must be worthy of it.

If, on the contrary, we apply this expression to the separate resurrection of the believers, then everything fits. Many will *not* be accounted worthy to partake in the resurrection from among the realm of the dead. Only the *elect* are also *elected* to this blessed event.

3. We must pay attention to Christ's expression "*children of the resurrection*" (Luke 20:36). Those who are accounted worthy of this resurrection are *God's* children, because they are children of *the resurrection.* If we said this of a general resurrection, the resurrected unbelievers would be called children of God. Only those who are considered worthy of the first resurrection are children of the resurrection.

This remarkable name is given to them for three reasons: a) Because they received their bodies by this resurrection. One is a child in the true sense of the word through the person from whom one receives one's existence. This bodily existence one receives from the resurrection. b) Because their adoption as children is then complete. As far as the body is concerned, this adoption is evident from what the Apostle says in Romans 8:23. c) Because the Savior wants to silence the crafty listeners with it. If these resurrected ones are children of God in the full sense of the word since the Lord Himself quickened them, they need no longer be children of a father and a mother. When in the fullest sense God is the Father of the righteous, and they are children in a perfect sense, then children can no longer issue from a marriage between a man and a woman.

4. Finally, we call attention here to the expression, "Neither can they die any more." This statement does not apply to the lost. For they will receive death in the fullest sense of the word, and become the prey of the second death. They arise unto damnation.

Even though this text does not pinpoint a different time for the two resurrections, it is a strong reference to the first resurrection. That is the way, and the only way Alford, Godet, Meyer, Nitsch, Olshausen, Van Oosterzee, Pfleiderer, Fausset, and other commentators explain it.

John 6:39-54

Four times in this section the Lord speaks of the resurrection.

1. He is speaking in each instance about the resurrection of the believers. In the preceding chapter the Savior also spoke of the resurrection of the wicked. If He had been thinking of a mixed and simultaneous resurrection there, it would have been strange that here He speaks exclusively and repeatedly of the resurrection of the believers.

2. This resurrection is not presented as a mere future fact, but as a special privilege. It will occur because the Father has given Christ a people of His own, and at the same time has given Him the task of saving them completely. Christ repeatedly calls attention to the fact that it is He who delivers His own from the grave. He is a complete Savior, both of the body and of the soul.

3. It will take place at the last day. This day is not to be viewed as a regular day of twenty-four hours, but as the great day of the Lord in contrast to the present day of man (cf. 1 Cor. 4:3 in the original language) and *the day of grace.* Since the Savior is speaking of the resurrection of the righteous, a delineation of time with regard to the wicked is unnecessary.

4. Ryle writes:

These words are a powerful argument in favor of the *first* resurrection as being a special privilege of the believers. For it is said here that the believers will be *raised up* and that this is a special honor and grace reserved for them. Nevertheless it is no less clearly stated in 5:29 that *"all* that are in the graves shall come forth," both the good and the evil. Hence it follows that there is a resurrection of which only the believers will partake, separated from that of the wicked. What else can this be but the first resurrection? (Rev. 20:5)

Romans 8:11

"But if the Spirit of him that raised up Jesus from the dead dwell in you, he that raised up Christ from the dead shall also quicken your mortal bodies by his Spirit that dwelleth in you."

1. The first resurrection is the fruit of the mystical union. No Scripture text teaches it more clearly than this one. The Apostle declares that the quickening of our mortal bodies depends on the indwelling of the Holy Spirit. It is the Holy Spirit who conforms them unto Christ, and He will one day cause them to experience fully the power of His resurrection. According to God's counsel and purpose, Christ and the Church are never separated. The Church shares with Christ in all His mediatorial glory.

2. It is said twice in this text that Christ is raised *from among the dead* (*ek nekroon*). In the same way, the Apostle says, believers will also be raised up. Just as Christ left many dead behind in their graves, so will they. We must realize that we can no more expect a delineation of time here than in John 6; nor is one needed.

Philippians 3:11

"If by any means I might attain unto the resurrection of the dead." This text offers more information than those previously quoted, since it contains a separate word for this matter in the original language.

First a brief word on the text itself. There are three different readings of this text. We shall attempt to illustrate this in English.

The word in all three readings is *resurrection from.* This is the only place in all of Scripture where this particular word is found. But the wording around it varies in different manuscripts as follows:

A) the resurrection of the dead

B) the resurrection from (among) the dead

C) the resurrection, namely, the one from (among) the dead.

The last reading is found in most and the best manuscripts. Such learned men as Scholz, Lachmann, Tischendorf, Alford, and many others accept it.

There are four main explanations of this word.

1. It denotes a spiritual resurrection. This is the teaching of Johannes Cocceius and many of his Reformed followers. Even in our day many continue in these footsteps. But this cannot be the meaning of this verse, since Paul had arisen from the sleep of sin's death and did not need to die in order to attain a spiritual resurrection. Moreover the context strenuously argues against this interpretation.

2. A second explanation is the one by Van Hengel. He believed that Paul thought he would continue living until the resurrection of the dead. Most rationalist exegetes followed him in that view. This opinion leaves the words unexplained, so needs no refutation.

3. Most Reformed theologians today say it refers to the general resurrection, but with the understanding that the emphasis is on one part of it, i.e., that of the righteous. But when viewed in this way, the words are not explained either.

4. The number of exegetes who apply it to the first resurrection is increasing. We mention only Alford, Meyer, Olshausen, Lightfoot, Ellicot, Ebrard, and Nitsch. And it is not just the Chiliasts, as is often derisively stated, who believe that here and elsewhere the first resurrection is taught in Scripture. We mention also Dr. S. Hoekstra, W. N. Stoit, and *Yearbooks of Scientific Theology,* pp. 543-595.

The viewpoint mentioned under point 3 above leaves unexplained how the Apostle could strive for the resurrection so fervently. Is not a general resurrection something that cannot be avoided? No one can escape it. If he was speaking of the blessed resurrection, then the question arises whether he was not fully conscious of his sonship. For the children of God have nothing else to expect but a blessed resurrection. Hence Paul is not referring in general to the resurrection, nor to the blessed resurrection, for the former is guaranteed him as a man, and the latter as a Christian.

What the Apostle does mean is a resurrection that is causally connected with this temporal life, and more particularly with the life of sanctification. It is one which would also be the gracious reward of conforming to Christ in all things. Compare this carefully with Revelation 20:4-8, Luke 14:14, and Hebrews 11:35. From these and other texts it is evident that Scripture does not isolate the resurrection from the context of this life, as is generally done today. That we will be judged according to our works will be evident in the resurrection body. The resurrection itself will be a part of the reward of grace.

Furthermore, if this text is viewed as referring to a general resurrection, then it does not explain the special choice and form of the words. If we can speak with certainty of the Church as *ekklesia,* an elect multitude in the world, why can it not be fully admitted that this *exanastasis* is an elect multitude from the mass of grave occupants? It is true that some are of the opinion that *ek* here refers to coming out of the earth, but then the question could be asked why this preposition *ek* is not always found when mention is made of the resurrection, since all dead must arise from out of the earth. For this reason we assume with many experts that *ek* refers to the elect multitude that will share in the first resurrection.

This explanation is by no means new. Dächsel, commenting on this verse, says, "Already among the Church Fathers there were some who did not apply this to a general resurrection at the last day, but to the first resurrection mentioned in Revelation 20:4." He adds that they saw it more correctly than most of the later exegetes.

1 Thessalonians 4:16

"The dead in Christ shall rise first."

There were some believers in Thessalonica who had no clear concept of the coming again of the Lord. For that reason their expectation of salvation was partly impaired. Currently many wrong views exist concerning the mistake of these Christians, and so we wish briefly to call attention to them.

1. Their mistake was not that they thought the deceased would have no part in Christ at His return. They knew better than that.

2. That they were jealous because they thought the living would precede the dead is equally unacceptable. Such childishness on their part would not be in good character, because the Thessalonian Christians were among the most advanced believers in the New Testament.

3. Their error apparently consisted in the opinion that their beloved dead would not be resurrected until the end of the day

of Christ, so that they would not be able to reign with Him in that day. The Apostle emphasized that the first act of Christ at His return would be the resurrection of the believing dead. The believers could be assured that they would share in the first resurrection.

Apparently shortly thereafter some easily shaken Christians believed that the day of the Lord was already *present.* That is the way, according to experts, the word *enesteeken* (2 Thess. 2:2) must be translated.

We have for the first time a clear statement regarding the first resurrection. We cannot concede that this text posits a contrast between an initial arising and a later being taken up in the clouds (1 Thess. 4:17). The following points argue against this notion.

1. Paul has already made this contrast clear in 1 Thessalonians 4:14 and 15, so he would be repeating unnecessarily.

2. Since this was not the problem of these believers, it was not necessary to emphasize it.

3. If Paul were talking about a general resurrection, he had no need to mention the dead in Christ only.

4. If the word *first* (v. 16) were restricted to *the dead,* first the dead would rise, and then the living. But this delineation of time applies to the entire sentence: "First the dead in Christ will arise."

5. Verse 14 says that Christ will bring the deceased with Him. There the first resurrection is already assumed, or it must mean that Christ will come with only the *souls* of the deceased.

6. Many Church Fathers, Olshausen, Stuart, and others see a contrast here between the first and the second resurrection, since only this conception provides an unforced explanation of Paul's words.

1 Corinthians 15:23-24

"But every man in his own order: Christ the firstfruits; afterward they that are Christ's at his coming. Then cometh the end."

It is evident from the entire chapter of 1 Corinthians that Paul is constantly thinking of the resurrection of the believers. The other resurrection lies, as usual, totally outside of his vision.

In this verse he is preventing an objection. In the preceding verse he said that as in Adam all die, even so in Christ shall all be made alive. This might evoke the question of why the believers did not immediately arise from the grave with Christ? To this the Apostle answers that the resurrection is not one single fact, but a three-staged one. Just as death itself consists of three parts, so also the resurrection from death. God has instituted an order here that cannot be changed or removed.

Every man in his own order. Paul is referring to everyone in his own army unit, group, cohort. The term is derived from the various regiments of soldiers. This contains the idea of succession, for the various army units do not march beside each other, but one after the other. Thus the Apostle is saying that the resurrection takes place in three different groups.

1. *The firstfruits, Christ.* Here we have the first unit of the army of the risen. The metaphor of firstfruits is derived from the life under the shadows (under the law—Heb. 10:1). At the ripening of the harvest, Israel took the sheaves of firstfruits to the temple.

In this context the metaphor has great significance and provides us the following ideas.

A) The entire harvest was sanctified in the firstfruits. By offering these to the Lord, Israel demonstrated that the entire harvest belonged to Him and must be consecrated to Him. Likewise believers are sanctified, i.e., separated and dedicated in union with Him who is the Firstfruits of those who will be raised. But separated from what? From the rest of the dead, in order to be consecrated to the Lord as a holy harvest.

B) This metaphor points also to the oneness of Christ and the deceased believers. For the firstfruits themselves were part of the harvest. Thus there is also a spiritual oneness between Christ and His people. By virtue of the mystical union there is between Him and His Church the closest solidarity. The metaphor excludes unbelievers.

C) The metaphor assumes that the believers resurrection must take place after Christ's. For the firstfruits preceded the harvest. They were a sign and guarantee of it. Christ's resurrection certifies the future resurrection.

D) Finally, this metaphor gives us the silent hint that there are others who have arisen with the Christ. The idea of firstfruits already contains the idea of plurality. The firstfruits consisted of a few sheaves and even of many ears. If we ask who then arose with Christ, we prefer to point to Matthew 27:52-53. As the firstfruit of His resurrection, *many* saints had already risen from their graves.

2. *Afterward they that are Christ's at His coming.*

A) Selectivity is also emphasized here: *They that are Christ's.* The first thing He will do at His return is to gather His jewels, which are scattered everywhere, deep in the seas and deep in the earth.

B) His people represent the full harvest of which He is called the firstfruits. The unbelieving dead are not sanctified by the firstfruits. That only His own will arise was already implicit in the metaphor of firstfruits, but it is once more reiterated for further clarification.

3. *Then cometh the end.* Here the Apostle refers to the third army unit. Perhaps the reason he does not elaborate on this is that only the wicked are in this group. Although Scripture teaches the resurrection of the wicked, it never speaks of it at any length. This resurrection is usually assumed rather than specifically taught.

Those who adhere to a general resurrection read the text here as though it says, "Then [that is to say, at Christ's return] the end will be." But the Greek word *eita* may not be translated this way. The first *afterward* (epeita) already included a period of almost two thousand years. What right does anyone have to translate this second *afterward* (eita), emphatic in the same context, with *then*? The word indicates a shorter or longer passage of time, depending on events referred to in the context (cf. Heb. 10:5-7). Neither may it be translated by *immediately thereafter, at once, seconds thereafter*. To indicate these ideas the words *exautees* and *eutheoos* are used.

Before leaving this text, we quote Van Andel, who was as brilliant as he was amiable, on this text.

> Hence this text does not speak of a general resurrection, but only of the living again of those who have the Spirit of Christ, for whoever does not have His Spirit is not His. This resurrection of believers is something special, something peculiar, which sets it apart from every other resurrection from the dead, whether that of those whom mankind returns to this earthly life, or that which takes place at the end of the

judgment. It is the fruit and continuation of Christ's resurrection; it is the manifestation of Christ's life in us; it is the perfecting and completion of Christ's spiritual body. Without the resurrection of His own, Christ would not be complete; His resurrection would, so to speak, without ours not materialize and come to its conclusion. If we do not keep this in mind, we may be in danger of underestimating our resurrection by considering it as something incidental, something that like an article of luxury can, if necessary, be dispensed with. Then we cease to strive with Paul toward the resurrection as toward a prize which we by the sanctification of our bodies try to obtain. It cannot be denied that the general way of thinking of this extremely important matter on the part of present-day believers needs a complete overhaul. So may all of us esteem the resurrection of the saints very highly, for it is the manifestation of Christ's glory and is indispensable unto the completion of our union with God.

Being totally unique, this resurrection is therefore also, as far as the time element is concerned, separated from the general resurrection. This is clearly evident from Revelation 20, where it is called the first resurrection, separated from the following one by the period of Christ's judicial reign over the nations of the earth.

This Christian philosopher and biblical Christian, who in Reformed circles occupies a place of prominence, accepts a non-simultaneous resurrection along with Alford, Bengel, Bloomfield, Burkitt, Da Costa, Meyer, Olshausen, Gill, Godet, Kling (in Lange), Von Hoffman, Girdlestone, and the English divines.

Hebrews 11:35

"That they might obtain a better resurrection."

1. The question here is what comparison is implied in *better*. There are three different thoughts on this:

A) Better than the resurrection mentioned in the first part of this verse.

B) Better than the offered deliverance from suffering.

C) Better than the resurrection of the wicked. Some of the ancient theologians held this opinion; and many think it today.

2. This is a reference to the seven brothers and Eliezer, of which Second Maccabees speaks. We know that the Jews in general and the Maccabees in particular were familiar with the idea of a first resurrection.

3. At the same time it also presents an instructive illustration of the rich comfort of this truth for the martyrs. Apparently martyrs will receive an especially glorious resurrection body. This would be wholly consistent with the law of retribution.

Revelation 20:5

"But the rest of the dead lived not again until the thousand years were finished. This is the first resurrection."

It is here that the first resurrection is most clearly taught. That is perhaps the reason why this text is often assailed and even mutilated.

As a proof text for the first resurrection, it distinguishes itself from all the previous texts in three respects.

A) It indicates the clearest of all the time that passes between the two kinds of resurrection. In these verses the thousand years are spoken of no less than seven times; three times it has the definite article, *the* thousand years.

B) It emphatically states who will be the partakers of the first resurrection.

C) It points out the purpose of the first resurrection: that the resurrected ones may rule with Christ for a thousand years.

This verse may be interpreted literally, or it may be symbolic or spiritualized.

Those adhering to the *symbolic* explanation vary greatly in their approach. For the sake of brevity, we mention only the main attempts at explaining these words according to this method.

1. Very generally, it refers to a glorious state of the Church in which the spirit of martyrdom is revived and the principles of the martyrs are loved again.

A) Unfortunately for this viewpoint, however, a spirit of martyrdom is not needed in days of great prosperity; at such times martyrdom is usually shunned.

B) The entire context contradicts it. For then we should really read, "Blessed and holy are the principles of the martyrs. The spirit of martyrdom will reign with Christ a thousand years."

C) More and more the absurdity of this false Chiliasm, which wants a glorious state of the church without Christ's presence, is being recognized, but all of Scripture runs counter to it. We need only to mention the teaching of the apostasy and of the Antichrist.

2. The marginal notes in the Dutch Authorized Version say that it is a resurrection from spiritual death. (See also Rev. L. J. Hulst, Dr. J. A. C. Van Leeuwen, and many others.)

The arguments against this are:

A) That it leaves the expressions totally unexplained.

B) That it is simply absurd, as the people mentioned were already blessed and holy and had already been martyred for Christ's sake.

3. Many theologians today see the first resurrection as the blessed presence of the deceased believers with Christ in heaven during this entire present dispensation. All John intends to say according to this view, is that the believers above are already blessed and hence do not have to wait for it, but immediately at death begin to live and reign with Christ. Thus Bavinck, Ten Hoor, Warfield, and others.

The arguments against this are:

A) The view leaves unexplained why John six times gives such an exact time indication. Emphasizing the blessedness of the body-less souls would have been sufficient.

B) It commits the hermeneutical mistake of unnecessarily explaining the same expression in the same context two different ways. Consistency demands that the second resurrection should also be spiritualized.

C) In verse 4 it is said that judgment is given unto these resurrected ones. And we know that the souls under the altar were crying loudly and longingly for God's judgment and revenge.

D) The assurance of the deceased about their immediate state of blessedness does not fit here at all and is taught in other places much more clearly and simply.

4. A unique explanation is offered by Abraham Kuyper. He interprets this entire scene as a chronological reference to eternity. From his point of view, this is probably the most consistent and at the same time the easiest interpretation. Many blindly follow him in this erroneous interpretation.

Let the reader kindly read these verses and substitute *eternity* for the thousand years every time they are mentioned. Then he will have to read, "Until eternity was ended"; "after eternity he must be loosed a little season"; "And when eternity has expired, Satan shall be loosed out of his prison."

Everyone must agree with the following positions:

A) Regardless of its meaning, the text speaks of a first resurrection.

B) These words must mean something specific. For Scripture pronounces no oracles with a double meaning or no meaning at all, as he did the oracle of Delphi.

C) It must be explained either literally or figuratively. A third way is not possible here.

It is a rule of exegesis that a word should be taken literally, unless the literal meaning is absurd. If it is agreed that a first resurrection is absurd, then of course this expression must be explained figuratively. But in that case we need positive proof from Scripture why a first resurrection would be absurd.

If this word is to be taken figuratively, as many still do, then, once more according to an uncontestable rule of hermeneutics, the so-called general resurrection in verses 12-14 must also be spiritualized. In that case there is no resurrection of the body at all. Then all the grim things Paul describes in 1 Corinthians 15:12-20 are true.

So we see that one can arrive at heresy. Most expositors recognized this and have openly admitted that at least here a first resurrection cannot be argued away, although in other respects they do not believe in a twofold resurrection. Thus, for instance, M. Stuart, Van der Palm, Charles Hodge, and others. There have been and still are others who, in order not to violate their exegetical conscience, have denied this entire book a place in the canon. Some Church Fathers and a few Reformers took this position. The famous Simcox remarks on verse 4, "Every viewpoint, with the exception of the literal one, is attended by insurmountable exegetical problems."

We conclude this discussion of the various scriptural prooftexts with a poem by Lange.

> Also death's sleep has its stages,
> There are also steps in the grave.
> Not until the end time does the Lord's Angel
> Descend to the countless dead.
> But the saints arise earlier
> From the chilly bosom of the earth,
> Into which they had sunk less deeply,
> For they were less dead.

Chapter 10

CONCLUDING REMARKS
ON THE FIRST RESURRECTION

From the Scripture texts we have discussed, it must have become clear that they say very little about the resurrection of the wicked and nothing of a mixed and simultaneous resurrection. On the contrary, much is said of the special resurrection of believers. Even the three texts (with their contexts), where the resurrection of both the righteous and the unrighteous is mentioned, the resurrection of the believers is spoken of first and deliberately separated from the other (see especially Dan. 12:12; John 5:20; Acts 24:15).

Over against these texts, three other texts make a distinction in time between the two resurrections (see 1 Cor. 15:23-24; 1 Thess. 4:16; Rev. 20:5). Many other texts assume it, partly because prophecy always emphasized the fact itself rather than the time. To these conclusions it can be added that the Scriptures indicate six times the passing of time between the two resurrections.

Linguistic Grounds for the First Resurrection

Those who deny the first resurrection do not take into account the peculiar form of the words used for the resurrection of the believers.

The expression *ek nekroon* (from among, from out of the dead) is never used for the resurrection of the wicked, but it is always used for the resurrection of Christ and of Christians. This expression appears about fifty times in the New Testament, but never in connection with the idea of a resurrection in general or of the wicked. In those cases, the particularizing little word *ek* is systematically omitted. According to Thayer, one of the highest authorities in New Testament Greek, the theory of a general resurrection is, under no circumstances, tenable. He says that *ek,* when preceding words in the plural, means "from the midst of many."

Edward Robinson, author of a famous Greek dictionary, explains *ek* when it precedes a genitive "as indicating a part taken from a whole." He believed in a first resurrection.

Some expositors are of the opinion that, in Scripture, expressions with and without the specializing preposition *ek* are used interchangeably, but this is not so. Christ's resurrection was a *resurrection out of,* whereby many dead remained in their graves. And that is why *ek* is always used for His resurrection. We point the reader back to what Ten Hoor writes about the expression *from the dead.* When Scripture speaks of the resurrection of John the Baptist and of Lazarus, it uses *ek* to indicate that many dead stayed behind. Sometimes *ek* is omitted (Matt. 22:23, 28; John 11:24; Acts 23:8). In such cases Scripture merely points to the future *fact* of the resurrection.

As a rule *ek* is omitted when the apostles are dealing with those who do not accept the special resurrection of believers. When Paul speaks of the resurrection to the mocking Athenian philosophers, he omits it (Acts 17:32). He also omits it when speaking of the denial of the resurrection by the Sadducees (Acts 23:6-8), and when he is speaking of the hope of the resurrection before the heathen governor Felix. In Acts 26:8 we find the same thing, as well as against the deniers of the first resurrrection in the church of Corinth, and in Hebrews 6:2 against people who regress in grace. In all these cases he omits *ek,* which refers to the resurrection of the elect, since all these people would be blind to this mystery of salvation anyway. When, however, he is speaking in the same context of the unique resurrection of the Lord (Acts 17:31; 26:23) he uses it again.

Many people agree that both expressions are carefully separated in Scripture and that *ek* is exclusively used of Christ and of those who are His. They also admit that *ek* expresses something special, but to them this means that the believers are transposed from the state of death into the state of glory. This word is also used metaphorically to indicate a *passage from* or *out of* a certain state into another one, and this would be the case with believers. But we cannot accept this meaning because it does not say in the singular, *from death,* but in the plural, *from the dead.*

Dogmatic Grounds for the First Resurrection

Earlier we pointed out that the particular resurrection is wholly in line with the election and separation of the Lord's people. Just as strongly as we see the idea of election in the *ekklesia* we must see it in the *exanastasis,* the resurrection *from out of.*

The Mystical Union Governs the Life of the Believer

Christ Himself is the *Resurrection* (John 11:25). The resurrection of believers is the fruit of their union with Christ. Because spiritually and covenantally they are comprehended in Christ, death cannot make a separation between them and their Savior. By His Spirit they are sealed unto the day of salvation. On earth, that which is sealed and that which is not sealed is carefully separated. The Holy Spirit will not allow the sealed "epistles of Christ" to be found in one mass with the non-sealed. Believers are chosen in Christ, live in Christ, are crucified with Christ, and will also arise with Christ. That is the way the apostles saw and presented it, when they preached the resurrection in Christ (Acts 4:2).

Of great significance is the expression, *first begotten of the dead,* which we find in 1 Corinthians 15:20, Colossians 1:18, and Revelation 1:5. Just as He arose as Conqueror of death and the grave, of Satan, sin, and hell—and in so doing left many behind in the realm of death—so also His people will one day, as conquerors in Him, leave many dwellers of the graves behind them. The metaphor of the firstborn clarifies the idea of the mystical union with respect to the resurrection. The power of His resurrection is already now the life of those who are His (Phil. 3:10). Upon His blessed return, this will become even more manifest.

The apostles never presented Christ as a solitary person from among the dead, but always as the First One, the Firstborn, the First (Acts 26:23). From this it must follow that more will arise from among the dead. Even their bodies will be fashioned like unto His glorious body (Phil. 3:21). Christians will be like Christ (Rom. 6:5-10; 8:11, 23; 1 Cor. 6:14, 20; 15:22-27; cf. Rev. 20:1-8; 2 Cor. 4:14). Olshausen notes on the expression *ek nek-*

roon: "The phrase would be inexplicable, if it were not derived from the idea that out of the dead some would rise first."

The Judgment of the Believers

Believers will rule the world with Christ. This, too, is the fruit of the mystical union. The Apostle Paul in 2 Corinthians 4 points out that he must suffer for Christ's sake. Indeed, that he is carrying the death of Jesus in his own body, so that the resurrection life of Jesus also might become manifest in his body. Paul comforts himself with the knowledge that he will become perfectly conformable to Christ's resurrection. He says elsewhere, "If we suffer with Him, we shall also reign with him," that is to say, judge with Him. The suffering and enduring in communion with Christ was literal and real, and thus will certainly also be the judging. Moreover, he emphatically teaches this in 1 Corinthians 6:1-10.

Before the believers will judge, they must first be resurrected. The believers will carry out the whole judgment upon the wicked in communion with Christ. So the resurrection of the wicked *is* already a judgment to the wicked. It would certainly be better for them if their bodies remained buried in the bosom of the earth. They arise unto damnation. Now if the believers judge with Christ, then it follows that their resurrection must already have taken place. The resurrection precedes the judgment of the world (Mal. 4:4-5; Rom. 16:20; 1 Cor. 6:2-3; Jude 14-15; Rev. 2:26-27).

On the basis of adherence to a simultaneous resurrection, one must do one of two things; either abandon the idea that the believers will judge the world—something Abraham Kuyper indeed does—or accept that first a resurrection of the righteous takes place. But if the latter, then there is only a gradual difference regarding the duration of time between the twofold resurrection.

Finally, we present for consideration the idea that Christ will come with all His angels. The Old Testament told us this (Zech. 14:5; cf. Jude 14-15; Col. 3:4; 1 Thess. 3:13; 4:14). This presupposes that the resurrection and the taking up into the air must already have taken place.

Benefit of the First Resurrection

If we now on these bases accept the first resurrection as a future act of salvation that is beyond all doubt, then the question is in order, of what profit is this doctrine? Why should we teach the doctrine of the first resurrection? Our answer is twofold.

1. Ministers of the Word, at their acceptance of their office, have solemnly promised before God and His Church, "that they shall thoroughly expound the Scriptures of the prophets to their flock, and that they shall appropriate the same, both in general and in particular to the profit of the hearers." They have promised that they will fight all errors that are repugnant to the pure doctrine of Holy Scripture.

2. This doctrine is of the greatest spiritual benefit. Those who adhere to the theory of a general resurrection see a general blessing in it. But they do not see a special and totally unique blessing, because the wicked arise at the same time and under the same circumstances. The only distinction will be that of life and damnation, just as in this life. This view is greatly at variance with Scripture, which considers the resurrection of the believers as a special blessing and of great influence upon the life of sanctification. We need only to remember the oft repeated statement by Christ in John 5, "I shall raise him up at the last day."

The benefit of the doctrine of the first resurrection is fourfold.

1. It casts a flood of light on election. Here we see that election is not merely a doctrine, but a divine reality that encompasses the bodies of the believers and reaches into eternity.

2. It clarifies the whole doctrine of the last things and all that it encompasses.

3. It makes the resurrection of the body an object of hope and of the greatest comfort.

4. Many Scripture texts are clarified by it.

Time Between the Resurrections

Now the question remains about how much time will pass between the two resurrections. The Apostle Paul does not speak clearly on this matter. This is why some hold the opinion that, since John in Revelation 20 indicates, in six instances, a certain time, there is a difference between Paul's teaching and John's. Henry Alford thinks that it had not yet been revealed to Paul, and that later John received the revelation concerning the definite time. (See his annotations on 1 Corinthians 15:23.)

Whatever the case may be, knowledge concerning a certain passage of time is not supplied until the end of the divine revelation. This difference tells us that the passage of time is not the most important thing; nor is this an example of increasing clarity and completeness of the divine revelation. The expression "the thousand years," although appearing in a vision, and therefore not to be taken rigidly literal in every respect, must nevertheless be understood in its self-evident meaning. Since "the rest of the dead" refers exclusively to those who have died outside of Christ, we conclude from it, that during the Millennium, there will be no more dying among the saints. Death will not have been destroyed yet, for it is the last enemy to be destroyed, but it will find no victims among the people of the Lord. Thus there will be a resurrection of the just at the onset and a resurrection unto damnation at the end of the thousand years.

This answers at the same time the question of who will partake in the first resurrection. In general there are two opinions on this matter.

1. Both in former as in later ages there have been those who think that only a certain class of believers will share in the first resurrection. They point to the example of Paul, who was assured of his full salvation, but according to Philippians 3:11, not yet of his resurrection. They also point to Revelation 20:4, which seems to speak exclusively of martyrs. This view loses sight of the fact that Scripture emphatically connects the first resurrection with the teaching of "the reward of grace." And just as there will be grades in that reward, so there will be a difference of grade with respect to the honor and glory of the resurrection bodies. And Paul, looking at the reward, by no means feared that the blessed resurrection as such would pass him by; but he did fear that he might miss out on the special honor of the gracious reward. For will there not be, according to his own words, preachers who will indeed be saved, but who will not receive the reward of grace?

We cannot go into this subject any further at the moment. A further development of this important matter will be given in the following chapter.

2. We believe, on the basis of the expressions, "the resurrection unto life" and "of the just," as well as on the basis of certain Scripture texts (Rom. 14:10; 1 Cor. 15:23; 2 Cor. 5:10; 1 Thess. 4:16; Rev. 20:6) that all the born-again people will take part in the final resurrection. This view is presently the most generally accepted one.

We conclude our discussion of the first resurrection with the words of an outstanding man, Joseph A. Seiss, and express our full agreement with his statement:

> The resurrection of the saints is totally separated, both in character and in time, from the resurrection of "the rest of the dead." If you delete it from the book of Revelation, we still find it in the epistles of Paul. Delete it from the epistles, and we still find it in the teaching of Jesus. Delete it from the entire New Testament and we still find it unmoved and unshaken in the holy oracles of Daniel and Isaiah. Nevertheless, let the hand wither that attempts to remove this doctrine from any part of God's Word. It is in there, clear and unmistakable, and gives the right to all saints to hope for the deliverance of their bodies and their corporeal glorification at the onset of the Millennium.

Part III
Believers

Chapter 11

THE RAPTURE OF BELIEVERS

Just as Scripture does not emphasize the *time* of the last things, so it does not emphasize the *sequence.* Only four texts in the New Testament offer in a general way some points of order. We list them here.

Acts 15:14-17. Here we find:
1. The calling of the Church out of all nations
2. The coming again of the Lord
3. The restoration of David's house and of Israel
4. The glorious results of it for the entire world (see also Rom. 11:15)

1 Corinthians 15:23-28. Here we find:
1. The first resurrection
2. The reign and judgment of Christ
3. The subjection of all His enemies
4. The delivering up of the Kingdom to the Father
5. God being all and in all

1 Thessalonians 4:16-17. This evidences:
1. The descent of Christ in the air
2. The first resurrection
3. The changing of the living believers
4. The taking up of the Church into the air
5. The bringing of the saints with Him

Revelation 20. This chapter points out:
1. The binding of Satan
2. The first resurrection
3. The reign of the resurrected saints with Christ during the kingdom of peace
4. The rebellion of Gog and Magog at the end
5. The second resurrection
6. The last judgment

It is evident from these passages that only the main aspects are given in the correct sequence. So if you hear persons give the sequence in minutest detail, as a rule you may put a question mark behind all they say. It cannot be emphasized enough that prophecy has not been given to satisfy human curiosity, for that is a sin against the tenth commandment, but unto instruction, refutation, correction, teaching, and for our greatest comfort.

When the Lord returns, there will be living believers. It will be a small flock. He will not find much faith on earth. The wise virgins will be sleeping, and the love of many shall have waxed pitifully cold. But not all believers will be resting in the grave.

The deceased believers will be raised first. It is sufficiently apparent that they will precede the living believers into glory. But there will pass no time between the first resurrection and the glorification of those still living.

The resurrection body will be like Christ's glorious body (Phil. 3:21). And if we want to picture something of this glory, then let us read and re-read the majestic description in Revelation 1. Christ was so superlatively glorious that John, who had known Him well before, fell as one dead at His feet. At that moment the beloved disciple still possessed flesh and blood which cannot bear the glory of the glorified. This resurrection body will, according to the description by Paul in 1 Corinthians 15, have five characteristics. It will be *incorruptible, glorious, powerful, spiritual,* and *immortal.* Not only will the resurrected saints receive such a body, but the living remnant will also. They, too, will be clothed with the body of glorification. All of this takes practically no time, for Scripture says emphatically (1 Cor. 15:52) that this change takes place *in a moment, in the twinkling of an eye,* that is, a split second.

With the receipt of the new body, their adoption as children is completed. At that moment their manifestation in glory will take place (Rom. 8:19; Col. 3:4; 1 John 3:2). Now the world sees a Church under the cross. Then, before the eyes of the whole astonished universe, Christ will reveal His Church together with Himself in glory and majesty. The so-called public justification will take place.

At that same indivisible moment, apparently all the elect will be gathered together. Let no one ask how that is possible, since a spiritual body, that is to say a body that is wholly governed by the Holy Spirit, will hardly be bound by time and place. We have only to think of the glorified body of Him to whom they will be made conformable.

Then the one, holy, catholic Church will no longer be an object of faith and hope, but a glorious reality. Another state of blessedness than this is not forthcoming. The true unity of the Church is not found in a federation, as is so ardently sought today, but in a sanctified union around the glorified Christ. Then, and no sooner, will there be one flock under one Shepherd (John 10:16). Everything will be gathered together under the one Head, Christ; all the saints together will fully understand what the breadth, length, depth, and height of the love of Christ is; there will be unity of the faith and of the knowledge of the Son of God (Eph. 4:13). And Christ will be fully glorified in all His saints and admired by all who believe in Him (2 Thess. 1:10).

After the gathering together of all believers from the four corners of the earth (Matt. 24:31), the gathering up, in other words, the taking up unto Him, takes place at the same moment (Matt. 24:29-31; John 14:2-3; 1 Thess. 4:17; 2 Thess. 2:1).

In this country, as well as in England, there are those who speak of a *secret rapture,* an invisible taking up of the Church into the air, of which the world notices nothing. We have not been able to find proof for this anywhere in Scripture. What we do find is proof for the opposite, for He comes *audibly* (1 Thess. 4:16) and *visibly* (Matt. 24:30).

It cannot be denied that there will be a rapture of believers. The last mentioned texts clearly point to this rapture. Evidently Christ comes first *for* and then *with* those who are His.

But, someone might object, this presents a twofold return of the Lord. To deny this we observe:

1. According to the ancient prophets, there will be only one coming of Jehovah to His people. The prophets do not even distinguish between a first and second coming, as we do now.

2. The term *twofold return* is not correct, since we are dealing with separate phases of His one return.

3. Everything takes place in the *one day of the Lord,* but this day is, as is generally agreed, not a day in the narrower sense of the word, but a longer period of time.

4. Christ at the rapture of the Church evidently does not come down onto the earth. The believers are taken up together to meet Him in the air (1 Thess. 4:17).

5. Scripture clearly teaches a difference between the coming of the Lord *for* His people and *with* His people. Read attentively 1 Thessalonians 4:14-17. The texts which say that He will return with all the saints presupposes that He has first come for them. He will stand on the Mount of Olives with those who are His.

6. The metaphors Scripture uses indicate this distinction. To His people He comes as the Bridegroom; as the Friend (John 14:2), the Savior (1 Thess. 4:16), the Rewarder (1 Cor. 3:8; Rev. 22:12). But with respect to the wicked we always meet up with thunder and lightning, storm and whirlwind.

7. Paul in Romans 11:25-26 calls this coming for the believer a *mystery.* Evidently this truth was revealed to Paul for the first time, so that we must not look for many clear texts about it.

Why would it not be possible for a little time to expire between the coming of the Lord *for* and *with* His own? Knowing that the day of the Lord will be an *aioon,* a dispensation, we must not make the mistake of wanting to shrink His future work to that of a twelve-hour working day.

The fact that Scripture does not specifically mention this time makes no difference, for there are more examples in prophecy of silence concerning a certain time. Thus, for instance, Isaiah 61:2 is divided by a comma, but this indicates a period of almost two thousand years (cf. also Luke 4:20)! And since Scripture could do this with regard to the first coming of the Lord, it can also be expected to do so with the second.

Most likely there is a span of seven years between Christ's coming *for* and His coming *with,* the believers, which is the final year-week of Daniel. This is what many students of prophecy think today. It is this year-week that terminates the times of the heathen and once more resumes the dispensation of Israel.

Undoubtedly this rapture of the Church will take place before the *great tribulation* (Jer. 30:7; Dan. 12:1; Matt. 24:21; Mark 13:19; Rev. 3:10; 7:14) which comes upon the entire world and which will be unlike anything in all of history. Israel will pass through this tribulation, as is apparent from the first two texts. But the believing Church will be saved from it, something the Lord has done often in the history of salvation (Noah, Lot, Red Sea, the destruction of Jerusalem). And only in that sense can the coming of the Lord be the joyful, inspiring, and constant hope for the Church which it could not be if the Church had to pass through the tribulation.

In the great tribulation, Israel and the world will receive due retribution for all their wickedness. The evil spirits will be cast out of the air to wreak havoc among the inhabitants of the earth. During this time the Church will have *rest* (2 Thess. 1:7) in companionship with its Lord. According to many, the air now cleansed from evil spirits will then be the Church's temporary home. There it will be presented before the judgment seat of Christ to receive the righteous reward for good works. More will be said on this in a following chapter.

This coming of the Lord to take up the Church is the essential hope of the Church, encompassing all other blessings. He Himself longs for it, for He wants His Church as His body to be where He is (John 12:26; 14:3; 17:24). He Himself is waiting for this (Heb. 10:13, Greek; Rev. 1:9). His Spirit cries out to Him, Come! He assures us in His last promise that He is coming speedily (Rev. 22).

Once Christ gave Himself to the Church out of unfathomable love, now He sanctifies it, and then He will present it before Himself and the Father, before the angels and the devils, indeed before the whole world as "a glorious church, not having spot, or wrinkle, or any such thing, but that it should be holy and without blemish" (Eph. 5:27). Then will be fully given unto us, as co-heirs with Christ, all things as an actual possession (Rom. 8:17; Eph. 1:22). At present, the Church possesses the firstfruits, but then comes the full harvest of glory, the harvest of an everlasting and perfect fellowship with the Lord and all the saints. "And thus we shall always be with the Lord." The reason that we can do without Him so well in our lives is because we comfort each other so little with these words. Only true love yearns for the full union. Only the pure bride longs ardently for the coming of the Bridegroom.

Chapter 12

THE REWARD OF GRACE

The Coming Judgment

Many believers have a problem with respect to the coming judgment. On the one hand they read in Scripture, "He that believeth on him is not condemned" (John 3:18) and, "There is therefore now no condemnation to them which are in Christ Jesus" (Rom. 8:1). On the other hand they read that we must all appear before the judgment seat of Christ (2 Cor. 5:10) and that the Lord will judge His people (Heb. 10:30). So they think they are faced with insoluble contradictions. This prevents them from finding out what is the actual situation. The Heidelberg Catechism question, "What do you believe concerning 'the forgiveness of sins'?" is answered: "That God, for the sake of Christ's satisfaction, will no more remember my sins, neither my corrupt nature, against which I have to struggle all my life long; but will graciously impute to me the righteousness of Christ, *that I may never be condemned before the tribunal of God.*"

A righteous person will never enter the judgment of God. Christ has been condemned for him or her and has thereby satisfied God's justice. God does not demand two satisfactions. By judicial imputation the righteous are in Christ. And no more than Christ can be judged can they who are in Christ be struck by the judgment of God. When the Apostle says in Hebrews 10:30 that the Lord will judge His people, Paul is saying that He will *avenge, do justice unto* His people over against their adversaries, as the context indicates.

This does not alter the fact, however, that we all must appear before the judgment seat of Christ, so that everyone may receive what is due him, according to what he has done, whether it be good or bad (2 Cor. 5:10). Those who teach a mixed resurrection usually see in this an indication that one day thick milling crowds of all the people must appear before the stern Judge on the great white throne. The teaching of a mixed and simultaneous judgment usually goes hand in hand with that of a simultaneous resurrection. But Scripture gives us not the least ground for this concept. Both views are usually held together, but both are equally unbiblical.

1. The word *all* in 2 Corinthians 5:10, according to the entire context, refers clearly to believers only. The judgment seat of Christ is something entirely different from the great white throne of Revelation 20. Before the former, only the believers appear and that at the beginning of the day of Christ, i.e., the kingdom of peace; and before the latter only the wicked appear at the end of the millennial kingdom of peace.

2. The idea of a variegated mixture of the glorified believers and the lost is absurd.

3. Not only the *time* but also the *location* is different. The *judgment seat of Christ*, the *bema*, will be in the air, into which the believers have been taken up; and *the great white throne* will be on the earth.

4. The purposes of the two judgments vary greatly. The purpose of the former is to hand out the retribution of reward according to one's works; the purpose of the latter is the consignment from before the face of the Lord to everlasting damnation. Here it is not the works but the persons who stand in the foreground.

Hence believers can fully rely on Christ's words when He says, "Verily, verily, I say unto you, He that heareth my word, and believeth on him that sent me, hath everlasting life, and shall not come into condemnation [judgment]; but is passed from death into life." They do not enter a general judgment together with the wicked, but judgment *will* be passed on their lives and works.

Appreciation for the Reward of Grace

As a result of a faulty eschatology (doctrine of the last things), there is an almost complete lack of the right appreciation of the glorious doctrine of the reward of grace. Even on the last page of the Holy Scriptures, however, the Lord calls out to His people, "I come quickly; and my reward is with me, to give every man according as his work shall be." Anyone who writes about the coming of the Lord may not keep silent on the reward of grace.

The Early Church gave too much importance to the meritoriousness of good works. Rome went even farther and committed the mistake of identifying the reward with heaven or eternal life. The Reformers, although they were aware of it, did not develop this great truth. In the later churches of the Reformation there was a fear of Rome's teaching on "good works." Rationalism ran all the way with the independent value of virtue for virtue's sake. Rationalists, of course, want nothing of a reward of grace. Kant's teaching on morals most definitely rejects it. Mystical and Antinomian groups were usually hostile to it, since as careless believers they had no use for good works and hence had no use for this incentive to obtain the reward of grace.

Generally speaking, the fact that people lived very little by belief in the coming of the Lord was the reason they had no eye for this comforting truth. If we have no eye and heart for the personal coming of our precious Savior, then, of course, we have no eye and heart for the work which He, as the Representative of the Father, will do at that time.

Thus, as always, one sin led to another, even though it was not a sin of commission but of omission. We intentionally speak of a sin, for the disregard of this truth has proven to be far from excusable and of incalculable damage to the Christian life.

Appreciation and development of this truth of the reward of grace is demanded for the following reasons.

1. Reverence is required for the Holy Scriptures as a whole and in all its parts. The doctrine of the reward of grace is a part of prophecy. No less than two hundred verses in the New Testament refer to this blessing, either directly or indirectly, or from a different angle.

2. This truth demands further development for the sake of the believers themselves. In His goodness it pleases the Lord to hold out this reward to the believers as a desirable prize for the runner in the race. If a cup of cold water given in the name of a disciple will be rewarded, then what comfort must this doctrine offer us when we are called to suffer for Christ! The Church

must know that God considers it an honor to reward His own at the coming of the Lord, and that He does not want to be served without bestowing the reward of grace.

3. We consider the development of these things urgently necessary because of the times in which we live. We are living in days when the battle of faith and life will become increasingly more difficult for those who fear God. The prophetic Word has predicted this. Because unrighteousness will increase, the love of many will wax cold. Satan's wrath will be great in the last days. The picture Paul again and again presents to us is bleak. To the extent that the cross will weigh heavier and heavier for the believers, to that extent they ought, more than ever, to direct their attention to the future retribution of reward. For only when we are constantly convinced that the cross will soon be exchanged for a crown by the Lord Himself can we be real cross-bearers.

What Grace Is

It is almost self-evident that the reader must not expect a complete treatment of this part of prophecy at this time. It can be discussed here only from the point of view on the last things. In order to shed light on the eschatological importance of this truth, and because of the great ignorance concerning this truth, it is necessary to consider briefly the *concept,* the *basis,* and the *nature* of the reward of grace.

1. The *concept.* The reward of grace is that free and favorable act of God whereby He, according to His promises, in the day of Christ and through Him, distributes to His people a special measure of glory according to the measure of their good works.

The concept of *grace* must be taken here in the sense of an unmerited act of favor on God's part, bestowed not on sinners who are still guilty and unsaved, but on sinners who have been justified. Hence the expression *reward of grace* contains a contradiction, for *grace* excludes the concept of *reward,* and *reward* excludes the concept of *grace.* These two concepts are absolute contrasts.

We must retain the concept of grace here in the above-mentioned sense, but the term *reward* needs further clarification. If we take this word in its usual sense, it is incorrect to associate it with grace. In the current sense it is understood as a certain sum of money which a laborer has bargained for beforehand and which the employer pays out to him as the amount he owes him. The concept of wages is equally unsuitable here, for that, too, is a previously stipulated payment for services rendered. So here, too, there is a mutual exchange or transfer of certain values. The word "tip" sounds too vulgar for this holy matter. Otherwise it would be the correct term for the matter under discussion, for what the system of tipping is in our human society, the reward of grace is in the Kingdom of God. The word that comes closest to "tip" is "reward." This word remains the most useful term to define the biblical concept.

It is useful first because "reward" implies the idea of freedom on the part of the rewarder. Nothing has been stipulated, nothing demanded, nothing negotiated and settled. It is wholly non-compulsory and optional, so that there is room for grace as the free favor of the rewarder. Also it is useful because the reward is to its recipient a token of appreciation for good deeds performed. Hence the expression *reward out of grace* is more preferable, because it is more correct than the expression *reward of grace.* The historical usage and brevity of this term, however, gives it the right of being maintained. For that reason we use it for the sake of convenience.

2. *Basis.* When we speak of grace in the sense of free favor, we might expect God to leave the good works of unbelievers without reward. This is usually the way we picture it, even though quite incorrectly. There is, on the other hand, an element of divine necessity in the payment of the reward of grace. The basis of the future payment is the retributive righteousness of God. Just as God *must* punish the evil, so He must, by virtue of His holy essence, reward the good.

It is a harmful onesidedness when we emphasize His avenging, but not His rewarding righteousness. In such a view God becomes a cruel judge of punishment who can have no pleasure in the good. He can no more leave the good unrewarded than behold the bad with impunity. This would undermine His throne, which is founded on justice and righteousness. God's righteousness entails the ordering and maintenance of the moral world order.

By virtue of the same principle that assigned Christ to the cross, believers are rewarded. Only Christ had to be crucified because the righteousness of God demanded punishment; believers are rewarded by virtue of His rewarding righteousness. To the believers, God's righteousness is the principle of their salvation and of all their glory. They are saved by justice, and by justice they receive the special measure of glory in the reward of grace. Hence there is an inevitability in the payment of the reward of grace.

We must not confuse *inevitability* with *necessity*. The latter comes from the outside, the former from the inside, proceeding from both justice and love. Even those who have advanced farthest in the Christian life do not by their good works present an obligation to God for which He must reward their good works. The inevitability of the reward of grace shows up nowhere stronger than in Hebrews 6:10 where we read this remarkable statement, "For God is not unrighteous to forget your work and labor of love, which ye have shewed toward his name, in that ye have ministered to the saints, and do minister." The text even specifies that God cannot forget their good works because He cannot be unjust. If God, even supposing that this were possible, could let their good work go unrewarded, then He could be unjust (cf. 2 Thess. 1:7).

Far from promoting service for reward, this idea cuts off all greed for reward, because we see that God, in granting the reward of grace, has Himself in mind first of all and most of all. That He is not unrighteous to forget our work must make us see that it is unrighteous on our part to forget His reward. He most definitely does not want to be served without granting this reward, for in so doing He obtains the glory of His retributive righteousness. It is for the sake of His righteousness that such believers as Moses and all the apostles had respect for the recompense of the reward. Those who reject this doctrine as being dangerous do not know what they are doing.

The question could be asked whether we, in the consideration of the inevitability of the reward, are not losing the concept of grace. Can we still speak of the free *favor* of it? Our answer is, "Most certainly."

A) Doing good works is of itself already a great grace. It is God who works in us both the will and the energy to do good works.

B) The fact that God acquainted us with the reward of grace as an inducement to godliness is proof of His boundless goodness. As the absolute Sovereign he had every right to demand and to command, without providing any motive or inducement. But in His goodness He always points out the advantages of serving Him, and the disadvantages of serving Satan. He prompts us with the pressure of love, and spurs His people on to holiness by pointing out the future glory as inseparably connected with our walk of life.

C) The contents of the reward of grace are obtained only by Christ and are imputed to us because of and in Him. By nature we were under the curse of death and damnation. Everything the sinner receives above and beyond it is pure grace. To this agree not only all upright believers on earth, but also the glorified ones in heaven, by casting their crowns at the feet of God (Rev. 4:10; 5:13; 19:4).

D) There is no contrast here between grace and justice any more than there is at the justification of a sinner. The reward also takes place by virtue of the satisfaction of Christ, and yet freely. There would be a contrast between these two, only if God Himself had not freely given the Christ with His satisfaction. God Himself by His righteousness ordained the reward of grace, while He imputes it by grace in Christ to the sinner. Their works *follow* those who died in the Lord. The works of believers do not, as the Roman Church in essence teaches, precede them in order to open the gates of heaven.

All greed for reward is abominable. It is the expression of a slavish spirit; it is also enmity against God, as it wants to make God into a debtor. This the God-fearing sense as though by personal observation, and therefore they have an insurmountable hatred of all service for wages. Moreover it is an everlasting impossibility for man to do something good for God. In order to do this, he would have to offer something of worth to God, which he does not possess.

3. *Nature*. Just as the theologians usually confuse the concepts of Zion, Church, Kingdom, Israel, and community in the

Old Testament, so in the New Testament they confuse the concepts of heaven, salvation, eternal life, heritage, and reward of grace. Especially with respect to the eschatological concepts there is often a gross confusion. We can only point out this fact, for it lies beyond our scope to go further into this now. Here we will call attention only to the difference between salvation and "the reward of grace." This expression appears nowhere in the Bible. Usually the concept meant by it is expressed in the word *glory*.

A) What is held out before and offered to the *unconverted sinner* is salvation, whereas believers are exclusively spurred on by the reward of grace. This reward is only for them as, for that matter, are all promises.

B) Salvation is a *gift* of grace, wherein work plays no role (Isa. 55:1; John 4:10; Rom. 6:23; Eph. 2:8-9); man is not even a factor. But with the reward of grace, it is an entirely different matter. There man does play a role (Matt. 6:1-20; 10:42; 1 Cor. 3:10-15; 9:1-27; 2 Tim. 4:7-8; Rev. 22:12).

C) With regard to the reward of grace, the free gift of salvation is presupposed; and it is also assumed that those who have received this gift can, by virtue of it, do work for the Lord. The gift of grace presupposes nothing but a creature worthy of damnation. For this reason the *gift* of grace must be carefully distinguished from the *reward* of grace.

D) Salvation is *the same for all,* for it is the fullness of eternal divine happiness. One heavenly citizen cannot be happier than another, because they are equally full of divine happiness. Therefore salvation expresses the state of equality for all. But, just as there are, as an old expression has it, larger and smaller completely filled vessels, so there will also be great variations in the degree and measure of glory. Now this is, according to Scripture, due to a causal relationship with the kind of life the believers lived on earth; but this is not the case with salvation *per se.*

E) Another point of difference is that salvation is not only in essence the same for all, but also that it is for all believers (the elect), whereas, on the contrary, not all believers receive the reward of grace. Paul in 1 Corinthians 3:10-15 teaches us that not even all preachers who are saved will receive the reward of grace.

F) The final difference is that salvation is already a *present possession,* whereas the reward of grace will be granted especially *in the day of Christ.* Certainly serving Him here and now in love is attended by happiness, but this does not alter the fact that when speaking of the reward of grace, we are dealing mainly with prophecy. After having tried to briefly clarify the concept and nature of this blessedness, we must now consider its prophetic aspect.

When Grace Is Given

When is the reward of grace given? This must have become clear to some extent during the preceding discussion. The reward is not given in its totality until the Lord comes for the complete deliverance and glorification of His people. But this future benefit of salvation already casts its light into our hearts and before our feet in this dark world; indeed we are saved in hope. But in the meantime the full benefit of salvation is waiting until the day of all days. No matter how we insist that godliness is profitable unto all things, and that serving the Lord regardless of its attending shame and self-denial can already afford the most blessed joys to the believing heart so that it can even sing Psalms in the night, all this does not alter the fact that we view the matter one-sidedly, when we call these human joys the reward of grace.

We human beings go easily to extremes, so that we are inclined to elevate one doctrine at the expense of the other. We often hear someone emphasize the present blessedness at the expense of the future one. Scripture does not warrant this. It is true that we can hardly esteem the present blessedness too highly. But we must never deprecate the fact that we are *saved in hope,* or that here we have only the firstfruits and that the full harvest is still forthcoming (Rom. 8:23), for only then will there be a place for the fulfillment of the blessed hope.

This wrong tendency of closing our eyes to Christ's future work affects this truth greatly. At funerals and in obituaries one frequently hears and reads that this or that God-fearing person has received the reward of the faithful. But whoever is motivated by the fervor of religious truth cannot be satisfied with this, because Scripture teaches us clearly that the day of Christ is at the same time the day of the retributive reward of grace. This is part of the judicial work of Christ. The day of wrath for the wicked is the day of the gracious reward for His people (Isa. 34:8; 35:4; 40:10; 59:16-20; 61:2-3; 62:11). The *public retribution* (Matt. 6:4, 6, 18) also points to a public judgment of believers in that day. Humility and generosity will be recompensed at the resurrection of the just (Luke 14:14). It is granted at the establishment of the Messianic Kingdom to Israel (Matt. 19:27-28; 24:45-47; 25:31-46; Luke 22:28-30).

The Apostle Paul did not expect his reward of grace until the day of Christ (1 Cor. 3:10-15; 4:5; Phil. 2:16; 1 Thess. 2:19-20; 3:7; 2 Tim. 4:8). The Apostle Peter had the same expectation (1 Pet. 1:7: 5:2-4). And in John we find the same thing (1 John 2:28; 2 John 7-8; Rev. 11:18; 14:13). The gracious reward of His people is one of the purposes of the Lord's return (Rev. 11:18; 22:12). This payment of the reward of grace is most closely connected with the resurrection of the righteous (Dan. 12:2-3, 13; Luke 14:14). In a certain sense the resurrection is part of the reward.

What the Reward Is

As far as the contents of the reward of grace are concerned, we must strenuously insist that it is Christ's reward, and that only in the closest union with Him is it given to believers in that day. Then the Father will *with Him* give us all things. In this term *all things* His reward is included. That is why He says on the last page of Scripture, "Behold, I come quickly; and my reward is with me, to give every man according as his work shall be." We know that He received a reward for the travail of His soul. Because He humbled Himself below all limits and depth, God also highly exalted Him (Phil. 2:9). Upon the deepest self-humiliation followed the greatest exaltation for Him. In all of this He is our perfect example and our protecting Surety.

He is our example, for here again the rule obtains that the body must follow the head. The law of justice also applies to His people, i.e., that the deepest humiliation is followed by the highest exaltation. Whoever humbles himself will be exalted. By His grace He makes His children small and humble, so that thereby He may exalt them all the more. In His looking forward to the recompense of reward He is also our example.

According to Hebrews 12:1-2, Christ looked upon His reward and, with His eye upon that, He endured the cross and despised the shame. From His prayer, "Father, glorify Thy Son," it is evident that He thirsted for the glory. Now to Christ this reward was not a reward of *grace,* to be sure. Nevertheless, as with believers, it was given to Christ by virtue of God's righteousness. Both issue from the same principle of the rewarding justice of God.

Christ the Mediator is not only given to us as an example in looking to the reward (Heb. 12:1-2), but also in receiving it. He is our Representative. By Him and together with Him the faithful receive the reward. Their relationship to Him determines it. The more they remain in Him, work for Him, and wait for Him, the greater the recompense of grace will be in that day. The measure of the reward is determined solely by their relationship to Him. Here the believers suffer the shame and suffering of Christ.

Moses already bore the affliction of Christ. Paul fulfilled in his flesh the remnants of the afflictions of Christ. To the Church, as the Body of Christ, is appointed a certain measure of suffering which *must* be endured. This is why the believers must enter the Kingdom of God through many tribulations. There is a moral, divine inevitability in this suffering, which can be deduced from the often-repeated little word *dei* (necessary), which is also used of Christ's suffering (cf. Luke 24:26; Acts 14:22; 1 Pet. 1:6). Texts like these do not merely contain prophecy, for then another word would have been used. We are rather dealing here with an inevitability that flows from the divine justice in connection with sin and glory. That which is logically the result of sin, God causes to work out in Christ to eternal glory. The light affliction, which is but for a moment, works for us a far more exceeding and eternal weight of glory (2 Cor. 4:17).

When we fully realize that the suffering of believers, which is borne on account of their relationship to Christ, is His own suffering, and that the seed of the serpent assaults Him in His members, then we shall also understand how it is such a great grace that we may suffer for Him. Scripture teaches us that whoever descends into the deep valley of humiliation and suffering with Him will also be glorified with Him. By the travail of His soul, He has been made Head and Heir of all things. So it is that whoever humbles himself here and bears His cross joyfully after Him, will, according to God's infallible Word, be co-heir with Him, and reign with Him.

That believers receive the same glory with Christ as the Mediator (not the uncreated glory of Christ as the Son of God!) Scripture teaches in several places. He is the Heir of all things, and those who overcome will inherit all things (Rev. 21:7). The glory He received from the Father, He gives to them (John 17:21). He has received a name above every name (Phil. 2:9), and believers receive it as well (Rev. 22:4). He will sit on His throne and they will sit with Him (Rev. 3:21). He has power over the nations; the conquerors do also (Rev. 2:26-27). Christ *is* the bright and morning star; they *receive* this morning star (Rev. 2:28). He walks in bright white clothing; they will walk with Him in bright white clothes. They will reign with Christ as prophets, priests, and kings. When the Apostle John says that we shall be like unto Him, this is not a Middle Eastern exaggeration but a glorious reality, for even their bodies will be fashioned like unto His glorious body (Phil. 3:21).

Meanwhile the question remains of what special nature this gracious reward will be. Who will dare make so bold as to answer with certainty? God will prepare unexpected surprises for His people, for neither eye nor ear has ever become cognizant of what He prepares for His people. Nevertheless, here, too, Scripture gives us some telling hints.

In the parable of the talents we are told that more talents will be added to the talents of the faithful servants. From this it may be concluded that the reward of grace will at least consist of an *increase* of the good things of grace already obtained. We find the same truth expressed in the parables of the faithful servant of the house and that of the pounds. And the same idea is found again in the promise given the faithful in Sardis. In that city were found a few names that had not defiled their garments, and now the Lord promised them that they would walk with Him in white, for they were worthy. Hence new undefiled garments will be added to the undefiled garments they already have. Therefore the reward of grace as the special degree of glory will, according to Scripture, consist of *a glorified extension and enlargement of the things of grace already received.*

Grace is glory in bud form, and through the coming appearance of the Sun of Righteousness, this bud will burst open into manifold splendor.

We can also say about the nature or character of the reward of grace that the good works of those who died in the Lord do not merely follow them (Rev. 14:3), but they specifically follow them *because* of what they are. Their good works do not just follow *after* them, but also *on account of* them. The works of faith, that is to say, *through* faith, done according to the law of God and to the honor of God, have been ordained from eternity (Eph. 2:10). They will not be affected by the ravages of time. They will endure throughout eternity and will honor the glorified believer. The Apostle Paul teaches us this in 1 Thessalonians 2:19-20, where he says that those to whom he gives birth through the gospel were his hope and joy and crown of rejoicing in the day of Christ. Those believers will add royal honor and glory to what he already possesses at the great day of retribution. They will be Paul's possession in a very special sense. They are his and he is theirs.

The Apostle teaches the same thing elsewhere. To clarify, we select only Philippians 2:16 where he says, "Holding forth the word of life; that I may rejoice in the day of Christ, that I have not run in vain, neither labored in vain." When believers bear the light of the Word before them in the world, they do so for the benefit of the world, and also for their own benefit. A third party also obtains benefit, Paul himself. This faithful servant will be acknowledged as the one who admonished the Philippians and spurred them on to perseverance and to shed forth their light. From those saints Christ will derive the material to praise His servant as good and faithful. And from that moment they will belong to the Apostle and he to them. They are *his* glory and he is theirs, and together they are the glory of Christ. Then the special relationship between the preacher and his congregation will be glorified and eternally confirmed and perpetuated. Hence the so-called "doctrine" of recognition of one another in heaven is assumed by the doctrine of the reward of grace, for all Paul said in this connection would have no meaning if the Apostle would not recognize his former sheep and if they did not recognize him as their former shepherd.

For this reason the good works of believers are not only the *fruits* of faith, but by God's order also the *seeds* of eternal glory, which He gives freely. The works of love are not the *ground* of the future reward of God's unmerited favor, but they do furnish the material for it. This need not amaze anyone, for it is a matter of course flowing forth from the world's moral order or, more correctly, from the rewarding justice of God.

It is a well-known and lasting ordinance of God that He has created in every seed, whether a natural or spiritual seed, the propensity and capability to produce its own multiple fruit and nothing else. That is an unchangeable law that does not allow for any exceptions. We never gather grapes from thorns or figs from thistles. Hence in that day the works of the believers, as so many spiritual seeds, bear exactly the fruits after their own kind. This idea is interwoven in all Scripture (see Ps. 41:1-3; Prov. 10:25; Jer. 32:19; Dan. 12:3; Matt. 25:14, 16; Rom. 2:6; 1 Cor. 15:58; 2 Cor. 9:6). Just as there is a proportional relationship between seed and fruit, so there is between work and reward of grace. The very highest glory follows the very deepest humiliation (Phil. 2:5-10). "Whoever sows sparingly will also reap sparingly" (2 Cor. 9:6). The great future will bring forth what we ourselves have sown. It will not merely follow in sequence of time after this life, but will be inseparably connected with it. Scripture could not have furnished a clearer metaphor to express this idea than that of sowing and reaping.

> In the past does lie the present;
> In the present what will be.

We ought not to work *because* of this reward but certainly *with an eye on* it. In so doing we safely follow in the footsteps of Moses, Christ, and the Apostles. This truth itself is of the greatest importance for both doctrine and life. It causes us to see that He gives grace for grace; He crowns His own grace, His own work in us. His sovereign good pleasure is glorified by it, for it is evident that "to whoever has, to him (or her) will be given." As with the first resurrection, it shows us the all-pervasive aspect of the mystical union. It sheds light on the great distinction between believers in this life, and the corresponding difference in glory in heaven.

But this truth is of special importance for life. It is mostly for this purpose that it has been revealed. The Lord takes into account in His Word that His people are of little courage and of weak strength, and are every moment ready to stumble and fall. For that reason He spurs them on to increasing effort in the race of faith.

False mysticism is deeply guilty with regard to this truth. Under the semblance of piety and humility, mystical people frequently make statements like this, "Even if there were no heaven as a reward and no hell as punishment, I would still wish to glorify God." This may be well meant, but it is an unwise statement that is dishonoring to God. It is incorrect in two respects.

First, heaven is not a *reward.* That became Rome's error early on. Good works are of no account with regard to salvation as such, nor are they in any way causally connected with it. But there *is* a connection between them and glory. Those two aspects may not be separated but must be distinguished from each other. We do not earn heaven as a reward, nor is it given as a reward of grace, for many will enter heaven without ever receiving a reward of grace. We are admonished, however, to *lay up treasures in heaven* by means of our good works (Matt. 6:19).

In the second place, such statements often reveal a lamentable over-spirituality and lack of knowledge. This indicates that the speaker thinks he knows better than the Lord Himself, who, taking into account our manifold weaknesses, knew that we would need prods on the way of salvation. But, of course, those who have exchanged the doctrine of man's powerlessness for the "stock-and-block" theory, must come to the idea that all spiritual incentives are superfluous. For it will not do any good to attempt to stimulate a block.

But oh what a beneficial incentive this truth affords if correctly understood and practiced! Initially it subdues the world and it brings heaven closer. It will remain the humble confession of all those who fear God. "Lord, we are but unprofitable slaves, and have done only what we must do." But He will say, "Well done, you good and faithful servants, enter into the joy of your Lord." And this will be to the threefold praise of His glory (Eph. 1:6, 12, 14).

Chapter 13

THE MARRIAGE SUPPER OF THE LAMB

In "the language of Canaan," the Supper of the Lamb is usually a poetic designation for heaven and eternal glory. In general, people assume that this expression refers to the glory and blessedness of heaven. In this view the heavens are the eternal wedding halls, the inhabitants of heaven are the wedding guests, and Christ is the Bridegroom. All this fits neatly together.

According to the natural view of prophecy, however, it means something specific. In Revelation 19 we find that the writer does not speak of the Marriage Supper of the Lamb as symbolic, but as something very real. Verse 9 says, "And he saith unto me, Write, Blessed are they which are called unto the marriage supper of the Lamb. And he saith unto me, These are the true sayings of God." This last assurance is striking. The Lord knew beforehand that the prince of darkness would attempt to rob this prophetic testimony of its power by making believers think that this language was nothing but a poetic reflection. No, says the Holy Spirit of prophecy, these are the true sayings of God. This brief declaration tells us that we must pay attention to the *words* and not merely think of symbols, poetry, or something of the kind. And He further tells us that these words mean exactly what they say. Does not truth demand the usage of unmistakably clear language?

Therefore, heeding this divine declaration, we wish to ask the following questions in order to get better acquainted with this important matter. *When, what,* and *where* will this Supper be, *who* will partake of it, and *how long* will it last?

When Will the Supper of the Marriage of the Lamb Occur?

Not presently in heaven, for:

1. His bride has not reached maturity as yet, and has not been made ready for it.

2. We do not read about it until after the return of the Lord Jesus Christ.

3. First the unfaithful bride, the whore which is Babylon, must be judged.

Nor will the Marriage Supper of the Lamb be celebrated eternally and forever. If that were the meaning, the metaphor would be ill-chosen indeed, for a wedding feast, especially the supper of a wedding, does not last very long. Yet the expression, "eternal wedding halls," originates from the assumption that this wedding will occupy all of eternity. However, Revelation 19 clearly teaches that this real wedding and this real supper come to an end. They are soon followed by the most terrible scenes of blood and slaughter in the Battle of Armageddon, the warfare of the great God. In this context the Supper of the great God is strikingly placed over against the Marriage Supper of the Lamb (vv. 9, 17).

We reject the idea of some expositors who think that the Marriage Supper of the Lamb will last throughout the Millennium. On the basis of Scripture, it must be placed at the beginning of the Millennium.

What Will the Marriage Supper of the Lamb Be?

Here we must be on our guard against two extreme viewpoints, namely, that of taking it too literally, and that of spiritualizing it. If we do the former, we end up with a Turkish or, more correctly still, a Mormon heaven; if we do the latter, everything goes up into a quasi-spiritual vapor and mist. We wish to emphasize further that we are dealing here with the pinnacle of the mystical union, and since the union itself is a mystery to us, the culmination point will be no less so. Hence we shall refrain from advancing unfounded speculations. For the sake of clarification we touch only on a few matters.

1. Christ Himself is the Bridegroom, as He has called Himself on several occasions (Matt. 9:15; 22:1-13; 25:1-10). The apostles also speak of Him as the Bridegroom (John 3:29; 2 Cor. 11:2; Eph. 5:22-32). We find woven into all of Scripture a spiritual bond between Christ and His people. This bond is of the greatest importance to all who love the Lord.

2. Next we must make a distinction between the marriage itself and the Supper taking place at that time. Strictly speaking, no mention is made of the Marriage *per se*, for which we refer to Ephesians 5:27-29, Colossians 1:22, and 2 Corinthians 11:2. The Marriage comes first, then follows the Supper.

3. The Supper indicates the unity, joy, rest, peace, and liberty of the redeemed. From early times all these ideas were combined in the happy idea of the last meal of the day.

Here we find the fulfillment of the Lord's Supper. The prophetic character of the Holy Table has been greatly neglected by the Church of Christ. Those texts in the New Testament that speak of the Lord's Supper—and they are by no means as numerous as is usually thought—point emphatically to the coming of the Lord. "I will not drink henceforth of this fruit of the vine, until that day when I drink it new with you in my Father's kingdom" (Matt. 26:29; Mark 14:25; Luke 22:16). The second main reference which discusses Holy Communion at length again connects it directly with the idea of the coming of the Lord. "Ye do shew the Lord's death till he come" (1 Cor. 11:26).

The reason so few believers derive the desired benefit from the Lord's Supper must be sought here. The Lord's Supper is thought of as merely a memorial meal, at which time His suffering and death are commemorated. But suppose Christ had suffered and died, but that He had not risen again. Then we would be, as the Apostle says, still in our sins and of all men most miserable. It is clear that the Lord wants the believer to cast his eye forward.

There must be a threefold look, first to the past, to the historic fact of salvation through His redeeming suffering and death. This remains eternally to the redeemed the greatest miracle of God's grace and the main cause of their salvation. For this reason the eye of faith must look in that direction again and again.

But the Christ is not a dead Christ. No, He was dead and became alive again and lives forever. Scripture demands that we not merely remember Him, but that we think of Him as the living Savior who is in heaven and still thinking of us in love. For that reason we must cast an eye of love on high, as the form for the celebration of the Lord's Supper enjoins us to do.

It is possible that even if both elements are present, many a God-fearing person does not derive the rich blessing which is still available. People correctly blame this on their sin, but they fail to identify the true nature of that sin.

The one important element that is lacking in the attitude of the partaker is *hope.* By hope the New Testament usually understands *faith as it directs itself with assurance, joy, and longing to the future, especially the future coming of the Lord and its attending blessing.* We must proclaim the death of the Lord *until He comes.* What does this mean? That Holy Communion may never be abolished? The future meaning indicates that it will be abrogated at the coming of the Lord. The shadows flee away when the Body appears, and the symbols disappear when Christ Himself is present. Believers no longer will need strengthening of their faith, fortification of their hope, and increase in their love.

But these words, *until He comes,* remind us that the Lord's Supper, itself already being the fulfillment of the Paschal meal, is in turn the prophecy and shadow of the Marriage Supper of the Lamb. Then the believers will see Him face to face in all His beauty. The Apostle tells us that believers must look with the eye of hope for His coming, when the holy meal will fully materialize. The celebration of the Lord's Supper must be seen as a blessed pledge and as a foretaste.

The Lord Himself refers to the same idea in Matthew 26:29 and related texts in the other Gospels. People have considered this statement as being fulfilled in the Lord's Supper, but that would mean that the Savior Himself partakes of the sacrament and spiritually drinks His own blood. Saying that the Lord is speaking of the fulfillment of the Jewish Passover makes even less sense. Some have held the opinion that these words were fulfilled when the Savior, after His resurrection and before His ascension, ate and drank with His disciples. But this explanation, too, is fraught with difficulties.

In the first place, it is by no means certain that He again drank wine, and new wine at that, with His disciples. The second objection to this idea is that it does not take into account the expression, "in the kingdom of my Father." Clearly the disciples did not believe that they were already in the Kingdom, for even after His resurrection they asked,

"Lord, wilt thou at this time restore again the kingdom to Israel?" We believe that these words have never obtained their fulfillment and will not materialize until the Marriage Supper of the Lamb. So it is not in eternity, but in the Millennium that the fulfillment of these words will be found. In eternity both hunger and food will have ceased, but not in the dispensation of the thousand years. Most expositors sense that expressions such as this cannot reasonably be applied to the past, nor to eternity. For that reason they prefer not to deal with such a text, or, if they do so, they spiritualize and apply it to the Lord's Supper or the heaven of glory.

Maintaining that we have here the *true sayings of God,* we explain this Marriage Supper of the Lamb as spiritual-corporeal reality, and as a great joy in the Millennium, especially at its commencement.

Where Will All This Take Place?

We can say very little about it, since Scripture provides few indications. But many texts give the impression that, at least for Israel, it will be in Jerusalem (Isa. 25:6-9; Ezek. 34:23-24; 37:21-28; Joel 3:17-20; Amos 9:13-15; Matt. 8:11; 22:11-13; 25:6; Luke 22:30). This is the most generally accepted idea. It contains nothing objectionable to those with an open mind.

Who Will Partake in All of This?

Christ and His Church, gathered from among all nations are, as the Bridegroom and the Bride, the main figures. But already the idea of a wedding feast tells us that there will also be other figures at this feast of all feasts. A careful reading of the Revelation of John shows us that this is indeed the case. One may compare also the Song of Solomon, Psalm 45, and the Parable of the Ten Virgins. After their judgment, the nations are also invited (Isa. 25). At this feast of feasts will be the greatest variety and at the same time the most perfect unity.

How Long Will It Last?

This is not specifically mentioned, but it is clear that it will not occupy all of eternity, nor the entire Millennium. It seems to us, together with many experts, that we are to think of the time that expires between the coming of the Lord *for* and *with*

His saints, hence seven years. While the world is being punished, the believers have peace and comfort.

Realizing we have not written exhaustively about this sacred mystery of the age to come, but being convinced that we have developed nothing but the *true sayings of God,* we hereby conclude our consideration of this matter.

Chapter **14**

THE BELIEVERS JUDGING WITH CHRIST

After believers have received the reward of grace, and after the unique Marriage between Christ and His pure, immaculate Bride has taken place, the believers will then judge with Christ. This takes place when Christ comes *with* all His saints. The last part of Revelation 19 describes this coming and judgment. The seer describes the vision of the Battle of Armageddon in three parts. First he introduces the righteous Judge. But He is not alone. He is followed by a shining multitude of heavenly beings dressed in clean, fine linen, in whom we recognize the saints of verse 8. We must reject the opinion that this verse speaks of angels.

Second, a solemn invitation is extended to the birds of heaven to eat their fill at the Supper of the great God.

Third, we find here depicted in a few bold strokes, the carrying out of the judgment. The kings of the earth have made the insane plan to fight the Christ in person. It becomes clear that all the nations are covered with a shroud and with a veil, so that they cannot see (Isa. 25:7). The nations have not accepted the love of truth; and for that reason God has sent upon them a strong delusion, so that they should believe a lie (2 Thess. 2:11). Thus Satan gets an ever stronger hold on them. He who has always deceived the nations succeeds, by means of the Antichrist and the false prophet, in hounding them on against the Christ, so that they march up to Jerusalem to fight against Him. But in so doing they rush headlong toward their ruin.

The Antichrist, who is the apparent leader of this conspiracy, is caught first and is cast alive into the lake of fire and brimstone. This is shattering to the minds of his followers, for they had thought that no one could do battle against him. "Who is able to make war with him?" they had confidently exclaimed. He who had already once caused His captors to lick the dust, takes him in plain view of all his worshipers and casts him into hell. The same thing befalls the false prophet, the servant of Antichrist. Whatever exquisite and miraculous power he may have possessed (Rev. 13), it is not able to save him now from the hand of the righteous Judge. Also their mighty armies are destroyed as in a moment by the sword of His mouth.

The saints partake in this judgment of the nations and their satanic firebrands, but not, of course, because Christ cannot handle it alone. Viewed correctly, He does do it alone. The idea that we see here some kind of cooperation between Christ and His people is erroneous. But where He is, there are also His servants. The lot of the Church is forever bound up with His own. Even the judgment by the saints is the result of the mystical union. Although He Himself is the great Representative of the Father and unto Him all judgment is given, He nevertheless will give to His Church, all things with Him. Hence the saints follow the Christ and are witnesses of His triumph. That they are not just passively looking on is apparent from most of the texts that refer to the judging by saints (Ps. 58:10-11; Dan. 7:21-27; Mal. 4:3-5; Matt. 5:5; 19:27; Luke 19:12-27; Rom. 16:20; 1 Cor. 6:1-10; 2 Tim. 2:12; 1 Pet. 2:9; Rev. 1:5-6; 2:26-27; 3:21; 5:10; 19:13; 20:4).

A few divines had the opinion that not all saints will partake in this judgment, but only those who have received the reward of grace. It is certain that judging and reigning with Christ is sometimes presented as an element of the reward of grace. To conclude from this that those who did not receive a reward of grace will, together with Christ, judge the world and the angels is going too far, it seems. The texts on which they base this opinion (Rom. 8:17; 1 Cor. 3:9-15; 2 Tim. 2:10-11) are by no means conclusive.

Scripture frequently refers to this truth in order to comfort and encourage God's people.

In this life they must bear a cross, but they will not be doing so forever. After a brief span of time everything will change. The suffering of the cross is not worthy to be compared with the glory that will be revealed in us. After having suffered for awhile, they will receive eternal glory in Christ. Therefore they must not, as followers of Christ and the Apostles, look on the things that are seen, but endure the cross and despise the shame.

From 1 Corinthians 6, it is evident that Paul gave the Church of Christ in general and the believers in particular a high sense of Christian honor. The situation in Corinth was sad indeed. Cases were not judged by those inside the Church. No discipline was exercised. On the contrary, people went outside their own circle in order to be judged by the world. A strife had arisen among the brethren about trivial matters. Instead of settling these matters in an amiable manner or resolving them among themselves, they went before a worldly court in order to obtain justice and to cause their opponents to suffer defeat.

How little they acted in the spirit of Christ who, when He was reviled, reviled not again, and when He suffered He did not threaten but committed Himself to Him who judges righteously. This was flagrant disobedience to His Word, which teaches that we must not tell the Church about the injustice done by a brother before having warned him repeatedly first. What a low opinion these people had of the Church of Christ! They threw away its honor to the world and gave the heathen cause to blaspheme the name of Christ.

The Apostle was indignant at such guilty activity. "Do ye not know that the saints shall judge the world? And if the world shall be judged by you, are ye unworthy to judge the smallest matters? Know ye not that we shall judge angels? How much more the things that pertain to this life?" (1 Cor. 6:2-3).

We sense here that the Apostle considers it of far-reaching significance that the believers will one day judge two worlds. The present-day Church, too, hardly takes account of this truth. But no one suffers more loss on this account than the Church itself. Some read these two declarations as though they refer to heathen judges, and that therefore they do not apply to present-day Christians. Such exegesis escapes the command expressed in these texts, i.e., that we should never take a brother in Christ to a worldly court, but to the Church. The Church will judge the world and therefore it must not allow itself to be judged by the world.

A lively consciousness of the future judgment by the saints will keep the believers from self-degradation and a life below their high status; it will keep them from worldly-mindedness and even widen the separation between the world and the Church; and last but not least, it will cause the believing heart to admire the great grace of God and to exclaim, "Who is like unto the Lord our God, who dwelleth on high, who humbleth himself to behold the things that are in heaven, and in the earth! He raiseth up the poor out of the dust, and lifteth the needy out of the dunghill; that he may set him with princes, even the princes of his people" (Ps. 113:5-8).

Many people believe that the judging by the saints will find its fulfillment in the heaven of glory, but that is an impossibility. The twelve apostles will sit on twelve thrones, judging the twelve tribes of Israel, and the twelve tribes are known as such only on earth. The faithful believers of Thyatira (Rev. 2:24-27) will receive power over the heathen. Do we believe that there will still be heathen in heaven? Even if it would be better to translate the word *heathen* by *nations,* the same objection still holds, for in the heaven of glory there will no more be separate nations than there will be separate families.

No, it is not in heaven, but on earth, that the believers will one day reign. We cannot fight against the truth, and this truth tells us clearly that the meek shall inherit the earth (Matt. 5:5), that they will reign upon the earth (Rev. 5:10; 11:15-18; cf. also Ps. 2; 22:28-31; 32; 72; Dan. 2:35, 44; 7:13-14, 27; Zech. 14:9). We consider ourselves conscience-bound to such statements of God's Word and we must oppose their spiritualization, as this would change the glorious expectation of salvation into darkness and imaginations. According to the demand of justice, the believers will one day reign with Christ before the eyes of the whole world, the same arena in which they at one time were the spectacle of the world in their suffering and struggle, and in their blood and tears. If it is the Father's good pleasure to give the Kingdom unto them, then we shall not take pleasure in robbing them of the comfort of this hope.

Following are the words of Seiss:

You may call this Judaism, if you like; you may laugh at it as though it were mere fantasy; you may consider it a carnal dream; you may label it as a heresy; but it is and remains the truth of God to which you and I and all men are irrevocably bound, and which has every prospect of being fulfilled before the next century will have passed. I long for this fulfillment and welcome it as the glorious expectation and the restoration of our fallen and deceived world.

We must keep in mind, however, that on this view it is not necessary to suppose that the saints at that time will have their permanent place on earth. The contrast that now exists between heaven and earth will then initially have been removed. Heaven will be opened, and the believers, being like unto the angels, will ascend and descend. Venerable students of prophecy such as Auberlin, Da Costa, Van Oosterzee, Van Andel, and numerous others usually refer here to the appearances of the Lord Jesus during the forty days before His ascension, which provides us an example and prelude of what is to come. At that time Christ was not fully in heaven yet, nor could He be considered an inhabitant of the earth in the actual sense of the word.

Furthermore, we must make a clear distinction between Israel and the Church. Israel is the eternal nation of the earth and will also then be on earth and, in contradistinction with the Church, lead a domestic and civil life. Jerusalem will be inhabited as an open village and its streets will be full of playing children. A suckling child of this people will play on the hole of an asp and a weaned child will put his hand on the cockatrice' den (Isa. 11:8).

"His soul shall dwell at ease; and his seed shall inherit the earth." We often sing solemnly, "E'en his children shall be blest, Safely in the land abiding," but do we also believe this as a future reality?

Meanwhile the believers' judging and reign cannot be described precisely and in detail. However, on the basis of Scripture, the following chief aspects are clear enough.

1. The believers' reign is the fruit of the mystical union, as are all the blessings of salvation (2 Tim. 2:12; Rev. 5:10).

2. It does not consist of merely condemning the wicked, but also of ruling and governing them. We are to think here of the old Israelite concept of a judge. The judges in Israel were not merely persons who pronounced people guilty or innocent, but they were also lawgivers and rulers (see Gen. 18:19; Ps. 98:8-9; Isa. 32:1; Jer. 23:5).

3. To the believers who suffered here with Christ it will be a reward of great honor and glory.

4. There will be differences and variety; some will reign over five and others over ten cities (see the Parable of the Ten Pounds, Luke 19:11-26). The twelve apostles will reign over the twelve tribes of Israel (Matt. 19:28).

5. This reign will last a thousand years (Rev. 20). At the end of this period, Christ will turn over His Kingdom to the Father (1 Cor. 15:24).

This presents a problem, however. Various Scripture texts tell us that Christ will reign forever, that His throne and scepter will last forever, and that He will be given dominion and power and glory forever and ever (cf. 1 Chron. 22:10; Ps. 45:6; 89:35-37; Jer. 23:5; Dan. 7:14, 27; Mic. 4:7; Luke 1:33; Heb. 1:8; Rev. 1:6).

This difficulty disappears, however, if we maintain the distinction between Israel and the Church as His body. He is King of Israel forever and ever. The angel says emphatically to Mary that the Lord God will give Him the throne of His father David, and that *He will be King of the house of Jacob forever.* Of this kingdom there will be no end. Israel will be the people of the earth forever. We shall not go any further into this question, since we shall write at greater length about Israel's future and destiny later.

Part IV
Israel

Chapter 15

ISRAEL AND THE CHURCH

When we study prophecy, we must make a distinction between Israel and the Church. Must not ecclesiastical self-knowledge be considered a prerequisite for the practice of godliness? Within the bosom of the Church itself many unscriptural ideas are held concerning its origin, nature, calling, hope, and future. Many believers consider Israel and the Church as being essentially the same. Or, to be even more precise, all the redeemed are considered together as being one class, one body.

We are convinced, however, that this idea is not according to Scripture. The Lord does not have one people, but two kinds of people; an earthly and a heavenly people. Israel is His earthly people with an earthly calling. The Church, as the body of Christ, is His heavenly people with a heavenly calling. This distinction was already made symbolically and typically at the calling of Abraham, the father of all believers (including the New Testament believers, which gives continuity of the covenant). He has seed as numerous as the sand of the seashore (Israel) and as the stars of heaven (the Church)

Scriptural References to Israel and the Church.
1. Nowhere in the Old Testament is mention made of the body of Christ. The body of Christ, however, is the essence of the Church. Therefore the essence of the Church is not proclaimed in the Old Testament.

To be sure, in the Septuagint translation we frequently came across the word *ekklesia,* the word that is always used in the New Testament for church, but this does not mean that the Church as the body of Christ existed or was known during the Old Covenant. For if that were so, then we would be justified in claiming that the Church of Christ existed in old Greece, because the word *ekklesia* was also used there. In the New Testament this word is also used for meetings other than the Church, but may we conclude from this that meetings of every kind are also the Church of Christ?

2. In the New Testament we come across the word and the idea of church or congregation in Matthew 16:18 for the first time. The Savior is not speaking here of the Church as something that is well known, as a historical institution, but as something in the future. He doesn't use the past or the present, but the future form of the verb, *I shall build,* not, *I build or have built.* That which still must be built has as yet no historical existence but lies in the future.

3. Scripture says repeatedly that the Church as the body of Christ is a mystery. It is particularly Paul who says this, because to him as the Apostle of the Gentiles, the ministry of this mystery was entrusted. In a Pauline sense a mystery is a truth that can be known in no other way than by special revelation (cf. Rom. 16:25-26; Eph. 3:1-10; Col. 1:24-27; 1 Tim. 3:16). This mystery was hidden during the preceding ages, was known to nobody, and was revealed to Paul. It was known during the old dispensation that some day the salvation of Israel's Messiah would dawn for all nations. Salvation in the coming Messiah would be not only for Israel but also for the nations. This is abundantly clear from a great number of texts. So it was not the salvation of the nations that constituted the mystery.

Then *what* did? *That by the suffering and death of Israel's Messiah a mystical body of the Messiah would come into being, comprised of Jews and Gentiles; and this would come about before the dispensation of the culmination of the Messianic salvation.* Even the prophets hardly dreamed of this whole dispensation. They always cast their eye at the Messianic bliss of the future. This entire dispensation is emphatically called a *dispensation of the mystery* (Eph. 3:9 in the original, according to the best manuscripts). We are now living in the days in which the hidden things of the Kingdom are unfolding (Matt. 13).

Hence the Church and the dispensation of the Church was not known in the days of old.

4. The Church is the body of Christ (cf. Eph. 1:22-23; 2:16; 3:6; 4:1-16; 5:23-32; Col. 1:18-24; 1 Cor. 12:12-27). The nature of the Church is that it is the body of Christ. It is nothing else, nothing more and nothing less. This distinguishes it from all other organizations.

Christ Himself is the Head of this body. He is called this in more than one place. But we are clearly taught that He became Head by His suffering and death and that His Headship is part of His reward for His deep humiliation. Hence we must accept one of two positions; either the Church was headless for four thousand years, or it came into being after the Head. As a rule God does not make headless things.

The Church follows Christ in all things. John expresses it thus, "As I am in the world, so are they in the world." The Church is an organism that is founded *in* the humiliated and exalted Christ (Eph. 2:21 and the preceding context). The Church is a body that grows *from* the Head (Col. 2:19).

5. When we look at the Holy Spirit, we come to the same conclusion. Within the Holy Trinity's internal activity, it is the Holy Spirit who forms the body of Christ. He formed Christ's human body in the womb of the virgin Mary, and He also forms His spiritual mystical body, the Church (1 Cor. 12:13). But the Holy Spirit was not active in this way in the days of the Old Covenant. He could not come before Christ was glorified. He builds only on the foundation of the sacrifice provided by Christ. He Himself does not bring about salvation, but He takes all things out of the full and glorified Christ. In the days of the old dispensation He did on occasion regenerate and save individuals, but not until Pentecost was He sent by the Father and the glorified Son to form a mystical body from both Jews and Gentiles.

6. The Church is built upon the foundation of the apostles and prophets. It is usually thought that this refers to the Old Testament men of God by that name. So it is supposed that this teaches that the Church was known by the prophets and so already existed during the Old Testament. But in every case in which the expression apostles and prophets appears in the New Testament, the prophets are mentioned after the apostles (cf.

1 Cor. 12:28-29; Eph. 2:20; 3:5; 4:11). From this we conclude with most exegetes that this does not refer to the Old Testament prophets but to those of the New Testament.

When this mystery of Christ, as Paul calls it, is not made known in any other age, but is revealed to His holy apostles and prophets (Eph. 3:5), it is unjustified to apply Old Testament promises to the Church.

When we consider all these things, it is clear that there *is* a difference between Israel and the Church.

Differences Between Israel and the Church

Now let us consider in which respects Israel and the Church differ.

1. The *calling* of the two is very different. The calling of Israel was earthly. Keeping this truth in mind, let us read the pronouncements of blessing and curse on Mount Ebal and on Mount Gerizim in Deuteronomy 27:12-26, and in addition Numbers 24:2ff; Deuteronomy 11:11-12; 28:1-18.

The calling of the Church is heavenly. Believers are called partakers of the heavenly calling (Heb. 3:1; see also 1 Peter 1:4; Eph. 2:6; Phil. 3:19-21; Col. 3:1-5; 2 Tim. 4:18; Heb. 10:34). This is important, for nature and disposition determine the calling of something. What is essentially similar has the same calling. If it can be proven that Israel and the Church have a different calling, then we can safely conclude that they differ in essence.

2. The *promises* were different. Notice what the dispensation of condemnation (2 Cor. 3:9) promises in Exodus 20:12, Deuteronomy 7:15 and 28:13. When Israel is obedient it always receives promises of prosperity—riches, honor, long life, numerous children, and a rich burial. But when the Church is faithful, it is persecuted. Indeed, to the extent that it is more faithful, it will be persecuted more. To the extent that it shows more obedience to its glorified Head, the world will hate and persecute it more. Meanwhile this suffering of the Church is not a sign of God's anger, but of His grace toward it. It is given the Church out of grace not only to believe in Him but also to suffer for Him (Phil. 1:19). Every believer agrees that faith is grace, but not that suffering for Christ must also be considered grace. This is little understood, and even less appreciated.

3. Israel was to a great degree *motivated and governed by the flesh.* The Church was *motivated by the Spirit* who dwells in it.

Whoever was born from Jewish parents in the olden days and was circumcised on the eighth day was thereby fully a citizen of Israel.

How totally different is the situation with regard to the Church. Nobody can be incorporated in this mystical body except he or she is born from above by water and Spirit. For Israel, the principle was obey and live; for the Church, live and obey. The Church, as the heavenly people, must cast its eyes upward. For there is its citizenship, and there it will be translated with Christ. It must first seek the Kingdom of God and His righteousness; it must lay up treasures in heaven; it must think of the things that are on high and not of those that are on earth; it must strive to enter into the rest that remains for the people of God; it must reach with both hands for eternal life.

We consider it a gross sin when preachers of the gospel try to weaken these demands in the Church of God. Quite often we get the impression that certain preachers fear that, when the faithful do all these things, they will neglect their earthly calling, or that they will become too heavenly-minded. That is one reason why today the Church exerts as much effort to get rich as do the children of the world. Oh that all heralds of salvation might understand, and that the entire Church might grasp, what it means to lay up treasures in heaven! It is to be feared that many hardly believe that this is possible, far less that this must be done, and even less how wonderful a thing it is.

4. The *armor of battle* for both was very different. Israel had to fight with material weapons; the Church must do battle exclusively with spiritual weapons, for unlike Israel, it must not fight against flesh and blood.

Israel had to exterminate the heathen; we must convert them. In Israel, the law of retribution prevailed. Elijah could call forth fire from heaven, but we may not do so. Samuel was allowed to hack Agag into pieces to the honor of God, but we may not do so. Esther was allowed to take revenge, we may not. In all of these things Christ Himself, as our Head, is our example, as we read in 1 Peter 2:23, "Who, when he was reviled, reviled not again; when he suffered, he threatened not; but committed himself to him that judgeth righteously." Compare also the following texts: Deuteronomy 7:1, 12; 28:7; 31:3-5 with Matthew 5:38-44; John 18:36; 1 Corinthians 4:12-13; 2 Corinthians 10:4; Ephesians 6:12.

5. Again we find essential differences in their *public worship.* These are not merely differences in ministration. Nowhere is the difference between "Moses' house" and "Christ's house" so manifest as here. Israel had an earthly sanctuary for a "house of God" and a "house of prayer." Israel had to travel to it from all corners of the country in order to pray and to sacrifice. Israel had its holy places, vessels, persons, and periods, but all these walls of separation have fallen for the Church. Its sanctuary is in heaven (Heb. 9:19, 24). All believers are saints, prophets, priests, and kings by virtue of their office as believers. Christ alone is the High Priest after the order, not of Aaron, but of Melchizedek. Concerning Israel, see 1 Chronicles 22:5; 2 Chronicles 6:38-39; concerning the Church, see 1 Corinthians 12:14-27; Hebrews 13:15; 1 Peter 2:5, 9: Revelation 1:5-6.

6. *Israel was God's servant in the form of a small child* not yet of age; the *Church* of the New Covenant *is of age.* In Israel was the slavish spirit of servitude (Rom. 8:15; Gal. 3:24; 4:6), but the Church may cry, Abba, Father. In Israel there was a ministry of condemnation; in the Church one of glory (2 Cor. 3). Israel had, and still has, a covering; we all behold with uncovered faces the glory of the Lord as in a mirror (2 Cor. 3:17-18).

7. That Israel and the Church are not identical can especially be concluded from the fact that the two are *always distinguished from each other in the New Testament.* With this idea in mind, read Acts, Romans, and Ephesians. In Ephesians the Apostle Paul presents the Christians from among the Gentiles as fellow citizens, fellow members of the same household, fellow heirs, and fellow partakers in the faith together with Israel. Historical Israel is not given a place in the house and membership of the Church, but on the contrary, the Church obtains its share and inheritance with Israel. It partakes of the root and fatness of the olive tree (Israel). It is not itself the olive tree but it is grafted in among the others as a wild branch. So the Church of the New Covenant sings correctly when new members make confession of faith:

When the Lord shall count the nations
Sons and daughters He shall see,
Born to endless life in Zion . . .

8. Finally, we point out that the *hope* of each was somewhat different. It was Israel's constant hope to be placed at the top of the nations with the Deliverer out of David's house. The hope of the Church is exclusively Christ's return. Israel as a nation knew of no cross-bearing as the Church does. The entire Church as a whole and every believer in particular must deny himself, take up his cross, and follow Him. If the people of the New Covenant refuse to be cross-bearers, they will never become crown-bearers. Here we must bear our cross after Him; there we shall wear a crown with Him.

As far as the hope of both is concerned, there is no essential difference. There may be a difference in hoping as an activity and with regard to a person's own salvation, but both to the Church and to Israel the *object of their hope* is *Christ, the King of glory, coming* to establish the Kingdom. Everything is waiting for the coming Christ. The groaning creation, blind heathendom, Israel, the Church, and the Holy Spirit—they all look with ardent longing for that day of all days. Only the day of establishment of the Kingdom itself, however, will the immense difference between the two become clearly manifest before the eyes of the whole world.

Thus we have seen the essential differences between the two groups of God's people. From all this, it is evident that we are not dealing with merely a difference of dispensation and ministry, but with an essential difference. Israel is another kind of God's people than the Church.

Two prerequisites are essential to understanding Israel's future—an insight into the essential difference between Israel and the Church, and the realization that this nation is Jehovah's eternal miraculous people in the special sense of the word.

The former we have briefly considered, now the latter demands our attention.

Chapter 16

ISRAEL: GOD'S MIRACLE PEOPLE

At present God has two kinds of people on earth, the Church (which has a God-given right to the heavenly Canaan) and Israel (the people of the earth, who have a God-given right to inherit the earthly Canaan).

Israel is a miracle-people. Whether we consider its origin in the gray past, its continuation during the course of centuries, its present manner of existence, its grand future, we can only view it as a miracle of God. This is the key to a correct understanding of Israel. It exists throughout the rolling ages among the nations as a wandering miracle and, to whoever denies the miracle, as a wandering enigma. At the same time it is the materialization of prophecy fulfilled and prophecy unfulfilled.

Israel's Past

Israel owes its *origin* to a miracle. The seed of promise was born from a mother who was both too old and too barren. Scripture calls attention to this double wonder both in the Old and the New Testaments. Humanly speaking, obtaining a seed of promise was impossible. And since Sarah looked at the matter purely from a human point of view, she simply laughed in unbelief. She thought that the Lord must have meant something different, so she got busy in a way that was not what the Lord intended. The Lord berated her by saying, "Is any thing too *hard* for the Lord?" Just as Sarah laughed in unbelief at the *origin* of Israel, so today thousands of Christians laugh at Israel's *future*. But even if the whole world were to laugh until it shook, it still cannot laugh away God's wonders.

Israel is a miracle of God in its *continuation*. This is almost a greater miracle than its origin, for here we are not merely dealing with a single or even double miracle, but with a long series of miracles spread over many centuries and nations. It is an unchangeable law of nature that whatever burns is consumed. Israel is an exception to this unalterable rule. Israel is the burning bush that keeps on burning throughout the ages and is never consumed. This bush had already burned and was severely scorched at the brick kilns of Egypt, but it kept on growing in spite of the leaping flames. It was uprooted from its fertile soil, but it still lives and bears many fruits.

Israel has existed under the most unfavorable circumstances; sometimes it lacked the right conditions to live at all. This nation has a history of blood and tears as no other. It is the spectacle and tragedy of the ages. It has never been able to mix with the nations, no matter how badly it wanted to do so at times. It remained, and still remains, according to the well-known metaphor, the drop of oil on the waters of the sea of nations. None of the other peoples can remain unmixed when living among strange nations, no matter how badly they would like to; but Israel remains, according to prophecy, a nation that dwells alone. Even though it is dispersed among the nations, it is not counted with them (Num. 23:9).

Israel's Present

When we consider Israel's *present-day existence* we again see a miracle of God's hand. For in its manner of existence it is a people of the most blatant and most painful contrasts. It is hated everywhere and yet sought after everywhere. It is hated because of its talents and cunning, and sought after for the same reasons. There is an instinctive repugnance in the bosom of nations for this unique people. If it is not oppressed or banished outright, it most certainly is not welcomed. Since the days of Egypt, the nations of the world have wrestled with the so-called Jewish problem. More than four thousand years ago Egypt was confronted with this problem, and the nations of today are still confronted with it. And it is as insoluble to the nations today as it was in Egypt. The shroud that covers many nations today prevents them from seeing that God Himself will solve this problem, but not until He dissolves all nations first.

Israel is wanted nowhere and yet wanted everywhere. To prove that the Jew in every respect stands in the limelight of attention, we refer the reader to S. B. Rohold's *The War and the Jew,* and to Abraham Kuyper's *Liberalists and Jews* and *The Jewish Problem.*

Jews are the biggest bankers and money lenders in England and France, and they could, if they wanted to, stop the war [World War I, Ed.]. And yet, it is their brothers according to the flesh who have had to suffer the greatest atrocities of the war. It must strike us again and again that these people are subject to the strangest contrasts. They manifest the contrasts of poverty and wealth, learnedness and ignorance, nobility and baseness of spirit, cruelty and humanity, conservatism and radicalism. The explanation of this phenomenon is that Israel is the bearer of both a curse and a blessing: of a curse when they forsake the God of their fathers, and of a blessing when they remain faithful to Him, especially when they throw themselves at the feet of the Messiah.

What a curse has emanated from the Dutch Jew, Spinoza, for the whole world! He dominates modern thinking and can justly be called the father of Bible criticism. And how the apostate Jew, Karl Marx, governs the social currents of thought! How the Italian Jew, Lombroso, has caused justice to stumble by his pestiforous doctrine that criminals are nothing more than examples of failure, a kink in the chain of the great process of world development!

Has not another Jew, Heinrich Heine, caused dreadful harm by his bewitching songs. The morally corrupt School of the Eighties in the Netherlands was also influenced by him, and the dreadful hater of Christianity, the Jew, Querido, may today be considered the prince of literature in that country.

The Jew, Cambetta, who has done much evil in higher politics, could be called the father of France's politics of revenge. The Reformed Jews dominate nearly all of the world press and, in America, the theater as well.

For centuries Jews have been accused of poisoning wells and water sources. This accusation is hateful and stupid. But by their spiritual and mental activity they have polluted and poisoned our moral and religious fountainheads. Both the signs of the times as well as the Word of prophecy give the impression that the Antichrist will be an apostate Jew, as the Roman

Catholic Church has believed on the basis of the opinion held in the first centuries.

Over against this curse stands the blessing, which Israel afforded the nations when it remained faithful to the God of their fathers. Viewed in the light of the Word, there are only two nations—Hebrews and Gentiles. Unbelieving scientists in Germany call Christianity Semitism, and correctly so, for our religion is Semitic through and through. We are not Semites, but we do live in the tents of Shem and worship Jehovah, the God of Abraham, Isaac, and Jacob. The great mistake of present-day Christianity is that it is more pagan than Jewish. To the extent that the Church of the Lord in the early Middle Ages became less Jewish, it became more pagan.

People sometimes speak with repugnance and deep contempt of the Judaization of the Christian religion. How careless such a statement is! We don't have to Judaize the Christian religion, for God has done that already! Our God is called Jehovah, the God of Israel. Our Savior is the King born of the Jews. As such He was crucified, and in that capacity He is coming back (Rev. 22:16).

The book from which we read three times a day is a Jewish book. It knows nothing of Americans or Englishmen or Hollanders. The church to which we belong is built on the Jewish foundation of apostles and prophets. Even the hallelujahs the redeemed in heaven sing are Jewish, the song of Moses and of the Lamb!

Lord Beaconsfield could with more than a semblance of justification say that one-half of the world venerates a Jew and the other half a Jewess, thereby referring to Protestantism and Rome.

So we need not have any fear of Judaizing. The mistake of the old Judaism was not that it was too Jewish, but that it was not enough Christian and too Pharisaic! Today there is, especially in our circles, a Judaism of which we should be afraid, and that is the disastrous delusion by which we identify the Church with Israel. People believe that some day kings will be the nursing fathers and queens the nursing mothers of the Church. The Judaizing of the Church in this sense has, more than anything else, robbed today's Church of its spiritual character. Says Bettex:

> The belief that they were Israel was the error that was frequently the downfall of such groups as the Huguenots, Puritans, and Camisards; and the heresy proclaimed from pulpits that the Church is the inheritor of the promises made to Israel has in various ways, through self-imagined exegesis, obscured and reversed the prophecies. [F. Bettex, *The Bible, the Word of God* (1904), pp. 185-187.]

We need not point out all the blessings the nations have inherited from Israel. The entire Christian religion is proof of it, all of history testifies to it, numerous writers enlarge upon it and nearly all nations make mention of it. A French scientist has shown that the Jews even had great influence upon Chinese literature some two hundred years before Christ. And the most glorious fact is that Israel's curse is only temporary and will soon be removed together with all other curses, whereas its blessing remains and before long will swell into a river of salvation, that to the entire world will be as a resurrection from the dead (Rom. 11:12-15). Israel is the *Am Olam*, i.e., the eternal people. It has not yet brought its full blessing to the world. According to Scripture it is hardly standing on the first rung of its ladder of destiny. For that reason it is immortal. For anything that has not yet reached its destination cannot die.

Israel's Future

Thus we have seen that Israel may be called a miracle nation. Not only in the sense that it has seen, heard, written down, preserved, and proclaimed God's wondrous deeds, but also in the sense that it is a walking miracle in its origin, continuance, and present form of existence. And by a miracle we mean an objective, extraordinary manifestation of God's providence in which the connection between cause and result cannot be subjectively understood by common reasoning. It is only natural that the sages of this world have set for themselves the task of unraveling the puzzle of the Jews. They have tried to explain it on the basis of Israel's rigid concept of God. But Mohammedans and Christians have the same concept and neither group can continue to exist separately. Others explain Israel's present-day separate existence on the basis of its history of suffering. The people's mutual oppression, they say, pulled and kept them together. But a common lot never resulted in a common religion, far less in a common relationship of blood. In addition, the Christian Church at times had to suffer as severely as Israel and yet the Church did not stay together. Still others deny that Israel is a separate nation and people, and they expect that increasing civilization will cause it to disappear.

Most historians, however, simply accept the Jews as an insoluble problem. Hegel was at his wit's end with what to "do" with the Jews. Although he was able to reduce the entire world to a few logical formulae, the Jews continued to perplex him. According to his own admission, they tormented him his entire life as a dark, insoluble riddle. The more he studied them, the more they perplexed him. Renan also was dumbfounded by this mysterious people. He wrote,

> In a certain sense the Jewish people have no longer any meaning or any right to existence after they produced Christianity. This people is a wandering skeleton that survived the sentence of death pronounced upon it . . . It is the strangest spectacle history has to offer us.

Usually the Church dismissed the matter with far less concern. The Greek Orthodox Church, at a Synod in 1542, promulgated that the only reason the Jews still existed was to remind the Christians of the bitter suffering of Christ, as if Scripture did not do this enough! In 1733 it repeated this and added as a second reason that this nation was to be viewed, by the Christians, as an example of God's vengeance. As if the waters of the Dead Sea and every cemetery are not proof of this as well!

Other writers are sometimes little more fair with regard to the Jews than the Greek Orthodox Church. Not infrequently they make the guilt of the Jews even greater than it actually is. When they say that the Jews have already had the time of their visitation because they have crucified Christ and hence will never have a future, they are wrong in two respects. Consequently their conclusion is wrong as well.

First, it is not correct to say that the Jews alone crucified the Son of God. Pilate was not only a worldly judge but also a world-judge. He judged and condemned in the name of the entire Roman world power. The world in miniature was gathered at the foot of the cross. It is self-righteous to put the blame of this criminal act on the Jews only. The beknighted and misguided crusaders did this in the Middle Ages. The result was that with burning hatred they cried, "Hep, hep!" The three letters of which this little word is formed are the first letters of the Latin cry, *Jerusalem must be destroyed!* While they wanted to save the city of Jerusalem from the hands of the Turks, they killed the children of Jerusalem by the hundreds as a result of the delusion that the Jews were the murderers of Christ. One may give the Jew most of the blame, but not all of it for—we must not forget—they did it knowingly, which is evident from Christ's prayer, Peter's statement in Acts 3 and Paul's words in 1 Corinthians 2. Israel did know that it murdered an innocent man, but not that He was the *Messiah!* So let us not weep with the daughters of Jerusalem for His misery, nor let us get angry with the Jews' guilt, but let us realize that we by our own guilt erected the accursed tree.

Second, it is unfair to Israel when we believe its past but not its future; this is a strange inconsistency! With respect to its past we believe all the miracles the Lord did among and to Israel. No matter how great and marvelous they are, we would not think of denying them, and whoever does deny them is considered an enemy, and correctly so! But the same people seldom give it a second thought that in the future even greater miracles will take place with regard to Israel. Or when they do read of them, they pay no attention, for they do not believe them. What is the reason, we may ask, for this different attitude—the miracles in the gray past are believed from beginning to end, but the future ones, which are no less clearly revealed, are not believed at all. Is it not due to a terribly sinful rationalism on the part of believing people? Should not the Savior cry out to our present-day Christianity, "O fools, and slow of heart to believe *all* that the prophets have spoken!"?

Exegetes, too, are unfair in their explanations of the prophecies regarding Israel. Those who concern themselves with prophecy are agreed that there are numerous prophecies for the Jews. Learned men such as Kuyper, Küper, Bavinck, Pierson, Rheim, Davidson, Delitzsch, and others are all agreed on that. The only problem is how those things must be explained. Modernists let them become the vapor of some dream about the triumph of truth, as they call it. The old Scottish Covenanters applied everything to themselves, as did the Huguenots and Camisards of France and the Puritans of New England. The Pilgrims wanted a visible theocracy on earth as is promised to Israel, but it is their country that became the breeding ground of Unitarianism and all kinds of soul-corrupting heresies. The Mormons explain these things so figuratively that they apply perfectly to their satanic synagogues. And the Anglo-Israelites claim them for the Anglo-Saxon race.

What do people in our circles do? [Reformed circles of Bultema's day. Ed.]. They tend not to touch these prophecies. Or they utter nothing but sounds and more sounds. Thoughtlessly they repeat the tale that came over from the modernist camp that there are but very few predictions, far less than is usually thought. This is definitely not true. There are many predictions, and apparently far more than the believing Church usually thinks. Again we hear the statement, "Prophecy is not fortune-telling," so that the hearers must get the impression that explaining prophecy is the same as telling lies. Also the statement that prophecy is not history written beforehand gives the impression that it is rather history written afterwards. The most objectionable mistreatment of Israel's prophecies, however, is to sort out the curses and blessings mentioned in the same context, so that the curses are applied to Israel and the spiritual blessings to the Church.

Finally, we point out the unfairness in zealously promoting missions to the heathen but not to the Jews. We must gratefully acknowledge that a change for the better is noticeable in this regard; there is a growing interest in missions to the Jews. But it is not enough. Three centuries ago our forefathers did more than we are doing now. They sheltered thousands of Jewish refugees from Spain and Portugal. At the Synod of Dordt a summons was made to convert these strangers, and at the University of Leyden a chair of Jewish Divinity was established. Do we indeed love the beloved for the sake of the fathers? Are we in our prayers truly followers of Him who prayed for them at the cross, or of the Apostle to the heathen who constantly beseeched God for their salvation?

Is not the command that we must begin at Jerusalem still applicable to us? This Jerusalem is not the city in which we live, nor even the country, but Jerusalem taken in the sense of the

Jewish people. Mission among the Jews is of the greatest importance for missions to the heathen, because converted Jews make the best missionaries. Such Jews are found in all countries and among all nations. They speak every language, tolerate every climate, and have unequaled tact and tenacity in removing stumbling blocks.

Israel is a divine miracle, a miracle in the past, the present, and the future. No philosopher can explain it, and no counterpart is to be found anywhere. Only God Himself can explain it, and He does so in His Word.

This is where we shall turn in order to obtain light on Israel's future. The light that shines in a dark place sheds light also on this matter. Whoever despises or obscures this light by not believing all that the prophets have spoken must of necessity let Israel go its way amidst the nations as a wandering and insoluble riddle.

On the other hand, whoever acknowledges that Israel is a miracle of God's hand can come to this conclusion, i.e., that Israel cannot be a miracle without a purpose, since God never performs miracles without a divine purpose. If Israel is a physical, national, and religious miracle, it must have a destination commensurate with it.

> No, answers the Word of God that never passes away,
> Israel will not forever remain the derision of the nations;
> Its King prayed for it at the shameful cross,
> And soon the Savior will come to the house of Israel.

Chapter 17

ISRAEL'S FUTURE
ACCORDING TO THE OLD TESTAMENT

The scope of this book does not allow us to deal extensively with the glorious subject of Israel's future. We shall show as briefly as possible that the entire Old Testament points to a glorious future which awaits Israel after all its wanderings. In so doing we shall let the infallible Word speak for itself as much as possible. Only a few hints will be given here and there.

Israel in the Books of Moses

Now the Lord had said unto Abram, Get thee out of thy country, and from thy kindred, and from they father's house, unto a land that I will shew thee. And I will make of thee a great nation, and I will bless thee, and make thy name great; and thou shalt be a blessing. And I will bless them that bless thee, and curse him that curseth thee: and in thee shall all families of the earth be blessed (Gen. 12:1-3).

We observe the following facts.

1. Abram was called at a time when Babylon aspired after human unity, power, and happiness. When the world attempts to bring things together in order to obtain power through unity, God separates them in order to emphasize personal holiness. It was a time when the world was sinking away in heathenism, i.e., into devil worship. In His mercy, God made a covenant with Abram and his seed against the devil and devil worship. Except for bestowing the blessings of His common grace, He let the world go. From now on Israel must be His prophetic people, to witness *for* Him and His service and *against* idolatry (Deut. 6:4; 33:26-29; 1 Chron. 17:20-21; Ps. 144:15; Isa. 42:10, 12). Israel must be the bearer of the Messiannic promise (Gen. 3:15; 21:12; 28:10, 14; 49:10; 2 Sam. 7:16; Isa. 55:3, 4; Matt. 1:1).

2. Notice the universal character of this promise. Israel will grow into a great nation. This is emphasized again and again (Gen. 13:14; 15:1-21; 17:6-7, 15-16; 18:18; 26:3-4; 28:3-4; 35:11-12; 46:3). Its seed will comprise many nations (Gen. 17:4-5; 28:3; 35:11; 46:3; Rom. 4:17). Abraham is the heir of the world. Kings will descend from him, from Sarah and from Jacob (Gen. 17:6, 16; 35:11). Who dares to claim that all these things have already found their fulfillment in the past?

3. Israel's enemies will fare badly. That has already been fulfilled literally in history—Egypt (Ezek. 29:14-16); Amalek (1 Chron. 4:43); Edom (Jer. 49:7-22; Ezek. 3; Obad. 3:1-4, 10-15); Moab and Ammon (Ezek. 25:3-11; Zeph. 2:8-11); Tyre and Sidon (Joel 3:4-8; Amos 1:9-10); the Philistines (2 Kings 18:8; 2 Chron. 26:6; Jer. 47); *all* nations (Joel 3:2-3).

4. Israel, however, is not chosen to be a curse, but a blessing unto the world. It will be blessed of the Lord and made into a blessing. All who do well to Israel as the people of God will be blessed for it (Gen. 18:18-19; 26:4; 28:14; Isa. 43:1; Zech. 8:23; Acts 15:13-17; Rom. 11:15-18). Israel is chosen for the grand purpose that all of mankind may come to know Jehovah, and the whole world may be filled with the glory of the Lord (Num. 14:21; Deut. 28:9-10; Ps. 67; Isa. 60:1-3; 61:6-9; 62:2; 66:19).

> Now therefore, if ye will obey my voice indeed, and keep my covenant, then ye shall be a peculiar treasure unto me above all people: for all the earth is mine: And ye shall be unto me a kingdom of priests, and an holy nation. These are the words which thou shalt speak unto the children of Israel (Exod. 19:5-6).

1. We are dealing here with a true covenant. All the elements of a covenant are present: two parties, a condition, a promise, and Israel's assent. This is not, however, the covenant of grace, for in that covenant no conditions play any role. It is nevertheless a fruit, a result of the covenant of grace. The condition does not say that Israel will be God's people if it is obedient. The basis of Israel being God's people is election and calling, neither of which are to be repented of. The question then is, with which covenant are we dealing here?

2. What we have here is a provisional covenant with the people, which means that when Israel as a nation is obedient, it will be God's precious jewel, the jewel of the nations. We are

dealing with a secondary stream of the covenant of grace. Israel is constantly reminded that it is God's jewel, lest it ally itself with the nations of the world (Deut. 7:6). It is God's special possession, hence it must not marry foreign women, it must circumcise its heart, not harden its neck (Deut. 10:16) and keep all His commandments (6:18).

3. Since Israel did not meet this condition, it has been rejected for many centuries as the jewel of the nations. Because it adulterously turned away from Jehovah, the children of Israel as a nation will:

> Abide many days without a king, and without a prince, and without a sacrifice, and without an image, and without an ephod, and without teraphim. Afterward shall the children of Israel return, and seek the Lord their God, and David their king; and shall fear the Lord and his goodness in the latter days (Hos. 3:4-5).

Although they are temporarily rejected as a peculiar people, they remain the beloved for the sake of the fathers by virtue of election and the covenant of grace. During Israel's rejection God has gathered unto Himself another peculiar possession from among all the nations, i.e., the Church. When the Church shall have reached its full number, then Israel's dispensation as a unique independent nation will dawn once again. Until that day, Peter can say of the Church that it is a royal priesthood, a holy nation, a peculiar people, to show forth the praises of God's attributes. The Lord is never without His very own people on earth.

> Then will I remember my covenant with Jacob, and also my covenant with Isaac, and also my covenant with Abraham will I remember; and I will remember the land. The land also shall be left of them, and shall enjoy her sabbaths, while she lieth desolate without them: and they shall accept of the punishment of their iniquity: because, even because they despised my judgments, and because their soul abhorred my statutes. And yet for all that, when they be in the land of their enemies, I will not cast them away, neither will I abhor them, to destroy them utterly, and to break my covenant with them: for I am the Lord their God (Lev. 26:42-44).

1. In the context of Leviticus 26, from verse 14 on, all the judgments pronounced upon Israel have been literally fulfilled. This section manifestly speaks of a long dispersion, which still continues. If the dispersion of Israel is literal and factual, will not the gathering up of Israel be equally so?

2. Scripture always makes a careful distinction between the various covenants pertaining to Israel (Rom. 9:4). The certainty of Israel's deliverance is firmly grounded in the indestructible covenant of grace, which is a fruit of election. God always uses His glorious covenantal name, Jehovah, when He speaks of Israel's future restoration. Thus here again He says twice, "I am the LORD," that is to say, the eternal and unchangeable One, who is married to My people.

Numbers 23:9-10 and 19-24 contains the remarkable prophecy of Balaam regarding Israel. This prophecy deserves our full attention in order for us to know Israel.

1. In Numbers 23:9, Balaam prophesies through the inbreathing of the Spirit that Israel will be a separated people and will not be counted or reckoned among the nations. This has been literally fulfilled even to this very day.

2. Israel will be a great nation and as such have a glorious future (v. 10).

3. It is a nation that is blessed and owned by Jehovah (v. 20).

4. Israel is indestructible. There is neither enchantment against Jacob nor divination against Israel. And the nation is indestructible because election and the covenant of grace are indestructible (vv. 23-24).

5. Israel's rest and peace, as that of an old lion in his den, does not come until all his enemies have been defeated and he himself will have dominion over his enemies. After this slaughter, the nations will be obedient to Israel's Messiah (cf. with Gen. 49:9-10; Mal. 4:3, and many other references).

And it shall come to pass, when all these things are come upon thee, the blessing and the curse, which I have set before thee, and thou shalt call them to mind among all the nations, whither the Lord thy God hath driven thee, and shalt return unto the Lord thy God, and shalt obey his voice according to all that I command thee this day, thou and thy children, with all thine heart, and with all thy soul; that then the Lord thy God will turn thy captivity, and have compassion upon thee, and will return and gather thee from all the nations, whither the Lord thy God hath scattered thee. If any of thine be driven out unto the outmost parts of heaven, from thence will the Lord thy God gather thee, and from thence will he fetch thee: and the Lord thy God will bring thee into the land which thy fathers possessed, and thou shalt possess it; and he will do thee good, and multiply thee above thy fathers. And the Lord thy God will circumcise thine heart, and the heart of thy seed, to love the Lord thy God with all thine heart, and with all thy soul, that thou mayest live (Deut. 30:1-6).

1. These promises refer to the future, because they will be fulfilled after the dispersion of Israel (see Deut. 28:49-52ff). It is almost unanimously agreed that this section describes the destruction of Jerusalem by the Romans, including the destruction by the Chaldees. There is nothing in the past that corresponds to these predictions.

2. In the preceding context mention is made of the dispersion. Just as this was a tragic reality for Israel, so will the re-adoption be a glorious reality, and hence these statements may not be spiritualized.

3. As usual, return and repentance go hand in hand. This is true to such an extent that the Hebrew verb for conversion comprises both concepts.

4. The certainty of Israel's future salvation is found in God's faithful covenant. These six verses contain the striking expression *Jehovah your God* no less than eight times.

Thus we have seen that Moses in all of his five books mentions Israel's future redemption. The books of Joshua, Judges, and Ruth contain many hints in the form of assumption, deduction, and shadowy allusion, but we shall not discuss these, as we wish to limit ourselves to the clearer references.

Israel and the Kingdom of David

In 2 Samuel 7:11-16 we find the so-called Davidic covenant. That covenant is not the same as the covenant of grace, just as the Ohio River is not the Mississippi River. But just as the Ohio River is a wide branch of the Mississippi River, so is the Davidic covenant a result of the covenant of grace. It concerns David and his descendants, though not exclusively, for Israel as a nation is the possessor of the covenants.

1. That we are dealing here with a real covenant is evident, since all the elements of a covenant are present, and since it is confirmed with a solemn divine oath (Ps. 89:3-4, 35-37; Heb. 6:17-18). Also it is often emphatically called a covenant with David.

2. The covenant comprises a threefold promise.

First, David will not build a house for the Lord, but the Lord will build a house for David, in the sense of kingdom.

Second, in that kingdom a son of David will reign eternally. The term "for ever" is used three times by Nathan and five times by David. This covenant will be irrevocable. Sin in David's house will be punished severely, but it will never destroy that house (see 2 Sam. 7:15; Ps. 89:20-37; Isa. 24:5; 55:3).

And finally, the son of David will be the Son of God. True, this is first a reference to Solomon, but the prophecy reaches much farther than to him. From 2 Samuel 23:1-7 it is evident that David himself looks far beyond Solomon. There he views Him as the Ruler who will extend His divine government over the whole world. David called a great One, among his descendants, his *Lord* and not his son (Ps. 110:1, Luke 20:42-44; see further the Messianic Psalms 2, 16, 18, 22, 72, etc.). In Acts 2:30 it is emphatically stated that David knew that God had sworn, with an oath, to him that of the fruit of his loins, according to the flesh, He would raise up the Christ to set Him on his throne.

3. This covenant has not been rescinded and will never be rescinded, since it is indestructible. These words may not be spiritualized in the same sense that Christ is *now* sitting on the throne of David, because:

A) The words *kingdom* and *crown*, when referring to the house of David, are always to be taken literally.

B) David himself, according to his swan song in 2 Samuel 23:1-7, understood these words in a literal sense.

C) The chastisements threatened in this covenant were literally fulfilled in the last days of Solomon, when the kingdom was rent, and when Israel and then Judah were carried into captivity. Why should we condense the blessings into something spiritual, but vague?

D) A literal exegesis is by no means absurd. It is absurd only to blind prejudice, but not to the little children who understand the word of the Father in its obvious and natural meaning.

E) We see in Luke 1:31-33 that the Lord has not forgotten this covenant and that it is His intention to fulfill it literally. Gabriel delivers to Mary a prophecy comprised of seven parts. Of those seven, the first five have already been literally fulfilled. The next two say that the Lord will give Him the throne of His father David and that He will be King over the house of Jacob forever. What gives us the right to spiritualize these last two parts of this one prophecy? With this method of exegesis we can make Scripture say, or deny, anything.

F) The disciples understood these words in a literal sense, as shown by their question in Acts 1:6. Christ did not berate their question as being wrong, foolish, or carnal. On the contrary, He encouraged them in their hope. If David, Gabriel, and the disciples take these words in a literal sense, should we not do the same?

G) In the last chapter of Scripture we are told that the Lord Jesus will return as the root and the offspring, and as the Lord and the Son of David. Only then, and no sooner, comes Israel's deliverance (see Isa. 2:1-5; 11:1-16; Jer. 23:1-8; Ezek. 37; Hos. 3:5; and numerous other places in Old and New Testament). Then the Kingdom of Israel will be established.

The Book of Psalms frequently mentions Israel's grand future. From practically every Messianic Psalm, something can be deduced regarding Israel's future, and many other Psalms mention it as well.

A particularly clear reference is found in Psalm 102:13-22. We shall not quote the entire passage, but will comment on a few details in passing.

1. Mention is made of Jehovah's arising and appearance in glory (vv. 13, 16).

2. He comes in mercy to Zion, i.e., the holy city Jerusalem, where the Lord will dwell forever according to His solemn oath.

3. He rebuilds the city, for He pities her dust (*Dutch Authorized Version*).

4. He delivers Israel from prison and looses those that are appointed to death.

5. After Israel's conversion follows that of the heathen. This is the continuous idea in all of Scripture (see Acts 15:17 and Rom. 11:12-15). This is the main topic of the latter part of Isaiah, chapters 40 to 66.

> This prophecy is a clear reference to the ultimate and final restoration of Israel and the addition of the fullness of the Gentiles, when the Deliverer shall come to Zion and the glorious state of the Church will dawn (Donner).

Except for the author's erroneous idea of a glorious state of the Church, this is correctly stated.

We should also compare Psalm 58:10-11; 68:24 and others with what Baalam predicted concerning the destruction of Israel's enemies. Although similar pronouncements have been partially fulfilled several times, most exegetes agree that their complete fulfillment must be looked for in the future.

Israel's Future in Isaiah

Isaiah provides such an abundance of material on this subject that we hardly know what to do with it. First we will select Isaiah 11:11ff.

> And it shall come to pass in that day, that the Lord shall set his hand again the second time to recover the remnant of his people, which shall be left, from Assyria, and from Egypt, and from Pathros, and from Cush, and from Elam, and from Shinar, and from Hamath, and from the islands of the sea.

1. This gathering takes place after the Lord has come to judge with righteousness and to smite the earth with the rod of His mouth (see vv. 1-5). This cannot refer to the return from the first exile, for it is emphatically stated that the Lord will gather His people a second time.

2. Those who apply these words to the gathering in of the believers in the Church also run into contradictions. Although the members of the true Church are gathered from all nations, the Church has not been in exile in Pathros (Upper Egypt), in Cush (Africa), in Elam (southern Media), and on the islands of the sea (all of Europe) and consequently must be returned. Moreover *his people* refers to Israel and not to the Church. For the Church He does not make a highway through the Red Sea, as He once literally did (vv. 15-16).

3. The only explanation that makes sense is the obvious one, namely, that the Savior upon His return shall gather together all Jews from all nations whither they have dispersed.

> He shall cause them that come of Jacob to take root: Israel shall blossom and bud, and fill the face of the world with fruit (Isa. 27:6).

1. It is sufficiently clear from the words themselves and from the context that this is not a reference to the Church.

A) The name Jacob always refers to historic Israel as viewed in its weakness and sin.

B) The Lord has never struck the Church, but Israel as an independent nation and kingdom has been smitten.

C) From the following context it is clear that this verse refers to Israel's exiles.

D) The church has never filled the world with fruit. The apostate Church does, however, fill the world with all kinds of abominations and whoredoms according to Scripture (see Rev. 17 and 18).

E) This verse speaks of affairs and events after the judgment of leviathan and Satan (see Isa. 27:1 and Rev. 20:1-8).

2. Israel has not obtained this flourishing condition as yet. Since the days of Isaiah, Israel has been a poor and despised flock. Scripture continuously teaches, however, that after the coming of the Savior it will blossom and become a blessing to all the nations of the earth (Isa. 2; Micah 4; also see Isa. 19:24-25; 45:4, 6; 55:1, 3; 56:3, 7; Acts 15:17; Rom. 11:15). According to God's decree and specific promises, Israel will be the channel through which flows the salvation of the whole world.

This has already been partially fulfilled through the Messiah and the spiritual treasures Israel has given the world, but it will be completely fulfilled only at Christ's return. The present partial fulfillment is our guarantee that all the rest will be completely fulfilled. The strong statement in Romans 11:15 shows clearly that this salvation can hardly be overestimated.

The second part of Isaiah, if viewed correctly, speaks of nothing but the future return and conversion of Israel and what is connected with it, including the first return after the seventy years of exile. Just as the prophets usually speak of the second coming of the Messiah with the inclusion of the first, so also here the first return is included in the second.

In our exegesis of this portion of Isaiah, we may not stop at the first restoration for the following reasons.

1. This restoration includes both Ephraim and Judah. In the return from Babylon only a small part of Judah took part, hardly totaling fifty thousand people.

2. This will be followed by a national repentance (Isa. 54:1-7 and other references). This by no means took place after the return from Babylon. Haggai and Zechariah, Ezra and Nehe-

miah, and Malachi teach us the opposite. Even at the time of Stephen, Israel was still uncircumcised in heart and ears.

3. This restoration will be eternal and never be followed by another disruption and exile, something that cannot be said of the first restoration (Isa. 43:7; 51:15, 21, and other places). The word *olam*, eternal, appears thirty-four times in this context in connection with Israel.

4. Israel will have dominion over the nations. The nations have had dominion over it for many centuries, but then the roles will be reversed (Isa. 51:10-22; 66).

5. Israel will pass on the blessing of its Messiah to all nations. Then the whole earth will be full of the knowledge and glory of the Lord (Isa. 66:19, 23; cf. 11:9; Hab. 2:14).

Again and again the Lord is presented as dwelling in the midst of His people.

Israel in Jeremiah

> In those days the house of Judah shall walk with the house of Israel, and they shall come together out of the land of the north to the land that I have given for an inheritance unto your fathers (Jer. 3:18).

1. *In those days* does not refer to the time after the exile, but to the time when the Lord Himself will sit on the throne in Jerusalem. This will be openly acknowledged by all the nations, who at that time will no more walk according to the imagination of their evil hearts (see v. 17).

2. Israel and Judah will be reunited. When these two kingdoms are mentioned together in Scripture, we are not to think exclusively of the first return (Isa. 11:12-14; Jer. 31:1, 31; Ezek. 37:6ff.).

3. The preceding and following context points to a future national restoration.

> Therefore, behold, the days come, saith the Lord, that it shall no more be said, The Lord liveth, that brought up the children of Israel out of the land of Egypt; but, the Lord liveth, that brought up the children of Israel from the land of the north, and from all the lands whither he had driven them: and I will bring them again into their land that I gave unto their fathers (Jer. 16:14-15).

1. *Therefore, behold, the days come.* Scripture usually does not use this expression to indicate the days that follow a certain age of a person, but a time in the far distance. According to

Ernst Wilhelm Hengstenberg, Jeremiah refers here to great and glorious future times.

2. This solemn oath would hardly be applicable to that poor handful of Jews after the first exile.

3. The *land of the north, and . . . all the lands* cannot very well apply to Babylon but, according to many, refers to Russia, where half of the present day Jews live [In the year 1917. Ed.].

4. The context points to the future restoration, since it speaks of the conversion of all Gentiles. Comparing these verses with 23:7-8 removes all doubt.

> Behold, the days come, saith the Lord, that I will raise unto David a righteous Branch, and a King shall reign and prosper, and shall execute judgment and justice in the earth. In his days Judah shall be saved, and Israel shall dwell safely (Jer. 23:5-6).

1. Generally the raising of the Branch is taken as the birth of the Savior. If that is so, then we interpret the deliverance of Israel and Judah as being in those days when the Messiah will personally do justice in the whole earth.

2. From this text, as well as from the context, it is clear that no salvation is forthcoming for Israel until the return of the Lord.

Jeremiah 30-33 deals almost exclusively with the salvation that is yet to come to Israel, and with the great tribulation which will be unlike anything it ever experienced in its turbulent history. We must not forget, however, that the prophets always connected far distant times with their own. Since this is not the place to discuss all the relevant texts in Jeremiah, we shall have a closer look at one among many.

> Behold, the days come, saith the Lord, that I will sow the house of Israel and the house of Judah with the seed of man, and with the seed of beast. And it shall come to pass, that like as I have watched over them, to pluck up, and to break down, and to throw down, and to destroy, and to afflict; so will I watch over them, to build, and to plant, saith the Lord (Jer. 31:27-28).

1. In the second part of Jeremiah 31:22 we read, "The Lord hath created a new thing in the earth, A woman shall compass a man." Some Church Fathers, Luther, and many Reformed theologians explain these words literally as having reference to Christ's birth out of the Virgin Mary. This is quite logical and

possible. And here we cannot level the objection that the text is not speaking of the former but the latter days, since it does not take into account the special nature of Messianic prophecy. But if we take this statement in its literal sense, it is no exegetical sin if we take all the prophecies regarding the glory of the future united Israel in the same sense and not symbolize them to their death.

2. The Lord has literally destroyed Israel. And *so* He will rebuild it. The word *so* precludes all symbolization.

Israel in Ezekiel

> And I will set up one shepherd over them, and he shall feed them, even my servant David; he shall feed them, and he shall be their shepherd (Ezek. 34:23).

1. The "one shepherd" is a reference to Christ. This does not mean that He feeds and watches over the Church in general, but that He shall rule as a Shepherd King over the future Israel.

2. This Messianic reign dawns after Israel has been gathered together from all nations and its enemies have been revenged (see the preceding verses).

3. This reign will result in the kingdom of peace (see vv. 24ff). Israel will dwell in safety and will be prosperous and nevermore be the derision of the nations, while even the wild animals will no longer devour it. Israel will not always be the tail, but will one day be the head of the nations.

> For I will take you from among the heathen, and gather you out of all countries, and will bring you into your own land. Then will I sprinkle clean water upon you, and ye shall be clean: from all your filthiness, and from all your idols, will I cleanse you. A new heart also will I give you (Ezek. 36:24-26).

1. This is one of the most misinterpreted texts in Scripture. Apparently without any compunction it is torn from its context in order to make it an explanation of the rebirth of a sinner, as if a sinner before his conversion had to be brought back from all countries and as if he would have to live in Palestine in order to be fruitful and prosperous.

2. If we explain this passage in terms of Israel, all absurdities vanish.

3. The same things must be said of chapter 37. Whoever explains this vision in terms of the conversion of a sinner must, if he wishes to remain consistent, arrive at the most terrible absurdities. Simply read and reread the entire chapter matter-of-factly and open-mindedly.

4. Both sections make it clear that Israel, in part at least, will return to Palestine in an unregenerate state. The national conversion, when on one single day the unrighteousness of the nation will be removed, apparently takes place at the coming of the Redeemer Himself.

Remembering that the reason for Israel's deliverance does not lie in Israel, but, as Ezekiel reminds us more than fifty times, lies only in Israel's God, His election, His calling, His covenant, and His covenantal name. We now take a quick look at the minor prophets.

Israel in the Minor Prophets

> For the children of Israel shall abide many days without a king, and without a prince, and without a sacrifice, and without an ephod, and without teraphim: afterward shall the children of Israel return, and seek the Lord and his goodness in the latter days (Hos. 3:4-5).

1. Hosea 3:4 has literally been fulfilled. As an unfaithful and totally forsaken wife, Israel has already been abiding in great shame for many days. It has sinned away its life and trodden under foot its great honor. Worse still, it has murdered its Lord and Sovereign King. Hence this royal nation no longer has a king, this priestly nation no priest, and this prophetic nation no prophecy and revelation. The three pairs of words contain contrasts. Israel has no God-given king, but as a nation it does not choose a ruler either; it has no God-given sacrifice, but it does not now erect images; it has no ephod, no means of revelation or true revelation, but it does not resort to the teraphim, i.e., false means of revelation.

2. It is again according to the demands of good exegesis that the conversion of Israel in the latter days (v. 5) be taken in the literal sense. Then shall the true David, the Anointed, reign over them as King either in His own Person or through a descendant and David as His regent.

For, behold, in those days, and in that time, when I shall bring again the captivity of Judah and Jerusalem (Joel 3:1).

1. The time of this return is the day of judgment of the nations (Joel 3:2), that great and dreadful day of the Lord when deliverance will be only on Mount Zion, as God Himself will be there with his own.

2. This prophecy does not refer to the Church, for the Church is not in captivity.

See Amos 9 and read the entire chapter carefully.

1. The first eight verses contain a gripping description of Israel's misery. No one will want to claim that Israel's miseries were only figurative.

2. Verses 8 through 15 show us, first, that Israel is not entirely wiped out by God's terrible judgments; second, that Israel will return to its country; and finally, that it will never be removed from its country again but will flourish gloriously there during the kingdom of peace.

Read Obadiah 17-21.

1. "House of Jacob" never means "people of God in general" but, without exception, always Israel.

2. Israel will become a fire that devours Edom and thereby causes revenge to descend upon its head.

3. This will take place after Israel itself has been returned and Jehovah has His throne in Zion.

4. Then Israel will greatly expand and become prosperous, in keeping with all that the other prophets tell us.

Read Micah 7:11-20, an important section worthy to be read and reread.

1. The walls of Zion are rebuilt. This takes place in the day when the nations are judged, as Joel and Obadiah also indicate.

2. Israel will then have dominion over its enemies. Here again all the prophets are in agreement. This proves the law of retribution.

3. Restored Israel will enjoy great fruitfulness in its country. This is also pointed out by other prophets.

4. The Lord will remove all its unrighteousnesses and cast their sins into the depths of the sea (Rom. 11:26).

5. Unfaithful Jacob receives all this glory, not on the basis of any merit, but on the basis of God's sworn faithfulness. (See in this connection Gen. 3:16, Luke 1:72-75, Rom. 11:25-36).

How often do we sing in our churches:

> Jehovah's truth will stand forever,
> His covenant bonds He will not sever,

while we don't believe a thing of it as far as Israel is concerned, even though Scripture teaches that the promises of the Covenant are mostly and in the first place for Israel.

Nahum contains a prophecy against Nineveh and consequently mentions Israel only briefly. But Nahum does connect the message of peace with the fall of Nineveh, just as Isaiah does with the fall of Babylon. The downfall of Nineveh availed Israel little, since the other world powers soon began oppressing the nation. Nevertheless the downfall contained comfort for the God-fearing people. Nineveh was destroyed because this proud city had oppressed God's people (Nahum 1:11-15). In the second place the destruction of this city is, as are all other judgments upon the nations, an example of the complete ruin of Israel's enemies and at the same time the guarantee of its own triumph over all its enemies. Thus the end of verse 15 must refer to the cutting off, not only of such oppressors as Shalmaneser, Sennacherib, and Rabshakeh, but also of Satan and the Antichrist. Even to this day it cannot be said of Israel, "The wicked shall no more pass through thee." Thus even Nahum points us to Israel's joyful future.

Of the prophet Habakkuk, Dr. Katwijk, in his excellent doctoral thesis, says correctly that his entire prophecy has an eschatological character. The prophet describes the apostate nations as laboring unto fire. Their evil activity is nothing but a gathering of fuel for the fire of judgment. They have corrupted the earth and therefore the Lord corrupts them. Even though the sinners are annihilated from the earth, the earth itself is not destroyed, but is filled with the glory of the Lord (Hab. 2:14; cf. Isa. 11:9).

Habakkuk 3 is a beautiful song that describes the coming of the Lord. The historical element contained in it only provides poetic images for future realities. Verses 12 to 16 describe the purpose of the Lord's coming—the judgment of the nations and the deliverance of His people Israel.

Of Zephaniah, it is said, "This book deals exclusively with eschatology," i.e., the last things. So writes Dr. Snijman in his doctoral thesis. For our purpose Zephaniah 3:9-20 is the most important section. It depicts in a few strong strokes the following matters:

1. Israel will be gathered from among all the nations and be brought back.

2. The Lord dwells in Zion in the midst of His people, and the nations turn to Him.

3. When Israel is returned from dispersion, it will be made a name and a praise among all people of the earth. "*The* nation among nations will be Israel" (Van Andel).

4. The whole context tells us, and the best exegetes agree, that these verses have never been fulfilled in history and will be so only in the future.

Haggai 2:6, 22-23 is a remarkable and instructive passage for our subject.

1. From the words themselves, as well as from their partial quotation in Hebrews 12:26, it is evident that they are speaking of the day of judgment. By now it must have become clear to us that the prophets give very little justification for the idea of a twenty-four-hour judgment day.

2. When all kingdoms have collapsed, the Lord will make the house of David (Zerubbabel here serves as a representative of this house) as a signet, i.e., He will not annihilate it, but cause it to glitter as a precious jewel. We are dealing here not merely with a word of personal comfort to Zerubbabel, but with a symbolic repetition of the Messianic promise made to David long ago and repeated in Psalm 89:28 (cf. also 1 Kings 15:24; Dan. 2:44; Matt. 1:12; Luke 1:33; Heb. 12:28). Refer also to what was written earlier concerning the Davidic covenant.

3. Haggai was not referring to matters that are connected with the return from Babylon, since he ministered after the exile.

Zechariah also ministered after the exile. He speaks more than any other prophet about that which lies in store for Israel. Among the many expositors who have written about the Book of Zechariah are A. C. Gaebelein in America and the Rev. T. J. Laan in the Netherlands.

Malachi, the last prophet of the Old Covenant, has no different message than what we have heard again and again. He emphatically tells the deeply guilty children of Jacob that they are not, and will not, be consumed because Jehovah changes not. Those who teach Israel's total collapse must come to the conclusion that the Lord does change. The last chapter of Malachi points out the following future facts of salvation:

1. There will be judgment on the wicked. The proud, who openly despise God's service, and all those who do wickedly will prove to be worthless and will perish like stubble.

2. The unrestrained fire of judgment will be a sun unto Israel. However, it will not be a sun that burns and scorches and causes sickness and death, but a Sun of righteousness with healing in His wings.

3. Israel will have dominion over all its enemies who for so long oppressed it. The law of retribution has the greatest significance for Israel as a nation.

4. The people will be one. The heart of the fathers will again be turned to the children and that of the children to their fathers. Says Van Andel, "Truly, this expresses beautifully and at the same time elevates the peculiar character of the Israelite expectation of salvation."

Israel and a Literal Interpretation of Scripture

Here then are a few examples, which could be multiplied many times, but which are sufficient to point out the similar tone in all the prophets. If we do not wish to ignore them, we can do one of three things with them; either deny them as being no more than dreams, wrench them into a system, or accept them as they stand with all the consequences. We deliberately choose the last of the three, because the texts we have considered simply cannot, with any semblance of justification, be explained in terms of the first exile, nor of the Church, nor of heaven in glory.

The expositors who spiritualize these things and explain them in terms of the glorious state of the Church are practicing two kinds of exegesis. They take the things regarding the first coming of Christ in a strictly literal sense, while they do not take the things regarding Christ's second coming literally, but exclusively in a spiritual sense. Oh that people in our circles [Reformed circles in Bultema's day. Ed.] would recognize how unfair this is and how little the meaning and intent of the Holy Spirit can thus be grasped! On what basis, for instance, dare we spiritualize Isaiah 9:7, which speaks of Christ governing from the throne of David, after we have first explained verse 6 in a strictly literal sense? Who gives us the right to spiritualize Isaiah 51, 52, and 54 when we read chapter 53 in a strictly literal sense? Galatians 4:27 does not do so by any means.

We give a few more examples of how people apply a twofold exegesis.

Isaiah 11:1 is interpreted as containing literal and real statements concerning the birth of Christ. Also verse 2 speaks literally of His extraordinary fullness with the Holy Spirit. Verse 3 is still explained naturally and as speaking of His innocence and righteousness. But when this chapter, beginning with verse 6, commences to speak of the glorious government of Christ and of Israel's restoration, some people get confused and begin, quasi-spiritually, to fence with wild world-end statements.

The same people quote Isaiah 35:5-6 to prove that it has been literally foretold that the Savior would perform glorious miracles. But why not then take the beautiful description of Israel's future return in the same literal and natural sense?

Isaiah 50:6 is seen as a literal reference to the people spitting in Christ's face, but when a few verses later the prophet speaks of Israel's future glory, all this seems to mean nothing to these people.

Isaiah 61:1-2 is explained as literally referring to Christ's anointing and to His preaching, but verses 3 to 11 are carelessly allowed to evaporate into meaninglessness.

The first verses of chapter 63 are often explained as literally referring to Christ's bitter suffering, but they are obviously speaking of His coming in judgment. Isaiah 65:2 is usually taken as a literal prophecy of Christ's pleading with the stiff-necked Jews of Jerusalem; but, we ask again, on what basis can the same people evaporate the superlatively beautiful description of verses 18 to 25? Does this show childlike open-mindedness with regard to the explanation of the words of God?

These expositors carry out the same reckless exegetical stunts with regard to the other prophets. This may become clear from these few examples.

Jeremiah 23:5 is accepted as literally referring to the birth of Jesus Christ; but when verse 6 speaks of the deliverance of Judah and Israel, it suddenly seems as though this chapter does not even contain these words.

Joel 2:28 is again and again explained literally on every day of Pentecost, but with regard to 3:1-2 a totally different exegetical approach is taken.

Every Christmas day Micah 5:1 is explained as having been literally fulfilled, but with regard to the preceding and following context an entirely different rule of exegesis is followed.

Perhaps no other prophet is dealt with so arbitrarily as Zechariah. His prophecies regarding the future cannot very well be explained in terms of the return from Babylonia, since he prophesied after the exile. Here Zechariah 3, 5, 6, 8, 9-14 are hard nuts to crack for those who wish to keep Israel in the grave of the nations.

Zechariah 9:9 is taken as a literal reference to His humble entrance into Jerusalem; but the remaining verses, which speak of His glorious appearance and reign over Jerusalem and the whole earth, are either systematically ignored or spiritualized.

Zechariah 11:12 is considered by the same people as a literal prophecy regarding the thirty pieces of silver; verse 13 is a literal prediction of the acquisition of a field for the price of His blood; similarly 12:10 is a prediction regarding the piercing of his side with a spear; and 13:7 is explained according to the same rule as a reference to the scattering of the disciples. But if we think that chapters 11, 12, 13, and 14 would also be explained in the same way, we would be sadly mistaken! At no cost are these people willing to explain these chapters according to the same rule, for then they would have to teach, as though it were the most horrible of horrors, the return and conversion of Israel!

We do not hesitate for one moment to label such exegesis of prophecy as exegetical highhandedness of the worst kind; indeed, we are convinced that this is removing the key of prophecy. Let no one misunderstand us here; we are not fighting against a literal explanation of prophecy with regard to Christ's first coming. The Holy Spirit Himself sets the example for doing so, and it is clear that everything that has been fulfilled regarding Him has been fulfilled precisely and literally. Neither are we breaking a lance for what earlier we called a rigidly literal explanation. But we do insist in the exegesis of prophecy that no double standard be arbitrarily applied, with a literal explanation when applied to His first coming and a figurative explanation when applied to His second coming and its implications for Israel's salvation. Such tactics result in robbing Israel of its rightful inheritance and in deluding the Church.

Simple believers often ask why the explanation of prophecy is not taken more seriously in our [Reformed] circles. They obviously long for that part of scriptural instruction and many would rather turn to any spiritual charlatan than to remain in utter ignorance regarding these things. The answer to this question must be that the key of prophecy has partly become lost in our circles. Let us not conceal this terrible fact. Countless members and leaders will readily admit that they don't know anything about these things, for it is a remarkable and undeniable fact that people are seldom ashamed about their ignorance regarding the last things and in some cases even boast about it. They feel that it is only the ignorant fanatics who know or think to know all about it. It is high time that this abscess is exposed. But even that is not enough, for exposure does not heal a malignant boil.

Hence in love we urge all who read this book to read the glorious predictions made to Israel and Judah. A great future yet awaits Israel. With wholehearted agreement we quote here what Dr. Chantepie de la Saussaye writes in his excellent book on the future.

> I for one, dear Sir, still continue to adhere to the politics of the prophets; and with regard to the promises made to Israel, I not only say, 'it is written,' but also, this written word is so closely connected with the entire structure of prophecy, that is to say, throughout all of Scripture,

that you cannot lift that part out of it without disrupting the total body; and, moreover, the future of Israel, more than anything else, determines the course of world history both politically and ecclesiastically.

With regard to Babylon's downfall and Israel's restoration, the prophet Isaiah gave advice that cannot be ignored with impunity. "Seek ye out of the book of the Lord, and read: no one of these shall fail, none shall want her mate: for my mouth, it hath commanded, and his Spirit, it hath gathered them" (Isa. 34:16).

Chapter 18

ISRAEL'S RESTORATION
ACCORDING TO THE NEW TESTAMENT

We could terminate our discussion of the Jews if it were not for people who believe that the New Testament teaches that Israel as a nation has no longer any expectation. And those who admit that Romans 11 does teach that Israel has a future usually explain that some day many Jews will be added to the Church through missionary activity. Both of these viewpoints must be rejected. For this reason we will now look at some texts in the New Testament.

Luke 1:67-80
1. In this Song of Zacharias we find a continuation of Old Testament prophecy, verse 70. It tells us that the redemption of Israel is not a matter of secondary but of primary importance. Also see verses 30-33.

2. The suggestion that we are dealing here with the carnal and Jewish ideas of Zacharias himself must be rejected. It is emphatically stated that he was filled with the Holy Spirit, who made him prophesy.

3. The opinion that this section is speaking of spiritual enemies is equally unfounded. But assuming it is such enemies the text is speaking of, we are still dealing with a prophecy that has not yet been fulfilled, for in that sense Israel has still not been delivered.

4. Here again the covenant of grace is presented as the solid basis of deliverance.

Luke 2:32

A light to lighten the Gentiles, and the glory of thy people Israel.

1. The first clause of this verse is quoted as frequently as the second is neglected. Why is the latter not used as often in connection with missions among the Jews as the former is in connection with missions among the heathen?

2. Van Andel comments:

> Israel is called a light but not glory. It has, in spite of its origin and destiny, sunk away in shame. But according to this text, Christ will save it. He will take away the shame of His people from the whole earth.

Matthew 19:28

> And Jesus said unto them, Verily I say unto you, That ye which have followed me, in the regeneration when the Son of man shall sit in the throne of his glory, ye also shall sit upon twelve thrones, judging the twelve tribes of Israel.

1. Christ's being seated on the throne of His glory will one day be reality, and this is closely connected with the seating of the apostles. Peter was thinking of a literal Messianic reward.

2. From these words can be concluded that the twelve tribes of Israel will exist after the coming of the Lord in glory.

3. This statement of the Savior is in complete agreement with the expectation of His contemporaries, as we can conclude from the Apocrypha. If these expectations had been wrong, then the Truth personified would not have strengthened them in their error.

4. This statement is in agreement with the language of the old prophets (cf. Luke 22:29-30).

Matthew 23:38-39

> Behold, your house is left unto you desolate. For I say unto you, Ye shall not see me henceforth, till ye shall say, Blessed is he that cometh in the name of the Lord.

1. This statement was not fulfilled in the procession of the next day, for it obviously refers to the time after the destruction of Jerusalem. Besides, the prophecy is too solemn for the occasion of the procession. Moreover, the Lord is speaking here to the representatives of Israel as a *nation*.

2. Today there are heretics who wish to promulgate the Universalistic error that even the hardened Jews who rejected Christ will one day be accepted again. But Scripture never

understands *all of* Israel in that sense. The elect Israel of the future will represent the entire nation.

> The house, the dwelling place of Israel, will be destroyed and as an exile the nation will wander among the nations of the world. But on account of the faithfulness of God a better future awaits Israel. The salvation of the Lord, after having blessed the Gentiles, turns again at the end of the ages to Israel (Roozemeyer).

Luke 21:24

> And Jerusalem shall be trodden down of the Gentiles, until the time of the Gentiles be fulfilled.

1. The *times of the Gentiles* is the entire period during which Israel as the people of God is rejected, and hence not the fullness of the elect from among the Gentiles. Prophecy is unanimous in its testimony that the masses of the heathen will be converted by the Jews (Ps. 102:13-22; Isa. 2; Jer. 6:19-21; Mic. 4; Zech. 8; Rom. 11:15).

2. Jerusalem's being trodden down will be a reality; so also will be its re-acceptance. "He that scattereth Israel will gather him" (Jer. 31:10). The prophets repeatedly remind us that both events occur with equal certainty. Whoever denies the one fact must also deny the other. And whoever accepts the one fact must accept the other as well; both stand or fall together.

3. The word *until* in Matthew 23:29 is paralleled in Luke 21:24 and Romans 11:25. This word alone forbids us to think of Israel's rejection and fall as being permanent.

Luke 21:29-33

> And he spake to them a parable; Behold the fig tree, and all the trees; when they now shoot forth, ye see and know of your own selves that summer is now nigh at hand. So likewise ye, when ye see these things come to pass, know ye that the kingdom of God is nigh at hand. Verily I say unto you, This generation shall not pass away, till all be fulfilled. Heaven and earth shall pass away: but my words shall not pass away.

1. We are dealing here with a parable. This parable is recorded three times, and every time in the same context and for the same purpose. Nevertheless most books on the parables hardly mention it. In most cases it is systematically ignored. The reason for this must be that this parable is at variance with

the authors' prejudices, since it deals with the restoration of Israel. Again and again it is obvious what an evil role prejudice can play in the exposition of Holy Scripture. As long as the fig tree is *unfruitful,* as in Luke 13:6-9, or is cursed, as in Mark 11:12-14, these expositors take delight in applying it to Israel's wickedness. They are more than ready to push the Jew into the grave of the nations and declare him to be dead. But when it is said of the same fig tree that it will bud and that this will be a sign of the imminent end, they are suddenly averse to this truth. The Lord teaches us, however, that Israel at present resembles a dormant tree in winter, but it will soon bud and turn green again. Today's Zionism is as the budding of the fig tree and consequently a significant sign of the times.

2. With a solemn *Amen* He says that "this generation," i.e., that of the Jews, shall not pass away, till all be fulfilled. This exegesis is the only natural one; it agrees with the context and with the rule of Scripture. It receives the seal of history, because Israel still exists as the miracle of God's hand. Many recent expositors share this viewpoint, as do the marginal notes in the *Dutch Authorized Version.*

Acts 1:6

Lord, wilt thou at this time restore again the kingdom to Israel?

1. Ever since the days of John the Baptist a longing for the manifestation of the Kingdom of God had been awakened in the hearts of the people. Jesus is referring to the same thing in Matthew 11:12, when He speaks of taking the kingdom of heaven by violence. This is not a reference to a powerful conversion, as is usually assumed, but to the fiery attempt to make the Kingdom of God visible for all to see; in the same sense as the social reformers of today constantly talk of "bringing in the kingdom." Even the disciples were not free from this enthusiasm. The Lord more than once rebuked them for this, and He does so here. He chides them for their impatience and high-handedness.

2. But the Lord by no means condemns the expectation of a kingdom of Israel as such. On the contrary, He silently allows for it and agrees with it. In this respect the great prophet could have no other viewpoint than that of all the prophets.

Surely, Israel will be restored again; the Lord does not deny this. He does not say that the thoughts and expectations of the apostles are erroneous. But He wants to lead those thoughts and expectations back to two very important subjects, on the one hand to a complete submission to the decrees of the Father, and on the other hand to the expectation of the Holy Spirit (Barde).

Acts 15:14-17

This is an important section as it points out the order of the facts of salvation.

1. First the Church must be called together as God's people from the nations.

2. When this has been completed, the Lord Himself will return.

3. For what purpose is He coming again? To build again the tabernacle of David, which is fallen down (cf. Amos 9:8-15).

4. The result of the Lord's return will be that the remnant of the people will seek the Lord. Then follows the conversion of all nations during the reign of peace.

Romans 11

The meaning of this chapter is so clear that it is not necessary to develop a specific argument on it. To say that Israel here means the Church, the spiritual Israel, does violence to the words themselves. It not only leads to insurmountable difficulties and forced, arbitrary exegesis. It also requires wrenching and mistreating the true contents, something one can lower himself to do, only when he allows himself to be motivated by a blinding prejudice against this truth.

Moreover there are three matters which forbid us to interpret Israel in any other way than the people that descended from Abraham.

1. The Apostle points out several times that the national privileges of Israel are everlasting (Rom. 3:1-4; 4:13-14; 9:4-5). Here he is not speaking in the past but in the present tense. In 11:29 he says that God will not withdraw His gifts of grace and His calling. Among these gifts of grace was Canaan (Gen. 15:18; 17:7-8; 26:3; 28:13).

2. Paul himself sets the example for interpreting certain texts in the prophets literally when they demand the inclusion of the restoration of the Jews, for instance Romans 11:26-27, which is

a quotation of Isaiah 59:20-21. This shows that the words of the Apostles are referring to historic Israel and a time that is still to come. See also Romans 15:10-12, which also contains quotations from the Old Testament.

3. The New Testament always adheres to the special names of Israel and the Gentiles. The word *Israel* appears seventy times in the New Testament and must, according to John Eadie, Brookes, Wilkinson, McCaul, and others, always be taken in its ordinary, literal meaning. Even in the Epistle to the Ephesians, which speaks exclusively about the Church out of the nations, Paul always makes a careful distinction between Israel and the Church as the body of Christ. The word *Jew* appears about two hundred times and always means a Jew in contrast to the *Gentiles.* According to Dr. Brookes, the word *Jerusalem* appears more than one hundred forty times, and every time for the literal capital of the Jews, except when such a word as new, heavenly, from above, or some similar adjective accompanies it.

Usually two texts are quoted to refute the above-mentioned position, namely, Galatians 3:28 and 6:16. The first reads, "There is neither Jew nor Greek, there is neither bond nor free, there is neither male nor female: for ye are all one in Christ Jesus." If this text is to prove that converted Israel ceases to be Israel, then this verse also proves that a slave who believes ceases to be a slave, as well as that a believing man or a believing woman changes sex. In Galatians 6:16 we read, "And upon the Israel of God." This is assumed to be a clear proof that the Israel of God is the Church. But we ask with Dr. McCaul:

> Is it according to the rules of hermeneutics to give the word a different meaning here than it always has? Would it be absurd to view Israel here as the descendants of Abraham? Would that be at variance with Paul's sentiments? Does not the context even demand that we think here of historic Israel? Can even one irrefutable proof be given that the word here must be taken to mean Church?

Is it not strange that those who believe that Paul is speaking of the Church here, explain in a strictly literal sense, the already fulfilled prophecy concerning Israel? Why should a different meaning be given to unfulfilled prophecy than to fulfilled prophecy?

It cannot be said often enough that the "wandering Jew" lives among the nations as proof of literally fulfilled prophecy.

A) They have been God's *witnesses* (Isa. 43:10, 12; 44:8); in spite of themselves they still are a standing testimony to God's holiness and faithfulness.

B) They *live among all the nations* (Deut. 28:64; Jer. 31:8-10).

C) They live a *strictly separated existence* in spite of their dispersion (Num. 23:9, Esth. 3:8). Their laws regarding food and their festivities enhance this strict separation.

D) There are *promised blessings* for those who bless Israel (Gen. 12:3; Num. 24:9; Ps. 122:6, 9). No other nation has for centuries blessed Israel as much as the Netherlands, and has there been another country so blessed religiously and politically as this little country?

E) There are *threatened curses* for its detractors. Have not Egypt, Amalek, Moab, Ammon, Edom, Tyre, Sidon and the various world empires experienced this in all its terrible seriousness? We read again that the Lord punishes them so severely because they have oppressed His inheritance. Frederic the Great observed that no nation ever flourished which persecuted the Jews.

F) Their *physical appearance* is literally fulfilled prophecy. "The shew of their countenance doth witness against them" (Isa. 3:9); their bent backs (Rom. 11:10), their fearful nature (Lev. 26:36), and their restlessness (Deut. 28:65) are mentioned in prophetic texts.

G) Their *unbelief* is a sad reality (Isa. 6:9-10; Matt. 13:14; Acts 28:26; Rom. 11:8; 2 Cor. 3:15).

H) Finally, their predicted *suffering* is all too literally fulfilled during their woeful history.

Thy Word is the truth, O Lord! must be the acknowledgement of our hearts every time we look at Israel's past and present. But who with even the slightest reverence for His infallible Word would dare to turn around and say with regard to Israel's restoration, Thy Word is poetic imagination!

So we have in broad outline shown that in the distant future Israel, although not every individual in it, but as a nation, will be converted and restored to its country. For many readers this poses more questions than answers. But already much is gained if, free from the hateful curiosity that is always more interested in the how than in the importance of the matter, we set ourselves to the study of the Word of the Lord. Particularly the prophetic part of it. Scripture also tells us something, although comparatively speaking, not much, about the manner in which the old covenant people will be re-accepted. We must always keep in mind, however, that, with all the prophets the emphasis is not on the time and manner, but on the matter itself. This rule we did not wish to disregard during our study thus far. Israel will be discussed again in connection with the Millennium.

At this point let it suffice to remind ourselves that as Israel originated, continued, and still exists through a miracle, so it will also, by means of one or more miraculous acts of God, be restored at the return of the Lord, whereby the dispensation of mighty and miraculous acts of the Lord will be ushered in.

Finally we refer all those who wish to make a serious study of the manner of Israel's restoration to the excellent books on Israel by Gaebelein, Geurs, Kelly, Seiss, Bickersteth, Saphir, Baron, Esser, Du Toit, Tris, and Da Costa.

Part V
Millennium

Chapter 19

THE MILLENNIUM OR THE THOUSAND-YEAR KINGDOM

De Genestet expressed the feelings of many regarding the subject of the Millennium in one of his short, so-called layman's poems when he said:

Whoever wants to talk about the Millennium,
Let him come back after a thousand years or so;
This question we can skip for the time being,
As we have plenty of other things to talk about first.

Regardless of how well intentioned this advice of the poet may be, we do not wish to follow it. On the other hand, it is with hesitation that we grapple with a subject which evokes such aversion and disdain, and which some of our greatest theologians brush aside with a single authoritative word.

Our soul is filled with sadness and is bowed down within us because, in spite of the rich development of Reformed theology, we are forced to venture into not only uncharted but practically barricaded pathways. If we were not driven by an unquenchable thirst for the incorruptible love of the truth, we would not have the courage to stand or move forward alone. On the contrary, we would give up in despair. But the truth of God makes one free and courageous, and causes him to face the unavoidable appearance of audacity. So here again we shall unconditionally put the axe of criticism at the old stumps of prejudice and error. In so doing we are encouraged by the unshakable conviction of faith, that when the Lord comes, He will not burn our work completely as wood, hay, and stubble, but will judge it to be if not as gold and precious stones, then at least as silver.

To begin, we offer a few words about the term. The term *thousand-year reign,* or *millennium,* is by no means the most preferable, because it calls attention more to the duration than to the concept itself. The main concept is not the thousand years, but the reign, the kingdom. *Kingdom of peace* would be a better name, and the best of all is perhaps *reign of Christ.* This indicates that the Savior as the King of kings is the main person in this kingdom. The name *thousand-year kingdom,* however, has by its long standing obtained a place of its own and is the more venerable because of the *reproach of Christ* attending it.

We wish to further some proof of the reality of such a reign, or kingdom, in which righteousness and peace shall reign on earth. Then we will discuss the different Reformed viewpoints regarding these matters. Finally we will examine some objections to the thousand-year reign of Christ.

In so doing we point out that human nature needs a glorious state of peace and bliss upon earth. Man falls deep within a need of painless happiness and imperturbable peace for himself and for all mankind. His yearning for this indispensable possession is part and parcel of his essence and being. And if this need is implanted in the individual, then it must also belong to all people, since all people are of the same essence. If this need were a result of sin, then a dying unto it would be required of us, as is required unto the world and our whole old nature; it has a right to exist not only as an innate phenomenon but also as an eternal power, since God never annihilates a thing He once created.

Such a yearning of the soul would be considered selfish, if it were merely a yearning and longing for one's own happiness. But this is not the case. On the contrary, this general and usually conscious need extends to everything that breathes. Thus, for example, in socialism we find people who are rich themselves, but by virtue of this natural need, strive after a paradise of happiness for all people.

Again the objection might be made that such a need is not universal, but is found only with a few eccentrics whose mental powers have been disturbed, or with a few privileged people such as poets and philosophers. This is not the case. It is true that this longing for perfection is manifested strongest by the noblest spirits of mankind, but it is nevertheless shared by all of mankind for the simple reason that all of mankind is created in

God's image. For that reason, too, it is not something accidental, but essential and irremovable in man at all times and in all places. History and ethnology confirm this in a striking manner. All nations in their myths, traditions, and legends have dreams of a glorious future. Even if unconsciously, they all believe in the ultimate realization of their deepest desires.

Now if it is God Himself who put this yearning for a universal salvation in man, then we may safely conclude that in His own time He will materialize this desire. To the little swallow which needs a place for its young He has also given the instinct to build a nest. Would He then never satisfy the poor and hungering human heart with all its sighings, yearnings, and longings? Did not Ten Kate sing correctly?

> We sway here between a smile and a tear,
> Our days are woven from cobwebs;
> Maybe the dream of this fleeting existence
> Is but a longing for life.

The Reality of the Millennium

Is it not true that God fulfills the needs He Himself has created? Now the question arises, how and when does He fulfill this hunger and thirst after the happiness of creation? Many will answer, in heaven. But we are not dealing here with the longing of the believer for heaven. This homesickness for heaven is of a much higher caliber. Both longings are worked by God, but with this difference, that the latter is from above and the former from below. For this reason God will fulfill the longing that is from above in heaven. The other longing which originates here below, he will fulfill on earth. From the fact that God has set the age in man's heart (Eccl. 3:11, *Dutch Version*), i.e., the golden age, we can deduce that the Lord of the whole earth will some day bring about a golden age here below. The whole creation, whose groaning and travailing in pain is mixed with great yearning, is looking forward to the day of the manifestation of the children of God. One day their sighing will turn into glad songs of deliverance.

Although it is by no means illegitimate to conclude the objective from the subjective (the Confessions do this frequently) we nevertheless wish to adhere to the method of letting Scripture speak for itself. For Scripture is the only source of truth, and for that reason we turn to it.

1. *God has never repealed the original destiny of man, i.e., to have dominion in the earth.*

This constituted the immediate object of the creation of man (Gen. 1:26). Man fell, and in his fall he dragged the earth and all that is on it along with him (Gen. 3:16-19). But in the promised seed of the woman a perspective on deliverance was opened. This perspective was repeatedly confirmed by the prophets in the ages following. God's counsel regarding this earth will not be frustrated by the sin of mankind. It is a maxim in theology that the second Adam, Christ, will restore what the first has lost. He will do *more* than that, but He will *also* do this. Both Testaments repeatedly allude to this, but especially the New Testament (Acts 3:19-21; Rom. 8:19-22; 1 Cor. 15:28; Heb. 4:9; Rev. 21:5).

The question is often asked, will there be animals in heaven? No, not in heaven, in the eternity of eternities when the Son will have delivered up the Kingdom, and the Father will be all and in all. There will be animals on earth during the Millennium. Just as animals have shared in man's fall and curse, so will they share in his blessings (Isa. 11:6-9; 65:25).

2. *Scripture gives no support whatever to the opinion that the present dispensation is the final one for mankind.*

The Bible clearly speaks of several dispensations. Due to a constantly recurring mistranslation, this is not evident from our *Dutch Authorized Version.* By translating *aioon* as *world* in many places, no room is left for a separate dispensation. Our godly and learned fathers by no means did this with an evil intent or out of ignorance regarding the Greek language. Rather, this translation is due to the total lack of insight into the coming dispensation of bliss. The common idea was, and still is on the part of many, that everything here on earth will calmly run its course and gradually move on, until some day Christ will come and suddenly ignite the world and burn everything on it to destroy the wicked and take believers to heaven. Then the course of the world will have come to an end, the goal of everything will have been reached, and the eternity of eternities will have commenced.

Scripture teaches us differently, however. (See Matt. 12:32; 13:39; the *Dutch Authorized Version* is incorrect here and leaves no room for a kingdom of peace. Why is it not translated the same way as in the preceding chapter?).

In Matthew 19:28 a distinctive future age is presented, in contrast to this present age, as the regeneration of all things. In 24:3 the disciples are not asking concerning the signs of the end of the world, but of this dispensation. They were thinking of the future Messianic dispensation of bliss. In verse 8 we read, "All these are the beginning of sorrows," so that this statement becomes a message of terror. But there is hardly any doubt that the Savior means this as a word of the greatest comfort. For He literally says that these things are the beginnings of *birth pangs*. Now we know from the prophets, the Apocrypha, Romans 8:22, and 1 Thessalonians 5:1-4 that the metaphor of birth pangs is the metaphor par excellence to indicate the end of the dispensation immediately preceding the Messianic blessedness.

Ephesians 1:8-18 speaks of the dispensation of the fullness of times when Christ shall gather together all things under one head. Again this refers to the Messianic reign of the future millennial dispensation, for He is not doing it now, nor will He do it in eternity when He shall have delivered the Kingdom unto the Father.

Peter calls the same period the *time of refreshing* and the *restitution of all things*. Note well that these expressions cannot refer to the present dispensation, for these times arrive at the coming of the Lord and the conversion of Israel. Nor can the various expressions for *time* refer to *eternity*, for such a longing for eternity was a totally foreign and unknown thing to a true Israelite such as Peter. Moreover, from Acts 3:21 it is clear that these times are of such great importance that the prophets spoke concerning them.

The author of the epistle to the Hebrews also speaks in Hebrews 2:5 and 4:9 of this world to come. In the latter text he literally speaks of a *sabbath rest* that remains to the people of God. The kingdom of peace is the great day of the world's rest.

Isaiah 14:7-8 also describes the earth at perfect rest. *Peace on earth* will not come to pass until Babylon is fallen, the kingdoms of this world ground to dust, and the devil crushed underneath the feet of believers.

3. *Without assuming a new dispensation of glory before eternity commences when God shall be all and in all, we cannot do justice to a great number of Scripture texts, especially those which speak of the conversion and glory of all the nations, indeed of the whole world.*

If such a conversion had always been fully understood, people would never have dreamed of a conversion of the world by means of missions or civilization. At present we are living in the dispensation of election. The gospel that is being preached to the nations is only a witness. The goal of missions is not to improve the world, because that would presuppose that the world is good. World improvement and progress is the goal of the god of this age. A civilized unconverted person is as unregenerate as an uncivilized person. No, Simeon told the Church council at Jerusalem, and James confirmed it, that God in this dispensation had no higher goal with the missionary activity than to gather unto Himself a *people from* among the nations. And when we consider the history of missions, we observe that God obtains this goal perfectly.

If it were His goal to convert the whole world at this time, then we are forced to speak of a complete failure, because there are far more heathen now than in the time of Paul. During the last half-century nearly two hundred million were added to their number [as of 1917. Ed.]. The so-called Christian nations return to heathenism faster than the heathen nations are being christianized. Never has a city or village truly been converted in the complete sense of the word. In America about fifty million people belong to no church at all. They are like the heathen, without God and without hope in the world. In the history of mankind there has never been so much spiritual and natural misery on earth as in our wretched days.

Those who at one time hoped for a world-wide conversion need a lot of "loving" optimism to hang on to this hope. In this hope, at least, they have *not* been saved. On the contrary, the nations are exterminating each other, the foundations are being undermined, all of life is increasingly being destabilized. Politically we are headed for a heathenistic deification of the state, and socially for the most horrible revolutionary craze. Many people who have given up on idealism are embracing all kinds of sensuality with the old slogan, "Let us eat and drink, for tomorrow we die."

But does Scripture not speak of glorious things for this earth and its inhabitants who are bowed down under the burden of sin and guilt? It most certainly does. The Lord has sworn by His holy name that the earth will be filled with His glory (Num. 14:21; Isa. 11:9; Hab. 2:14). From the last two references we learn that this will take place after the judgment of the nations and not until the reign of Christ's peace.

All nations will call Christ blessed (Ps. 72:17). All the ends of the earth will turn to the Lord. All they that are fat upon earth, i.e., all glorious and great ones, will worship Jehovah, the God of Israel (Ps. 22:28-30). Ethiopia, i.e., dark Africa, will hasten to stretch out its hands to God (Ps. 68:31-32). All heathen will honor Him (Ps. 86:9; 87; 96; 97; 98; 99; 100; 102:15-22; Isa. 42:1; 43:9; 45:22; 65:22-23). This idea is repeated over and over, especially in the second main division of Isaiah. "Everything that hath breath, praise the Lord!" is the basic note of all Old Testament prophets and psalmists, and this will become glorious reality some day.

In the New Testament it is not any different. John the Baptist points to Christ as the Lamb of God that *taketh away* the sin of the *world*. Let us not stint these words, but take them as seriously as any other statement in Scripture. Christ speaks of the new birth, Peter of the restoration of all things. Every knee will bow unto Jesus. Philippians 2:10-11 does not apply to this age, nor can it refer exclusively to punishment, as is often wrongfully concluded. This text, too, is to be taken as a reference to a future age. Christ will save the world (John 3:17). His name is Savior of the world (1 John 4:14). We must accept what these texts say and not force them into the straitjacket of a system. The idea of a universal salvation is unbiblical, but that does not alter the fact that a natural explanation of this text, and of many others as well, fully justifies the statement that Satan will not carry away the majority of souls as his prey.

Dr. Abraham Kuyper was aware of these texts in both Testaments. In order to do justice to the broad scope of the long row of texts, he tried to cover this by his extensive development of the doctrine of common grace. Many of his followers carry this to the extreme and greatly misapply it. Nevertheless this great thinker comforted himself with the thought that the tree of mankind will be saved. We agree with him here, but on the basis of his standpoint this is then a strange tree indeed. However, on the basis that a massive conversion of heathen will take place, this can indeed be said.

Nations will be saved and the kings of the earth will bring their glory into the new Jerusalem. All *nations* will still be blessed in Abraham (Gal. 3:8). Abraham is not called the heir of the world for nothing. Salvation, and note well that it does not say the Savior only, is of the Jews. This is an urgent reason for all the nations and especially for all Christians to appreciate Israel. For what end does God still cause the Jews to endure? He Himself says by the mouth of one of His prophets, "Destroy it not; for a blessing is in it."

After the return of Christ, Israel, delivered and restored, will carry the light of salvation to the ends of the earth. When we ask, "*by what* will the nations be converted," the answer must be, "by Israel" (Ps. 67:7; 102:16; Isa. 9:6; 27:6; 43:21; Mic. 5:6-7; Zeph. 3:19-20; Zech. 8:13). And when will they be converted? The answer to this question must be, "after the coming of the Lord when Israel itself is first converted" (see Acts 15:17, Rom. 11:12-15, and numerous texts in the Old Testament, especially Ps. 67).

4. *In the Psalms and the prophets we find numerous references to certain future events.*

These events have never yet been fulfilled in the past, cannot be fulfilled in the present dispensation, and cannot refer to eternal glory (Ps. 72; Pss. 96—100; Isa. 2, cf. Mic. 4; Isa 11:12; 25; 26; 35; 40—60; Jer. 31:31-34; 33:14-22; Ezek. 6:4-8; Dan. 2:44-45; 7:13-14; Hos. 14:6-9; Joel 3:16-21; Amos 9:13-15; Obad. 17-21; Nah. 1:15; Hab. 2:14; Zeph. 3:16-20; Hag. 2:22-23; Zech. 9:10-17; 10:6-12; Mal. 1:11; 4:2-3). All biblical experts, even the most radical critics, agree that glorious things are said of Israel. According to them, all those grand expectations have been given the lie by the outcome. They proceed from the assumption that such a miracle is impossible. They do not understand Israel and usually hold the opinion that its history has come to an end. Whoever denies miracles finds none with regard to Israel, for it is the miracle-nation par excellence.

Even J. H. Bavinck agrees that according to the prophets the Anointed of the Lord will lead Israel back from the country of exile, that this will be a glorious occasion and will coincide with the conversion of Israel and the restoration of the temple and its worship, and that the prophets predict a golden age in which not only Israel but also the Gentiles will share. If one thinks that this professor believes all this, he is sadly mistaken. No, according to him the prophets are only using earthly images and sensuous forms into which they pour eternal contents; the shell becomes a carrier of an imperishable core, which at times even in the Old Testament breaks through to the surface. Israel's great mistake was that it did not penetrate to that core. And thus chiliasm originated, which is therefore of Jewish and even Persian origin. The strength of this chiliasm seems to be the Old Testament, but in reality this is not so; the Old Testament is absolutely not chiliastic. With its Messianic kingdom it depicts the completed Kingdom of God that is without end and lasts forever. That is more or less Bavinck's presentation.

It must immediately strike anyone who has studied prophecy that there is a striking resemblance between this viewpoint and that of the moderate critics. How in this manner can the texts applied to Christ's first coming be said to have been literally fulfilled? It is impossible to explain these glorious descriptions of the future with any just semblance of eternal glory. For we must hold then that throughout all eternity there will be *heathen, animals, sinners,* and many more things, which are simply unthinkable as being in eternal glory. Even the last enemy, death, would never be annihilated. Or is death perhaps part of the shell in which the core of eternal glory is hidden?

Dr. Bavinck can know that all prophecy insofar as it has been fulfilled has always been literally fulfilled. He can know that God Himself holds up a literal fulfillment as the touchstone of true prophecy over against false prophecy. It cannot be unknown to him that the apologetic value of prophecy vis à vis unbelief lies exactly in its most exact and precise fulfillment. Hence what right and justification does he have to speak of shell and core with regard to unfulfilled prophecy?

We request our readers to read carefully the texts referred to above together with the exegesis given by this learned professor, who in other respects is to be esteemed so highly, and they will find that this exegesis must lead to the most horrible absurdities. Whereas on the other hand all these matters can be explained quite naturally as speaking of a separate dispensation in which the world is only partly glorified.

5. *Revelation 20 alone is sufficient proof for this teaching.*

We are referring here to what was said earlier about this chapter in connection with the first resurrection. In addition we quote the observations made on this chapter by Henry Alford, Dean of Canterbury, who himself is not a fulfledged chiliast. It is the testimony of someone who is more than qualified to express his opinion concerning exegetical matters, which he does as follows.

> On one point I have ventured to speak strongly, because my conviction on it is strong, founded on the rules of fair and consistent interpretation. I mean, the necessity of accepting literally the first resurrection, and the millennial reign. It seems to me that if in a sentence where two resurrections are spoken of with no mark of distinction between them (it is otherwise in John v. 28, which is commonly alleged for the view which I am combating),—in a sentence where, one resurrection having been related, 'the rest of the dead' are afterwards mentioned,—we are at liberty to understand the former one figuratively and spiritually, and the latter literally and materially, then there is an end of all definite meaning in plain words, and the Apocalypse, or any other book, may mean anything we please. It is a curious fact that those who maintain this, studious as they generally are to uphold the primitive interpretation, are obliged, not only to wrest the plain sense of words, but to desert the unanimous consensus of the primitive Fathers, some of whom lived early enough to have retained apostolic tradition on this point. Not 'til chiliastic views had run into unspiritual excesses, was this interpretation departed from.

Reformed Viewpoints Regarding the Millennium

Those who call themselves Reformed have divergent views on Revelation 20, which points out the need for a natural and obvious meaning of terms. For those who desire an excellent summary of the different theories concerning the Millennium, we refer to *Explanation* by Moses Stuart, to Schaff in his American edition of *Lange's Commentary,* S. J. DuToit, *Unfulfilled Prophecy,* and to the article "Millennium" in the Schaff-Herzog Encyclopedia by C. A. Briggs. We are interested here only in the different explanations by Reformed writers. The most important views among them can be reduced to four, and these can, in connection with the time of fulfillment, be divided with regard to the *past,* the *present,* the *future,* and *eternity.* Here follows only a brief statement regarding each of these views.

1. *With regard to the past we find among Reformed writers mainly three views concerning the Millennium.*

A) According to Augustine's theory, the kingdom of peace started with the first coming of Christ. Owing to à Marck's influence, this view has always had many adherents. Augustine, however, understands the number thousand in a figurative sense as referring to all of the present dispensation, whereas à Marck ends the Millenium in the eleventh century.

B) Others say the thousand years began with Constantine the Great about the year 300, and ended in the year 1300, with the wars against the Waldensians, and the rampage of Turks and Tartars. This is more or less the view of Pieter, Jacob Keur, Hugo Grotius, and Johannes Cocceius.

C) Ernst Wilhelm Hengstenberg starts the Millennium in the year 800, with the reign of Charlemagne, and ends it with the French Revolution. Only very few followed him in this respect.

The pointed criticism by Isaac Da Costa is applicable to all of these views when he says,

Professor Hengstenberg says that the Millennium has already been here. Well, then it must have taken place in a dream, for nobody has noticed anything of it.

2. *The number of those who place the Millennium in the present is legion.*

The far-reaching influence of Augustine in this regard is unmistakable. This view, too, appears in various forms. All consider the figure *thousand* as symbolic for this entire dispensation. Nevertheless opinion differs greatly regarding the nature of the Millennium during this dispensation. Mainly speaking, there are again three opinions.

A) J. H. Bavinck explains that the reign of the believers during the Millennium refers to the presence of the departed souls with Christ in the intermediate state. More or less of the same opinion are Charles Hodge, Benjamin B. Warfield, Vos, Ten Hoor, and Danhof.

B) Others believe that this dispensation of grace under the reign of Christ is the Millennium. This is the actual view of Augustine, adopted by Rome and many Reformed theologians. They identify the Church with the Kingdom of God and so the Church can say, "I sit a queen," or with the Reformed university professor E. Böhl, "We are surrounded by it" [the Millennium].

C) Finally, many consider the practical and subjective experience of the grace of Christ in the heart as being the Millennium, i.e., Helenius De Cock, Kohlbrügge, and many more.

> Whoever knows the sweet reign of grace is living in the Millennium, which is still being looked for by those who have not purified their consciences from dead works and hence have not entered into the rest of God (Kohlbrügge).

The main objection to these views is that no serious attempt is made at coming to grips with the message of Revelation 20. One does not get the impression that an honest, conscientious effort is made to understand what the Spirit is teaching there. For it certainly may be considered worthy of everyone's attention (a) that we are dealing here with a brief and succinct declaration by the Holy Spirit, and (b) that the divine Author so strongly emphasizes the number thousand that in a few verses He repeats it six times. When someone points out the same thing again and again, I conclude that he is serious about the matter. Why then are people so unfair with the great Author of the Word? Are they not grieving Him by so doing?

3. *The number of those who view the thousand years as a future state of bliss for the Church on earth is also very great.*

The Arian, Daniel Whitby is usually considered the father of this expectation. In the Netherlands, Campegius Vitringa must be considered the chief spokesman for those who entertain this expectation. His famous commentary on the Revelation of John is considered the leading one of all those that followed. In the main, Brakel, Groenewegen, Koelman, Janszoon, Klinkenberg, and Hendrik de Cock (the father of the Secession) agree with him.

This view is known in English-speaking countries as postmillennialism. The first term indicates the expectation of Christ's coming after the Millennium; the second is the name for the teaching that Christ will be coming before and for the purpose of instituting the thousand-year kingdom. If we can still speak of any theological controversy in England and America, then it is concerning this matter. It is indeed of far-reaching significance. Although many are not conscious of this fact, in Reformed circles these principles vie silently for priority. Concepts infiltrate, even though their names may be unknown to us.

Our objections to postmillennialism are too great and too many to enumerate briefly. Yet for the sake of completeness we list a few.

A) Postmillennialism does not take sin and Satan seriously and consequently fosters a superficial and pernicious optimism.

B) It identifies the Church with the Kingdom of Christ and thus walks in the fatal footsteps of the Roman Church.

C) It ignores the clear pronouncements by Christ and the apostles that the condition of the world and the Church will be indescribably woeful at the return of the Lord.

D) It fails to recognize the various dispensations. All the clamor of *claiming the whole world for Chirst,* which more or less agrees with the English expression *bringing in the Kingdom,* is, regardless of how well intentioned, nothing but sinful anticipation, and a premature reaching for the future dispensation of bliss.

E) It entertains the error that the entire counsel of God has already been fulfilled with the first coming of the Messiah. Particularly His cry on the cross, "It is finished," is explained as though He had already completed all His mediatorial *work.* This error is by no means as innocent as people think. It is detrimental to the life of hope.

F) It does not take the doctrine of the Antichrist seriously. He is usually identified with the pope. If, on the other hand, we still expect a distinct man of sin, then he must manifest himself while Satan is bound; but the Revelation of John teaches that Antichrist receives all his power from the dragon.

G) This theory does not do justice to the Jews. And if its adherents still mention a literal restoration of Israel as a nation in Canaan, they do so in spite of their view and contrary to it.

H) Christ has repeatedly said that believers must watch, as they do not know when He will be coming. According to Scripture this watching for Christ is no less important than being on our guard against the devil. There is no salvational act from which Scripture derives so many motives for a godly walk as from watching and waiting for the Lord's return. It must be obvious, however, that if before the Lord's coming there will first be a millennium, then He cannot very well be expected by His own.

4. *Finally, we note Dr. Abraham Kuyper's views on the thousand-year reign.*

According to him, this designation of time is nothing but a symbol for eternity. Undoubtedly many people who prefer that others do their thinking for them will adopt his views, as has Dr. R. L. Haan, to our amazement. One must read Revelation 20:3-8 on this view, revising as follows:

> And cast him into the bottomless pit, and shut him up, and set a seal upon him, that he should deceive the nations no more, till *eternity* should be fulfilled: and *after eternity* he must be loosed a little season. ... But the rest of the dead lived not again until *eternity* was finished. ... And when *eternity* is expired, Satan will be loosed out of his prison, and shall go out to deceive the nations which are in the four quarters of the earth, Gog and Magog, to gather them together for battle.

We thus arrive at the greatest absurdities. If this exegesis did not originate with such a great mind it would not be worth a refutation.

In this tangle of contradictory opinions it creates a strange impression and fills us with amazement that chiliasm is being ridiculed from every side. Again and again it is the recipient of unkind jabs. All kinds of loose and unproved accusations are slung at those who hold to the simple words as they are recorded in the Word of God. If the matter were not so serious we might compose an amusing list of contradictory accusations which could fittingly be returned to the addresses from which they came.

Objections to the Millennium

Throughout the centuries there has been no "heresy" against which such an unfair and unreasonable battle has been waged as against chiliasm (the Millennium). It was called absurd without first examining whether it might be true. It would be wise to learn the lesson taught by history. Israel's sages considered it absurd that the Messiah should suffer, die, and be buried. Celsus, the Mocker, considered it repulsive that the Son of God would be born of a woman. Modernists considered the resurrection ridiculous. It does not behoove us to call something absurd without full examination, especially when the opponent adheres to the true words of God.

Today people are no longer as vehemently opposed to the thousand-year reign as they used to be. They have not been able to deny the glorious fruits from this tree. It must be known to those who keep up with the times that the most faithful preachers in England and America are usually chiliasts. Willem Bilderdijk and Isaac Da Costa in the Netherlands constituted as it were the brass wall against apostasy at the time of the Awakening there. This does not alter the fact, however, that Dutch theologians in particular still continue to fulminate unreasonably against this teaching. Fairness demands that we briefly listen to the grievances that are continually launched against chiliasm.

1. *Daniel in his second chapter says nothing about the Millennium, nor does Christ mention it in His discourse on the Mount of Olives.*

This is a strange accusation. These same people attack higher criticism's *argumentum ex silentium,* the argument from silence, as being superficial and one-sided. But is this not the case with their own argument here? Besides, did not Daniel in 2:35-37 speak of a kingdom? Did not the stone grow into a great mountain that filled the whole earth? According to the metaphorical language of Scripture, this mountain is the image of a kingdom (cf. the Scofield Reference Bible note on this and also on 7:27). Only the thousand-year duration of this kingdom is, understandably, not indicated here. The demand that Daniel and Christ should have mentioned it is the more surprising since these people have first denied all power of proof to Revelation 20:5. Besides, if we must demand several indubitable scriptural proofs for every doctrine, then we shall have to abandon several other doctrines (see Kuyper, *Encyclopedia,* II, 244). In addition, Christ never spoke of the covenant of works, original sin, Antichrist, and numerous other truths. May we justifiably conclude from this fact that these doctrines are not based on Scripture?

2. *It has always led people to fanaticism and enthusiasm.*

History contradicts this. That which a few heretical hotheads have perpetrated may not be charged to this teaching, for then we could with equal justification accuse the doctrine of election of false passivity, fatalism, and what have you, since that kind of misuse has been made of this doctrine. The fanatics of Munster and the nudists of Amsterdam were postmillennialists. If it must be admitted that shameful misuse has been made of this teaching, then this very fact points to its excellence, because the most excellent things in the world are subject to Satan's resistance.

3. *It treats Scripture in an arbitrary manner.*

With full conviction we cast this serious accusation into the face of the accusers, for this accusation has never yet been proved. Also, it has been frequently shown that the accusers deserved the accusation themselves. The same thing can be said about the accusation that chiliasts differ widely in their views. The *truth* is that we are dealing with a rare unanimity hardly found anywhere else. Here a Reformed man like Van Andel and a Confessional man like Gunning, Jr., have the same views as the Methodist Blackstone. Here we do not find different views but only one, i.e., that the Lord is coming for the purpose of founding a kingdom of peace.

4. *The teaching of the Millennium proves too much and is fraught with insurmountable difficulties.*

It is unreasonable to demand of premillennialists that they furnish answers to all kinds of difficult and curious questions. Every truth leaves unanswered questions. This may be said particularly about the last things, where more than anywhere else we gaze from the temporal things into the fathomless depths of eternity.

Those who make this accusation usually think of two things:

A) The restoration of the heathen nations. If Israel is to be restored as a nation, they object, then also there must be a restoration of the heathen nations of Ammon, Moab, Elam,

Egypt, Assyria, and even Sodom (see, for instance, Isa. 11:15-16; 19; Jer. 49:39; Ezek. 16:53-55). In response, we ask, what objection can there be against believing that in the "times of restitution of all things" these nations will also revive and flourish? We know that there will be nations in the Millennium, so that we are not compelled to adopt the ungodly doctrine of a second probation. The restoration of these nations will pose no greater miracle to the Almighty than the restoration of the Jews. Is it not remarkable that this kind of Bible text is systematically ignored? We are more than willing to exchange our view for a better one.

B) They think even more about the temple of Ezekiel, so carefully and exactly described in the eight final chapters of his prophecy. Willem Bilderdijk thought the system of the chiliasts so attractive that he was amazed that it was not generally accepted. Next to the terror of the Munster fanatics, nothing frightens Reformed people more than this temple. We admit that it is difficult to explain these chapters. Therefore, we make the following brief observations.

(1) This one difficult section, Ezekiel 40—47, cannot render the many clear texts on the subject powerless. The difficulty here is partly the result of prejudice and partly of laziness. Biblical theologians have as yet spent very little time and effort on this section. Only the hand of the diligent maketh rich.

(2) Ezekiel 40 through 47 is not speaking of the Church. At the same time this suggests that the Reformed explanation is unsatisfactory, for it usually considers them a description of the Church.

(3) Nor do we find here a description of heaven. For then it would not be true that "Eye hath not seen, nor ear heard ... the things that God hath prepared for them that love him." So this explanation, too, does violence to the words and can therefore not be the right one.

(4) This temple has a specific meaning and must therefore explain something specific. We must accept it, because the Holy Spirit did not do superfluous work here. If all of Scripture is given by inspiration and is profitable, then so is this section. If not, then let someone prove this and we shall

cut this section out of the Bible or add it to the Apocrypha. If no proof can be given, then, out of reverence for the Word of God, we must have serious regard for this section.

(5) We must not ignore and despise the clear indications given by God Himself, but joyfully accept them to help us with the explanation. We find then that the vision of this temple is described in relation to a certain *people,* a certain *time,* and a certain *place.*

The context and the subject matter demand that we conclude that the temple is for the *nation of the Jews* and in the *land of Israel* (see Ezek. 40:2). But learned men such as Orelli, Volck, Abraham Kuenen, and others, have shown that nothing in the history of Israel corresponds to this description. Hence the conclusion is unavoidable that we must expect a future fulfillment. Moreover the context (Ezek. 39:27-29) tells us clearly that this vision will become reality after the judgment of the nations, after Israel has triumphed over Gog and Magog, and after Israel is converted and lives in its own land.

(6) But what about those sacrifices? These do not detract anything from the only perfect sacrifice of our precious Mediator. But why cannot these sacrifices have a retroactive power to show Israel its guilt over against the precious blood of the Lamb? At least that is the thought held by a long list of able and godly exegetes.

5. *This view of millennialism makes Christianity materialistic.* If this were the case, then we should reject it with contempt and even vehemently combat it. We are merely following what Abraham Kuyper wrote in *De Heraut* of July 7, 1912.

> What objection could be made to the fact that when this earth is going to perish one day and a new earth under a new firmament takes its place, also on that earth, but then in a far more glorious form, again a new realm of nature would shine in far greater abundance, and among this also an animal kingdom?

When the Rev. G. Hospers quotes this statement, he says, "Truly, Dr. Kuyper is, to quote a word from Scripture with a chiliastic application, not far from the Kingdom of God."

The opponents of chiliasm give the impression that they are fighting a specter they have conjured up in their ignorance and fear. It would not be difficult to compose an anthology from the writings of the opponents of the chiliasts in which would be found the elements of a pure biblical chiliasm. Thus Johann Keil in his commentary on Ezekiel attacks it extensively, and yet he, too, teaches a first resurrection of the righteous, a return of the Jews, and that the day of Christ is a dispensation of a thousand years. When one admits these three matters, then one is to all intents and purposes a biblical chiliast.

6. *An objection often heard and closely connected with the preceding is that it would be a humiliation for Christ.*

This objection is based on a misconception and proceeds from the assumption that the glorified Christ one day will actually come to reside on earth during this sinful dispensation. This is by no means the case. No one emphasizes Christ's exaltation and glory more than a biblical chiliast. "The kings of Sheba and Seba shall offer gifts. Yea, all kings shall fall down before him: all nations shall serve him" (Ps. 72:10). None of these things shall be a humiliation for Christ.

7. *And finally it is thrown in the face of chiliasm that not a single Confession mentions this teaching.*

The claim that it should be found in the confessions would be valid, if the Church had painstakingly developed a doctrine of the last things, as it did other doctrines, but she never did so. Moreover the confessions are strictly ecclesiastical, often high-ecclesiastical, whereas chiliasm emphasizes the Kingdom more than the Church, the Scriptures more than the confessions.

It cannot rightly be said that chiliasm has been rejected by all confessions or appears in none. The Nicene Creed seems to be strongly advocating this teaching. At the first general assembly of the Church in A.D. 325, no less than three hundred and eighteen bishops from all countries were gathered together. At this assembly a general creed was composed for the universal Church of those days. In this creed all heresies are attacked, but chiliasm is not attacked by a single word. On the contrary, the closing lines of this creed state, "And I look for the Resurrection of the dead, and the Life of the world to come." The council explained this article thus:

> The world was made less on account of God's providence, for God knew beforehand that man would sin. For that reason we look forward

to new heavens and a new earth according to the Holy Scriptures: the appearance in the Kingdom of our great God and Savior, who will become visible to us. And as Daniel says, "The holy ones of the Most High shall receive the Kingdom." And there will be a pure and holy earth, the land of the living and not of the dead, of which David, seeing with the eye of faith, is speaking (Ps. 27:13): "I believe that I shall see the goodness of the Lord in the land of the living"—the land of the meek and humble. Christ says, "Blessed are the meek, for they shall inherit the earth." And the prophet says (Isa. 26:6), "The feet of the meek and lowly shall walk in it."

The word *millennium* is not used, but the matter is obviously meant.

Those who appeal to the testimony of the confessions are usually referring to the Lutheran Confession of Augsburg and the Second Helvetic Confession adhered to in Reformed circles, both of which, so these people believe, condemn chiliasm. It is clear, however, that both contain a refutation of Anabaptism, which is unbiblical postmillennialism in its most devastating consequence and manifestation.

After having considered the proofs for and the objections against the thousand-year kingdom, our conclusion can only be that it is a glorious object of hope to the believing heart and a great comfort in our troubled days.

Chapter 20

QUESTIONS AND VIEWPOINTS REGARDING THE MILLENNIUM

The scope of this book compels us to be as concise as possible. For this reason we will answer briefly a few questions and consider the Millennium from several points of view.

In what manner is the thousand-year kingdom coming?

The answer must be, first, in the negative, *not by the hand of man* (Dan. 2:34). Enumerate all the excellent Christian activities you can think of, such as missions, Bible distribution, Christian education (both higher and lower), all these things will not usher in the kingdom of Christ. The Lord Himself is coming to establish it. When we pray, "Thy kingdom come," we are praying for that coming. Postmillennialism, which expects a state of bliss on earth for the Church in this dispensation, which bliss its adherents consider to be the kingdom, must lead to the greatest disappointment. The stone that rolls down from Zion's mountains is cut out without human hands. All effort to usher in this kingdom is nothing but an activity rooted in the covenant of works, a denial of the future work of Christ, an overestimation of mankind, and Pelagianism on a grand scale.

The kingdom of Christ is coming with and through the *parousia* (the personal presence) of Christ. Ezekiel predicted in 21:26-27 that the crown would lie overturned, until He would come who has a right to reign. As long as He is absent there will be strife and ill-will among the nations. The kingdom is wholly dependent on the King.

Before the coming of the kingdom of peace, the two most terrible events that ever befell the world will take place, namely, the *judgment of the nations* and the attending *great tribulation*. Regarding the former, see Daniel 2:34ff; Joel 3; and Revelation 11:17-19; 14:15-20. Note especially the preceding context in these passages which speak of the kingdom of peace. Actually all the plagues mentioned in Revelation 6—19 belong to this period.

What the judgment of the nations is to the world, the *great tribulation* is to Israel. Although still unconverted at that time, Israel will have been partially gathered from among the nations in its own land. Isaiah 18 and 60 give the impression that one or more maritime powers will aid the Jews in this respect. Gog and Magog and the Antichrist will fearfully oppress Israel. (On the great tribulation, see Jer. 30:4-8; Ezek. 38; 39; Dan. 9:26-27; 12:1, 9-11; Matt. 24:14-28; 2 Thess. 2:1-12; 13:11-16; 17:7-14; 19:21, and also the preceding contexts of the various descriptions of the kingdom of peace.) A small-scale example of these judgments occurred at the beginning of Solomon's reign; the evildoers were removed before the kingdom of peace began to flourish. Neither is there any Universalism for Israel.

How must we picture the nature of the reign of Christ?

From of old, poetic spirits have let their imaginations run wild on this matter, but all unbiblical and excessive speculations are to be strictly avoided here. We must keep in mind the essential difference between Israel and the Church. The result of identifying the one with the other is confusion.

This confusion concerns the *King,* the *reign,* the *partners,* the *place,* the *glory,* and the *duration* of this kingdom. On each of these items I will give a brief observation.

1. *Christ is indeed the King, but of Israel, and not of the Church.*

Between Him and the Church there is a much closer relationship. It is sad to realize that many believers think they are honoring their Savior by referring to Him as their King and the King of the Church. Since it is mostly the language of love that speaks thus, the Lord, who looks at the heart, will consider it as such, but we are dealing with a gross error of the mind.

Christ is the King of Israel and the Head of the Church. He will restore again the kingdom to Israel (2 Sam. 7:8-16; Ps. 110; Isa. 4:2; 9:6; 11; 32:1; Jer. 3:12; 23:5; Zech. 6:12; 9:9; Matt.

19:28; 27:11, 37; Luke 1:32-33; Acts 1:6). To understand the Millennium we must first look at Israel. "From that moment on He again restores the kingdom to Israel" (Van Andel).

2. *This distinction also casts light on the reign of Christ.*

He reigns *with* His Church *over* Israel, and thus over the nations. The Jews are the people of the earth and remain so eternally. As a nation, Israel does not go to heaven but has Canaan as an everlasting possession. The theocracy will be restored; Israel will receive its own state, society, judges, counselors, and king from the house of David (see Ps. 45:17; Isa. 1:26; 32:1; 60:17-22; Jer. 23:4; 30:9, 21; 33:17; Ezek. 34:23-24; 37:24-25; Hos. 3:5; Obad. 21).

None of these things can be said of the Church, however. Her glory exceeds all this. As high as the bride of the king is above the people of the king, so high is the Church above Israel.

3. *In the Millennium there will not be just one people of Christ, but three totally different classes of people.*

These three classes are: A) the *Church,* B) *Israel,* and C) the *nations.* It is regretable that our Bibles often have the word *heathen* where the word should have been translated *nations.* The Church is like the glorified Christ, so she will have the greatest glory.

> Israel as heir of the world will have dominion over all the nations; it will be a nation of prophets, priests and kings, without which sword or spear and only by spiritual power will have dominion over the nations of the world (Van Andel).

The tables will be turned; the nations lie at the feet of Israel because Israel itself has fallen down at Messiah's feet. (See Ex. 5:22; Deut. 28:13; 1 Chron. 21:21-22; Isa. 31:6-7; 40—66; Ezek. 37:13; Zech. 8:23; Rom. 11:26. The Psalms constantly point this out, see Pss. 3, 9, 22, 25, 67, 68, 72.)

Then, and only then, does Israel receive the fulfillment of all its promised blessing and prosperity. If the prophecies concerning its suffering and the destruction of its land have been literally fulfilled, then we may expect the promises of blessing and prosperity to be just as literally fulfilled. One day Israel will cry out in ecstasy, "This land that was desolate is become like the garden of Eden; and the waste and desolate and ruined cities are become fenced, and are inhabited" (Ezek. 36:35).

4. *Where will the reign of Christ be?*

This is a matter of great concern to some people. They abhor the idea of Christ being an earthly king. But let them put their minds at ease. For in the first place, *on the earth* is something quite different from *earthly*. His kingdom is never *of the world*. No one emphasizes this truth as strongly as does a true biblical chiliast. The happiness of man shall not be born from the sea, i.e., from the womb of the nation. The stone rolls down from on high out of Zion's mountains.

We must also remember that the contrast between heaven and earth which, due to sin, still exists, will have been removed. Christ Himself will restore all things again and gather them under one Head into an absolute monarchy, to which all of creation looks forward. We must not picture the Lord of lords and the King of kings as a crowned head in this present wretched dispensation.

Scripture gives us sufficient indications that Christ's actual dwelling place and majesty are *above the heavens* (Ps. 8:1). Heaven is His proper dwelling place (1 Kings 8:49). From this place of glory He reigns, together with His Church, over Israel and the nations to whom He apparently will also manifest Himself constantly. The reign of Christ will be in heaven, on earth, over all nations, but particularly over His people Israel.

5. *The reign of Christ will have both heavenly glory and earthly glory.*

When we maintain the eternal difference between Israel and the Church, we shall comprehend that in the thousand-year kingdom there will be neither exclusive heavenly glory nor exclusive earthly glory, but both—for the Church, heavenly glory and for restored Israel, earthly glory. The Church is blessed with all spiritual blessings in heaven in Christ and its destination is not to dwell in Palestine, for that is Israel's destination (see 1 Cor. 15:40-42).

6. *As for the duration of Christ's reign, we are not yet dealing with eternity, and so it has an end.*

The Scriptures indicate in Revelation 20 that this kingdom will last one thousand years.

Not a single irrefutable proof can be forewarded as to why this delineation of time, which is repeated six times, should be spiritualized. The Church of the first three centuries understood it literally. Even in the Middle Ages people understood the number *thousand* literally. A literal interpretation of this number agrees with the symbolism of numbers in Scripture; the thousand-year Kingdom is the celebration of the sabbath of Israel and of the whole world. It is the year of Jubilee of all Jubilees, the year of the good pleasure of the Lord.

But if we do take this expression to mean a thousand years, we are faced with a problem. Numerous texts tell us that the kingdom and reign of Christ will be eternal (see 2 Sam. 7:16; Ps. 10:12-18; 18:46-50; 45:3-6, 17; 68:1, 3, 16; 89:2-5, 23-37; 145:6-21; Isa. 9:3-7; Jer. 33:14-26; Ezek. 37:24-28; Dan. 2:44; 7:10-14, 27; Mic. 4:1-7; Luke 1:30-33). How can the thousand-year reign and eternity be reconciled with each other? Many cannot reconcile them and therefore reject the thousand years. To solve this difficulty, we must make a distinction between Israel and the Church, and recognize Israel's position. When we do this, the difficulty disappears immediately. Christ will be King over *the house of Jacob forever.* Gabriel assures us emphatically in Luke 1:33 that His kingdom on the *throne of David will have no end.*

So Christ's reign over the *nations, sin, Satan,* and *death* comes to an end. The kingdom of peace is at the same time as the day of judgment. In reality that kingdom will be as we have everywhere found it announced by the prophets, both preceded and followed by the judgments. On this point both 1 Corinthians 15:24-26 and Revelation 20 are helpful. When the nations, sin, Satan, and death have been done away with, Jesus will deliver up the *reign over the world* to His Father, but He Himself remains forever the King over the *house of Jacob,* that is to say, *Israel.* And in this sense His Church as His bride will, of course, reign eternally with Him.

Moreover, to understand the reign of Christ correctly, we must make a distinction between Christ Himself as the King of the Jews, and the *ruler* as David's descendant. Far too often the difference between these two illustrious personalities has been overlooked. That is the reason things have been ascribed to Christ that can only be said of an earthly ruler. Ezekiel 45 and 46 speak most extensively of this ruler. But we meet him again and again in prophecy (see also, for instance, Isa. 11:10; 32:1;

Jer. 30:9, 21; 33:17; Ezek. 34:23-24; 37:24-25; Hos. 3:6; Mic. 2:13). Sometimes things are said of this prince which cannot apply to Christ, but only to a mortal man (see, for instance, Ezek. 45:22; 46:18; 48:21). Students of prophecy, such as Arno C. Gaebelein, Bromet, Esser, and others, assume that the prince mentioned does not refer to Christ, but to a descendant from David's house who, as a perfect theocratic ruler, will be the true vicar of Christ. Hence the ages-old dream of Rome in this regard will then also come true.

How must we picture the earth as the dwelling place of man?

The curse will be initially removed. As the earth shared in the manifestation of the glory of the children of God (Rom. 8:19-22), then Christ will do what has been sung by little children, "Who unites together heaven and earth." It will be a time of the greatest fertility (Deut. 28; Ezek. 34:26-27; Hos. 2:20-22; Joel 3:18; and many other texts). Then the knotty problem of the Middle East will be solved. There will be an abundance of peace, and militarism will no longer impoverish nor vex the nations. The nations will no longer learn war (Ps. 72; Isa. 2:4; Mic. 4:3).

The animal kingdom will celebrate together with man. Their cruel, predatory nature will change into gentleness (Isa. 11:6-8; 65:25).

In spite of all the glory, however, death will still be found on earth. It is the *last enemy* to be annihilated. Satan will have already been bound, while this enemy still persists. If we picture the day of Christ as a day of twenty-four hours, then this statement by Paul makes no sense. But when we see that death continues on, while Christ as reigning King has already done away with all other enemies, all dominion, all power, and all strength, then a surprising light is shed on this word (1 Cor. 15:24-26).

We must not forget that death is a servant of God on account of sin. Apparently the children of God will not die. At least Scripture does not say anything about it. It does say that a sinner being a hundred years old shall be accursed (Isa. 65:20). There are some who hold the opinion that saints like Enoch will be changed alive or, after having died, will be immediately raised again. But where Scripture is silent it behooves us to be the same.

In any case it is clear that sin will not have disappeared altogether, so that death cannot be dispensed with as yet. Some nations will only feign their submission to Christ, so that after his release Satan can again organize a revolt against the Lord.

Even though death may not have disappeared altogether, this strong enemy will to a large extent have lost its power. The lives of men will be miraculously lengthened. That death will be a scarce occurrence, even among the unconverted, can clearly be concluded from Isaiah 65:20. A person already a century old will be considered a child and death will be seen as a special judgment of God.

In spite of almost two thousand years of preaching, the earth is still covered with the darkness of ignorance and error, but then the earth will be full of the knowledge and the glory of God as the waters cover the sea. How often do we hear these words in the prayers of the godly, and how little it is realized that these prayers will never be answered in this dispensation, but only in the coming dispensation of bliss. The covering of the face that is still cast over all people will then be removed. Idolatry will no longer be found. Isaiah 2:20 reads, "In that day a man shall cast his idols of silver, and his idols of gold, which they made each one for himself to worship, to the moles and to the bats" (see also Zech. 14:9; Mal. 1:11).

The devil will be bound during the thousand-year reign; this means much for he is the prince of this world, the god of this age who leads the whole world astray. There is almost no truth he has obscured more than the truth concerning himself. Especially when one denies the thousand-year kingdom, he seldom arrives at a correct view of the devil. His unique power is underestimated during this entire dispensation. People speak of his "last convulsions," his "bruised head," or he is called a "muzzled dog" or a "chained lion." The Apostle Peter, who had had an actual encounter with him, calls him a roaring lion, walking about, seeking whom he may devour. But when, on the other hand, Scripture speaks of a future binding of Satan, people think this has a figurative meaning. So when he is running loose, they put him in chains, and when he is really bound with chains, they let him run loose!

It is a comforting thought that man does not have to curtail Satan's power, for this situation would be hopeless. The God of peace shall soon bruise Satan under the feet of God's people (Rom. 16:20). Not until the return of the Lord will the "mother promise" of Genesis 3:15 be fulfilled.

At the end of the Millennium, the kingdom of peace comes to an end.

This is described in Revelation 20:7-10.

> And when the thousand years are expired, Satan shall be loosed out of his prison. And shall go out to deceive the nations which are in the four quarters of the earth, Gog and Magog, to gather them together to battle: the number of whom is as the sand of the sea. And they went up on the breadth of the earth, and compassed the camp of the saints about, and the beloved city: and fire came down from God out of heaven, and devoured them. And the devil that deceived them was cast into the lake of fire and brimstone, where the beast and the false prophet are, and shall be tormented day and night for ever and ever.

It is a fearful thought that the kingdom of peace must end in such a release of Satan. There are some who derive from this an argument against the thousand-year kingdom itself but this is more an argument of frustration than anything else. There is a divine necessity for this loosing of Satan from the bottomless pit. It is emphatically told to John, "After that he must (*dei*) be loosed a little season." Why this *must* be done we are not told. The deepest reason seems to lie in the justice of God, at least not in the devil or in man as is usually thought. There has been much speculation regarding this loosing and the subsequent uprising, but it seems to us that we cannot nor do we need give a theodicy, that is to say, a justification of the ways of God. One thing is certain, God has His own wise reason for and purpose with it, so that with this loosing He will give a justification for His ways. The event will make clear that Satan cannot bring one accusation or complaint against Him and that His creation will not be in perfect condition until He Himself is all and in all.

As soon as Satan is free again he goes to the four corners of the earth. If he were to go to Jerusalem, the center of the earth, he would, as he apparently knows only too well, run up against the holiness of its inhabitants, for that city is called Jehovah Shammah, i.e., *the Lord is there*. Were he to go to the nations around Jerusalem, he would find them too much under the influence of the beloved city of God. For that reason he goes to the uttermost ends of the earth where people evidently have merely feigned submission to the prince out of the house of David. Hence, in spite of a thousand-year imprisonment, his nature and strength and cunning and influence have remained the same. His hellish plan succeeds. He gathers the nations together and fills and moves them with hatred against Jerusalem.

This plot suddenly comes to an end. A battle never ensues. The moment the seething hordes want to lay siege around the camp of the saints and the beloved city, fire descends from God out of heaven and consumes all of them. This revolt of Gog and Magog, or of the northern and Asiatic nations, is not the same as the one mentioned by Ezekiel. The latter takes place *before* the Millennium, the former *at the end* of it (see Ezek. 38 and 39).

After the victory over Gog and Magog follows the final judgment of the devil. Just as in the case of death, he who has the power of death experiences the final judgment in three stages. First, he is cast from heaven upon the earth, then from the earth into the bottomless pit, and finally from the bottomless pit into hell. There he finds his erstwhile willing servants, the beast and the false prophet.

The resurrection unto damnation of "the rest of the dead" takes place immediately afterwards. They are judged by the Judge on the great white throne according to the subjective standard of their works committed during their entire lives and according to the objective standard of His severe justice. Now also the last enemy, death and the grave, gets its turn. Heaven and earth are now perfectly cleansed and Christ delivers up the Kingdom to His Father.

Many believers have tormented themselves throughout the ages with this judgment of the great white throne. Yet believers are not even in the mind of the writer; they are not as much as mentioned in these verses. Before the judgment seat of Christ only believers are found, and before the great white throne only the wicked. The former event takes place before the thousand-year reign, the latter after it. This is really the *last* judgment. Immediately after this final judgment Christ delivers the kingdom up to His father. As man He had gone away in order to receive the kingdom (Luke 19:12). As the Son of man He has kept it intact and purified it from all evil powers so that He can finally say, "I have glorified thee on the earth: I have finished the work which thou gavest me to do." With these words He then returns to the father that which had been given Him, i.e., the heathen as His inheritance and the uttermost parts of the earth as His possession (Ps. 2:8). Israel, the nation of nations, was *His* in a special sense (John 1:11), and it remains His forever and ever (Luke 1:32-33). Then God will make all things new. The results of sin will be forever removed. Nowhere in Scripture are we given an extensive description of the eternal state. For this is not an object of prophecy as is the thousand-year kingdom (Acts 3:21). Only Revelation 21:1-5 tells us something about it, and what is said there is sufficient to justify the lines by Da Costa:

> When the Lord God is in all,
> And in all the One and All,
> Then it will be light forever,
> And no night will ever fall.

Chapter 21

THE MILLENNIUM AND THE ETERNAL STATE DISTINGUISHED

It will not be superfluous to call attention to the distinction between the Millennium and the eternal state. By its very nature not much can be said about this matter, since Scripture speaks little about the eternal state of glory. For clarity's sake we will touch on only a few things.

Revelation 21 and 22

The last two chapters of Revelation are perplexing to the exegetes of prophecy. The looming question here is whether these two chapters give us a further description of the thousand-year kingdom or whether we are dealing with a description of the state of eternal glory. In the main there are four viewpoints.

1. Many consider Revelation 21 and 22 a further development of the Millennium. Professor Joan van den Honert, T. Hz., in his analysis of Revelation often printed in the front of the commentaries by the old English divines, gives several reasons why these chapters cannot refer to the state of eternity. He considers them to be referring to the glorious state of the Church at the endtime.

2. About an equal number believe that the last two chapters of Revelation are speaking of the eternal state of glorified believers, for which many reasons are given. No one speaks as clearly and convincingly in defense of this view as Du Toit.

3. Many students in this field divide these chapters into several time segments and say that 21:1-8 speaks of eternity, while all the following verses speak of the Millennium.

4. Finally there are those who believe that the Millennium and the eternal state are running together. Much can be said in

favor of this view, for the prophets often do not take into account a specific time, place, or other circumstance.

To decide here in favor of any one of the four is difficult. We believe that in the future more light can and will be shed on this subject. The actual study of prophecy is hardly a century old, so we may expect a more painstaking and prayerful examination, whereby Scripture will be compared with Scripture to shed much light on these chapters. If we had to choose one of the four views, we would give our preference to the third. We think it is rather certain that 21:1-8 gives a brief description of the state of glory. But we believe that thus far no conclusive proof has been given that all the rest is speaking of conditions and situations in the Millennium.

The difficult expression in 22:2, "the leaves of the tree were for the healing of the nations," can mean, according to the experts, *to the maintenance of the nations.* There can be no healing in the real sense of the word in eternity, for healing presupposes sickness which is part of death, and death in turn is the wages of sin. Neither can there be heathen anymore. That the nations are maintained points out the truth that man has no existence in himself but is borne by the eternal power of God.

Three Future Stages

It must be admitted, however, that Scripture speaks very little of eternal bliss. Almost daily we hear pious believers quote Scriptures which they apply to eternal bliss, but actually the texts refer either to the non-physical intermediate state or to the Millennium. At least it must be considered curious that seldom, if ever, is a distinction made between these three states: a) the bodiless souls from the day of death to the return of the Lord; b) the condition of the believers in the Millennium; and c) the eternal bliss in the heaven of heavens. Scripture says enough of all three, so that treating all three as identical is an error.

The Millennium is the great subject and the glorious vista of prophecy. It is the age of the Messianic salvation, the golden age of Israel and the nations. The golden age of nations lies in the past, but Israel's lies in the future.

It is fair to say, however, that the state of eternal glory can hardly be called a subject of prophecy. If the eternal state is mentioned in Old Testament prophecy at all, it is only in two places, i.e., the last two chapters of Isaiah (Isa. 65:17; 66:22). The New Testament speaks very little about eternal glory. A few times it is indicated by way of contrast with eternal damnation. Revelation 21:1-5 is the principal place which in a few words says much about it. The description of eternal glory is almost exclusively negative in nature. The Millennium is always described in positive terms, frequently even the details. Hence these negatives are instructive, because they afford much material for contemplation to the soul who loves Him and hates sin.

1. Revelation 21 states that the first heaven and the first earth have passed away. Verse 11 of the preceding chapter says that the earth and the heaven fled away and there was no place found for them. Many people, both in times long past as well as today, did and do now believe that the heaven and the earth which now exist will be totally annihilated, but this is by no means the case. The *fashion* of this world passes away. The present heavens and earth are kept in store, according to 2 Peter 3:7, and reserved unto fire against the day of judgment and perdition of ungodly men. What is said in Revelation 20:11 is the same as what Peter describes in these awesome words, "But the day of the Lord will come as a thief in the night; in which the heavens shall pass away with a great noise, and the elements shall melt with fervent heat, the earth also and the works that are therein shall be burned up" (2 Peter 3:10). That the earth will not be destroyed but is eternal is more than abundant from Scripture.

A) It is emphatically called eternal in contrast with the disappearing generations of mankind (Eccl. 1:4): "One generation passeth away, and another generation cometh: but the earth abideth for ever." "Who laid the foundations of the earth, that it should not be removed for ever" (Ps. 104:5). "Thou hast established the earth, and it abideth" (Ps. 119:90). "And he built his sanctuary like high palaces, like the earth which he hath established for ever" (Ps. 78:69).

B) The reason the earth is eternal is that it is the Lord's possession (Exod. 19:5; Deut. 10:14; Job 38:33; Ps. 24:1; 50:12; 1 Cor. 10:26, 28). It is His possession in the fullest sense of the word, because He made it. God never forsakes the works of His own hands. This also means that He never destroys what He once has made.

C) No text says that the earth as the dwelling place of man will be destroyed. Those texts that speak of the *end of the world* are not speaking of the *kosmos* but of the *aioon,* which means this present dispensation. And when the Bible speaks of the *perishing* or *passing away* of the world, or of the earth and the heavens, then the Greek verb *parechomai* means the transition from one place, form, or condition to another. And even when the words *dissolved* or *flee away* are used, the context makes clear that we are not to think of a total annihilation.

D) The world will be *reborn* (Matt. 19:28). Just as an individual at regeneration will not be destroyed to be created anew afterward, so will this not take place with the world. Hence when the Lord says, "Behold, I make all things new," and then it is said that there is a new heaven, this does not mean a totally different creation, but the same creation that is renewed. The essence of all that the Lord has made remains, but the form and the sinful propensities change completely.

E) The character of the Jewish nation presumes an eternal earth. Israel is elected by God as the eternal people of the earth (Exod. 19:5-6); Israel is the nation that will possess the earth eternally (Ps. 37:9, 11, 29; Isa. 60:21; Jer. 31:36; Ezek. 37:25; Dan. 2:44; 7:14, 27; Matt. 5:5; Rom. 4:13). The perishing of the earth by fire refers to the complete cleansing of the earth. Fire was used in Israel as the effective cleanser of things that were extremely unclean. The fact that not only the earth but also heavens shall "pass away" must be ascribed to their unity with regard to sin. Sin seems to have originated there. In any case the heavens, too, are said to be impure in His holy sight, so that this necessitates a new heaven as well as a new earth. Christ's satisfaction and reconciliation are also of the greatest significance for heaven (Eph. 1:10; Col. 1:20).

2. *And there was no more sea. (Rev. 21:1).* This statement is often taken in a figurative sense as meaning the sea of nations or as a metaphorical expression for the idea of *separation* or *upheaval;* but the immediately preceding and following context compel us to accept a literal interpretation. The salty sea is the collecting trough and garbage bin of this earth. The rivers carry dirt and rotten things to the sea. Much of it may be eaten

by fish, but not enough to safeguard the water against corruption. We must admire the wisdom of the Creator for salting the waters of the sea so strongly, for that counteracts the decay. No harmful and pestilential vapors arise from the sea to jeopardize the health of man and beast. Such a sea is not necessary in eternal glory. Since sin and death are no longer present, there will not be any corruption either. According to Peter's statement, the earth is *of water* and *in the water,* but evidently the earth will then no longer exist in that manner or be so composed.

Scripture teaches us, however, that in the thousand-year kingdom of peace, the sea still exists. The wicked dead who did not partake of the first resurrection lay all that time on the bottom of the sea, but at the final judgment we saw that the sea gave up the dead which were in it (Rev. 20:13). During the kingdom of peace He who is greater than Solomon will have dominion *from sea to sea* (Ps. 72:8; Ezek. 47:8, 15, 17).

It is a question, however, whether together with an eternal glorified earth there will not be also such a sea. It seems to us that we are almost compelled to accept this idea, since the sea is a creation of God and not the result of sin (Gen. 1; Exod. 20:4, 11; Deut. 5:8). Now the Lord does not forsake the work of His hands, nor a part of it. His honor over against Satan does not allow this. Nor can we think of any reason why the sea could not undergo a similar regeneration and glorification to that of the earth. The present treacherous sea, which is the garbage bin of a sinful world and a wall of partition between the nations, most certainly will then no longer exist. Neither need we fear that in the sea there will be devouring sharks.

3. In the eternal state God dwells with men. "Behold, the tabernacle of God is with men, and he will dwell with them, and they shall be his people, and God himself shall be with them, and be their God" (Rev. 21:3). The holy city, new Jerusalem is, according to Revelation 21:9, the Church of Christ. After the defeat of Gog and Magog and the cleansing of the world, she descends from God out of heaven, prepared as a bride adorned for her husband. In the Garden of Eden the Lord frequently visited Adam; now, for wise reasons, He hides His face from the godly. In the kingdom of peace He will do again what He did in Paradise, and through Christ, manifest Himself. But in

the blissful life of glory, He dwells forever and ever *in* His Church. In her He will be all to her. The Church as the wife of the Lamb will continue to occupy her own unique place of privilege forever. In the eternal state she is the tabernacle of God *with men.* In the day when God lives eternally with men, the Church will have the incomparable privilege of being the eternal dwelling place of God.

But the idea that the distinction between Israel and the Church will have come to an end finds no support in Scripture. On the contrary, Scripture calls Israel not only an *eternal people,* but it also teaches emphatically that Israel will continue to exist as a separate nation with Christ as its eternal King. Isaiah 66:22 removes all doubt in this regard, for there we read, "For as the new heavens and the new earth, which I will make, shall remain before me, saith the Lord, so shall your seed and your name remain" (cf. Isa. 65:17-19). The greater glory of God, however, will through Christ Jesus be manifested forever in the Church (Eph. 3:21). When it is said in 1 Corinthians 15:28 that God will be *all in all,* this does not imply that God is *in all in the same manner.* He hates a gray uniformity in all His works, and as the Unchangeable One, He will continue to do so eternally. There will even be nations saved and ruled by kings who will bring the honor and the glory of their nations into the New Jerusalem (Rev. 21:24, 26; 22:2).

4. In the eternal state all tears will be wiped from people's eyes. Now the Lord gives unto His children psalms in the night, but then the cause for all tears will have been removed. The Heidelberg Catechism correctly calls life a vale of tears. Through sin, this life has become so terrible that we are consumed by His anger and troubled by His wrath. According to Job, man that is born of a woman is of few days, and full of trouble.

The somber picture of this temporal life furnished by many biblical writers represents a far healthier view of life than that given by present-day superficial Christianity which, even now, when life gets sadder from one day to the next and nothing but fearful suffering stares us in the face from every side, still continues to dream of peace and no danger. Blessed are they who mourn. Their sorrow will soon be changed into eternal joy, for there is a world without tears, which will be eternally their portion. At the return of Christ, all the tears of the Church disappear. In the Millennium there will still be tears found in Israel and mainly among the nations, since the last enemy, death, has not yet been annihilated.

5. In the eternal state, however, *death* will be no more. In Revelation 20:14 it was said that *death and hades were cast into the lake of fire.* It is not hell which is cast into the lake of fire, but *hades,* that is to say, the realm of the dead. This realm could not be entirely dispensed with in the kingdom of peace, because from time to time sinners still had to descend into it. Death is the last enemy that is to be destroyed. We refer once more to what we have said about this in the chapter on the two resurrections. We are further reminded that together with death, all mourning, wailing, and trouble will have passed away. These, too, are but elements of death, just as is the grave.

6. The *devil* will have been cast into the lake of fire and brimstone. This place has been especially prepared for him and his angels (Matt. 25:41). In the thousand-year kingdom he had been bound, but not yet completely finished off and cast into his own place. Evidently during all that time he retained his inner strength, although the full deployment of his power among the nations had been taken away from him. After the thousand years had come to an end, he was released again, and immediately he succeeded in organizing a revolt against God and His people on earth. Our Savior is manifested, however, that He might destroy the works of the devil (1 John 3:8). And in that glorious purpose He will not fail. By His death He will destroy him that has the power of death, that is, the devil (Heb. 2:14). People often read this text as though it means that Christ by His death has already destroyed Satan. Satan is, to be sure, an already conquered enemy, but he is by no means done away with. Not until the end of the kingdom of peace is he consigned to hell. He will not be annihilated there, as many think today, but will be tormented forever. And all those who have willfully turned away from Christ and gone after Satan (1 Tim. 5:15) will share his fate forever. Why are people driveling about an annihilation of the wicked or a restitution of all things? The last pages of Scripture clearly teach us differently.

But the fearful, and unbelieving, and the abominable, and murderers, and whoremongers, and sorcerers, and idolators, and all liars, shall have their part in the lake which burneth with fire and brimstone: which is the second death (Rev. 21:8).

Since we are dealing here with a contrast to eternal bliss, the one stands or falls with the other. If one thing is clear in Scripture, it is that there is an eternal punishment in hell.

The place of perdition evidently is not a part of the new heaven and the new earth, for it is emphatically called *the outer darkness.* "For *without* are dogs, and sorcerers, and whore-mongers, and murderers, and idolators, and whosoever loveth and maketh a lie" (Rev. 22:15).

Moral Distinction

From the few differences mentioned above, it must be clear that there is a distinction between the Millennium and the eternal state. Frequently the moral distinction between the two is expressed in two words, namely, that in the thousand-year kingdom righteousness will *reign,* because there will still be sin, whereas in the eternal state righteousness will *dwell,* since sin will have been put away forever. The Millennium is the preparation for eternal glory and as such is perfectly in agreement with God's usual manner of working. Just as death comes in stages, so full salvation comes in stages. "It doth not yet appear what we shall be" (1 John 3:2). We are still looking through a glass, darkly. But it is clear that the children of God are headed for a glorious future. Oh, that then they would not look at the things which are seen!

We conclude with a word of the now blessed Isaac Da Costa, which he addressed to his "precious spouse".

Although there may be clouds, somber clouds, in the sky;
Although clouds may hang low above the church, the country, our home,
And although there may be much round about us that cries out to us:
Bend your shoulder underneath the cross!
Well then! O may this future beckon! For that cross provides, at the same time, the hope!

Chapter 22

A LOOK INTO THE REVELATION OF JOHN

Without laboring under the delusion that we can solve all the difficulties in the Book of Revelation, we consider it nevertheless useful to cast a chiliastic look into it. The best commentaries and explanations of this book are, without exception, from the pens of chiliasts. We are thinking here of those by Joseph A. Seiss, Lord, Kelly, Grant, Darby, Lincoln, Ford Ottman, Arno C. Gaebelein, and Walter Scott in English, and by Gunning, Voorhoeve, Maasdam, and Esser in Dutch. *Blikken in de Openbaring* (*Looks Into the Revelation*) by Van Andel is also instructive. The more recent books by Greydanus and De Moor are valuable, but, alas, the authors allow themselves to be frightened off by the specter of their own making, what they call the heresy of chiliasm, and to a large extent they also remain victims of the antiquated method of exegesis.

We offer here only a few general observations regarding the *character*, the *division*, and the *exegesis* of this prophecy.

The Character of the Book of Revelation

1. *As far as the character of this prophecy is concerned, we are dealing with a book of comfort for the Church.*

Revelation is a book of comfort from beginning to end, and also to the end of this dispensation. The Church was in need of comfort in the days of John, for the Roman eagle was at the point of striking its claws at Jesus' lambs. The Church needed no less special comfort in the Middle Ages, when she was afflicted unto death by so-called Christian Rome; and at the dark end of this dispensation she will no less need the comfort of the Head of the Church.

History shows that the purpose of this last book, namely, providing comfort to the oppressed believers, did not fail. The first Christians, as well as the Albigenses and Waldenses, comforted themselves with the numerous promises of this book. Not until the Church imagined herself to be rich, was in need of nothing, and dreamed of a state of bliss upon the earth did this book seem to be a superfluous luxury sitting way in the back of the Bible.

What constitutes the special comfort of this book? This comfort is evident in various ways.

A) Believers know that their bodies will be made like unto Christ's glorious body (Phil. 3:21; 1 John 3:2). On the first page of Revelation the heavenly glory of the Mediator is shown to them. Prior to that, they did not yet know how He looked in His full glory and majesty, but now they could know how their own bodies would soon be changed.

B) This book speaks more often and in greater detail about the reward of grace than any other book of the Bible. The word *victory* appears more often in it than in all other Bible books together. All His and their enemies are presented here as vanquished.

C) The greatest comfort for the Church of the cross is undoubtedly that the Lord is presented time and again as coming soon. And as long as He tarries He watches over His flock, for He walks in the midst of the golden candlesticks, and in His right hand He holds the stars, i.e., the teachers of the Word, and no one can pluck them out of it.

D) The Lord is coming back to establish a thousand-year kingdom of peace in which the believers will reign with Him as kings on earth. The cross-bearers will become crown-wearers. So let them do what He has done, endure the cross and despise the shame because of *the exceeding and eternal weight of glory.*

2. The Lord Jesus Christ at His return is, in a special sense, the center of this prophecy.

Unfortunately the title does not sufficiently express this. The correct title should be, *The Revelation of Jesus Christ to John.* The glorified head of the Church Himself emerges here in all His regal glory and splendor. The word *apocalupsis* tells us that the veil of heaven, which hides Him from His people, will one day be removed. The same word appears in Luke 2:32; Romans 2:5; 8:19; 16:25; 1 Corinthians 1:7; 14:6, 26; 2 Corinthians 12:1, 7; Galatians 1:12; 2:2; Ephesians 1:17; 3:3; 2 Thessalonians 1:7; 1 Peter 1:7, 13; 4:13.

These two general qualities, comfort and the centrality of Christ, are significant for the exegesis of this book. It is imperative that a word of comfort convinces us that it is unambiguous and absolutely true. The only correct exegetes are those who express its comfort and avoid a maze of historical events. Many explanations give the uninformed reader the impression that Gibbon or some other historian furnishes the best commentary on these divine words. And with regard to the second characteristic, all those exegetes who pay more attention to the angels than the One who looses the seals, who call more attention to the Antichrist than to the Christ, who dwell more on the Beast than on the Lamb and more on the harlot than on the bride of the Lamb, greatly commit exegetical sins. Christ is the Sun of righteousness who sheds abroad His light upon everything and everybody. Only those who know Christ in all His fullness can truly learn to know the Antichrist and his followers.

3. *The most solemn and formidable subjects are treated in the form of Old Testament symbols.*

This requires that here more than anywhere else its exegesis must be based on comparing Scripture with Scripture. Those exegetes who are aware of this give the best explanation. Thus, for instance, the candlesticks, the sea of glass, the incense, the temple, the ark, the sacrifices, the firstfruits, the precious stones, and the tree of life find their entire or partial explanation in the Old Testament. Ford Ottmann in his new commentary takes this into account. The voluminous book by the famous student of prophecy, Dr. A. Keith, *The Harmony of Prophecy,* deals exclusively with this subject, and we recommend this book to all who are interested.

This Old Testament "color" of the Revelation is not simply a historical curiosity, as is often thought. It incontestably assures us that Israel's institutions, as frequently mentioned in the Old Covenant, are *eternal.* This Old Testament coloration at the same time evokes the idea that in Revelation, Israel is again the subject of prophecy. Whoever looks *only* for the Church in this last book of the Bible is mistaken. With regard to Israel,

Revelation links up with Daniel's great prophecy regarding his people and his city in Daniel 9:24-27. But more on this later.

The Division of the Book of Revelation

The *division* of this book is given by Christ Himself. Practically everyone agrees that verse 19 of the first chapter provides us a divine division with these words, "Write the things which thou hast seen, and the things which are, and the things which shall be hereafter."

This provides a threefold division.

1. *The things which thou hast seen.*

This refers to the appearance of the glorified Christ to John described in the greatest part of the first chapter. Viewed correctly, every detail of this grand description speaks volumes about the inexhaustible glory of the Savior. And what a thought that we may know we shall be made conformable to Him!

2. *The things which are.*

This refers to the seven churches, which in John's day were a historical reality. Nevertheless the letters to the churches have a prophetic character. Today this is generally acknowledged and is evident from many facts.

A) All of Revelation is called at the beginning and at the end (1:3 and 22:7) a *prophecy*. The main idea of the entire book is the *coming of the Lord*. Each of the letters contains a reference to that coming.

B) The number *seven* is a prophetic number. There were more churches in Asia Minor, but evidently seven are chosen to express the idea of completeness.

C) The moral sequence of these churches not only points out the intention to pronounce a divine judgmental evaluation of the entire historical church, but at the same time agrees with the history of the Christian Church. This has been extensively shown by Lincoln, Pember, Brookes, Grant, and others.

D) Only when looking at it this way do many things in the letters themselves become clear. Then we shall understand why this series ends so somberly and dismally with the lukewarm Church of Laodicea. This agrees wholly with the great apostasy at the end of this dispensation and with the picture given us by Christ and the Apostles. Laodicea is an apostate church where Christ stands outside the door and is ready to spew her out of His mouth. Much more could be said about this, but we rather quote what Dr. J. H. Bavinck writes about these churches:

> They depict conditions in the churches as they were found in those days and which at the same time are typical of the entire Church of Christ, hence conditions that occur again and again in the Church and which will especially return at the end of time. For it is clear that all of them are written under the impression of the imminent persecution and return of Christ. All of them contain a reference to the return of Christ, and with that in view they admonish the Church to be watchful and faithful.

In view of the division and the explanation of "the words of this prophecy" it is of the utmost importance to keep this constantly in mind.

3. *The things which shall be hereafter.*

This is the third part of Revelation. In the second and third chapters we see the entire historical Church in her suffering and struggle, in her responsibility and failure. The third part deals with the terrible judgments upon the world and the apostate church, right after the true Church will meet the Lord in the air (1 Cor. 15:51; 1 Thess. 4:17). The third part covers the rest of Revelation, beginning with chapter 4.

The true Church, as the body of Christ, is, from chapter 4 on, no longer on earth but in heaven. Not until chapter 19 does she come with Christ to earth to judge it in righteousness. Since this division of the book is most closely connected with its exegesis, we next wish briefly to call attention to this matter.

The Exegesis of the Book of Revelation

On the *exegesis* of the last book of the Bible, it is hoped that readers will be satisfied with a few remarks.

1. *Beginning with chapter 4, the Church is no longer on earth.*

Whoever looks for her on earth and sees all the events described as pertaining to her will never come to any clarity and comfort as far as most of Revelation is concerned. Such explanations do not in the least increase our knowledge about the *coming of the Lord,* which is the main subject and object of Revelation. Meanwhile the possibility exists that many will not agree that the Church is no longer found on earth in the third main part of Revelation. For this reason we feel obligated to advance some proof for this statement.

A) It is evident from the words that are used in Revelation 1:19, *the things which shall be hereafter. Hereafter* is not a translation of the indefinite *usteron,* i.e., afterward, but of the definite *meta tauta,* meaning after the previous things have come to an end. This specific expression we meet again in 4:1, where the third part of the book begins. Thus these expressions point out that the dispensation of the Church has come to an end and another dispensation has begun, i.e., the day of Christ and its attendant events. Then the "times of the Gentiles" will have been completed.

B) That in these chapters we are dealing with a dispensation different from the present one is evident from the many matters described therein. For example, 11:3-6 speaks of the two witnesses of God who will prophesy for twelve-hundred sixty days. They are described in these words:

> And if any man will hurt them, fire proceedeth out of their mouth, and devoureth their enemies: and if any man will hurt them, he must in this manner be killed. These have power to shut heaven, that it rain not in the days of their prophecy: and have power over waters to turn them to blood, and to smite the earth with all plagues, as often as they will (Rev. 11:5-6).

Now it must be clear that we are not dealing here with the dispensation of reconciliation. The Savior berated the sons of thunder because in their zeal they wanted to call down fire from heaven upon the Samaritans. Here, however, we see strict adherence to the law of retribution. In the present dispensation the Church may not avenge itself, not because vengeance is to be considered as something from the devil, but because it is from the Lord. "Vengeance is mine; I will repay, saith the Lord." This fact we see verified again when the day of wrath has come.

C) The Lord does not save His people *in* or *during* the hour of temptation which will come upon all the world, but *from* it (3:10). *The hour of temptation* means the great tribulation when the devil will have been cast out of heaven upon the earth.

At present the Church is engaged in battle against the spiritual wickedness *in the heavenly regions,* but then *she* will be in heaven and Satan out of it (see 12:10-12).

D) Again and again we find the Church in heaven represented by the twenty-four elders, clothed in their long white robes and with golden crowns on their heads. They sing there the new song saying, "Thou art worthy to take the book, and to open the seals thereof: for thou wast slain, and hast redeemed us to God by thy blood out of every kindred, and tongue, and people, and nation" (Rev. 5:9). It is generally believed today that they are the representatives of the entire body of Christ. Again and again we see the Church on high, crowned and glorified, while on earth the most dreadful judgments are raging. See Revelation chapters 4, 5, 6, 7, 11, 14, 15, and 19.

E) It is not until Revelation 19 that mention is made of the marriage of the Lamb. After that we read in verse 14, "And the armies which were in heaven followed him upon white horses, clothed in fine linen, white and clean." So there it is stated that the glorified Church partakes with Christ in the judgment on earth. If one is willing to read the "*words* of this prophecy," he finds many proofs for the opinion expressed here. And wherever one may look, he will not find the Church anywhere on earth. Our conclusion is that chapters 4 through 22 are speaking of things that lie still in the future, although with the understanding that the so-called historical school is correct that the future events already now cast their shadows on the history of the Church and the nations. Although there is a progressive fulfillment of prophecy, we must not consider these shadowy things as the actual fulfillment.

2. *A close connection is shown between Revelation and the prophecy of Daniel.*

This connection is so close that it could almost be called a continuation of Daniel. That they are closely related is a commonplace understanding, and yet we fear that it is little realized *how* they are connected.

A) Both speak of the *times of the Gentiles,* i.e., the time when Israel as a nation will be rejected. In Daniel 2 and 7, Daniel speaks about the beginning and the end of those times. In the dream of Nebuchadnezzar, all the kingdoms of the world are shown to him. The "times" begin with Nebuchadnezzar and end with the stone cut, without hands, out of the mountain, which must not be understood as a reference to Christianity or the first coming of Christ, but to the second coming unto judgment and the establishment of His kingdom on earth.

There is, however, a great difference between the views of the two books. Whereas Daniel mentions in few words the beginning and the end of these times, John exclusively and extensively dwells on the end of them. Daniel speaks of all four world powers, whereas John limits himself to the last one, namely, the Roman-Germanic. According to Daniel the destruction of these world powers is a matter of a moment, but John shows that this takes place gradually. Another difference is that whereas Daniel has an eye only for the Jews as the people of God, John also knows of the Church as the body of Christ.

B) Revelation joins mainly with the great prophecy of Daniel concerning the *seventy year-weeks*. We find this prophecy in Daniel 9:24-27. Because of its great importance we quote it in its entirety.

> Seventy weeks are determined upon thy people and upon thy holy city, to finish the transgression, and to make an end of sins, and to make reconciliation for iniquity, and to bring in everlasting righteousness, and to seal up the vision and prophecy, and to anoint the most Holy. Know therefore and understand, that from the going forth of the commandment to restore and to build Jerusalem unto the Messiah the Prince shall be seven weeks, and threescore and two weeks: the street shall be built again, and the wall, even in troublous times. And after threescore and two weeks shall Messiah be cut off, but not for himself: and the people of the prince that shall come shall destroy the city and the sanctuary; and the end thereof shall be with a flood, and unto the end of the war desolations are determined. And he shall confirm the covenant with many for one week: and in the midst of the week he shall cause the sacrifice and the oblation to cease, and for the overspreading of abominations he shall make it desolate, even until the consummation, and that determined shall be poured upon the desolate.

Anyone who has prayerfully studied this momentous prophecy will praise the illuminating action of these words of God. Here we are given one of those keys God offers us in His Word.

But just as this prophecy is received upon prayer, so can it be clearly explained only by prayerful examination. Without going into details, we wish to look at it for a moment in order to better comprehend the connection between this prophecy and Revelation. It deals with Daniel's people, i.e., the nation of the Jews. In fact, Daniel knew no other holy city than earthly Jerusalem.

The seventy weeks are *year-weeks*. This does not detract anything from the truth stated earlier that all time indication in Scripture must be taken literally. For the word translated *weeks* literally means *units of seven* or simply *sevens*. Hence the word can mean days, months, or years. Only the context can determine this; and it decides at this place for *year-weeks*, thus also the partial and literal fulfillment in the first coming of the Lord. In this connection the text speaks of the seventy years of the Babylonian exile. So we are not dealing with the so-called prophetic substitution of a day for a year. The theory that a day stands for a year is unbiblical. We are not dealing here with weeks in the usual sense of the word, but with *units of seven years*.

The seventy units of seven years total up to 490 years. And they are divided into three parts in the following manner: (1) Within seven year-weeks or forty-nine years the city and the sanctuary would be rebuilt. In Ezra and Nehemiah we can find the literal fulfillment of this. (2) There follows sixty-two year-weeks, or 434 years. According to the famous chronologist Ussher and other experts, the Messiah was slain exactly 434 years after the rebuilding of the city and the temple. Only the Modernists deny the literal fulfillment of this prophecy. (3) But seven plus sixty-two year-weeks still leave one year-week unaccounted for. That week is mentioned in verse 27. This year-week, too, just like the others, must be taken to mean a literal period of seven years.

Now the question is, where is that one week of Daniel to be found? People have looked for it, like the "missing link" of Darwin, everywhere, but found it nowhere. They will not find it in *history* since it still lies in the future. For the "he" in this verse is not the Messiah but the Antichrist, as is evident from the fact that he oppresses Israel as well as from the fact that this verse speaks of *the end*. The context also favors this idea. When we compare this verse with Isaiah 28:15 and Matthew 24:15, we come to the same conclusion, that the text is not speaking of the Christ but of Israel's great enemy of the last days who will sit in the temple as a god (2 Thess. 2:4).

Old Testament prophecy does not at all concern itself with the *times* of the Gentiles during which Israel will be dispersed and the Church gathered from the world. Between those sixty-nine year-weeks and that seventieth week already lies a period of more than 1900 years. During this intermediate dispensation, the Church is gathered from among the nations. When the bride of Christ has been called from the world, then *the times of the Gentiles* will be accomplished and the fullness of the Gentiles will have commenced. And this seventieth week will not begin before the bride of Christ will have been caught up into the air to meet her heavenly Lord. According to the best biblical manuscripts, the Apostle Paul in Ephesians 3:9 calls this dispensation *the fellowship of the mystery, which from the beginning of the world hath been hid in God.* This dispensation is a parenthesis. It is not Israel that constitutes an interim dispensation, but the Church. This dispensation of grace is just as hidden to the writers of the Old Testament as the body of Christ itself is.

But someone may ask impatiently, what have these seven years to do with the Revelation of John? Our answer is, this year-week is the brief period during which all the terrible judgments mentioned in Revelation 6 through 19 take place. What is briefly referred to in Daniel is described at great length here. This period terminates the times of the Gentiles and continues the interrupted history of Israel and the establishment of the thousand-year kingdom.

3. Revelation is a closed book if we insist on explaining it only in terms of the Church and the Gentiles.

Whoever wants to exclude Israel from Christ's future work understands little of that future, since Israel will not merely return to the scene as a converted part of the Church but specifically as the center of God's counsel regarding this earth. The Song of Moses (Deut. 32), which is so significant that it is still sung in heaven by the redeemed, casts a surprising light on the central and eternal character of the people of Israel. Note specifically Deuteronomy 32:8; see also Revelation 7:1-8. The second major part of Isaiah points out this truth again and again. Israel's fall resulted in the calling of the Church. The fall of the false church and the rapture of the true Church result in the restoration of Israel.

> For God is able to graft them in again. For if thou wert cut out of the olive tree which is wild by nature, and wert grafted contrary to nature into a good olive tree: how much more shall these, which be the natural branches, be grafted into their own olive tree? (Rom. 11:23-24).

And in connection with Israel's restoration, the city of prophet-killers, which now is still called spiritual Sodom and Egypt, becomes again the *beloved city* (Jer. 3:17; 30:17-18; 31:38-40; Zech. 8; 12:6; 14:11). Jerusalem is the city of the great King, the King of Israel. The King is eternal and His reign is eternal, for He will be King over the house of Jacob forever. For this reason the residence city of the King will also be eternal.

But before that comes to pass, Jerusalem during the final seven years must first become the residence of the Antichrist and the main seat of apostasy of the whole world. There the wrath of God and of the nations against the Jews must reach its pinnacle. This is the period of the great tribulation, which will cover the second half of the seventieth week. Also during that time the two witnesses mentioned in Revelation 11 will do their work. These are two persons who bring a message to Jerusalem for apostate Israel. This occurs immediately prior to the coming of Christ with all His saints to destroy the Antichrist and to save His people Israel. Lo-ammi then becomes Ammi again and Lo-ruhamah, Ruhamah.

4. *The Book of Revelation must be explained literally as much as possible.*

A strong futurism allows far more literalism than any other standpoint. To put the minds of some people at ease, it is important to remind them that the literal explanation does not preclude a faithful and correct explanation of the symbols and metaphors.

Undoubtedly no one ever met an exegete who believes in a literal fulfillment and who insisted that all the symbols and metaphors be explained in a rigid, literal manner. It is not reasonable to say that in Revelation everything is symbolic and that consequently everything must be symbolized when explaining this book. If one were to say this, he would be as far from the truth as one who claims that everything must be explained in a rigidly literal manner. Scripture itself usually provides sufficient indication when a statement or vision must or must not be taken in a literal sense.

It is particularly important that the time indications found in Revelation 11, 12, and 13 be understood in a literal sense. They are presented in three forms as follows: a) 1260 days; b) a time, times, and half a time; c) 42 months.

Time here stands for a year, *times* for two years, and *half a time* for half a year. So we have here one and the same period of three and a half years. When checking the various places where these time divisions are given, we see that John gives a literal indication of the second half of the last year-week in Daniel. It is the time of the actual raging of the Antichrist and of the great tribulation. For a further discussion of the literal explanation we refer the reader to what has been said about this subject earlier, "Blessed is he that keepeth the *words* of this prophecy" (see Rev. 1:3; 22:7, 18-19).

Chapter 23

THE CALLING OF BELIEVERS
IN THE LIGHT OF PROPHECY

It is a sad fact that many Christians allow their views to be shaped by public opinion rather than by the light of prophecy. Whereas public opinion by and large is poisoned, we obtain an unbiblical view of things and allow ourselves to be tossed to and from by the changing opinions of the day. Prophecy has two primary characteristics calculated to point out the solemn calling of believers: prophecy is a *light* and it is *firm.* As a light it gives us a true view of our calling in these dark times. Its firmness gives us solid ground in the midst of all that changes and totters around us.

PROPHECY IS A LIGHT

Whoever has observed present-day Christianity with a discerning eye in the light of the Word must conclude with grief that many "Christians" have become worldly-minded and that the few who live separated from the world often pursue their course without much comfort and hope. Today there is pitifully little joyous assurance of faith. Particularly there is a lack of joyful, invigorating *hope.* People hardly know what it is to rejoice in the hope of the glory of God. They have heard that there is something like experience-working hope, but they have not experienced it.

They do believe that hope makes not ashamed, but this thought gives litttle comfort (Rom. 5:2-5). They are saved by hope in the sense that they wish that one day they may be saved (Rom. 12:12). To abound in hope (Rom. 15:13) is something they have hardly heard of. They do not know the hope that made Paul bold in speaking and writing (2 Cor. 3:12). A waiting for the hope of righteousness by faith is not found with them (Gal. 5:5). They allow themselves to be moved far away from the hope of the gospel (Col. 1:23) because they do not yet hope in Christ as the hope of glory. The Christian fight of faith is often evaded because people have not put on the hope of salvation as a protecting helmet (1 Thess. 5:8). The reproach of Christ is borne so little because His people hope so little in the living God (1 Tim. 4:10; 5:5; 6:17; 2 Tim. 3:5).

In Hebrews 6:17-19 hope is depicted as an anchor of the soul, sure and steadfast. The cable that holds this anchor is unbreakable. There are many dangers in the sea of life—hidden rocks, sandbars, storms, fogs, and whirlpools. In all these dangers, an anchor is of the utmost importance. In the same way, hope is of inestimable value to believers.

Let us not deny the fact that all too often hope is lacking in the life of God's children. This is a terrible calamity. For what is hope? It is the aspect of faith which looks forward with great assurance and joy and longing to the coming of the glorified Christ. If this anticipation is lacking, the believer has lost much spiritual power; he is like a warrior without a helmet and a ship without an anchor. Under these conditions there is little assurance, little joy of faith, and little certainty of God's love.

Closely connected with hope is the Christian virtue of *patience.* In these days of spiritual decline, patience, too, is almost a forgotten virtue, even with true believers. In recent years Christendom has dreamed and talked and preached about little else than doing great things. Whoever still dared to speak of the Christian virtue of patience was considered to be somewhat of a Baptist or Labadist. For must not Christendom claim the whole world for God, and must it not lay at Jesus' feet again that which Satan had pillaged, and do all kinds of similar great things? But these are all things of which we read nothing in Scripture, and which proceed only from the hearts and minds of men. But as long as God is still called the God of patience, Christendom will not be able to discard this virtue (Rom. 15:5). We must possess our souls in patience (Luke 21:19). Especially in the affliction of these days believers must understand what it means to be patient in tribulation. Tribulation must work patience (Rom. 5:4; 12:12; James 1:3).

That patience is not without fruit is evident from Luke 8:15. The Apostle wants believers to be strengthened unto all patience (Col. 1:11). They must run with patience the race that is set before them (Heb. 12:1-3). It must have a perfect work in believers (James 1:4). It is of great significance even for society (James 5:7-8). In the days of Antichrist, it will prove to be indispensable (Rev. 13:10). The glorified Christ praises patience and considers it to be equal with laboring for His name's sake (Rev. 2:2-3). In Titus 2:2 it is mentioned together with soundness in faith and love. In 2 Peter 1:6 it shares a place of honor with love, virtue, knowledge, temperance, and godliness. The Apostle Paul, too, frequently gives it a place among all other Christian virtues (see 1 Tim. 6:11; 2 Tim. 3:10). Ministers especially cannot do without it (2 Cor. 6:4; 2 Tim. 2:3, 10, 24; 3:10).

Now what is meant by this patience that is mentioned so often? A comparison of the texts and contexts in which the word appears shows us that it is the grace that is cultivated by the expectation of the coming of the Lord (see, for instance, Rom. 8:22-25; 1 Thess. 1:3; 2 Thess. 3:5; Heb. 6:11-18; James 5:7-8). It originates on the part of man from suffering. It must not be identified with indolent passivity, for it has nothing in common with this. It is not simply a passive virtue; but it is true that it is more internal than external.

Patience presupposes the humble acknowledgement that the disciple is not above the Master, that through much tribulation we must enter into the kingdom of God, that here we must continue to bear our cross in self-denial. It is that grace of God in the soul of the believer whereby he willingly and in self-denial accepts the cross and perseveres in carrying it after Jesus, because he looks for the day when that cross will be eternally exchanged for the crown of glory. It prevents the soul from impatiently and prematurely grasping for what God has promised or from penetrating into what He has covered and hidden. "It teaches you two things: to bear whatever burden God wants you to bear, and to wait patiently for what God has promised you" (Dr. Sillevis Smitt).

The Greek word that is often used for this idea means literally, *to remain underneath*. This indicates that as believers we must constantly remain beneath the cross. And the possibility of doing this with joy and perseverence, regardless of how heavy it is and how painfully it cuts, is given with the hope with which it is most closely and repeatedly connected. Believers can stand much suffering and even love their cross since it makes them conformable to Christ's suffering, provided they may have the calm assurance within that after a light affliction will dawn a far more exceeding and eternal weight of glory.

The Hebrew Christians experienced a great regression in grace. This is the reason the holy author constantly and repeatedly points out to them that they must hope and be patient. "Ye have need of patience," he tells them (Heb. 10:36). Oh, that this call would sound forth from every pulpit to the backsliding Christians of today! Perhaps there has never been a time when the practice of patience was more necessary than the present. For we need not wear a prophet's mantle to know that our hard times will become increasingly harder.

What we are observing in the world today can be considered mild compared to what is coming. And the believers will be increasingly vexed and oppressed by the world powers, the monetary powers, the trade unions, and all forms of sin. Let us therefore cultivate the courage of a martyr by a hope that enables us not only to live but also to suffer. Only the light of prophecy can be a safe guide for us here. No little tract, no meditation or political speech can arm the believers for the battle of the future, only a steadfast look of hope upon Him who is called the Hope of glory. The expression "where there is no hope there is no life," applies not only to the individual but also to the Church as a whole.

Psychologists of renown have claimed that present-day man is no longer receptive to or drawn by religion. Maybe here or there someone's mind may be convinced a little or his will may be touched somewhat, or his feelings may be set in motion, but man as a whole, and especially males, simply cannot find any pleasure in religion in our enlightened days. Those learned men forget, of course, that the gospel does not appeal to natural man and that no more persons will believe than have been ordained to eternal life. But apart from this, the psychologists' observation contains much truth. The aspiration of living hope, which at the same time includes immovable certainty, longing, and joy, is not cultivated practically in present-day religious life.

The prophets were stalwart men such as have not been seen since then. They were at the same time men of longing for righteousness. There is no true religion without a full, deep, and tender longing for God. A Christianity that exclusively revels in the ever-evaporating present is not the right kind of Christianity and will also lose itself in the present. Hence it cannot be denied that many God-fearing people live a comfortless life and are just as anxious and concerned about the cares of life as the children of the world, and just as afraid of death as they are. This should not surprise us, considering the present-day situation, for the light of prophecy leads to the conclusion that an element is lacking in spiritual life.

In addition, prophecy repeatedly admonishes us to be *sober*. In various places the prophets teach us that, toward the end of time, the nations will be made drunk with the wine of the fury and wrath of God. The Apostle John in the last book of the Bible speaks of the false church who, as a drunken whore, sits on a scarlet-colored beast. When everyone around us overindulges in alcoholic beverages, then we must be very sober indeed not to participate in it. It is for this reason that the Lord repeatedly and solemnly admonished His Apostles to be sober (Luke 21:34; 1 Cor. 15:34; 1 Thess. 5:6-8; 1 Peter 1:13; 4:7; 5:8). With these warnings, the Lord wants to impress upon the hearts of His children that they must view matters in the right light. And do we ever view things in the right light, if we do not view them in the light of eternity?

Life in the light of the Lord's coming will also be *watchful*. "Watch therefore: for ye know not what hour your Lord doth come." This warning resounds constantly in the instruction of the Lord (Matt. 24:42; 25:13; Mark 13:33; Luke 12:40; 21:36). "Behold, I come as a thief. Blessed is he that watcheth, and keepeth his garments, lest he walk naked, and they see his shame" (Rev. 16:15). The believers must watch for two very important reasons, *against* the wiles of Satan and the temptation of sin, and *for* the unexpected coming of the Lord Jesus Christ. This watching must be done *before* prayer (Matt. 26:41) and *by* prayer (1 Pet. 4:7; 5:8).

All those who have written in a Scriptural manner about the coming of the Lord are unanimous in their testimony that this truth has an extraordinarily sanctifying influence on the lives of believers. And how could this be otherwise? Gazing upon the glorified Christ, who was dead and is alive again, must produce the richest fruit. We have the words of the Apostle as proof that it changes our image from glory to glory (2 Cor. 3:18), makes us heavenly minded (Matt. 16:26-27; Phil. 3:18-21; Col. 3:1-5; Titus 2:11-13), pure and holy (Phil. 1:6; 1 Thess. 3:12-13; 5:23; 2 Pet. 3:11-12; 1 John 3:3), and bold and faithful in confessing and witnessing (Mark 8:38; 1 Tim. 6:13-14; 2 Tim. 4:1-2; Heb. 10:35-37; 1 Pet. 5:2-4). It offers the richest comfort (John 14:3; Acts 1:11; 1 Thess. 4:13-18) and makes us faithful in the service of the Lord (Matt. 25:19-21; Luke 12:42-44; 19:12-13).

> Working, watching, praying, and waiting every hour
> Is the secret of all spiritual power.

PROPHECY IS FIRM

The word of prophecy is not only a shining light that points out our calling and causes us to distinguish between false and true light; it is also a *very firm* word. When we adhere to it, we are not soon *shaken in mind* (2 Thess. 2:2). Prophecy points out the certainty and fulfillment of God's counsel. When we look at the present time, it seems as though the world is governed by fate or chance, so that injustice continues to triumph. But prophecy shows us that the all-wise hand of the invisible God moves and guides the wheels of world history, even though they seem to run contrary to each other. It is not the powerful rulers of this age who rule the world, but the servants of the Lord by whose hand the pleasure of the Lord shall prosper. Soon, when the times of the Gentiles have sped by, He will show Himself worthy to take the book of God's judgments and to open its seals.

Note well that it is a *book*; in a book there is a plan, thought, order, and a goal. We find these things even in the terrible judgments that are now already on the earth and which will continue to increase. And the book of judgments contains not only a most certain plan but also a wise and glorious goal. All things must work together as the awe-inspiring means to establish His royal government over His creation here below, so that every creature that is in heaven, on the earth, and under the earth will eternally offer thanksgiving, honor, glory, and power to Him who sits on the throne and unto the Lamb.

This pointing of divine prophecy to the "ever wise counsel of the Lord," which stands firm forever and which one day will be perfectly fulfilled at the end of time, is very comforting. But if we had no certainty that all these things would actually and literally be fulfilled in the future, this comfort would, to a large extent, if not totally, be gone. However, the Lord has provided this certainty in the prophecy that has already been fulfilled. Everywhere in His Word we come across instances where an appeal is made to the exact fulfillment of His predictions (Deut. 18:22; Isa. 41:23; Jer. 28:9; 2 Peter 1:19-21). Judging by the word of the faithful Witness, we can unreservedly depend on everything the prophets have spoken. The main argument of Peter's speeches on the Day of Pentecost, then in the porch of Solomon, and later in the house of Cornelius, was his appeal to fulfilled prophecy. The Apostle Paul and eloquent Apollos had no surer foundation for their preaching. Prophecy, with the exception of the many metaphorical and symbolical utterances, is literally inspired, literally meant, and always literally fulfilled; so it will also in the future be fulfilled, not merely in essence, but to the last tittle and iota.

Then too, in our day there are many matters that demand the attention of every believer. In our own confined, ecclesiastical circle alone we constantly hear a clamor about the urgent demand for missions, Christian education, Christian mercy, and about the battle in politics and society. For various reasons all these voices are important. But there is one voice that drowns out all other voices and yet is seldom listened to. It seems to resemble the voice of one calling in the wilderness, and yet it is the voice of Him who testifies to the truth of prophecy and says, "Yea, I come quickly." Oh, that soon the day might dawn when the prayer of the entire Church reverberates like a mighty echo, "Amen. Even so, Lord Jesus!"

And, furthermore, there is a voice for those who extend His Kingdom,
A call to prepare the way of the King,
To the innermost part of the heart first of all.

Finally then, we have reached the end of our task. On the last page of Scripture it is said, "Behold, I come quickly; and my reward is with me, to give every man according as his work shall be" (Rev. 22:12). What we have written we leave in the hands of Him who is coming soon. He will not withhold His reward of grace from whatever, by His grace alone, is good in it, and that which is wrong in it, through our own sin He will surely burn. Meanwhile may He bless that which is good and render harmless *and* forgive that which is bad.

> Turn to God and Christ, the Lord,
> And believe His saving Word;
> Live a pious Christian life,
> Soon will end all earthly strife.

Maranatha!

APPENDICES
History

Appendix 1

THE LESSON FROM HISTORY

We have set ourselves the task to give here a brief historical survey of the living expectation of the coming of the Lord. We are not guilty of exaggeration when we say that this history almost completely coincides with that of Chiliasm in one form or another.

PURPOSE OF THIS SURVEY

1. *We wish to point out the power of the coming* of *our Lord Jesus Christ* (2 Peter 1:16).

The admonitions of the New Testament are driven home with the argument that the Lord is coming. The history of Christ's Church teaches that no other doctrine has such an unparalleled influence upon one's head and heart, faith and life. We can touch upon this only in passing.

2. *We wish to break a lance here for Chiliasm which is often poorly understood and badly maligned.*

The accusations against it are innumerable. Among other things, the Chiliasts are accused of expecting a glorious state of the Church on earth before Christ returns. But this accusation demonstrates ignorance concerning the true historical Chiliasm. This reproach would be better directed at many of the older Reformed theologians and at present-day postmillennialists. The accusation of fanaticism and enthusiasm is also well known. The history of Chiliasm points out that many of its adherents embraced wild notions. But what does this prove against Chiliasm *per se*? Nothing at all! We are dealing with the same circumstances which surround the doctrine of election. Ever since the days of Paul, how much sin has been committed against this comforting truth, both from the right and from the left! But all its abuse proves nothing against it but rather much in favor of it. Hell does not break loose on account of insignificant matters. Only where there is bright light are there dark shadows. It is unfair to attack Chiliasm because of the fanaticism which attended false Chiliasm, or of the abuse of it by carnal men. Thus, for instance, today Mormonism adheres to a false form of Chiliasm, but for that reason we cannot call Chiliasm Mormon, or even consider it co-responsible for this pernicious heresy.

3. *It is our intention that this brief survey will be at the same time, at least partly, a biography.*

It makes not the least claim to being a complete profile or scientific-historical exposition. We shall mention a few sources which we have consulted. In addition to the books by present-day Chiliasts, which we shall mention shortly, we owe much to various books on dogmatics, histories of doctrines and church histories, as well as to numerous articles. Indispensable sources for the study of the history of Chiliasm are those of Maitland, *The Apostolic School of Prophetic Interpretation;* Silver, *The Lord's Return in History and Scriptures;* and Robertson, *Regnum Dei.* We regret that we were unable to peruse the volumes of Corrodi on Chiliasm. The cloud of witnesses for historic Chiliasm is so great, however, even from the camp of its opponents, that one witness more or less does not matter.

We first take a brief look at the old history of the Chiliast expectation of the Lord's coming, then at its history during the Middle Ages, in order finally to pause briefly at the modern history.

STATEMENTS BY NON-CHILIASTS

Today it is well-nigh incontestable that the Church of the first three centuries was Chiliastic. There is hardly any contradiction to be found of this fact; on the contrary it finds more and more confirmation by all new historians. As is evident from his excellent thesis, Dr. F. W. Grosheide apparently does not want to admit this yet. To support our claim we quote here a few statements by non-Chiliasts.

The modern Dr. S. Hoekstra writes in his *Christian Doctrines:*

The expectation of the return of the glorified Christ among Christians was nearly absolutely general in the earliest times; this went hand in hand with the belief that Christ would come again to establish an earthly kingdom of the Messiah.

Gieseler, in his *Church History,* Volume I, page 166 (quoted in the well-known *History of Dogma* by Hagenbach), writes:

In all the writings of that time (namely, the first two centuries) Chiliasm comes so clearly to the fore that we may view it as the commonly held belief.

Semisch, in his well-known article on Chiliasm, expresses himself thus:

During the first centuries, with which we are dealing here, Chiliasm formed a basic element if not of the general belief of the Church then at least of scholastic orthodoxy.

This statement is incorporated in the *Patristic-Biographic Dictionary* of Torenbergen-Klein, from which we have derived many particulars.

Harnack in his article "Millennium" writes as follows:

Indeed, the coming of Christ to establish the millennium was in the early centuries connected with the Gospel itself.

Similar statements are made by such men as Gibbon, Hase, Robertson, Shedd, Bush, Schaff, Mosheim, Knapp, Crippen, Barnes, Burton, Tailor, Muncher, Newton, Whitby, Kitto, Maitland, Charles Hodge, Milner, Chillingworth, Alford, Gresswell, Trench, Hooikaas, Seeberg, Zahn, Loofs, Sheldon, Fisher, and others.

Not only do they admit that Chiliasm was part and parcel of the teaching of the early Church, but they also agree that it had the most blessed influence on the conduct of believers. Domela Nieuwenhuis in his *Van Christen tot Anarchist* (*From Christ to Anarchist*) says:

The belief in the return of Christ incontestably gave the earliest Christians such a great amount of trust and courage that they were capable of unparalleled self-sacrifice, that they even considered life of little value and sometimes longed to be in a position and to be allowed to bring this sacrifice.

Shedd, Gibbon, Bush, and many writers of the most divergent opinions express themselves in the same vein. According to Shedd and others, Chiliasm became stronger to the extent that persecution became more vehement. This is another fact that points out the divine truth of this doctrine. For it can hardly be expected that the indwelling Spirit in the Church would have comforted Jesus' flock under such heavy oppression with a lie or a false belief.

STATEMENTS BY CHILIASTS

We mention now a few Apostolic Fathers and Church Fathers who entertained a Chiliastic expectation of Christ's return.

Barnabas, who is usually considered to be the well-known co-laborer of Paul, left a general epistle, which seems to have been written after A.D. 70, since it assumes the destruction of Jerusalem. This is of great significance, for if Barnabas had given wrong views on the future, John would not have supported them twenty years later in Revelation 20. Barnabas' writing was so highly esteemed that for a long time it was read in the Christian assemblies, and the Codex Sinaiticus incorporated it as part of Holy Writ. Barnabas writes:

> Take heed, my little children, why the Word says, *He finished in six days. This means* that the Lord God will complete all things in six thousand years, for as He testifies with Him one day is as a thousand years and a thousand years as one day. Therefore, my little children, in six days, i.e., in six thousand years, all things will be completed. *And He rested on the seventh day.* This means that when the Son will come and destroy the lawless and the wicked, and when the sun, moon and stars will be moved, then He will gloriously rest on the seventh day.

According to him this day is the true Sabbath of a thousand years when Christ will reign.

Clement of Rome is by many considered to be the same person as the one mentioned in Philippians 4:3 as having his name in the book of life. His writings, too, were highly esteemed; for a long time they were thought to be infallible. He is considered a Chiliast by Hamilton, Seiss, Haldeman, Silver, and others.

Hermas was most likely the same person as the one who is greeted by Paul in Romans 16:14. Hermas wrote a famous book as the result of a vision in which Christ in the garb of a shepherd appeared to him. As is the case in all prophecy, the keynote of this book is *turn ye unto Him!* with the urgent reason, *the Lord is coming!,* according to Van Koetsveld. In the first vision Hermas explains that the earth will be renewed and in that future age the righteous will dwell in it. He is generally considered to be a Chiliast.

Papias was a pupil of the Apostle John. Eusebius in his *Church History* speaks of him as if he were a petty-minded weakling, but elsewhere he calls him eloquent and mighty in the Scriptures. He had opportunity to know the views of the Apostle John regarding the last things. Eusebius says of him that he taught, "There will be a certain thousand-year kingdom after the resurrection of the dead when Christ will reign bodily upon the earth." Eusebius was strongly anti-chiliast and interpreted Papias' view on the basis of an already incorrect interpretation of Revelation. According to him, Papias did not see the mystical and figurative meaning of Revelation.

Polycarp had been ordained as bishop of Smyrna by John. He is most likely the angel of Smyrna mentioned in Revelation 2:8. He was one of the youngest disciples of John and became the teacher of Irenaeus. The latter called him "the blessed" on account of his piety. When Polycarp spoke of his intimate relationship with John, his face shone with joy. He died a martyr. Irenaeus relates of him that he taught on the authority of John that the earth during the Millennium will be fruitful. Thus two of John's disciples, Polycarp and Papias, are in agreement on this matter.

Justin Martyr was ten years old when John died. He had been philosophically trained. At the kind recommendation of an aged Christian he started to study the prophetic Scriptures. He soon acknowledged that in them was to be found the only trustworthy and useful philosophy. In his famous *Dialogue with Trypho the Jew,* the object of which was to convince the Jews that Jesus is the true Messiah, he develops, as he emphatically insists, *the doctrine of all Christians.* On the basis of the prophets he believes in a rebuilt, decorated, enlarged, and inhabited Jerusalem and in a thousand-year reign of Christ.

Ignatius. It cannot be proved with certainty that this Apostolic Father was a Chiliast, although this is likely. He paid attention to the signs of the times and lived in the expectation of the return of the Lord; he combated the antichristians of his day, and had respect unto the recompense of the reward. Without wishing to claim that this combination of beliefs can be found only with Chiliasts, it is undeniable that they are seldom found elsewhere.

Irenaeus, the main interpreter of the practical biblical school at Antioch, had heard from the mouth of Polycarp what John had told him. When Irenaeus speaks of the recompense of the believers at the resurrection of the righteous, he expresses himself thus:

> The blessing just mentioned undoubtedly refers to the times of the Kingdom when the righteous will rise from the dead in order to reign; when all of creation, renewed and glorified, will bring forth abundant fruit.

On the duration of the kingdom he says:

> In the same number of days in which the world was created, the world will in the same number of thousands of years be completed. God finished on the sixth day all He had made and He rested on the seventh day from all His works. This is a history of the past and at the same time a prophecy of the future, for the day of the Lord is as a thousand years.

So we have here an unbroken tradition. John was the beloved disciple of the Lord. Most of the persons mentioned here had known and heard him speak personally about the future things. And those, such as Irenaeus, who had not heard the Apostle, still spoke with authority on the Millennium because they had known the disciples of John.

Tertullian lived until about A.D. 200. He was one of the most remarkable men of the early Church. The steadfastness of the martyrs had been the reason for his embrace of Christianity. He wrote a Chiliastic book, *The Hope of the Believers,* which is no longer extant. In his book against Marcion he writes:

> We confess that we have been promised a kingdom before the perfect state in heaven, and in another situation, since this will be after the resurrection, for a thousand years in divinely rebuilt Jerusalem. After these thousand years have passed, during which time the resurrection of the saints, who according to their merits will arise sooner or later is completed, the judgment and burning of all things will take place.

Cyprian was the famous bishop of Carthage. He devoted himself with great zeal to the study of Holy Scripture and interpreted it simply and naturally, including Revelation 20:1-6. He believed, as did nearly all of his contemporaries, that the seventh millennium for this world, in conformity with the seventh day of rest at creation, would be the great sabbath day of the world.

Tertullian and Cyprian were the main representatives of the North African school in Carthage. The nature of the teaching of this school is usually called practical-ecclesiastical. It rejected philosophical speculations and adhered to positive Christianity.

Hippolytus is renowned as one of the most fertile and versatile writers of the Western Church. Not philosophy but Scripture was the object of his study. In addition, he was a pupil of the strong Chiliast, Irenaeus, and so we could hardly expect anything else from him. In his tract on the Antichrist, he reveals himself as a strong proponent of Chiliasm.

QUALIFIED STATEMENTS ABOUT CHILIASM

Clement of Alexandria can justly be called the father of the Alexandrian school. The representatives of this school were already dizzy with philosophical speculations. Clement is known as a fiery opponent of Chiliasm, for he, together with his famous disciple Origen, corrupted exegesis in the Church for many centuries. The Jewish-Greek doctrine of the Logos was to him the focal point of religious-philosophical reflection. Professor Berkhof in his *Hermeneutics* writes of him:

> Clement of Alexandria was, so it seems, the first who in all of Scripture, both in the Old and in the New Testament, discovered a parabolic meaning and declared the principle: All of Scripture *must* be explained allegorically (that is to say, symbolically, spiritually).

Nevertheless, if we may believe Seiss, Clement also taught a world sabbath on the seventh day of the world.

Nepos. This man is usually considered a terrible heretic, although he had done nothing wrong. His passionate opponent *Dionysius* admitted that he had great respect for Nepos' piety, his study of Scripture, and his merits with regard to church hymnology. But this bishop of Egypt interpreted Scripture, and also prophecy, literally and naturally, and for that reason he became a Chiliast "heretic." He wrote a book against the Bible corrupters of the Alexandrian school entitled, *The Refutation of the Allegorizers.* It is strongly Chiliastic, but according to many people not excessively so. A biblical Chiliast knows how to differentiate between a moral and a sensuous kingdom. This book became popular with the Christian ministers in Egypt. Even in the sixth century, some people named themselves after him.

It was against this book that *Dionysius* of Alexandria fulminated. He was a disciple of Origen and completely saturated with the latter's spirit. In the church he represented a group with a lax attitude; his doctrine contained "an indefinite breadth of view and a flexible elasticity of concepts." Significant also are his arguments against the Chiliasm of Nepos. They reduce to the following:

1. A heretic, not John, wrote Revelation.
2. This Book of Revelation can never be understood.
3. Holy Scripture must not be understood literally, but allegorically.

Lactantius was a productive writer, erudite, and a fiery opponent of heathen philosophy. He is often called the Christian Cicero. He writes:

> Just as the Lord made such great things in six days, so must the service of Him and His truth do their work during these six thousand years; there must come (a time of) rest and peace from all the trouble the world has endured for so long. The King and Conqueror Himself will reign on earth with them (His saints) and He will build the Holy city, and this Kingdom of righteousness will last for a thousand years. The earth will bring forth all its fruit without the toilsome labor of men. The wild animals will abandon their ferocity and become tame. The snake will no longer have poison and no predatory animal will devour other animals any more.

Commodianus was a poet and historian. Born and reared as a heathen, he was won over to Christianity by reading the Bible. His two great books show that he believed in the first resurrection and in the millennial glory on earth. In vivid colors he describes the end of this dispensation.

Melito of Sardis, a diligent, wise, and divinely enlightened bishop of the Church in Asia Minor, walked in the Holy Spirit and received a letter from the glorified Savior. He was a man of great activity in every field, but his many writings have not been preserved. According to reports, from his writings on the Revelation of John and on prophecy, he reveals himself as a proponent of realistic interpretation of Scripture and therefore as an opponent of the spiritualizing championed by the Gnostics and the school of Alexandria.

Methodius vehemently opposed the spiritualizing theology of Origen. He was a staunch advocate of the verbal exegesis of Scripture and consequently he must be considered a Chiliast. He died a martyr in A.D. 311 during the persecution under Emperor Diocletian.

Victorinus of Pettau (304 A.D.) wrote, among many expositions, an interpretation of Revelation. According to the testimony of Jerome, he believed in the Millennium. Victorinus, too, was counted worthy of the crown of martyrdom.

Sulpicius Severus likely did not die until after 420. He is lauded as an excellent orator, fine stylist, and orthodox writer on ecclesiastical matters. He had an eye for the signs of the times, was an opponent of the allegorizers and upheld the general view that after six thousand years the world sabbath would dawn.

CONCLUSIONS ABOUT THE EARLY CHURCH

From this shining row of faithful witnesses, we believe that four matters become sufficiently clear.

1. During the first three centuries, Chiliasm was taught everywhere by the most erudite and godly men; by Papias in Phrygia, Justin in Palestine, Clement of Rome in Rome, Irenaeus in Gaul, Nepos in Egypt, Cyprian and Tertullian in Carthage, Hippolytus and Lactantius in Rome, Victorinus in Pettau, and so on. Chiliasm was the teaching of the entire Church.

2. Chiliasm was not taught on the basis of any philosophical principle, but on the basis of oral tradition which had been received from the mouth of the apostles themselves. Barnabas, Clement of Rome, and Hermas were the pupils of Paul, and Papias, Polycarp, and Ignatius of John. Hence it was more than merely well known.

3. This truth had a strong influence on their hearts and lives. "The Apostolic Fathers give almost nothing but an uninter-

rupted series of admonitions for the life of the Christian" (Dr. F. W. Grosheide). Many of those mentioned above remained faithful until death. Indeed, such a sanctifying influence proceeded from the expectation of the Lord and related events that many unbelieving historians explain their practice of virtue solely on the basis of this expectation. See, for instance, Hooikaas, *De Ascese der Eerste Christenen* (*The Ascesis of the Early Christians*). According to Dr. S. Hoekstra the concepts *Chiliasm* and *martyrdom* are closely connected, indeed so closely that when martyrdom ceased, interest in Chiliasm ceased with it.

4. This doctrine was not contradicted by a single orthodox Church Father. According to Mosheim, *Caius* of Rome was the first to launch an attack upon it. But since this teaching is found in Revelation, he rejected Revelation as a "composition of monstrous fables." He had the opinion that it taught a vulgar, sensuous, and carnal millennium. According to him the author was not the Apostle John but the heretic Cerinthus who, in order to have his errors accepted, ascribed them to the venerable Apostle John.

Dionysius was not sound in doctrine and was also not able to successfully combat Chiliasm except at the expensive price of rejecting the last book of the Bible. *Clement* of Alexandria in his exposition of Scripture proceeded from totally wrong principles and was philosophically speculative in doing so. Eusebius was half-Arian and does not have, for many reasons, a good name as a teacher of the Church. Soon we shall say more about Jerome, Origen, and Augustine. Except for *Cerinthus,* who apparently expected some sort of a millennium as the Mormons do today, it was the most pernicious sects such as the Alogi and the Gnostics who opposed this doctrine.

Many attempts have been made to derive an argument against Chiliasm from the silence on this subject in the writings of Ignatius, Tatian, Athenagoras, Theolphilus of Antioch, and others; but apart from the extreme weakness of such an argument, experts such as S. Hoekstra, Semisch, Hagenbach, and others have the opinion that their silence on this doctrine must not be construed as a denial of it, but rather is to be attributed to caution, since no doctrine was more repugnant to the Roman Empire than this.

The argument derived from silence on this doctrine in the Apostolic Confession means just as little, for:

A) These articles have not been written by the Apostles, as Rome teaches, but after the heyday of Chiliasm, possibly not until the fifth century.

B) This piece of writing is short and gives only a brief explanation of the form of baptism, so that many other truths are missing in it, such as, for instance, that which forms the heart and core of the Reformed faith.

The Council of Nicea gives us a strong indication that Chiliasm was the general view of the believers of the first three centuries. In the year 325 Constantine the Great, who then already was the visible head of the Church, convoked the first council at Nicea. Here 318 bishops from all Christian countries came together. For that reason this Church assembly is called an ecumenical council, i.e., a Church assembly that represents the entire Church and also speaks authoritatively for the entire Church.

These bishops had been called together for the purpose of refuting and combating heresies, particularly Arianism, but also any other error. If this Council had considered Chiliasm a heresy or error, it would certainly have raised its voice against it. We find nothing of the kind, however. Rather the opposite is true; the explanation that is given of the last article may be considered Chiliastic in nature, even though the word "millennium" does not appear.

Meanwhile it will be difficult to find a stronger proof for the veracity of Chiliasm than that which its enemies afford us. For if the Church's book of comfort *par excellence,* to the readers of which the Lord pronounces and promises a special beatitude, was rejected by the Alogi, Caius, Origen, Dionysius, the Council of Laodicea, and a large part of the Eastern Church in their fight against Chiliasm, this not only puts these antagonists in an unfavorable light but the case which they propagated as well.

The Alexandrian school was the most fearsome bulwark in the battle against Chiliasm. It is of the greatest importance to know that the real opposition originated in this sector and that this school especially must be blamed for the decline of the doctrine. What was the most characteristic trait of this school?

It engaged in philosophical and often unbridled speculation, Scripture distortion, and much philosophical pride.

Origen was the most erudite representative of this school and its chief interpreter. He was vehemently opposed to practical-biblical Chiliasm and viewed Revelation as a collection of wild dreams which nobody could understand. With all his erudition, he comes to us through all the ages as the grand master of spiritualization. In doctrine he was a radical Universalist and even entertained the hope of the salvation of the devil. With Hymenaeus and Philetus, he denied the bodily resurrection. This arch-heretic and distorter of Scripture strongly resisted the doctrine of the Millennium.

Because of its influence, the school of Alexandria became famous for his erudition. The natural heart of man has always been inclined to bow before the goddess of reason and knowledge. That is the way it is now and it was that way then. The evil principles championed by Origen and his school made such inroads that, in the year 360, the Church assemblies of Laodicea, out of antagonism against this doctrine, excluded the last book of the Bible from the canon. As a result, a general prejudice arose against this book, which, even in the days of the Reformation, had not altogether disappeared and is sometimes still noticeable.

The *Rev. H. Hoekstra* accuses Origen of having destroyed the Eastern churches, who were, among other things, his Greek-philosophical and spiritualizing followers. He then goes on to say:

> The attack against Chiliasm by these dissenters cannot meet with our approval, for they placed their speculation above the Word of God and distorted it according to their grandiloquent ideas, denying the resurrection of the body and the future glorification of the material world, which was also created by God; for according to them the material world, matter, contained sin from which the spirit of man must liberate itself. It was only natural and a matter of course that they were very much against Chiliasm, but they threw away, as a German saying goes, with the bath water the baby also. They were of a kind with Hymenaeus and Philetus who had departed from the truth, saying that the resurrection was past already (2 Tim. 2:17). The success of the pernicious principles of this school was the first and chief cause of the decline of Chiliasm.

Another cause of its decline must be sought in the conversion of Constantine the Great and, as a result, the elevation of the Church to a State Church. Opinions on the character of this ruler vary greatly. He seems to have been a strange mixture of heathen and Christian. Many feel that he served Christianity, so that it in turn might render him beneficial services. He was definitely a cruel man. He murdered his own son, Crispus, and his second wife, Fausta. Not until a week before his death did he receive the sacrament of baptism. He ascended to the throne of the Caesars in the year 323. From then on he was considered the *Pontifex Maximus,* the high priest of the Church of Christ.

The Church secretly congratulated itself because the persecution now came to an end. She began to feel rich and powerful and began to forget both her origin and her future. Gradually she let go of her heavenly Head in order to cling to earthly things. She now felt at home here below, and whoever imagines that he has an abiding city here no longer seeks for a future one. Since she imagined that she had her citizenship here on earth, she no longer expected the Lord from heaven. To be true, she continued to adhere to the confession of His return, but this no longer had a blessed influence on life. It was the time of which we often hear people say, "When the churches were (made) of gold, the people were (made) of wood." The once scornfully persecuted Church became the queen of the earth, and "those legs are strong indeed, which don't buckle under luxury."

Once again we listen to the youngest antagonist of Chiliasm in the Netherlands, the Rev. H. Hoekstra:

> The main reason why Chiliasm receded to the background, however, must be sought in the reversal which took place in the affairs of the Christian Church since Constantine the Great. From a persecuted body the Church became a ruling body. Christianity, until then the sect that had been hated by the official world, became the religion of the state. That did not benefit the spiritual character of the Church. What need was there now to look for the return of the Lord? The incentive for it—the misery of the times—had disappeared. The Church obtained peace; it looked as though gradually the kingdom of glory had already dawned. It was believed that from now on the Church of Christ would slowly extend herself victoriously over the whole earth. From that time on the earlier stance of the Church disappeared during which she had, as it were, with girded loins and burning lamps, been waiting for the coming of the Bridegroom. And so there was quite naturally no longer any soil left in which Chiliasm could survive.

Is it not obvious how excellent a compliment here is given to
the Chiliasm of those centuries? When the Church in her right
attitude was working with girded loins and waiting with burning lamps for her Lord, this was the soil in which Chiliasm
could thrive. But when the Church secularized, Chiliasm could
no longer flourish. It is a heavenly plant indeed that can thrive
only on this kind of soil! It *must* be a heavenly cutting that
without the proper soil can thrive in darkness!

A third cause of Chiliasm's slow decline must be sought in
some of its adherents themselves. Heretics especially threw
suspicion upon Chiliasm. Not only the Jews but also the
Jewish-minded sects such as the *Ebonites* and the *Nazarenes*
were proponents of a vulgar, sensuous Chiliasm. The very
dangerous heretic *Cerinthus,* who by many is thought to be the
father of Gnosticism, also made of the Millennium a luxurious
land of plenty. The Montanists were one-sidedly enthusiastic
about it, and the Donatists, who might be called the Anabaptists of those days, were also usually adherents of a vulgar,
sensuous Millennium.

Not only the sects but also excellent men such as Papias,
Irenaeus, Nepos, Commodianus, and Lactantius at times
expressed themselves too carelessly. This evoked contradiction
and provided mockers with a cane with which to beat the
doctrine. All these things, however, are by no means an argument against Chiliasm as such; for in a certain sense it can be
said of all Christianity, that it has no greater enemies than
careless Christians themselves. This has always been the sly
method of the devil. If he cannot reason away sound doctrine,
he corrupts it. If he cannot thwart the good seed in its growth,
he sows bad seed which looks much like the good seed.

As a final cause for the decline of this doctrine we are to
think of the work of the two great Church Fathers, Jerome and
Augustine, especially the latter. Jerome lived until the year 420.
He is considered the greatest Roman Catholic Church Father.
He possessed more knowledge than nobility of character. For a
long time he was the secretary of Pope Paul Damasus. Pope
Damasus issued a proclamation against the writings of Papias,
Nepos, Victorinus, and Sulpicius Severus, all of whom had
written about the Kingdom of Peace. One of the results was
that the Council of Rome in 373 condemned Chiliasm as

heretical and officially rejected it. Rome has always hated Chiliasm, but this need not surprise us. It wants to be the Kingdom of Christ itself.

Jerome wrote a famous and sound book about the prophecy of Daniel. The reason that he did not publish an interpretation of Revelation was his aversion to the doctrine of the Millennium. Most of the errors of Rome can be found in the books of Jerome. It is surprising that even this Church Father believed that a sabbath rest will dawn for the world after six thousand years. Although he was filled with repugnance for this doctrine, according to Semisch, he did not have the courage to express publicly a condemnation of it "over against the cloud of old-orthodox defenders and the definite favor of public opinion." He wrote:

> There is a difference of opinion on the future events and how they must be viewed and how the Revelation of John must be understood. If we interpret it literally, then we end up in the way of the Jews. If we interpret it spiritually, as it is intended to be understood, we seem to come into conflict with many of the old theologians. The majority of our people in these parts (namely, Palestine) adhere to belief in the Millennium so that I sense beforehand that I will incur the anger of many... We do not agree with it, but we cannot condemn it, for many men in the Church and many martyrs said these things.

Thus, indirectly and in spite of himself, Jerome, too, testifies strongly in favor of the Chiliasm of that time.

Augustine, more than anyone else, determined the ecclesiastical fate of this doctrine. "His arguments against Chiliasm were like hammer blows" (H. Hoekstra). He lived in turbulent times. The lamentable results of the State Church were beginning to manifest themselves on every side. The ministers became the great men of the world and a biblically ordered life began more and more to belong to the exceptions. In these trying times Augustine at first entertained expectations of a millennial kingdom of peace. But when he saw the Roman Empire, which had been called eternal, fall under the blows of the Nordic barbarians, while the Church not only remained intact but daily increased its influence on the nations of the earth, his idea of the High Church was born. He then relinquished his expectation of a future kingdom, while he became the victim of the illusion that the Millennium had already

commenced with the first coming of Christ and now manifested itself in the Church. His most important book, *The City
of God,* is actually nothing but a development and glorification
of the idea of the High Church, that the Church is everything.
On the basis of this idea he finds the Church everywhere in
Scripture, consequently she is at one and the same time Zion,
Judah, Israel, Jerusalem, Jacob, the bride of Christ, the Kingdom of Christ, and so on.

According to *The City of God,* the devil is presently bound,
and driven out of the heart of the believers; the saints already
reign and conquer with Christ over sin and the devil; the
Antichrist, the beast, is nothing but the evil world, and his
image is hypocrisy. Indeed, in reaction to the carnal fanaticism
of some Chiliasts and the Donatists, he allowed himself to be
swayed in principle to the standpoint of Hymenaeus and Philetus, who said that the resurrection had already taken place.

The identification of the church with the Kingdom is a fatal
error which has unleashed a sea of woes into the world and of
which we daily still see the disastrous results. Experience
teaches us that once a person accepts this concept of the
church, he yearns for earthly greatness but does not thirst for
the living God. This concept of the Church (for do we not see
the results of it with the Mormons, with the so-called Christian
Socialists and the Federation and Reform movements, and
with all earthly-oriented Christianity?) means death to the
living hope, the true yearning, the real homesickness. As soon
as one accepts this view, he doffs his pilgrim's mantle and lays
down his pilgrim's staff, for he is home already. Thus one loses
sight of the goal of the Church and has the opinion that the
Church's calling is to convert, and rule the whole world. This
view limits our attention to the past and the present, and causes
us to lose sight of the future work of Christ. Satan must be
pleased with this system, for it hardly reckons with him any
more, and what could be more satisfying to him?

These then are the "hammer blows" Augustine dealt to
Chiliasm. We cannot refrain from remarking here that these
blows, far from convincing, are flimsy arguments indeed. True,
on the one hand they are hits because they satisfy the flesh of
sinners. For did not Rome gladly appeal to Augustine? Every

Romanist priest still parrots Augustine's words. But on the other hand, it is deeply humiliating for the opponents of Chiliasm, that they are unable to produce more solid and Scriptural arguments against it. We do not hesitate, on the basis of God's holy Word, to brand Augustine and all who are of the same opinion on these issues as *false* Chiliasts.

Appendix 2
THE MIDDLE AGES

Lately it has been asserted that the Middle Ages need not be called dark; but with regard to the expectation of the Lord's return, they were very dark. How could it be otherwise? The ruling Church was a sworn enemy of any future reign of Christ. Jerome and Augustine controlled the eschatology of the Middle Ages. The latter has, far more than is often suspected, pointed out harmful ways for the Church to follow in these matters. Furthermore, there was only one person in a thousand who could read.

Consequently, the people could not examine prophecy for themselves. And their spiritual leaders never preached on prophetic themes except occasionally in order to arouse fear. In general, little study of the Scriptures was made, since the learned men knew no Hebrew and not much Greek, and because Rome inherently valued heathen philosophers and tradition higher than the Holy Scriptures. The church scrupulously withheld the Word from the people, so that in Europe, shortly before the Reformation, a New Testament was hardly obtainable at any price.

Toward the year 1000 a dreadful fear and terror arose among Christendom, as it was generally thought that the day of judgment would dawn at the end of the year 1000. Augustine had taught that the Millennium had begun with Christ's first coming. People thought it would end after one thousand years and would be followed by the last judgment. Rome speculated on the superstition of the people and extracted money for its coffers from the general upheaval and confusion. It succeeded in convincing many to sell all their possessions and bequeath the money to the Church in order to put their consciences at peace. This upheaval resulted in the Church becoming richer than ever and gaining possession of almost half of Europe.

In a few old church hymns, mention is made of the expectation of the return of the Lord, usually in connection with the last judgment. In general people shunned the light of prophecy and of the bright and shining Morning Star; they were afraid of Rome. The State Church is a moral monstrosity, whether it is advocated by Rome or Protestantism. Inevitably such a church corrupts rather than saves the souls of its members.

The only resistance to the teachings of Rome was Chiliastic in nature. Whenever people's faith became hope and turned to the future, they clashed with Rome, which claimed to be the Kingdom of God on earth. Dissatisfaction, hope, and mysticism were usually the hidden motivations that directed the sects away from Rome. The chief motivation seems to have been hope. The Chiliasm of the Montanists and Donatists of the first centuries, as well as that of Nepos and other strong Chiliasts, made its influence felt until deep into the Middle Ages. Although Chiliasm had officially been rejected by Rome, it never disappeared altogether.

We shall now briefly mention a few persons and sects in order to draw some conclusions.

Bernard of Clairveaux, who died in 1153, was the most beautiful figure of the Middle Ages. Although he was guilty of nearly all the errors of his day, he had a living hope *for,* an upright faith *in,* and a burning love *of* Christ. In his hymns he speaks of the imminent coming of the Lord. Apparently he did not expect a blessed state of the Church prior to Christ's coming. The evil times in which he lived were to him the sign of the approaching coming of the Lord. Some call him a Chiliast, but in our opinion he cannot bear this name in the sense implied at that time, namely, a heretic.

Arnold of Brescia was born at the beginning of the twelfth century. Study of the Bible opened his eyes, not only to the shortcomings of the Church, but also to how she ought to be, and one day would become. He could not recognize the apostles of Christ in those proud princes of the Church, who in magnificent attire rode on horseback with sword clanging at their sides. Thus grew the decision in him to stem this degeneration. He was a man of his word, of action, and of a serious nature. He traveled throughout the country as a prophet of penitence, painting in vivid colors the judgments of God upon an apostate Church. The pope eventually had him hanged and ordered his corpse burned and its ashes scattered in the River Tiber. It cannot be said with certainty whether he was an adherent of Chiliasm, but he is usually so considered.

About 1200 *Joachim of Fiore* was convinced that God's judgments on an apostate Church, which was already to him the whore of Revelation 17, could no longer be averted. He, too, was a man who had read his Bible. He is called one of the greatest exegetes of the Middle Ages. He made an extensive study of the prophetic writings. He was a Chiliast and expected the Millennium of Revelation soon. The Fratricelli, who belonged to the Franciscan order, adopted his views and disseminated them. According to Luther, Munzer derived "his high-minded ideas" from Joachim's exegesis of Jeremiah.

Peter of Bruys fulminated against the externalization of the churches, again as the result of studying the Scriptures. Prior to the Reformation, there were no more formidable enemies in the mind of Rome than those who allowed themselves to be enlightened by Scripture. Peter was not in every respect sound in doctrine, but nevertheless insisted that the Word of the Lord be held high as the only valid touchstone of theology. As an itinerant preacher, he announced that the Kingdom of God on earth was approaching. Rome ordered him burned at the stake in 1224.

Henry of Lausanne became his successor. He, too, received light from the Lord. Even his enemies spoke highly of him as being mighty in the Scriptures. Taking John the Baptist as his example, he traveled from city to city as a prophet of repentance. In him we also discover a Chiliast vein.

The Albigenses. Usually different sects in the south of France are grouped together under this name. They called themselves the Cathars (the pure). They were not altogether pure in doctrine, although some historians remind us that the reports concerning them came from their bitter enemies. Pope Innocent III preached a crusade against them. The result was that during a murderous war, that lasted twenty years, they were practically exterminated. They were considered Chiliasts by Rome. In any case, they dared to resist Rome and endure death for Christ's sake.

The Waldenses were closer to the evangelical truth than the Albigenses. Today many people question that they derived their name from Peter Waldus and even claim that their origin must be looked for much earlier, indeed as far back as the Apostolic days. Their knowledge of Scripture was extraordinary. They all could read and write. They were not surpassed in knowledge of Scripture. Even their enemies testified that their walk and conduct was most praiseworthy. Nevertheless Rome raged in a hellish manner against these simple and godly people.

Today there are still many Waldenses in Italy. Their zeal for the Kingdom of God is renowned. The old Waldenses, as well as the present-day ones, are Chiliastic.

This scant survey is sufficient to make the following remarks on Chiliasm.

1. Chiliasm was the result of an unbiased study of the Holy Scriptures, especially prophecy. This is significant in the face of the scornful claim that Chiliasm is Jewish and leads us back to Jewry. But these leaders did not arrive at this doctrine by reading the Talmud or the Apocrypha, but only by reading Scripture. These people did become anti-Romanist, but not anti-Jewish.

2. Their enemies frequently testify to their exemplary conduct and walk. To know this is of great importance in judging their true character.

3. They were virtually the only opposition to Rome's abominations during the high Middle Ages.

4. In many instances they allowed themselves to be tortured for Christ's sake and they remained faithful to Christ and their Chiliasm unto death.

Apart from all this, it must be said of these and other Chiliastic sects that they sometimes committed the error of premature anticipation and ran ahead of things which God will bring about in His own time. The Scriptural injunction, "Ye have need of patience," was applicable to many of them. And some, such as Savonarola, allowed themselves to personally prophesy instead of explaining prophecy to others. But these sects, however mistaken, were far better than Rome. Generally speaking, Chiliasm was one of the most refreshing phenomena in the dark Middle Ages.

Appendix 3

FROM THE REFORMATION
TO THE PRESENT

THE REFORMERS

The blessed Church Reformation of the sixteenth century was a definite victory over Rome's errors. The bright light of the Word was removed from underneath the bushel and placed on the candlestick. With regard to the expectation of the return of the Lord, a revival erupted.

Luther concerned himself with the coming of the Lord. In the important things in his life he believed to see the signs of the immediate end of all things. He hoped that Christ would hasten the day of His coming to end the quarrels on earth and to "pulverize the entire earth to dust." He expected that wickedness would become rampant until life for the believers would become unbearable and their crying would arise from every place for the coming of the Lord in judgment.

He often attacked false Chiliasm, which always expected a blessed state of the Church on earth in a carnal sense and apart from the return of Christ. That he did not expect much good from the world outside of Christ is evident from the following quotations:

People continue to rage and become more wicked by the day, which is truly a comfort to the weary soul, for this shows that the glorious day of the Lord is at hand. The world is left to its own ways, so that the day of its destruction and of our delivery might be hastened.

Some people say that before the last days the entire world will become Christian. This is a lie forged by Satan, so that he might obscure sound doctrine. Therefore be on your guard against this deception; for we must always bear the cross, while those who persecute the saints are always in the majority.

Ever since the gospel has been revealed, the world has become very obstinate and stubborn and is starting to crack. I hope that soon it will burst and collapse by the coming of the day of judgment, for which we look with great anticipation and sighings of the heart.

He constantly heeded the signs of the times, as is evident from the following statements.

How Satan rages everywhere against the Word! I consider this to be in no way the least sign of the approaching end, namely, that when the day of the Lord is at hand, Satan is at work and belches forth his final fury.

I constantly see this day before me, for I am certain that this day must be at the door; for all the signs, foretold by Christ and the Apostles, have been fulfilled.

Nothing is more certain than this, namely, that only by far the smallest part of mankind shows any concern about such signs; in general people could not care less. Hence it is to be feared that this day is nearer at hand than we believe. The signs are multiplying.

Although he refrained from making any calculations, and at times even hoped for better times, the day of the Lord was always on his mind. He even expected that he would not be able to finish his Bible translation before the Lord would come upon the clouds of heaven.

According to Seiss, who wrote a book on Luther, he also taught that Christ will personally reign as King of Zion on the renewed earth, and also that after six thousand years of strife the thousand-year day of rest will dawn for the world. During the first years of the Reformation he entertained great expectations regarding the Jews, but later he inveighed against them in his impassioned way.

A Jewish heart is so stick-stone-iron-devilish hard that it cannot be moved. They have been hatched by the devil and are doomed to hell. To convert these children of the devil, as some dream can be done, is, according to the Epistle to the Romans, impossible.

We would not have expected such a judgment from the man who himself had been delivered from the shackels of Rome and who always strongly emphasized God's omnipresence. Psychologically, however, this is more easily accounted for. The Jews disappointed Luther severely. At first he had expected that Israel, which had always been oppressed by Rome, would in its entirety welcome and join the Reformation. Nothing of the sort happened. On the contrary, some left Rome and went to the Synagogue. For that reason in 1543 he wrote a vehement pamphlet, *The Jews and Their Lies.* Add to this that Professor Carlstadt, the Zwickau Prophets, and Munzer and his Anabaptists advocated a false Chiliasm, opposed him strenuously, and even jeopardized the entire work of the Reformation, and it will be clear to what extent such Chiliasm became repugnant to him.

At the same time it cannot be denied, regrettably, that from his point of view he could not very well embrace a biblical Chiliasm, since he always connected the return of the Lord with the end of the world and the general judgment. His lack of differentiation between true and false Chiliasm and his deep repugnance of the false kind of his day was part of the reason why Luther ended up rejecting the last book of the Bible. He was an adherent of literal interpretation, so it was clear to him that he would not be able to use this book to deny the Millennium. He declared that in Revelation he found much that was neither prophetic nor apostolic, nor did he find any proof for its inspiration. Taking everything into consideration, we can say of Luther that unconsciously he held many true Chiliastic ideas, and that he was an excellent opponent of false Chiliasm, but that he did not possess sufficient light on Chiliasm as it was found during the first three centuries and today.

Melanchthon's teaching about the last things was similar to Luther's. Like Luther, he expected that the world would exist only six thousand years. He wrote this as a memorandum on the first page of Luther's Bible. Like Luther, he did not expect a state of bliss for the Church in this dispensation, and he believed that the end of all things was very close. Like Luther, he was a fierce opponent of false Chiliasm. He is the composer of the *Confessio Augustana,* the most important Confession of the Lutheran Church. In Article 17 he expresses himself thus on the matter: "We condemn those who today spread the Jewish ideas that before the resurrection of the dead the godly will rule the world after all the wicked everywhere have been subjugated." It is obvious that this expression refers to the contemporary fanatics and Anabaptists, as is generally assumed today. Franz Delitzsch, who was as witty as he was learned, says, "I am a Chiliast, but the *damnamus* of the

Augustana does not touch me." Lange, Richter, Steffann, Rinck, Ebrard, Brookes, and others, are of the same opinion.

The same things can be said about the second *Reformed Confession* of Switzerland. It was composed by Bullinger, the successor of Zwingli, and approved by Beza, the successor of Calvin. Article 11 of this Confession says, "We reject the Jewish fantasies that before the day of judgment there will be a golden age on earth and the believers will accept the reign of the world after the subjugaton of the wicked, their enemies." This statement has often been quoted to refute the expectation of a Millennium as such. We and all present-day premillennialists can with all our hearts agree with this article, for it is nothing but a denunciation of that false expectation which today is known by the name of postmillennialism.

In his otherwise excellent lecture on *The Millennium,* Dr. R. L. Haan gives the impression that premillennialism expects the Millennium before the return of Christ. If this were the case, then this article would be directed at present-day Chiliasm. The fact is, however, that the premillennialism of today hates nothing more than the abominable error that a millennium of any kind is still to be expected before Christ's return. For the sake of our esteem for Dr. Haan, we hope that he made a mistake in terminology.

Calvin has seen, believed, and embraced from afar. The evidence in his books is abundant that he, like Luther, concerned himself much with the return of Christ. In his *Institutes* he expresses himself thus: "Let us not forget, however, to desire the return of the Lord as the greatest of all events, the happiest event, with sighing and groaning." But he went no farther than any other Reformer in developing a doctrine of the last things. Like Luther, Calvin constantly fights against the false, but the true he does not know. Hence he, too, often throws out the baby with the bath water. In his *Institutes* he says, "The Chiliasts limit the time of Christ within a thousand years, but their invention is too childish to need or merit any refutation." Again, he does not touch present-day Chiliasm, for he teaches on the basis of Daniel 2:44, that Christ will have an *eternal* Kingdom. He will be King over the house of Jacob forever, and there will be no end to this Kingdom (Luke 1:33).

We heartily agree with the great Reformer that Chiliasm would be childish, if it were to limit the Kingdom of Christ, contrary to Scripture, within the thousand years. Every age brings its own calling, and obviously it has not been the calling of Calvin to interpret prophecy. In general we can say of Calvin:

1. The coming of the Lord was to him a matter of utmost importance and not, as to many of his followers, a secondary matter.

2. He combatted false Chiliasm while many of his followers actually *are* false Chiliasts because they expect a state of bliss for the Church in this dispensation. Although he was too much a proponent of the spiritualizing method of interpreting prophecy—he applies the promises made to Israel to the Church and the curses to the Jews—he nevertheless did not believe that a conversion of the Jews was impossible according to his exposition of Romans 11.

4. His vehement aversion to Rome and the heretics prevented him from coming to an objective development of eschatology.

THE CHILIASM OF THE SEVENTEENTH CENTURY IN ENGLAND

What is true of the eschatology of Luther, Melanchthon, and Calvin generally applies also to Zwingli, Bullinger, Beza, Knox, Latimer, and other Reformers. Especially in England, where the study of prophecy usually did *not* take a back seat, there were in the seventeenth century many famous theologians who were definitely Chiliasts; we mention three.

Joseph Mede is considered by many to be the father of the study of prophecy. In 1677 he published three books on Revelation, an exposition of 2 Peter 3, and a book on Daniel with a treatise on the apostasy of the last days. His sole purpose was to discover the right meaning of the prophetic Scriptures. To that objective he applied all his comprehensive learning. He was a professor at the University of Cambridge and taught history, Jewish antiquities, and chronology. He was so famous that many foreigners visited the university to see him.

Dr. William Twisse was the president of the Westminster Assembly held in 1643 and one of the men who composed the

Presbyterian *Westminster Confession*. He also was a learned and godly theologian. His published material consists of three folio book volumes. At first he was a strong opponent of the doctrine of the Millennium. One day, after he heard that Mede had preached that the seventh thousand years must be considered as the day of Christ, the day of judgment, during which the Messiah will reign on earth, he was, according to his own words, so inflamed with anger that he decided to lay all other study aside and dedicate himself exclusively to the task of refuting this error. Thereupon he went to see Mede. The result of this visit was that Mede convinced him that this doctrine was Scriptural. Just as Lord Littleton and Gilbert West lost their unbelief, so Twisse's hatred of and opposition to biblical Chiliasm disappeared. Later Twisse wrote prefaces for several books in which Mede contended for the doctrine of the Millennium. He said of Mede, "Many exegetes have done an excellent job, but Mr. Mede surpasses them all."

James Ussher, the famous chronologist, was a close friend of Mede. By his book on the chronology of the Old and New Testament he rendered inestimable services to the study of prophecy. He was as humble as he was learned. After his death in 1650 his mortal remains received a place of honor in Westminster Abbey. In an anonymous pamphlet he was even called a prophet. He is generally known as a Chiliast.

The *Baptist Confession* composed in Britain in 1660 apparently leans toward Chiliasm, for Article 22 gives expression to the expectation that Christ, after His return, will reign as King on earth and His people with Him. This symbolicum was signed by all the Baptist ministers and was believed and confessed by twenty thousand members.

Other famous Chiliasts in England at that time were John Milton, Jeremiah Taylor, Samuel Rutherford, John Bunyan, and Burnet J. Leade. In the eighteenth century Isaac Newton, Thomas Newton, Doddridge, Watts, Robert Hall, Fletcher, Toplady, Cowper, Coke, both Wesleys, and numerous excellent men, all of whom adhered to Chiliasm, prospered in the field of learning.

CHILIASM OF THE
REFORMED CHURCHES IN THE NETHERLANDS
DURING THE 17TH AND 18TH CENTURIES

It is quite evident from the Confessions and formulary prayers that in earlier times the Reformed Churches in the Netherlands were thinking—and living accordingly—far more about the return of the Lord than is the case today. It is usually said by such men as Bavinck, H. Hoekstra, and Haan that the theologians Cocceius, Witsius, à Brakel, à Marck, Moor, Alting, Groenewegen, d'Otrein, Vitringa, and others advocated a *milder* form of Chiliasm. The fact is that these men were nothing else than our present-day postmillennialists. They did expect a millennium, but before and apart from Christ. Out of a full conviction we must call this an unbiblical, indeed a highly pernicious error.

Pièrre Jurieu (d. 1713) deserves mention here because he was summoned to ecclesiastical court for his Chiliasm. As a professor at the High School in Rotterdam he wrote a book in French in 1687 on *The Fulfillment of Prophecy*. According to him, papal Rome was the antichristian kingdom. He considered its collapse to be imminent. And immediately after this downfall the blessed reign of Christ on earth would commence. This book brought him much trouble. The Synod of North Holland insisted on examining ecclesiastically whether he had violated the teaching of the Church with respect to the Millennium. It brought this to the attention of the Walloon Synod which convened the same year in Balk, but the result of the examination was that Jurieu was acquitted of any suspicion of being unorthodox.

Pièrre Poiret (1646-1719) was a different kind of Chiliast who, as a Frenchman, spent most of his life in the Netherlands. He was an exceptional man, a philosopher, theologian, mystic, and a man of immense energy and feverish diligence. In his *magnum opus* of six volumes on *De Goddelijke Huishouding* (*The Divine Economy*) he reveals himself as an adherent of the doctrine of the reign of Christ on earth. Poiret already saw clearly that not only Revelation 20 but the whole Bible was full of this truth. Also this tree did not bear such bad fruits, for in Rijnsburg, where he lived for more than thirty years, he was held in great esteem by all on account of his honest heart and upright godliness. He cannot, however, be considered orthodox in every respect.

Jean de Labadie (1610-1674) was an eccentric but important personality in the ecclesiastical history of the Netherlands. It seems to us that thus far he has not been fully understood. He has been judged and evaluated in the most divergent ways by friend and foe, both during his lifetime and afterward. The most serious accusation which is usually leveled against him from the Reformed side is not his stark Chiliasm, which had already been attacked by the renowned theologian Koelman in his book on Revelation, but that he wanted to establish a pure Church; this is in any case a better accusation than an impure one. But in spite of all his peculiarities, his mysticism, and his lack of wise discretion, both friend and foe vie with each other in admitting that he was very capable and loved his Savior dearly. He was a man who desired to live according to Scripture and ceased to attend regularly the services of the State Church, which became increasingly more worldly.

Robert Fleming is another foreigner who studied and preached in the Netherlands. In 1701 he published a book on Revelation. This book became famous because it predicted, a century before it happened, the collapse of the French throne. He thought that the Millennium would commence in the year 2000. This is the opinion of many students of prophecy.

Generally speaking it must be said of the Dutch State Church, in the 17th and 18th centuries, that very little joyous hope in the blessed return of the Lord was found. People looked back to Dordrecht more than forward to Christ. Apart from a few exceptions, we find, with nearly all the old exegetes, the expectation of a state of bliss for the Church on earth, which obscured rather than clarified a right view of the last things. This expectation of a state of glory of the Church in this dispensation is often called a moderate Chiliasm in contrast to the Chiliasm that was base and inordinate; but, viewed in the light of the Word, this expectation is false. Moderate Chiliasm may not be vulgar or base, but a fine error is no better than a flagrant one. We find little that is uplifting and enriching in the life of the Church in those days. Dr. A. W. Bronsveld in his thesis on *De Oorzaken van het Rationalisme in Nederland* (*The Causes of Rationalism in the Netherlands*) says:

> How accurate was the picture given in those days:
> "People pinch and bite; they hew and hack to pieces;
> They pull and pick and tear and rob and pillage;
> Godliness itself is spit upon its face—
> We see it, but we look at it with eyes full of pity."

THE REVIVAL OF THE STUDY OF PROPHECY

1. In the Lutheran Churches

Johann Albrecht Bengel (1687-1752), professor at the seminary at Denkendorf, and renowned exegete of the pietist movement, deserves the greatest place of honor for his studies of prophecy. The revived Lutheran interest in prophecy dates back to him. His influence is incalculably great even to this day, especially abroad. He lived in the arid days of Rationalism, so that we need not wonder why this sensitive soul had to lament, "It looks as though in spiritual matters winter is at hand; we live in a miserable, cold time; we need an awakener."

God ordered it so that Bengel himself became that awakener of his contemporaries by opening the prophetic Scriptures to them. His daily activity was searching the Scriptures. While doing this he forced himself to follow three rules (which still may be considered worthy to be imitated): A) Let the Bible be your source—not books, not great men, not public opinion, but only and alone the whole Bible. B) Read nothing *into* the Bible; this shows an unbiased and childlike way of studying Scripture. C) Do not ignore anything in the Bible, for all of Scripture is given by inspiration of God. His main books on prophecy are *Eene Verklaring van de Openbaring* (*An Interpretation of Revelation*) and *Ordo Temporum,* a treatise on chronology. His *Gnomon* [now published as *New Testament Commentary,* 1982, Kregel Publications] or Guide to the New Testament is his *magnum opus.* It is almost inevitable that he should be a Chiliast when we remember that he diligently studied prophecy according to the above-mentioned rules.

It cannot be lamented enough, however, that Bengel fixed the date for the return of the Lord and the beginning of the

Millennium as 1838. He entertained and proclaimed the idea that the Lord later revealed the time of His return to John. The Adventists and other sects seem to have adopted this idea from him. This considerably diminished his fame and caused him to be numbered among mysticists and fanatics, although he was among the purest and soberest of souls. Because of this one mistake, many people have now arrogantly rejected all of his work. In any other area people would not act so stupidly, but in the realm of prophecy, they usually make the strictest demands.

2. In the English-speaking World

In the English-speaking world the honor of having launched the present-day study of prophetic Scriptures and its attendant hope for the return of the Lord is awarded to Manuel Lacunza, a Chilean Jesuit. This priest wrote a book in Spanish, entitled, *The Coming of the Messiah in Glory.* It is to this day a standard work on the coming of Christ to found the Kingdom of Peace. It appeared in 1812 and was soon translated into French and Latin. In 1826 it came into the hands of Edward Irving, the well-known founder of Irvingism. He was so elated with it that he at once decided to translate it into English. The next year he published his translation in two large volumes. Everyone is agreed that this book by Lacunza evidences a rare knowledge of the Bible. As a Jesuit in Chile, he instructed the people from the Bible, and it is evident that he was in love with the Scriptures. He wrote under the Jewish pseudonym of Ben Ezra, and therefore many people believe that he was a Jew. But this is by no means certain, although there are two things that argue in favor of it. He has a Jewish appearance, *and* he has a Jewish insight into the Scriptures. His book will be read until the return of the Lord.

Since the beginning of the 19th century, the Spirit of the Lord has guided thousands in Europe to a renewed study of the Scriptures, especially prophecy. And almost without exception the result has been, that they began to long more ardently for the coming of Christ to take up believers into the air.

In England during the 19th century, there were many excellent representatives of the Scriptural expectation of a Millennium on earth. *Alexander Keith* wrote famous books on *Fulfilled Prophecy, Harmony of the Prophetic Word,* and *Signs of the Times. Robert Murray McCheyne,* a much loved writer in Reformed circles, wrote on the subject. *Edward Greswell* wrote a standard work of five volumes on the Parables showing that he is a Chiliast. *Richard C. Trench,* who wrote on the Parables and the Miracles, in his *Christ, the Desire of All Gentiles,* reveals himself as a Chiliast. *Henry Alford,* the excellent exegete, in his annotations on Revelation 20 makes himself known as a proponent of Chiliasm. *Samuel P. Tregelles,* whose exegetical and critical contributions are highly esteemed by all, wrote an exposition on Daniel and Revelation, and adhered to the Chiliasm of the Plymouth Brethren to which group he belonged.

Charles J. Ellicot in his excellent commentaries frequently gives Chiliastic explanations and is usually counted among the Millennialists. *John Cumming* preached on little else but the return of Christ and everything connected with it. The same can be said of *Grattan Guinness. John Charles Ryle,* the well-known expositor of the Gospels, manifests himself in his *Future Facts and Present Duties* and other books as an ardent Chiliast. *Thomas Chalmers,* the father of the Secession in Scotland, who was a profoundly learned man and excellent student of Scripture, was a convinced Chiliast. (See the Preface by Capadose to Hebart's *Eschatology.*) Chalmer's successor adhered to the same expectations regarding the future.

But where would be the end if we wished to tell you about the two Bonars, Bickersteth, Birks, Brooks, Beverly, Bellett, Darby, Kelly, Mackintosh, Wigram, Elliot, the Wilkinsons, the McNeils, Saphir, Spurgeon, Haslam, Andrews, Fausset, Guthrie, Müller, Campbell, Meyer, Pember, Baxter, Anderson, Walter Scott, Baron, and dozens of others in that country? They are all men of great ability, zeal, and godliness, and convinced premillennialists.

With a few exceptions, all those who are still orthodox in the English State Church adhere to this view, and not in a milder form, as people prefer to call it. They oppose the so-called moderate form of Chiliasm as unbiblical postmillennialism that dreams of a kingdom of peace apart from the King of Peace. But to accuse present-day premillennialism of base or even sensuous Chiliasm is even more unjustified. Reformed circles have seldom paid any attention to Chiliasm and hence they seem to wish to deny the possibility, in any case the reality, of a moral and spiritual (literal) Chiliasm. They now frequently make a distinction between *moderate* and *sensual* as if there were such a thing as moderate sensuality.

3. In France and Other Countries

Chiliasm has one characteristic which cannot be denied by even its bitterest enemies and that is its *catholicity*. It is found in all ages, all places, and among all classes of men. No matter how much it is derided by proud science or narrow-minded orthodoxy, it boldly appears again and again, fully assured of its justification. It is fully convinced that it rests on the unshakable foundation of Scripture.

Since the days of the Reformation, France never lacked witnesses to this truth. The famous commentary of Charles Daubuz was Chiliastic. Not only in France but throughout all Europe it was considered a standard work. Often the persecuted Huguenots adhered to this truth; the Camisards also, although they sometimes committed the sin of anticipation of the promised state of bliss. During the Awakening the three brothers *Monod, de Presencé, Guers,* and others, were proponents and preachers of it. In Switzerland venerable men such as *Malan, Gaussen,* and *Godet* were witnesses to this maligned truth. In South Africa must be mentioned *S. J. du Toit, Professor N. J. Hofmeyer,* and *Lion Cachet,* the author of *Naar het Land der Vaderen (To the Land of the Fathers).* Du Toit wrote the excellent treatise on *Onvervulde Profetie (Unfulfilled Prophecy.)*

The missionaries of these later years have carried Chiliasm to the ends of the earth. *Karl Guttzlaff* carried this truth, accompanied by Da Costa's Chiliastic poems, to the millions in China; *Bettleheim* of Hungary to Japan; *Alexander Duff* of Scotland to India; *John Eliot* to the Indians; *John Paton* to the New Hebrides; *Josef Wolf* to all countries were there were Jews; *Josef Rabbinowitch* and *Lord Radstock* preached it in Russia.

It will be difficult to mention ten great missionaries who succeeded them who did not adhere to this truth. This, too, is a constant and everywhere-recurring characteristic of Chiliasts. They are always warm friends of missions.

Franz Delitzsch, professor in Germany, who died in 1890, aroused great interest in the mission among Jews by his *Institute for Jews.* Following his example, similar institutes were inaugurated in Leipzig, Erlangen, and Christiania. *Grattan Guinness* is the founder of the great School of Missions in London, which by the year 1888 had sent out more than five hundred missionaries. *The Christian and Missionary Alliance* in America under the leadership of the deeply spiritual A. B. Simpson, who is frequently considered the main interpreter of American premillennialism, sent out dozens of missionaries to all countries. The missionary church of the Rev. H. W. Witteveen in Ermelo sent out numerous messengers of peace to Sumatra, Java, Egypt, and other countries. Actually there has been only one Chiliast community, i.e., that of the *Hernhutters,* which at the same time is well known as the most excellent missionary church. Regardless of the above facts, which are sufficiently known historically, the accusation is nevertheless made, in writing or orally, that premillennialism is the death of missions.

CHILIASM IN AMERICA

It is impossible to strive here for comprehensiveness because a complete history would be equal to about half of the American Church History. We would have to commence with Colonial times for, according to Taylor, Silver, and others, Puritans and independents were Chiliastic. From the earliest times are mentioned *John Clark, Increase* and *Cotton Mather, John Eliot, Thomas Price, B. Gale, Joshua Spalding.* The German pietists brought with them an expectation of a kingdom of peace in *Het Ware Christendom* (*True Christianity*) by J. Arndt, the writings of Bengel, and Stilling's *Die Berlenburger Bibel* (*The Berlenburg Bible*), a work in four folio volumes which contains Chiliastic explanations.

In addition to these, mention must be made as definite defenders *Philander Chase,* president of Cincinnati College and founder of Kenyon and Jubilee Colleges; *C. P. McIlvaine,* university professor in New York and later the head of Kenyon

College; *Mark Hopkins,* president of Williams College; and *Nathan Lord,* president of Dartmouth College. But the false expectation of a state of bliss, entertained by *Jonathan Edwards,* has done much harm in this country; he is the American Augustine. As the main representatives of the last century the following must be mentioned:

Dr. George Duffield, minister of the First Presbyterian Church of Detroit. His book on *Prophecies Concerning the Second Coming of Jesus Christ* (1842) is a standard work. His most ardent opponent was Moses Stuart, who is nevertheless frequently considered a Chiliast because he was a convinced proponent of literal interpretation of Scripture and, remaining true to himself, gave a Chiliastic interpretation of Revelation 20. *Prof. J. T. Duffield* of Princeton is often called the father of present-day premillennialism. The two Duffields must not be taken for one and the same person, as is quite often done.

Dr. Joseph A. Seiss was the chief American interpreter of Chiliasm in the Lutheran Church. He was a man of talent, study, energy, and zeal. For many years he was the editor of *The Lutheran,* the official paper of the Lutheran Church. His books on *Revelation, Daniel, The Last Days,* and *The Millennium* are at present well known throughout all of Europe.

Dr. A. J. Gordon of Boston can safely be considered to have been for many years the best representative in the Baptist Church. He was an ardent champion of the verbal inspiration and literal interpretation of Scripture. His book *Ecce Venit* (*Behold, He Cometh*) will ever remain worthy reading on the return of Christ. At present Dr. Haldeman is the most important Chiliast spokesman for this church.

Dr. William Nast, the father of the German Methodists, was the main interpreter of eschatology in those churches. He was a man of vast learning and indefatigable fervor; he wielded a fluent pen. He was editor of *Der Christliche Apologete (The Christian Apologist)* and promoted with word and pen both in German and English the doctrine of the kingdom of peace. *Dr. L. W. Munhall* is the most ardent champion of this teaching in the Methodist Episcopal Church. His book on *De Wederkomst van Christus (The Return of Christ)* is very instructive. He is at the same time the strongest opponent of the worldly-minded current in the Methodist churches. His book *Method-*

ism Adrift! demands respect and admiration for the man who has the courage of conviction to accuse his entire denomination of apostasy and unfaithfulness.

Dr. W. J. Erdman was for many years the outstanding witness for Chiliasm in the Congregational Churches. Dr. Erdman devoted himself to this cause and wrote several larger and smaller books on it. These churches are almost totally secularized through higher criticism and the teaching of evolution, but the few faithful witnesses who remain are champions of the millennial kingdom of peace on earth. In this connection must also be mentioned the influence of the famous *Dr. G. Campbell Morgan.*

Dr. W. G. Moorehead, president of the seminary at Xenia, Ohio, was an energetic fighter for orthodoxy in the United Presbyterian Church. He was the soul of many a *Prophetic Conference.* He was one of the summoners of the conference held in Chicago in 1914. He did not conceal it from his students, but taught it to them as the truth of Holy Scripture. His book on Revelation is excellent. He was obviously "mighty in the Scriptures."

Dr. W. R. Nicholson, bishop of the *Reformed Episcopal Church,* was a champion of this teaching and was as capable as he was courageous. The Episcopalian churches are commonly enamored with the high-church idea of a state church. For this reason it must amaze us all the more that this group of churches has produced its equivalent quota of representatives of millennial teaching. Usually from this section came strong opposition. At the Conference of 1878 there were 43 Presbyterians, 27 Baptists, 7 Methodists, and 15 Episcopalians who were proponents of the Millennium.

We skip here the numerous sects that are wholly or partly Chiliastic in hue and in some cases propagate the most pernicious errors. We must nevertheless mention the name of a man who is considered to have done more than anyone else for the development of the teaching concerning the last things in the sense advocated here. We are referring to *Dr. James H. Brookes.*

Brookes graduated from Princeton Seminary. For more than twenty-five years, he served a large Presbyterian congregation in St. Louis. For some twenty years he was the editor of

The Truth, which is considered a goldmine for the knowledge of Holy Scripture. By means of word and pen he obtained a name for himself far beyond the borders of this country. His *magnum opus, Maranatha,* is one of the most outstanding studies on the return of the Lord. His study on *Israel and the Church* is possibly the most illuminating book ever written on this subject. In a tract he wrote how he became a Chiliast or, as it is commonly called in this country, a premillennialist.

During the early years of his ministry he had almost an aversion to the last things. One morning, when he had deliberately avoided reading from Revelation at his family devotions, he asked himself why he was doing this. And since his conscience condemned him, he decided from henceforth to read Revelation prayerfully, the more so since the beatitude of Revelation 1:3 does not speak of *understanding* but of *reading* and *hearing.* Revelation led him to Daniel, and the latter in turn to the other prophets. The result of his prayerful study of Scripture was that he became fully convinced of these three facts: A) The Lord Jesus Christ is coming back bodily and visibly; B) One day a kingdom of peace will come on earth; C) This glorious kingdom is not coming before but after the return of the Lord. Like *Dr. Arthur Pierson* and others, he also expresses it as his experience that this truth is the key to the correct understanding of the Scriptures.

Gaebelein, Scofield, Gray, Torrey, Riley, Jennings, Pettingill, and *Blackstone* are among the most excellent authorities on the prophetic Scriptures and advocates of Chiliasm.

It certainly is no exaggeration to say that with the exception of the Seminary at Princeton and the Reformed Churches, all who are still positively adhering to the verbal inspiration of Scripture in this country are Chiliasts. At first strong opposition to Chiliasm emanated from the Reformed Church, but today we hardly hear about it.

Also a powerful headwind blew from the Presbyterian Church, but there, too, the wind has considerably died down. Not since *Dr. D. Brown* of Scotland has anything new been leveled against it, not even by such capable Presbyterian scholars as *Rice, Patterson, Charles Hodge, Warfield, Vos, Rankin,* and just recently *McKnight.* By far most of the objections of these men originate from a false principle of exegesis, namely, the lamentable spiritualization of unfulfilled prophecy. They are perfectly correct when it concerns an ill-advised, almanac-like literalness. But between these two lies the golden mean of literal exegesis which at the same time wants to take into account the abundance of metaphorical language and the poetic garb of many images.

Methodists such as *Dr. D. Steele* and *George W. Wilson* combat Chiliasm for entirely different reasons than the Presbyterians. These two Armenians point at the "pernicious Calvinistic character" of Chiliasm. We are compelled to admit here that biblical Chiliasm is totally in line with election. If Calvin and Luther lived in our day they would undoubtedly be full-blooded Chiliasts.

An accusation that is frequently heard in this country is that among Chiliasts there are as many ideas as there are heads. The fact is, however, that those men mentioned above as the principal spokesmen of the various denominations were all agreed on the following points:

A) A bodily return of Christ before the Millennium.

B) A bodily resurrection of the believers at His coming.

C) The devil will be bound for a thousand years.

D) The resurrection and the judgment of the wicked will be at the end of the kingdom of peace.

In this connection it is almost amusing to a Chiliast that the opponents of Chiliasm are not agreed on very important, indeed essential, matters. We just mention in passing:

A) A Congregational minister, who does not mention his name, in attacking Chiliasm interprets the coming again of the Lord as the coming of the Holy Spirit into the heart of a sinner. (See *The Coming of Christ in His Kingdom,* p. 79).

B) *J. Stuart Russell* in his *Parousia,* which is a critical examination, attacks Chiliasm but teaches that Christ has already returned at the destruction of Jerusalem. *Dr. Agar Beet* in his *The Last Things* attacks both this teaching and Chiliasm.

C) *Moses Stuart, S. M. Merrill,* and *D. Steele* in their books against Chiliasm (Rev. 20:4-5) speak of a literal first resurrection, whereas *G. W. Wilson* in his *The Sign of Thy Coming* protests correctly that it is the Chiliasts who teach this.

D) *H. T. Adamson, George W. MacMillan, George Bush,* and *R. L. Haan* all wrote books on the Millennium in an anti-Chiliast vein, but their viewpoints vary widely when it comes to saying what exactly the Millennium is.

We could enlarge on this striking disagreement among anti-Chiliasts, but we have no desire to do so now. If it had not been a fact that this accusation is constantly made by these opponents, we would not even have mentioned it at all. We have already adduced enough proof here to be convinced that the true unity of viewpoint is on the side of those "who wait for the Kingdom of God."

The sin of which Chiliasm has lately been accused is that it refuses to help reform the world and society. To this we can answer that biblical Chiliasm is deeply convinced: A) that it is not God's purpose to improve the world in its present condition; B) that nowhere in Scripture is an injunction or example given to *reform*. James 5:1-8 provides the divine and infallible way to deal with social evils.

CHILIASM IN THE NETHERLANDS DURING THE LAST CENTURY

No one who loves the Reformed Church will consider it unimportant to dwell on this subject for a while. We must first have a look at the men of the *Reveil* (Awakening) and then at the *Secession*.

1. The Chiliasm of the Reveil

By the *Reveil* we mean the religious awakening as it manifested itself among the upper class in some larger cities in the Netherlands about a century ago. The religious awakening there as elsewhere brought with it also a revival of the doctrine of the last things or, more correctly, a life of expectation of the coming of the Lord. The eschatological character of the *Reveil* is the most outstanding one of this entire movement. This explains three other characteristics of the *Reveil;* i.e., it was less ecclesiastical, less national, and more poetic than was the Secession.

First, it was less ecclesiastical. We cannot simply say that the *Reveil* was totally non-ecclesiastical as is sometimes said. But whereas the men of the Secession by and large wanted a return to Dordt, the men of the *Reveil* reached out for the future. And whereas the Secession clung tenaciously to the Church-idea at the expense of the State-idea, the *Reveil* did exactly the opposite. The men of the *Reveil,* especially Da Costa, viewed the Church of this dispensation as an embryo that would not be born until the rebirth of all things.

Its less national nature is explained by the eschatological character of the *Reveil.* For it is probable that eschatology was nowhere less developed than in the Netherlands, in spite of the enormous dogmatic work done by the forefathers. The Dutch national character does not seem to be favorable to the study of the last things. In any case, the eschatology of England, Switzerland, and Germany had a noticeable influence on the *Reveil.*

The striking poetic nature of this revival must be explained partly as the result of future expectations and partly from the fact that both its father and its principal spokesman were poets. It is a psychological and historical fact, however, that the living expectation of the return of the Lord creates poetry both in heart and life. Today Bilderdijk is generally acknowledged as the spiritual father of the *Reveil.* It can be proved that he was even the precursor and pioneer of the Secession. Hence we wish to take a brief look at his expectations regarding the future, in order to pause and take a look at Da Costa and a long line of his followers.

Willem Bilderdijk was a genius of the first rank; he was great in every field. In the big *Gedenkboek* (*Memorial Volume*), published in 1906, his greatness is reviewed from every angle by capable men. It is regrettable that in this book his theological significance is not mentioned, for in this respect he was of greatest importance. He had never studied theology at a university; but he did study his Bible diligently. Add to this that his nature, principle, and juridic studies prevented him from spiritualizing prophecy, and nothing else could possibly be expected than that all of his theology be Chiliastically oriented. As a theologian he can best be compared to Jung Stilling who himself had great influence on the religious life of the higher circles in the Netherlands, during the first years of the nineteenth century.

Bilderdijk viewed all of world history as a preparation for the coming and the Kingdom of the Lord. He saw that everything in his days was preparing itself for the "new society." He carefully watched the signs of the times. He saw signs where no other mortal ever saw or would see them. For example, he saw in the Jewish substitution of the name *Israel* for *Judah* a sign that Shiloh would come soon; perhaps he was not far off the mark for the fig tree is already budding. According to him the great apostasy began with the French Revolution and was rapidly increasing. In the scientific knowledge of his day he saw Anti-christianity systematized. Hence out of fear of the abominations of heathenism he did not dare to let his little son, Lodewijk, study Latin. "Believe me," he wrote to Da Costa, "I tremble for fear of learning, when I consider the situation of today."

This gloomy bard became joyful in the Lord when he observed that people began to pay more attention to Revelation and that they generally heeded the signs of the times more than before. And it made him happy that his beloved friend, Da Costa, had "so gloriously comprehended the coming of Christ." He considered very few Christians ready for this "glorious prospect" on account of the false spiritualizing method of interpreting prophecy. This was, according to him, an annihilation of prophecy. Regardless of how speculative in nature Bilderdijk was, in these things he was objective and was afraid of teaching anything outside the Word of the Lord. "Let us not arrogate to ourselves too much detailed description of the future," he wrote to Da Costa, whom he frequently admonished to calmness and carefulness with regard to future things.

Bilderdijk was through and through a child of hope and longing. The imminent coming of the Lord was to him, from an early age, no mere speculation of the mind, but a joyful hope which kept him going, during his suffering, in the days of his exile. In his preface to the second volume of his letters and essays, Da Costa writes, "This expectation, ever more definite and developed, filled most of his Christian poems since the days of his exile, and animated and encouraged him in his long and many-sided battle against the apostasy and lie of his age."

This expectation also prompted him to constantly study prophecy. He has left us an abstract of Revelation. Because of his expectation of the coming Kingdom of Israel's Messiah, he became the means in God's hand of the conversion of Da Costa and Capadose. According to him, the orthodox Jews were deeply guilty but by far not as guilty as the apostate Christians of his day. He loved the Jewish people for the sake of the Lord. Of Israel's future he wrote:

> The Lion of Judah lives and carries the scepter of heaven and earth,
> And approaches for the second time.
> Look for Him! Yes, He approaches,
> As wide Megiddon already gathers its eagles,
> Which smell the smoke of blood,
> Which from the undulating vale of slaughter shall rise far and wide
>   unto heaven,
> When His avenging arm shall destroy the heathen,
> United in the Hope of Israel with the erring descendants.
> Bewail your temple until then; mourn, yea mourn;
> Soon the veil will be torn from your countenance.

Elsewhere he speaks of the coming of the Lord to establish the kingdom of peace.

> Hear, thou earth, yea hear me foretell!
> The decisive moment explodes into destruction,
> The pregnant womb of the ages, swelling in the pangs of labor,
> The pregnant womb of the ages is opening up,
> The King of Peace descends, bow down
> Ye nations! Rulers, bow, and lay your scepters down!
> It is Jesus whom ye expect, you have your Savior again,
> O earth, O mankind, yea, kneel down;
> The glory is His, the power with the scepter of heaven and earth!

And on another page he expresses himself on the same subject thus:

> This clump of clay shall soon have run its erratic course;
> Heaven declines again to reunite with earth,
> And shoots its laughing beams through the nebulous mass of clouds.
> The morning dawns, the Sun of uncreated truth
> Breaks through and the wide universe glimmers with its clarity.
> The blasphemous clump of worms that grub in its dunghill
> Hide in vain their heads at the appearance of that blaze.
> He draws near, the God-Man drawn near in the divine omnipotence
> That causes the earth to cringe at the look in His eyes,
> As the breath of His breast melts mountains and rocks,
> And with His lightning power rushes across the whole earth,
> He draws nigh, the Savior draws nigh;
> He is the hope for which we look,
> To reunite the brethren with the brethren.

The whole *Reveil* with all its different nuances was contained in the powerful personality of Bilderdijk. His expectations about the future passed on to his principal disciple, Da Costa, and through the latter to all of the *Reveil,* the favorable influences which are still noticeable in the Netherlands. We now take leave of this great Chiliast with a word of Bavinck: "All the desires of his heart melted together in the prayer, 'Come, O Savior, come, O come!' " We are compelled to dwell a little longer on Da Costa as he is generally acknowledged to be the main spokesman, the "Prophet of the *Reveil.*"

Isaac Da Costa (1798-1860) is still far too little known as a theologian. Reformed people seem to have the opinion that he was merely a versatile poet and a pious man. The fact is, however, that Da Costa was first and foremost a theologian, and that is what he wanted to be. Writing poetry was a heavy task to him. If the ardent longing for Christ's return had not always burned in his heart, his name as a great poet would most likely never have been known, for the remark has been made, that on his lyre he had but one string, and that he always plucked it.

This string was not religion in general, nor merely the love for Christ, but more particularly his ardent longing for "the day of the glory of God." Anyone who desires to read his poems from that point of view will notice that almost without exception every poem ends with, *"Lord Jesus, come!"* in one form or another. Though we do not go so far as to claim that this expectation of salvation made him a poet, we do believe that this hope made him a *unique* poet. If we lost sight of that fact, we get little out of his poetry.

After his conversion, this expectation of salvation was the basic note in all his songs. Like the psalmists of old Israel, he calls on all nations to prepare themselves for the day of Christ.

> Cast, nations, at this coming, away
>   Your gods of wood and stone,
> With their imagined authority forced upon them,
>   And their seeming righteousnesses,
> For the King will bring you
>   Righteousness and peace!
> But woe to superstition, unbelief, false faith
>   And imagined enlightenment!

And expect salvation from Him,
    Great and small, sinners and nations.
In that rending of His clouds
    A judgment is threatening, a voice is calling.
Let everything pay homage to Him,
    Sing hymns to Him, bow the knee to Him!
Unto Him, the Judge; let the earth tremble!
    Unto Him, the King; let the earth shout for joy!

We "lukewarm Westerners" can hardly imagine such ardent longing for the coming of the King of Peace as is manifested by this son of Abraham. By way of further characterization of this faithful witness we quote a few more lines:

Hasten, great God, this most blissful of all days!
    Almighty One, Thou who canst slow down the time
Or speed it up, with one wave of that invisible hand,
    Which keeps the whole world in motion and in check.
We live in the hope of Thy promises!
    We languish from longing for the divine judgment, which tarries!
Let the fire make haste, so that our eyes may satisfy themselves
    (If it may be) with Thy beauty; that we may bathe
In the light that beams forth from Thy face, O God!

Many will be inclined to consider such language as the result of mere poetic moods or the dream of an overheated imagination; but we find these expectations expressed not only in his poems but in all his essays, brochures, and Bible lectures. His whole view of life was Chiliastic and that *on the basis of God's promises.* And here again this plant bore the most excellent fruits. Just as he himself testifies about Bilderdijk, so this hope was also to him a constant, animating stimulus to witness of the Lamb that was slain and will come again, and against the antichristianity of his day. To Da Costa applies fully the words of Scripture when it says, "They that wait upon the Lord shall renew their strength," for with a weak body and many cares he indefatigably toiled and fought in many areas.

The modern Professor Van Gilse praised Da Costa for the fact that when he had acknowledged the Bible to be the Word of God, he also proclaimed with fervor the coming of Christ. For this doctrine, he said, although it is to us modern people an absurdity, is proclaimed on nearly every page of Scripture. It is a great neglect to ignore it, while at the same time claiming to be a Bible-believing Christian. Da Costa's expectations about the future explain four facts in his personality and life.

First, he had an almost fanatical love for Bilderdijk. He knew Bilderdijk's shortcomings better than his enemies did, but in spite of that he loved him with a love that is seldom equalled. It is usually thought that this love can only be explained on the basis of a common congeniality of faith and mind, so that Bilderdijk can be called the spiritual father of Da Costa. But this congeniality of faith does not quite fully explain his veneration of Bilderdijk.

Between these two there was something that is all too frequently lacking in present-day Christianity—*the fellowship of hope.* In principle it is present in all believers, but in full reality is found only rarely. Da Costa saw that prophecy was neglected everywhere by everyone, but he saw that Bilderdijk studied it diligently. His ardent longing for the day of glory was not understood by others, but his spiritual father found all his comfort and strength in it. Both were fully convinced that in the return of Christ "they possessed the true key to all the histories of the world as well as to the sacred predictions in both the Old and New Testaments." Both were ardent Chiliasts. Hence it is the similarity of their expectations regarding the future that bound Da Costa so closely to Bilderdijk and his writings.

Second, from Da Costa's expectations about the future we understand the peculiar and prophetic character of the products of his pen. He was one of a kind in all of the Netherlands. Many of his religious contemporaries despised prophecy as being *obscure,* but he paid heed to it as to a light shining in a dark place. Holland has never settled its account with Da Costa; it has neither refuted him nor accepted his message. We consider Da Costa to be irrefutable. The booklet by the Rev. H. Hoekstra is new proof of that. For Hoekstra (who is praised by Dr. H. H. Kuyper, Rev. Sikkel, and Rev. Doedes as a preacher of the full gospel and mighty in the Scriptures) should, as a Dutch anti-chiliast, have attacked and defeated his fellow countryman. Instead, when he discusses Da Costa we hear nothing but praise for him and his Chiliasm, which ends with these words: "We can honestly say that if we ever could become a Chiliast, then it would be Da Costa who could make us one. Everyone who knows his Bible lectures knows that in many places they are like a string of sparkling precious stones."

Third, we can only in the light of this expectation understand and at least partly appreciate the position Da Costa took with regard to the so-called "address movement." It is well known that he abstained from signing when the seven men from The Hague in two addresses insisted on maintaining the Three Formularies. This action on the part of Da Costa was considered strange and is interpreted in various ways. It has been attributed to his stubbornness, his medical standpoint, or even to his lack of a true Reformed spirit. But it seems to us that not one of these explanations nor a combination of all three is valid. Dr. Oosterhof's dissertation on *Da Costa as a Polemicist,* which in other respects make for pleasant reading, did not shed any light whatsoever on this aspect. Whoever reads Da Costa's writings notices practically nothing of this *medical standpoint,* which is referred to again and again, and even less of his not being full Reformed.

True, Da Costa had some objection to the Formularies. Why should we deny this? To him they were not a complete expression of the whole truth since they are practically silent on inspiration, history as the basis of dogma, the eternal generation of the Son, the doctrine concerning the future, and unfulfilled prophecy. Especially the last-mentioned item weighed heavily with him, for it was his wish that in his time the doctrine concerning the return of the Lord would be developed. We are convinced that the real cause of Da Costa's attitude lies in his expectation of the future.

He did not expect anything good for the Church, state, or society, from anything or anybody except from Christ Himself. As is evident from his *Rekenshcap van Gevoelens (An Account of My Sentiments),* in his early age he believed that he must seek the cure of the existing evil in the Church and theology in a return to an earlier situation in the Church, but after 1843, he saw that a cure was only possible in the way of progress toward a new, divinely promised future. Earlier he contrasted the old with the new; now the new provided him with weapons against the old. What he means by this *deliverance* and by what he calls *the new* is clear to anyone who knows him. He emphasized that he did not consider the Church to be his friend, but the Kingdom. Dr. Oosterhof says on page 256 of his dissertation:

His looking forward to the *ecclesia gloria,* (i.e., the glorified Church), is satisfying and pleasant. The question may be asked, however, whether the glorious expectation regarding the future of the Church did not make him too complacent regarding the present situation. The abnormal condition became to him something almost inevitable, we would almost say, something normal!

This learned man, in spite of his voluminous study, shows that he understood Da Costa very little indeed, for even posing this question is a misunderstanding of the man, who from 1822 on, when he "cast his *Objections* as a fire rocket into the army of the enemy," fought with such heroic courage to his last breath against the spirit of the age. Beets said correctly of him that he possessed a heart "that took a consuming part in *all* that our times bring forth." But he did not make the mistake of delving into the ecclesiastical situation in hope of effecting a normal situation in this sinful dispensation.

Finally, we can also explain from Da Costa's Chiliasm his stance with regard to the Secession. Just like his friends Groen and De Clerco, he did have moments when he was strongly inclined toward the Secession. His heart always went out to the Separatists, because his friends Scholte, Wormser, and Van Hall belonged to them. But there was something that barred the way to a full affinity of the spirit between the Secession and Da Costa. It bothered him extremely that the cast-out and oppressed believers in many instances adhered more to the Formularies than to the Word and, above all, that they often looked back with nostalgia to the past rather than forward with joyful longing to the coming Savior. If this were not the only reason, it was nevertheless one of the main reasons why he did not close ranks with them. The Messianic expectation of salvation was as strong in him as weak in the circles of the Separatists. And like his pupil H. P. Scholte afterwards, he could not call anyone really totally orthodox who did not order his life in the light of the coming of the Lord. Hence we see that almost all that is characteristic of Da Costa can be reduced to his Chiliastic view of life.

As far as we know, the modern Professor Scholten is the only one who attacked Da Costa on his Chiliasm. This again is characteristic and the more so since Scholten himself agrees:

A) That the prophets expected a political-theocratic restoration and unification of all of Israel, that is to say of the twelve
tribes under one King out of the house of David.

B) That John also envisaged this when he wrote Revelation,
but that this Apostle later learned to view the matter more
correctly and that everything must be understood in a spiritual
sense.

By saying these things he placed sufficient ground under the
feet of Bible believers to accept the doctrine of the millennial
reign of Christ on earth. Da Costa did not fail to give a reply to
these statements. In his *Bedenkingen tegen het Synodale plan
eener nieuwe Neder-Duitsche bijbelvertaling van het Nieuwe
Testament* (*Objections to the Synodical Plan for a New Dutch
Bible Translation of the New Testament*) he discusses the
matters Scholten brought against him. The latter had, among
other things, accused him of not being Reformed, as the Helvetic Confession makes mention of *Jewish reveries*. He reminds his opponent:

A) That at the Synod of Dordt, 1618-19, such men as *Alsted*
and *Bisterveld* who believed in the teaching of these Jewish
dreams, were not expelled for deviation from the Reformed
faith.

B) That at that time Chiliasm was not yet a subject of special
study, and for that reason was not dealt with in the Formularies and hence was neither condemned nor accepted.

Now we must briefly say something about important men in
whom the influence of Bilderdijk and Da Costa can be traced.

Abraham Capadose must be mentioned first. Together with
his friend Da Costa this Israelite had learned to know the
Promised One of the Fathers through Bilderdijk's instruction
and had received the sacrament of Holy Baptism together with
him. He is considered the father of the Dutch Sunday School
movement and the mission among Jews. The story of his
conversion is told in every language of Europe. He wrote
several booklets on the last things: *Overdenking Over Israel's
Roeping en Toekomst* (*Reflection on Israel's Calling and Future*), Rome en Jeruzalem (*Rome and Jerusalem*), *De Hoop
der Uitredding* (*The Hope for Delivery*), *Zijn Hand Is Niet
Verkort* (*His Hand Is Not Shortened*), *De Groote Verdrukking
Aanstaande* (*The Great Tribulation Imminent*), and others.

Willem de Clerco was the improvisator of the *Reveil.* This talented and lovable Apostle-John personality is called by Dr. A. Piersma the Melanchthon of Da Costa. He cast a much deeper look into the soul of Da Costa than did Groen, who in other respects was so very astute. His attitude towards the Secession was about the same as that of Da Costa. In his diary he writes about the Secession, for it greatly touched his tender and deeply sensitive heart. The reasons that kept Da Costa from joining it can be seen in Kohlbrügge's negative attitude toward it as well; both were of great influence on him.

J. H. Koenen was a jurist of amazing erudition. Like most men of the *Reveil,* he was also a poet, while he theologized much. For quite some time he, together with Da Costa, was one of the editors of the periodical *De Nederlandsche Stemmen* (*Dutch Voices*). He wrote an extensive and beautiful biography of his friend, and published all the latter's essays in two volumes. His book on *De Joden in Nederland* (The Jews in the Netherlands) is the principal source on this subject. He shared the expectation of his friend and differed from him only in the manner of doing battle.

J. F. Schimesheimer is the man who provided us with Da Costa's Bible lectures. He did not belong to the higher classes but had extraordinary talents. By self-instruction he reached the point where he knew most of the languages of Europe. For a decade he published a weekly against Modernism. In order to learn Scripture he copied the whole Bible twice. In his *Levensbericht* (*Biography*) of Da Costa he informs us that he told nothing about Da Costa but the things he was in agreement with. In each volume he tells us much about Da Costa's Chiliasm. From this we conclude that he agreed with it. One portion of the spirit of Da Costa had fallen on himself!

Among the ministers who were influenced by Da Costa about the future must first be mentioned *C. C. Callenbach,* minister at Nijkerk. He was actually still a disciple of Bilderdijk, and as a student was a capable preacher of the gospel. He was a warm friend of Da Costa and joined the *Reveil* wholeheartedly. He has been compared to the moon which in lovely beams reflected the eastern blaze of Da Costa's sun. He was a diligent student of the prophets; he wrote a booklet on *The Return of the Lord* and another on *The Future of the Jews,* which sufficiently reveal that he was a kindred spirit of Da Costa.

H. P. Scholte, the well-known founder of Pella, Iowa, can still be considered as belonging to the school of Bilderdijk. Dr. Wagenaar, in his dissertation on the *Reveil* and the Secession, correctly calls him a disciple of Bilderdijk and a friend of Da Costa. We find all the traits of Bilderdijk and Da Costa reflected in Scholte. A man of spirit and talent, he was a courageous fighter who carried sharp arrows in his quiver. In his book, Wormser has not succeeded in acquainting us fully with this singular person for the simple reason that Scholte, like Da Costa, found in Chiliasm his own view of life, which compelled him to live in the light of the future. Wormser had no eyes to see this.

L. J. van Rhijn, although not learned, was a well-liked preacher in those days. Groen and Da Costa loved to hear him preach. In 1852 Da Costa wrote to Groen, "Van Rhijn has said it well: to a Christian it is not a question of looking forward or backward but heavenward." This statement typifies the whole person of van Rhijn. Shortly before his death he translated K. Rohr's *Concise Biblical Eschatology,* which shows that he was influenced by the Chiliastic *Reveil.* Of course we must not overlook the fact that Chiliasts like Stilling, Hess, Menken, Haas, Hentzepeter, and others also asserted their influence.

J. de Liefde was a prolific, popular writer for both adults and children. He excelled in everything. He was a gifted writer, poet, composer, orator, and historian. He wrote a pamphlet against *Richting en Leven* (*Direction and Life*) by A. Pierson, in which he shows that Modernism owes its origin to the lack of a living hope. He was a follower of Da Costa and ardently expected the coming of the Lord to take those who are His to meet Him in the air and to establish His Kingdom of Peace. When he first spoke in Amsterdam, Da Costa said of him, "A prophet has arisen amongst us."

Dr. C. Schwartz worked for years as a missionary among the Jews in the Netherlands. He called Da Costa his *dear fellow clansman and kindred spirit.* He labored indefatigably with word and pen in several countries in the interest of Israel. He wrote articles in German for the *Heraut,* which were translated into Dutch by Looman. He wrote a book on prophecy and a preface to the book by Geurs on Israel's future.

W. Jamieson, an Episcopal minister, declared at the graveside of Da Costa that he owed more to him than to anyone else on earth. He shared Da Costa's expectations of salvation. The same thing can be said of *Thelwall,* the Episcopalian missionary among the Jews, *Pauli,* and *the Rev. R. Engels* from Niewolda, who in an address to Synod urged the delegates to maintain the characteristic doctrines in the spirit of Da Costa. See also J. C. Rullman, *Reveil en Afscheiding (Awakening and Secession).* They all were heavily indebted to Da Costa.

L. Tinholt was a child of the *Reveil,* a pupil of Da Costa, and was called at his graveside, "Reformed in heart and soul." He was blessed with a clear mind and a rich spirit, and he possessed a comprehensive knowledge in almost every area of science. It was always an honor and joy to him to bear reproach for his expectation and preaching of the Kingdom of God in the sense mentioned above.

J. Ph. van der Land was for several years a minister in Rotterdam. In his youth he had faithfully followed the Bible lectures of Da Costa and, as a result, had obtained a deep insight into the prophetic character and cohesion of Holy Scripture. He closely observed the signs of the times, expected the return of the Lord soon, and courageously testified against the Modernist apostasy from God and His Word. As is true of all Chiliasts, he believed that the restoration of Israel was intimately related to all other great problems of the world. He saw that as long as Jerusalem lies low in shame, Rome with her daughters, or, if one wishes, Babylon, will flourish.

J. P. Hasebroek, the poet and writer of *Waarheid en Droomen (Truth and Dreams)* called himself a son of Calvin and a child of the *Reveil.* He was under the spell of Stilling, Bilderdijk, and Da Costa. He often lauded the coming kingdom of peace in glorious verse.

Ten Kate, the poet, also considered himself to belong to the school of Bilderdijk and Da Costa. He was a diligent student of prophecy, wrote beautiful poetry on the future kingdom of peace, and is known as a defender of Chiliasm.

J. J. le Roy, minister at Oude Tonge, was one of the few orthodox preachers in these days. Van Oosterzee calls him "the famous Kantian," since in some respects he was a follower of Kant and had written often about him. He produced several solid books promoting the *Reveil.* Toward the end of his life he studied prophecy more than philosophy. He wrote *Beschouwing der Voorzeggingen des Ouden en Nieuwen Testaments Betreffende het Nog Toekomstige* (*Reflection on the Predictions in the Old and New Testaments Concerning That Which Still Lies in the Future*). He also wrote *Openbaring van Johannes* (*Revelation of John*). In both he reveals himself to be a full-fledged Chiliast.

H. W. Witteveen cannot be considered as belonging to the *Reveil,* but he may nevertheless be mentioned here since he was wholly permeated with the spirit of that spiritual revival. He advocated in writing, poetry and sermons a Chiliasm which by no means can be called *moderate,* as it is often termed. That this did not make him an idle dreamer can be attested to by the many missionaries he sent out to the ends of the earth from Ermelo, which he liked to call *Erbarmelo.*

Even men of great learning experienced the beneficial influence of this revival. We mention here first of all *Dr. J. J. van Oosterzee.* In his diary he writes, "What is being called the 'Theology of the *Reveil*' has also had its remarkable influence on me, which many consider, as I do, a blessed influence." Kuyper calls Van Oosterzee *a man of ten talents.* Da Costa exerted a special influence on him. In his *Iets Over Da Costa* (*Something About Da Costa*) he says that "this poetic dilettante-theologian has at times seen and brought to light more of the glorious harmonies of Scripture than many a theologian by profession, who are as gray as the dust on their books." According to his *Dogmatics* and his *Christology of the New Covenant,* he fully shared the Chiliasm of Da Costa. English and American Chiliasts like to appeal to Van Oosterzee as "the great Dutch theologian."

Dr. J. I. Doedes was for many years a friend and colleague of Van Oosterzee, of whom he also published a brief biography. Together they published for many years the *Jaarboeken voor de Wetenschappelijke Theologie* (*Yearbooks for Scientific Theology*), while later they wrote many articles in the *Nieuwe Jaarboeken* (*New Yearbooks*). Dr. Doedes was an active opponent of Modernism. His logic is irrefutable. In foreign coun-

tries he is well liked for his critical studies and concise hermeneutics. In his evaluation of the (Dutch) Confession of Faith he
attacks, on the basis of Revelation 20, a single general resurrection. It is often alleged that only poetic minds believe in a
Millennium, but here we have a businesslike, rational, and
critical man of learning who, like many others, accepts it and
that on the basis of the infallible Word of God.

Dr. D. Chantepie de la Saussaye, Sr. Da Costa greatly
influenced this Father of the Ethical School. His first publication, in French, was inspired by Da Costa and dealt with the
future of the Jews. For years he combatted Modernism as a
courageous warrior. He was the principal contributor to *Ernst
en Vrede (Earnestness and Peace)*, the publication of the Ethicals. In 1868 he toured the Netherlands to hold four lectures on
the future, *Israels Roeping (Israel's Calling)*, *De Messias (The
Messiah)*, *Het Wereldrijk en de Antichrist (The Kingdom of
the World and the Antichrist)*, and *Het Duizendjarig Rijk (The
Millennium)*. From the last lecture, which was most instructive, we quote the following expression.

> It is by no means subject to doubt that, just like the Apostolic church,
> so also was the persecuted Gentile Church during the first centuries,
> indeed even later, even after the persecution had ceased, Chiliast.

Dr. N. Beets is often called the preacher of the *Reveil*. He
was a poet of merit and an inimitable writer of prose. By his
edifying writings he exercised much influence in those days. He
was one of the speakers at the graveside of Da Costa and spoke
there as follows: "Rest in peace, fiery son of the East, inspired
singer, humble confessor, patient sufferer, faithful witness of
Jesus Christ the crucified One!" In a general sense it may be
said that he was a kindred spirit of Da Costa, but it is difficult
to establish how much he adhered to the doctrine of the Millennium. His ironic nature made him fearful of extremes.

P. Hugenholtz. Van Oosterzee in his biography says, "The
venerable colleague P. Hugenholtz in Rotterdam has born the
burden and the heat of the day." His booklet on *De Teekenen
der Tijden (The Signs of the Times)* reveals him as a Chiliast
who was tired of all the strife in the Church and yearningly
looked for the blessed coming of the Lord.

Dr. J. J. Toorenenbergen also attended for a long time the
evening gatherings at Da Costa's home. Later he became a

contributor to the periodical *Ernst en Vrede*. However, he was more orthodox Reformed than the other Ethicals. He was a man of considerable learning. As is evident from this *Handboek der Christelijke Geloofsleer (Handbook of Christian Doctrines)* he was a Chiliast in the same sense as Da Costa and the entire *Reveil*.

Dr. J. H. Gunning, Jr. was a man of profound learning among the younger generation of the *Reveil*. What attracted him most in "his" Da Costa, as he called him, was that the latter always proclaimed the coming of the Lord with fervor. He himself proclaimed it courageously, at the expense of his scientific fame, both in speaking and writing, both from the pulpit and the lectern, for more than half a century. He was a man of prayer and passed through life mostly misunderstood and as a stranger here on earth. According to him, Church restoration was impossible, hence his spirited battle against Groen and Kuyper. He believed that the Millennium was close at hand. His strongly Chiliastic view of life sheds a surprising light on Gunning's personality which in other respects was quite mysterious. No publication of his saw the light without reflecting this view. His booklet on *Prediking van de Toekomst des Heeren* (*Preaching the Coming of the Lord*) is as precious as gold. In *Blikken in de Openbaring* (*Glimpses Into Revelation*) his Chiliasm manifests itself most clearly. Through the influence of Chantepie de la Saussaye the entire Ethical movement bears a Chiliastic hue.

Dr. J. H. L. Roozemeyer was a grateful and outstanding disciple of Chantepie de la Saussaye, whom he considered unforgettable. He was a greatly beloved minister in the Reformed Church. He revealed himself as a bright theologian in his commentary on the Gospel of Matthew and in his reader on *Het Christelijk Geloof* (*The Christian Faith*). As is evident from the latter, to him, too, Chiliasm was "no earthly reverie."

Dr. J. H. Gunning, III, is, like his father J. H. Gunning, Jr., a remarkable and important man in the Netherlands; and was appointed as an evangelist among the educated. He was a man whose outlook was as broad as it was sound; he was a favorite preacher and writer. His periodical *Pniël* (*Penuel*) had many readers. He wrote biographies of Budding and Witteveen and his popular expositions of some Bible books are well known not only in the Netherlands but also among us. We consider his exposition of John's Revelation to be one of the best, if not the best, in the Dutch language.

We further mention here the following names as well-known proponents of Chiliasm in the old fatherland.

T. M. Looman may be considered one of the younger leaders of the *Reveil.* Although he was not a theologian by profession, he accomplished more in the field of theology than many theologians of renown. His merits in more than one area cannot be described in a few words. To him, too, Chiliasm was not just a matter of secondary importance but an indispensable element in his view of life. This cannot come to us as a surprise, because in his Bible exegesis he adhered to literal interpretation. He expresses it thus.

> The literal meaning is the one that is immediately evident from the words of Holy Scripture, in their original meaning. In order to be literal, the sentence must be true, that is, it must neither conflict with the context nor with any other incontestably clear meaning. From this we can conclude: (1) that every text in Scripture has of necessity a natural meaning. Luther says: "The literal meaning of Holy Scripture is the whole basis of our faith, the only thing that stands firm in calamities and temptation." (2) This meaning cannot be wrong, because it is the one which the holy writer wishes to convey directly to the mind of the reader, and which, as understood according to the laws of rhetoric, emanates from his words. The literal meaning, being the one which issues forth from the actual meaning of the expressions, according to the demands of the usage of language and the context of speech, can usually be known with certainty; and as soon as that is proved, it has the power of proof.

M. S. Bromet was a Jew who was baptized in 1855. He wrote several instructive booklets on the last things, of which are best known: *De Wederkomst en de Regeering van den Heere Jezus Christus* (*The Return and the Reign of the Lord Jesus Christ*), *Kort Overzicht van Eenige Gelijkenissen des Heeren* (*Brief Survey of Some of the Lord's Parables*), *De Eerste Opstanding in Verband met de Wederkomst des Heeren* (*The First Resurrection in Connection With the Lord's Return*), *Het Nationaal Herstel en de Bekeering van Israel* (*The National Restoration and the Conversion of Israel*), and *De Toekomende Heerlijkheden* (The Future Glories). We cannot recommend the last-mentioned booklet enough for the study of the last things. It consists of seventy-five pithy questions and answers.

E. Gerdes, the well-known poet of *Er ruischt langs de wolken* (*A Lovely Name Resounds in the Clouds*), the writer of more than two hundred children's books, was a disciple of the Rev. Johan de Liefde and, like the latter, he spoke and wrote much about the blessed return of the Lord to take up His Church in the air and to establish the millennial kingdom of peace.

I. Esser, the well-known friend of missions and open-air preacher, endured much contempt for Christ's sake. By his bold witness concerning the Savior, he commanded great respect even from the mocker, Multatuli, and the anarchist, Domela Nieuwenhuis. The latter calls him "a man who must be given the honor of being a believer of the right stamp." Esser did his utmost to convert Domela Nieuwenhuis. Kuyper wrote in *De Standaard* that Groen van Prinsterer venerated Esser and was as happy as a child when Esser visited him again, and prayed with him. He made a thorough study of prophecy, and he contemplated much on the coming of the Lord. For quite some time he published the periodical *Maranatha.* He also wrote an excellent *Verklaring van de Openbaring* (*Exposition of Revelation*) and *Het Lot der Joodse Natie* (*The Fate of the Jewish Nation*). In his *Straat-prediking* (*Street Preaching*) he recounts his experiences as a street preacher.

W. van Oosterwijk Bruin is also considered one of the younger advocates of the *Reveil.* As the father of the young men's societies and editor of the *Jongelingsbode* (*Young Men's Messenger*) he was well known. He also contributed articles to the *Heraut* (*Herald*). His books on the *Reveil, Uit de Dagen van het Reveil* (*From the Days of the Reveil*) and *Het Reveil in Nederland* (*The Reveil in the Netherlands*) made him one of the authorities on this religious revival in the Netherlands. Whoever reads his books will soon become convinced that he was totally permeated with the spirit of Bilderdijk and Da Costa. He, too, places the future Kingdom more in the foreground than does the Church of today. And he also had poetic talents—a characteristic of all of the men of the *Reveil.* He wrote many beautiful poems.

A. J. Hoogenbirk was a man of broad knowledge, and the Johan de Liefde of his time. For many years he, together with J. A. Wormser, was an editor of the illustrated periodical, *Excelsior.* In the *Heraut* he always wrote the articles for children. From his periodical, as well as from his article "Parousia" in *Om de Kunst* (*For the Arts*), it is sufficiently evident that he was a Chiliast.

J. A. Wormser was the son of the older Wormser who was such a warm friend of Groen and Da Costa. He was an excellent writer on theological subjects. He was a co-editor of *Excelsior*. His exposition of John's Revelation is a valuable booklet on the last book of the Bible. He teaches Chiliasm, albeit in a somewhat toned-down and changed form.

Here, then, is a cloud of witnesses who will forever belong to the most eminent men in the history of the Dutch Church. One cannot but consider it an honor to find himself with his Chiliasm in the company of such great men.

Meanwhile it certainly is most remarkable that today the deeply religious spirit of the *Reveil* disappears more and more by the day; and the complaint is heard that the churches are externalizing, and that Chiliasm is languishing or retreating to the sects. Perhaps Rev. H. Hoekstra would say that Chiliasm *has no longer a soil* on which to thrive. At least one can convince himself that Chiliasm does not thrive in arid soil, and that it does not produce such bad fruits. And if we then apply the biblical rule that a tree can be known by its fruits, we may boldly testify that this tree is good.

2. Chiliasm in the Circles of the Secessionists

In a broader sense of the word, the Secession [in the Netherlands a group that seceded in 1834 from Dutch Calvinism over matters of doctrine and discipline—Ed.] is part of the general religious revival of the beginning of the nineteenth century. In a narrower sense a great difference exists between the *Reveil* and the Secession. The latter was more church related, more national, less individualistic, less poetic, and less aristocratic than the former. The most striking difference between these two movements, however, is in eschatology. The *Reveil* leaped forward, the Secession backward; the *Reveil* was Chiliastic, the Secession considered this as heresy; in the *Reveil* more songs were heard about the coming of the Lord, in the Secession more sighs about one's own corruptness. Just as the father of the *Reveil* put the stamp of his spirit on this whole movement, so also did the father of the Secession, H. de Cock, assert his influence there.

De Cock considered the Chiliasm advocated by Rev. H. P. Scholte in the *Reformation* to be contrary to the Formularies and the Word of God. He did believe that great events would soon take place; he even believed that Israel would be returned as a nation to the land of its forebears. He saw in the railroads and steamboats, which came into being during the last years of his life, one of the means by which the prophecies regarding the great world events would be fulfilled. He pictured the near future as being grave and expected oppressive times for both the world and the Church. He constantly repeated the text, "Blessed is he that watcheth, and keepeth his garments." However, he had no clear concept of coming things. His son *Helenius de Cock* says in his biography of his father that the latter always pictured the Kingdom of Christ as a spiritual Kingdom which had nothing in common with the kingdoms of this earth.

But Scholte did not teach that the Kingdom of Christ was carnal and sensual and had something in common with the kingdoms of the world. He believed in a spiritual corporeality. The elder de Cock expected, so continues his son, that one day the Lord would be victorious over all His enemies and make His Church a praise in the earth. If we take this expression in connection with some statements by Hendrick de Cock, and with what *Kok* in his book says about this father of the Secession as to his expectations about the future, then it is sufficiently evident that he entertained the idea of a state of bliss for the Church on earth apart from Christ's personal coming and Kingdom. This is what our present-day postmillennialists teach. This expectation is absolutely unbiblical and pernicious; it is the false Chiliasm condemned in some Confessions.

It is understandable that the men of the Secession opposed Chiliasm so vehemently, because Satan in those early days of the Secession succeeded in supporting a miserable caricature of pure Chiliasm as it was found in a few Chiliastic sects before their eyes. *Jan Mazereeuw,* a prosperous farmer and former mayor of Opperdoes, succeeded in 1825 in gathering a group of followers around him. He became fanatic about the doctrine of the Millennium and taught that the time of baptism and the Lord's Supper had passed. Nevertheless, it is said, that for the rest he was strictly orthodox in doctrine and modest in demeanor. Kuiper discusses him in *Geschiedenis van het Kerkelijk Leven in Nederland* (*History of Church Life in the Netherlands*).

The excessive disturbances at Spijk, Bierum, Zandt, Uithuizermeeden, and Bunschoten, in which sometimes Chiliastic elements took part, and which brought nothing but derision and persecution upon the Secession, filled the simple godly people in the northern part of the country with a deep abhorrence of everything that even resembled Chiliasm.

Perhaps the pantheistic and sensual Chiliastic sect known as the Zwijndrecht *Nieuwlichters* (*Newlighters*) filled the usually simple and ignorant people of the Secession with a fear of Chiliasm. This sect, under the leadership of Mulder and Maria Leer, toured throughout the Netherlands in those days, lived a communistic life, and taught that everything, sin included, proceeded from God, that everything was dissolved in Him, and that therefore there was neither a hell nor a devil. In Friesland, the small but influential sect of Jan de Blauw, baker at St. Jansga, was very active. He was accompanied by a woman who was said to be a prophetess. He believed that Christ's return was imminent and considered himself to be called to act as His forerunner and preparer of the way. It is no wonder then that Reformed people felt fearful aversion to everything that even as much as hinted at the doctrine of the last things.

In connection with these affairs they had heard people proclaim the most detestable heresies and had seen the wildest fanaticism. What they totally lacked was a well-developed eschatology. Moreover, they still remembered well the excesses of the Anabaptists and the Labadists; and now this again! To them these events spelled nothing but delusion and heresy! These were the thoughts that settled in the minds of the Secessionists. And to this very day most of them still entertain these ideas. Add to this that there are always many poeple who think that Chiliasm, even when it is not inordinate, is a complicated, obscure, and mysterious doctrine, and it need not surprise us that people shrink from it.

Yet the Reformed Churches in the Netherlands have never lacked eminent witnesses to this truth. Convinced that history can best be known by looking at living personalities, here again we mention briefly some representatives.

H. P. Scholte has already been mentioned in connection with the *Reveil.* It is undoubtedly due to his influence that the so-called Scholtians of the Secession were often Chiliasts. He himself was already a Chiliast when he joined the Secession and daily became even more so. In *De Reformatie,* the paper of the Secessionist Church, he testified to this doctrine, which was so dear to him.

H. Klein was tutored by him to become a minister. After Scholte's departure, Klein became his successor in the church in Utrecht. Shortly after 1850 Klein, too, departed for America. He was such a strong Scholtian that he desired nothing more ardently than to be allowed to rest beside Scholte on God's acre. That he was a Chiliast comes as no surprise.

A. C. Tris was first a notary public and even wrote a *Handboek voor Notarissen* (*Handbook for Notaries*). In 1842 he went to Arnhem to study under Professor Brummelkamp. He belonged to the Scholtians. After having been a minister of the oppressed Secessionists for a few years, he departed for America in the spring of 1851. Before he left, he visited Da Costa with whom he had corresponded about Israel's future. Da Costa embraced him and said, "I thank God that I have found a man among the people who is so bright in the prophecies!" He gave him a letter of recommendation to take to Dr. Thomas De Witt, who helped in the settlement of many Dutch immigrants in America.

Tris first became a minister of the Dutch Reformed Church at Albany, but soon left that church because of its toleration of freemasonry. Shortly thereafter he became the first missionary among the Jews in New York. There he labored a long time in four different languages. He wrote several sound booklets on *De Toekomst des Heeren* (*The Coming of the Lord*) and everything connected with it. To him, too, Chiliasm was an energizing view of life and found in him a talented advocate.

A. M. C. Van Hall was not a preacher but a young jurist who consciously chose the part of the outcasts and who considered the reproach of Christ more precious than the honor of men. At the meetings in the home of Da Costa he had become acquainted with Scholte. Later they found themselves called upon to plead for freedom of conscience and religion for the oppressed Church. For quite some time Van Hall was a contributor to *De Reformatie*. When the fathers of the Secession forsook Scholte, Van Hall remained faithfully at his side. When many years later Scholte in his beloved Pella, Iowa, told about his experiences in his earlier years, he could not find enough words of esteem for Van Hall, who had been so noble and kind to the harassed and persecuted people and who had supported him so faithfully. Van Hall shared Scholte's views regarding the coming Kingdom of Christ. An excellent booklet on Van Hall has been written by the Rev. J. Bosch of Steenwijk.

J. Van Dijk was first a minister of the Christian Reformed Congregation at Doetinchem. But he felt limited, because he was not allowed to preach that the Lord is coming back bodily to reign for a thousand years on earth. At the same time he longed to have fellowship with all Christians. He was, for instance, a proponent of the Evangelical Alliance and wrote a brochure on that subject entitled, *Allieeren door Alliantie (Associating Through Alliance)*. He seceded and founded a training school in Doetinchem in which he trained more than two hundred preachers for the Reformed Church. Hence his Chiliasm did not turn him into an idle dreamer but, on the contrary, made him gird his loins.

J. G. Smitt was one of the first Secessionist ministers in Amsterdam who had much fruit from his labors there. He was a Chiliast. It has always been a characteristic of biblical Chiliasts to practice as much as possible full communion of the saints with all believers, even though that means climbing over high church walls. This was the case with Rev. Smitt, and soon he was suspect and summoned before Classis. At the advice of his consistory he then decided to separate and become independent.

M. Sipkes was a minister of the Christian Reformed Church at Winterswijk. He diligently searched and studied the prophets. He wrote several booklets in defense of the pure truth against Modernism. His booklet on *De Toekomst des Heeren (The Coming of the Lord)* saw several reprints. It is one of the most excellent writings in Dutch on Chiliastic views of the return of the Lord.

J. W. A. Notten, the well-known writer of *De Held der Hulpe* (*The Mighty Helper*), *De Ernst des Levens* (*The Seriousness of Life*), and many other popular books, believed in the Kingship of Christ over the Jews and the future restoration of Israel. Whoever believes in this but not in the Millennium contradicts himself, for these two things are absolutely inseparable. Rev. Notten was the son-in-law of Professor Van Velzen, who also believed in the return of the Jews to Palestine. The students at Kampen had an argument about the Jews one day. There was one student who pointed at another, saying, "Professor, he believes in the return of the Jews! Is that not heresy?" "Why, no," Professor Van Velzen answered, "he has read that in the Bible. Are you not reading your Bible?"

J. Van Andel is a name that is kept in great honor by all Reformed people. It is generally agreed that his was a spirit of more than ordinary depth, intellect, and taste. Added to these talents was a true, godly mentality and love of the Word of the Lord. He considered himself called by the Lord to explain Scripture, which in his opinion had not been revealed to the learned but to the simple, for the benefit of the quiet and silent ones in the land. This goal he pursued to the end of his life. Professor ten Hoor once wrote about him, "During the last twenty years we know of no writer who has guided us more deeply into the organic cohesion of Scripture than the Rev. J. Van Andel."

The fact that such a spirit was a fully convinced adherent of Chiliasm to the end of his life is not a small argument in its favor.

If we are not mistaken, it was due, among others, to Van Andel that about 1860 this question was discussed from time to time at ecclesiastical assemblies. It was his great aspiration to make clear to the churches that there is a biblical Chiliasm, but regrettably the churches refused to accept his message. *Rev. Bulens* of Varseveld and *Rev. D. Breukelaar* of Aalten stood at Van Andel's side as convinced Chiliasts.

Thus we have almost come to the end of this gallery of faithful witnesses to the Lord Jesus Christ. We would not have tired the reader with the seemingly monotonous account of this list if it were not that the impression is constantly given by the Reformed camp that Chiliasm belongs to ignorant sectarians and in practical life is useless. It is an undeniable fact, however, that in history, Chiliasm or rather, the living expectation of the coming of the Lord, has always proven to be a hidden motivation to successful activity. Among the many venerable men whom we omitted because we have limited ourselves as much as possible to the *Reveil* and the Secession, we mention a few now in passing.

Dr. P. Van Ronkel can rightly be said to belong to the school of Da Costa. While studying at the University of Gröningen he began to read Da Costa's poems with great satisfaction. He was baptized in 1856, at which occasion Da Costa was one of the witnesses. For many years he was the greatest orator in the Reformed Church.

Pierre Dammes Huet was a remarkable figure in ecclesiastical Holland. He was an orator, a popular writer, and a poet. His Afrikaans poems will always be cherished. For quite some time he was an editor of *Het Eeuwig Leven* (*Eternal Life*). If we are correctly informed, he lived, like his earlier namesakes and kinsmen *Pierre Jurieu* and *Pierre Poiret,* a life of expectation of a kingdom of peace on earth.

We consider the Darbyite concept of the church an error; it can not be denied, nevertheless, that such Chiliasts as *Willink Van Bennebroek, G. P. Bronkhorst, J. A. Donker, H. J. Lemkes* and especially *Jakob Voorhoeve, H. C. Voorhoeve, Jzn.,* and *J. N. Voorhoeve* were men who have worked hard in our apostate times to shake the believers awake and point to the coming of the Lord. The same may be said of the brothers *Arend* and *M. Mooy* to whom the leadership of the Free Congregations is entrusted.

Finally we wish to point out that the biblical Chiliasts throughout all ages and in all countries remained consistent. Dr. A. Robertson writes in his *Regnum Dei* concerning the Chiliasm of the first centuries that it agreed on the following points:

A) A dreadful manifestation of sin against the Church of Christ.

B) The imminent return of Christ.

C) Christ will destroy the world power and establish His glorious Kingdom on earth.

D) The first resurrection of the believers, to have their share in this Kingdom.

E) At the end of the Kingdom of peace the general resurrection and judgment will take place.

As secondary and at times slightly varying elements, he mentions:

A) The belief that the world will exist seven thousand years because at creation "seven days" are mentioned.

B) Different views on the enemies of the Kingdom of Christ and the Antichrist who will be their leader.

C) The *place, duration,* and *extent* of the Kingdom of Christ. Justin, who taught that it will be established in Jerusalem, held, according to Robertson, the generally accepted view.

We cannot but gaze with amazement at the rare unanimity found here. For the same things Robertson mentions about the Chiliasts of those early centuries can still be said of those of today in every country. The lesson from history points out three things:

A) The catholicity of Chiliasm.

B) The missionary zeal of Chiliasm.

C) The uniformity of Chiliasm.

In the short sketches of the adherents of this doctrine we could not every time point out the details of their views. Nor was this necessary, for apart from a few exceptions they were all agreed on the aspects pointed out by Robertson. In the biblical expectation of the Lord's return and Kingdom we see the initial fulfillment of the prayer, "that they all may be one."

BIBLIOGRAPHY

Arndt, Johann, *Het Ware Christendom.*
Augustine, *The City of God.*

Bavinck, J. H., *Dogmatics.*
———, *Magnolia Dei.*
Beet, Agar, *The Last Things.*
Bengel, Johann Albrecht, *New Testament Commentary,* 2 volumes, (Grand Rapids: Kregel Publications).
———, *Eene Verklaring van de Openbaring.*
———, *Ordo Temporum.*
Berkhof, Louis, *Hermeneutics.*
Bertholdt, *Christologia Iudaeorum.*
Bettex, F., *The Bible, the Word of God.*
Bilderdijk, Willem, *Gedenkboek.*
Blackstone, W. E., *Jesus Is Coming.*
Bromet, M.S., *De Eerste Opstanding in Verband met de Wederkomst des Heeren.*
———, *De Toekomende Heerlijkheden.*
———, *De Wederkomst en de Regeering van den Heeren Jezus Christus.*
———, *Het Nationaal Herstel en de Bekeering van Israel.*
———, *Kort Overzicht van Eenige Gelijkenissen des Heeren.*
Bronsveld, A. W., *De Oorzaken van het Rationalisme in Nederland.*
Brookes, James H., *Israel and the Church.*
———, *Maranatha.*

Cachet, Lion, *Naar het Land de Vaderen.*
Calvin, John, *Institutes of the Christian Religion* (Grand Rapids: Wm. B. Eerdmans).
Capadose, Abraham, *De Groote Verdrukking Aanstaande.*
———, *De Hoop der Uitredding.*
———, *Overdenking Over Israel's Roeping en Toekomst.*
———, *Zijn Hand Is Niet Verkort.*
Cellenbach, C. C., *The Future of the Jews.*
———, *The Return of the Lord.*
Cumming, John, *The Millennium.*

Da Costa, Isaac, *Israel and the Nations.*
———, *Bedenkingen Tegen het Synodale Plan Eener Nieuwe Neder-Duitsche Bijbelvertaling van het Nieuwe Testament.*
———, *Rekenschap van Gevoelens.*
De Liefde, Johann, *Richting en Leven.*
Delitzsch, Franz, *Institute for Jews.*
Doedes, J. I., *Jaarboeken voor de Wetenschappelijke Theologie.*
———, *Nieuwe Jaarboeken.*
Duffield, George, *Prophecies Concerning the Second Coming of Jesus Christ*
Du Toit, S. J., *Unfulfilled Prophecies.*

Esser, I., *Het Lot der Joodse Natie.*
——, *Straat-prediking.*
——, *Verklaring van de Openbaring.*
Eusebius of Caesaria, *Church History.*

Gaebelein, Arno C., *Daniel* (Grand Rapids: Kregel Publications).
Gerdes, E., *Er Ruischt Langs de Wolken.*
Geurs, *Israel and Her Future Restoration.*
Gieseler, Johann Karl, *Church History.*
Gordon, Adoniram J., *Ecce Venit: Behold He Cometh.*
Gray, James M., *Home Bible Study Commentary* (Grand Rapids: Kregel Publications).
——, *Prophecy and the Lord's Return.*
Grosheide, F.W., *New Testament Exegesis.*
Gunning, J. H., Jr., *Blikken in de Openbaring.*
——, *Prediking van de Toekomst des Herren.*

Haan, R. L., *The Millennium.*
Hagenbach, Karl R., *History of Dogma.*
Haldeman, J. M., *History of Premillennialism.*
Hasebroek, J. P., *Waarheid en Droomen.*
Hebart, *Eschatology.*
Hoekstra, H., *Chiliasm.*
Hoekstra, S., *Christian Doctrines.*
Hooikaas, *De Ascese der Eerste Christienen.*
Hugenholtz, P., *De Teekenen der Tijden.*

Jurieu, Pierre, *The Fulfillment of Prophecy.*

Keith, Alexander, *Fulfilled Prophecy.*
——, *The Harmony of the Prophetic Word.*
——, *Signs of the Times.*
Koenen, J. H., *De Joden in Nederland.*
Kok, J., *The Coming of the Son of Man.*
Kuenen, Abraham, *Prophets and Prophecy in Israel.*
Kuiper, *Geschiedenis van het Kerkelijk Leven in Nederland.*
Kuyper, Abraham, *The Jewish Problem.*
——, *Liberalists and Jews.*

Lacunza, Manuel, *The Coming of the Messiah in Glory.*
LeRoy, J.J., *Beschouwing del Voorzeggingen des Ouden en Nieuwen Testaments.*
——, *Betreffende het Nog Toekomstige.*
——, *Openbaring van Johannes.*
Lord, David N., *Laws of Figurative Language.*
Luther, Martin, *The Jews and Their Lies.*

Maitland, Samuel R., *The Apostolic School of Prophetic Interpretation.*
Martyr, Justin, *Dialogue With Trypho, the Jew.*
McCheyne, Robert Murray, *Christ, the Desire of All Gentiles.*
Munhall, L. W., *De Wederkomst van Christus.*
——, *Methodism Adrift!*

Nelson, D., *Unbelief, the Greatest Malady of Our Times.*
Nepos, *The Refutation of the Allegorizers.*
Nieuwenhuis, Domela, *Van Christen tot Anarchist.*

Notten, J. W. A., *De Ernst des Levens.*
———, *De Held der Hulpe.*

Patton, William, *The Judgment of Jerusalem.*
Pierson, Arthur T., *A Study on the Writings of Israel's Prophets.*
———, *Many Infallible Proofs.*
Poiret, Pierre, *De Goddilijke Huishonding.*
Preuss, *The Antichrist.*

Riehm, *Messianic Predictions.*
Robertson, Archibald, *Regnum Dei.*
Rohold, S. B., *The War and the Jew.*
Rohr, K., *Concise Biblical Eschatology.*
Roozemeyer, J. H. C., *Het Christelijk Geloof.*
Rullman, J. C., *Reveil en Afscheidung.*
Russell, J. Stuart, *Parousia.*
Ryle, John Charles, *Future Facts and Present Duties.*

Schaff, Philip and Herzog, Johann J., *Encyclopedia of Religious Knowledge.*
Schimsheimer, J. F., *Levensbericht.*
Seiss, Joseph A., *The Signs of the Times.*
———, *Daniel.*
———, *The Last Days.*
———, *The Millennium.*
———, *The Apocalypse* (Grand Rapids: Zondervan Publishing House).
Sikkel, *Holy Scripture and Its Exegesis.*
Silver, Jesse Forrest, *The Lord's Return in History and Scriptures.*
Sipkes, M., *De Toekomst des Heeren.*
Sparenburg, P. A., *Prophecies Concerning the Messiah and Their Fulfillment.*
Stilling, Jung, *Die Berlenburger Bibel.*

Tertullian, *The Hope of the Believers.*
Toorenenbergen, J. J., *Handboek der Christelijke Geloofsleer.*
Torenbergen-Klein, *Patristic Biographic Dictionary.*
Trench, Richard C., *Christ, the Desire of All Gentiles.*
———, *Notes on the Miracles of Our Lord* (Grand Rapids: Baker Book House).
———, *Notes on the Parables of Our Lord* (Grand Rapids: Baker Book House).
Tris, A. C., *De Toekomst des Heeren.*
———, *Handboek voor Notarissen.*

Van Andel, J., *Blikken in de Openbaring.*
Van Dijk, J., *Allieeren door Alliante.*
Van Oosterwijk Bruin, W., *Het Reveil in Nederland.*
———, *Uit de Dagen van het Reveil.*
Van Oosterzee, Jan Jakob, *Christology of the New Covenant.*
———, *Dogmatics.*
———, *Iets Over Da Costa.*
Warfield, G., *The Apocalypse and the Millennium.*
Wilson, C. W., *The Sign of Thy Coming.*
Woltjer, J., *The Word: Origin and Explanation.*

Zeegers, *Logica.*

INDEX OF NAMES

INDEX OF SCRIPTURE TEXTS

Due to the more than 1700 Scripture texts mentioned in the book, we have only indexed those about which an explanation or an important reference is given.

INDEX OF SUBJECT MATTER

An * before a word indicates that the word that follows has a listing in this Index.

COMMENTARY ON ISAIAH
by Harry Bultema

Isaiah has been called the "greatest of all Old Testament prophets". No book is more complex than the book of Isaiah or unfolds as many prophetic events as Isaiah. Concepts concerning the suffering Savior, the last days, the coming Kingdom, the terrible Tribulation, and the Millennial Kingdom are all contained in its 66 unique chapters. Isaiah flows with warnings and judgments, history, comfort and salvation.

In this, one of the greatest commentaries ever written on the book, Harry Bultema is careful to place each scene in its proper eschatological position. Writing from a premillennial and pre-tribulation viewpoint he unfolds the book of Isaiah to us in a spiritual, scholarly manner. His chapter-by-chapter commentary pays worthy tribute to one of the great prophetic books in the Scriptures.

His commentary pulsates with helpful information for every student of the Word. It is permeated by the author's human touch with life, his ardent love for the Savior, and a pastor's heart blended with a reformer's courage.

"... with evangelistic zeal seasoned with clarity and concern of the prophet, Bultema unfolds the spiritual insights of Isaiah and distinctly enlightens applications of these truths to your life today."—*Baptist Standard*